December 26, 1998

Howard,

with love to a wonderful brother

Sowell

Innovations in
Practice and Service Delivery
Across the Lifespan

Innovations in Practice and Service Delivery with Vulnerable Populations

Series Editors:

David E. Biegel, Ph.D.
Arthur Blum, D.S.W.
Case Western Reserve University

Innovations in Practice and Service Delivery Across the Lifespan,
David E. Biegel and Arthur Blum

This series is sponsored by the Mandel School of Applied Social Sciences, Case Western Reserve University.

Innovations in Practice and Service Delivery Across the Lifespan

Edited by

David E. Biegel, Ph.D.
Arthur Blum, D.S.W.

Case Western Reserve University

New York   Oxford
Oxford University Press
1999

Oxford University Press

Oxford   New York
Athens   Auckland   Bangkok   Bogotá   Buenos Aires   Calcutta
Cape Town   Chennai   Dar es Salaam   Delhi   Florence   Hong Kong   Istanbul
Karachi   Kuala Lumpur   Madrid   Melbourne   Mexico City   Mumbai
Nairobi   Paris   São Paulo   Singapore Taipei   Tokyo   Toronto   Warsaw

and associated companies in
Berlin   Ibadan

Published by Oxford University Press, Inc.
198 Madison Avenue, New York, New York 10016
http://www.oup-usa.org

Oxford is a registered trademark of Oxford University Press

Library of Congress Cataloging-in-Publication Data

Biegel, David E.
    Innovations in practice and service delivery across the lifespan / David E. Biegel, Arthur Blum.
        p.   cm.   —   (Innovations in practice and service delivery with vulnerable populations)
    Includes bibliographical references and index.
        ISBN 0-19-511155-9 (cloth)
    1. Social service—United States.   2. Medical social work—United States.   3. Medical care—
United States.   I. Blum, Arthur.   II. Title.   III. Series.
HV91.B54   1999
361.973—dc21
                                                                                                        98-9710
                                                                                                        CIP

Printing (last digit): 9 8 7 6 5 4 3 2 1

Printed in the United States of America
on acid-free paper

In Memory
Henry L. Zucker
1910–1998
Social Welfare Pioneer
and Friend

Contents

Acknowledgments

The idea for this volume grew out of the efforts of the Center for Practice Innovations at the Mandel School of Applied Social Sciences, Case Western Reserve University. Our involvement with this Center over the past six years convinced us of the need to address the growing segmentation and compartmentalization of knowledge both within and among disciplines and professions and to emphasize the benefit of interdisciplinary approaches to synthesize the development and application of knowledge concerning practice and service delivery innovations across both problems and populations. We hope that this inaugural volume in our *Innovations in Practice and Service Delivery with Vulnerable Populations* series will encourage both thought and action in this area.

This volume would not have been possible without the combined efforts of a number of individuals. First and foremost, we would like to thank the authors of this volume for their excellent contributions and for their willingness to work together with us in shaping their chapters to best meet the purposes and foci of this volume. The twenty-five authors of the thirteen chapters in this book represent a variety of disciplines and professions. We believe that their combined efforts demonstrate the value and importance of interdisciplinary and interprofessional perspectives. They have helped make the idea for this volume become a reality.

Work on this volume was aided by the support of the Codrington Charitable Foundation, the George Gund Foundation, the Nord Family Foundation, and the Premier Industrial Fund, core funders of the Center for Practice Innovations at the Mandel School. We would also like to acknowledge the encouragement, support, and assistance that we received from our editors at Oxford University Press, Gioia Stevens and Layla Voll, respectively, in the development of this series and volume. Carol Hughes and Leslie Ray are thanked for their secretarial assistance.

Innovations in
Practice and Service Delivery
Across the Lifespan

Introduction

The past three decades have been marked by major changes in the nature of society in the United States, an explosion of knowledge concerning social problems, and the development of new theories that provide greater understanding of vulnerable populations. High rates of poverty and homelessness, especially among women and children, increasing alcohol and drug abuse problems, the needs of the growing numbers of high-risk infants, high rates of teen violence, inadequate services for persons with severe and persistent mental illness and an increase in the aged population and the need of this population for care are just a few of the human service needs that have captured attention.

Attempts to deal with these vulnerable populations through traditional human service programs have not proven effective. Vulnerable populations are defined as "those individuals or groups who have a greater probability than the population as a whole of being harmed and experiencing an impaired quality of life because of social, environmental, health, or economic conditions or policies." Characteristics of this population include a multiplicity of needs, the presence of severe and long-term problems, and an unlikelihood of an improvement in their quality of life without assistance. Despite these deficits and constraining circumstances, vulnerable populations have a capacity for resilience, growth, and change. Interventions by social workers and related human service and health professionals with vulnerable populations encompass interventions on individual, family, and community levels.[1]

The terms "practice" and "service delivery" in the title of this volume may have differing meanings in different disciplines. As used in this volume, "practice" or "direct practice" is defined as "work with individuals, couples, families, and small groups, consisting of helping or social treatment through services such as therapy, counseling, education, advocacy, provision of information, referral, and certain aspects of community organization such as social action and mediation" (Pinderhughes, 1995). As used in this volume, service delivery encompasses all those activities that an agency or organization must perform to fulfill its mission. These activities include the following eight components:

---

[1]This definition and population description is an adaptation of those by R. L. Barker (1995), *The social work dictionary* (3rd ed. p. 404), Washington, DC: National Association of Social Work, and J. Rothman (1994), *Practice with highly vulnerable clients* (pp. 5–8), Englewood Cliffs, NJ: Prentice-Hall.

defining and performing a needs analysis of the population to be served; case finding; screening clients for services offered within the organization; making referrals to other agencies for services not available within the organization; establishing assessment procedures and outcome goals; creating linkages among services and to other organizations; doing follow-up; and monitoring the system and evaluation of outcomes (Blum, 1994).

Dramatic changes have occurred in direct practice and service delivery in response to our greater understanding of the needs of vulnerable populations. New, specialized programs and new practice methods have been developed that better address unmet human needs. Many programs and methods have been lumped together under the rubric of "innovation." However, minimal analyses of the nature of these innovations and of their similarities and differences have occurred.

Webster's Third New International Dictionary defines "innovation" as "something that deviates from established doctrine; something that deviates from established form" (p. 1166). If one substitutes the word "theory" for doctrine and the word "structure" for form, two separate dimensions of innovation emerge. New programs can be based on new theory but still maintain old structures, or they can maintain old theories but change structure, or both theory and structure can change. Thus, to analyze new approaches to vulnerable populations, systematic analyses of both theory and structure must take place.

While there is no litmus test as to when an innovation should no longer be considered innovative, in general, two criteria can be utilized: first, when there has been sufficiently widespread adoption of the innovation that it represents what now might be considered standard practice; second, when there are no more major refinements in any of the essential elements of the innovation. Under this definition, of course, a former innovation that is now considered standard practice can again evolve into an innovation if it changes substantially over time to reflect either changing needs of the population or changes in knowledge related to developments in theory, empirical research, or practice wisdom.

It should be noted that while today's innovation may become tomorrow's orthodoxy, often developments in human services seem to proceed in a circular fashion. Thus, the innovative movement to home-based services represented in elements of child welfare and mental health practice, discussed in this volume, seems, in part, a return to the roots of social work practice in the early twentieth century, albeit with greater sophistication based on increased knowledge and experience gained over the past three-quarters of a century. It should also be noted that innovation in human services proceeds at a fairly slow pace, often taking a number of years or decades to move from innovation to standard practice. Of course, once a form of practice is accepted as standard, even the presence of new empirical data that cast doubt on the effectiveness of the intervention may have difficulty dislodging it from widespread use.

Our recent literature search of a large number of databases found no systematic approaches to the analysis of innovations in relation to theory and structure. Rather, the literature contained program descriptions that reflected the authors' idiosyncratic approaches and seldom included empirical evidence of the effectiveness of changes in direct practice or in service delivery.

A second finding of the literature review was that the new knowledge concerning vulnerable populations was extremely segmented. Beginning in the l960s, service delivery approaches were designed either to address particular problems (i.e., poverty, substance abuse, mental illness, family violence) or to meet the needs of specific populations (i.e., children, adolescents, the aged). Professional education also moved toward creating greater specialization in relation to problems or populations. Thus, for example, social workers in direct (clinical) practice may specialize in a problem area such as mental health or alcohol and/or other drug use, in a population area such as children, families, or the aged, or in a combination of both problem area and population.

One of the positive consequences of this approach has been the development, at a very rapid rate, of greater knowledge concerning vulnerable populations. Most of the current literature is problem- or population-specific. In addition, a number of new journals that are problem- or population-specific have been developed.

A negative consequence of this development has been an increasing isolation among specialists. Innovations in direct practice and service delivery that have relevance across problem areas or population groups often are not shared. Each group of specialists approaches what are often common issues in direct practice and service delivery as if they were specialization-specific. Few attempts are made, for instance, to take a common concern such as case-finding techniques (which are critical for all vulnerable populations) and to analyze innovations across problems or populations as to the viability of particular approaches. This isolation among specialists has led to a primary assumption of difference and uniqueness, rather than a search for commonness and a shared utilization of new knowledge and new approaches to direct practice and service delivery. In addition, knowledge development is occurring at such a rapid rate that both practitioners and faculty have a difficult time trying to keep up with current developments within these specializations.

New knowledge concerning vulnerable populations repeatedly stresses the need for a multidimensional approach in planning of direct practice and service delivery innovations to meet the multiple needs of target populations. To do this successfully requires drawing upon knowledge from a variety of academic disciplines, such as sociology, anthropology, and economics, and involving a number of professions. The social work profession historically has had the most extensive involvement with vulnerable populations of any single professional discipline. This involvement spans many fields of practice, such as child welfare, mental health, and aging. However, the nature of both practice and service delivery with vulnerable populations requires the involvement of a number of professions, including psychology, psychiatry, nursing, and allied health professions. In addition, others involved with vulnerable populations have professional degrees offered in fields, such as counseling and gerontology, that cut across traditional disciplines.

A negative consequence of the "specialist" approach to problem and popula-tion is the high degree of isolation that exists among disciplines and professions. An unmet need in developing innovations is the sharing of knowledge and approaches and the development of practice and service delivery program innovations that bring together the variety of disciplines and professions necessary to engage successfully the multiple needs of vulnerable populations. Thus, *there is currently an urgent need for interdisciplinary approaches to synthesize the development and application of knowledge concerning practice and service delivery innovations across both problems and populations.*

Focus of the Volume

In response to the needs we have outlined, this volume, the first in the *Innovations in Practice and Service Delivery with Vulnerable Population* series, takes an interdisciplinary approach to the examination of innovations in direct practice and service delivery. Innovations are presented that address a range of problems and/or illnesses across the lifespan—that is, with children and adolescents, adults, and the elderly. This volume places emphasis on the following:

- presentation of innovations that are conceptually sound and for which, to the degree data are available, there is empirical evidence to undergird the innovations
- systematic presentations of innovations in relation to their theory base, structure, and use
- presentation of a range of innovations that have relevance for specific problem areas and/or populations
- presentation of the limitations of innovations in practice and service delivery, with a focus on future research needed to enhance knowledge development
- discussion of the policy implications of innovations in practice and service delivery.

Organization of the Volume

This volume is divided into four sections. Part I, *Theory and Conceptual Framework*, contains two chapters; the first focuses on a wide range of theories of practice that have applicability for understanding innovations in practice, and the second discusses issues in organizational innovativeness.

In the first chapter of the volume, Francis J. Turner discusses the roles and diversities of current theories and focuses on helping the human service practitioner to better understand how theory can be utilized in working with vulnerable populations. Turner notes that we have moved from theoretical orthodoxy to the acceptance of a wide range of different theories that can be called upon to help us understand reality. After discussing the reasons for these changes over time, he discusses the applicability and utility of theory for work with vulnerable populations. Rather than suggesting the use of one or two or several theories for use with vulnerable populations, Turner suggests that a variety of different theories can be helpful in particular situations and then presents an analytical framework for comparing theories and analyzing their differential use. The chapter ends with a discussion of questions for future research and challenges for the future.

In chapter 2, the focus of attention moves from vulnerable individuals and groups to organizations that serve vulnerable populations. The chapter focuses on the question of why some organizations are innovative and others are not. Jack Rothman and JoAnn Damron-Rodriguez discuss innovation from an organizational perspective in this empirically based chapter, which is based on an extensive review of the literature in which the authors identify variables associated with organizational innovation. These variables are organized around two principal themes, organization factors and dynamics. Organizational factors that have been found to be associated with innovation include seven variables: external relationships and funding, goals, organizational size, professionalization, leadership and group participation, task environment, and job satisfaction. In addition to these organizational factors, Rothman and Damron-Rodriguez note that innovation is also affected by what has gone before, by the stages of innovations, and by the actors involved in the organization. Six key variables are identified that pertain to organizational dynamics: previous experience of the organization with innovation, organizational discontent, the type of innovation, communication and contact by organization members with the innovation, the innovation actors, and factors associated with the implementation of an innovation.

Parts II through IV of the volume focus on innovations in practice and service delivery with children and adolescents, adults, and the elderly, respectively. Collectively, the chapters in each part of the volume discuss significant problem areas experienced by the population group in question in which there have been important developments in innovative practice, service delivery, or both. For continuity throughout the volume, authors of each of these chapters were asked by the editors to cover the following four topics in their chapters:

1. *A definition of the vulnerable population and its characteristics, both demographically and conceptually.* Are there significant subpopulations whose characteristics require differential approaches in practice or service delivery? Are there different conceptual approaches as to the cause of problematic behaviors (i.e., a disease explanation versus a psychosocial explanation in substance abuse) that dictate different practice or service delivery innovations?

2. *Issues in practice and service delivery and areas in which innovations are needed.* What is the current state of knowledge concerning the identified population? What evidence is there which is driving the need to innovate? What evidence is there as to the success of various innovations? What is the rationale behind different innovations? As would be expected, the chapters in this volume reveal considerable variation in the extent to which innovations have been subject to empirical testing as well as considerable differences in the quality of such research. Thus, as noted later, each of the chapters in this section also discusses implications for future research.

3. *Overview of the types of innovations that are currently taking place in the field and a more detailed presentation of one or more innovations as examples of innovative responses in practice and service delivery.* For the particular innovation(s) described, what is the rationale for the innovation(s), what aspects of practice or service delivery are being changed, what evidence is there of its effectiveness, and what are some of the barriers to change?

4. *Implications for practice, service delivery, policy, interdisciplinary education, research, or some combination of these.* Each chapter includes a discussion of implications in relation to one or more of these areas. In some cases, this is an overview of implications arising from a variety of innovations that are taking place in the field or a focus on the implications of the innovation(s) upon which each author concentrated major attention.

Part II, *Innovations in Practice and Service Delivery with Children and Adolescents*, contains four chapters, each focusing on a particular vulnerable population. In chapter 3, Lynn T. Singer, Sonia Minnes, and Robert E. Arendt provide an extensive review of innovations in practice and service delivery that have been developed to address the needs of three particular groups of high-risk infants, namely, infants born after fetal exposure to maternal substance abuse, infants with chronic illnesses diagnosable in infancy, and preterm infants with low and very low birthweights. For each of these subgroups, the authors provide a definition and description of the population and its associated problems, discuss issues pertaining to practice with these populations, and then review a variety of the innovations in practice and/or service delivery that have been developed to address the identified problems. While there is a large amount of empirical data about these interventions, as the authors point out, there are a number of weaknesses in current and past empirical work and considerable gaps in knowledge remain.

In chapter 4, Victor Groza discusses innovations in adoptions of vulnerable infants and children. The chapter begins with a discussion of the heterogeneity of the adoption population. It identifies seven subpopulations of adoptees, including such vulnerable groups as children with physical or developmental disabilities, victims of abuse and neglect, and international adoptees. For each of the groups presented, Groza provides a description of the population, discusses the population's areas of vulnerability, and presents an overview of needed services. Groza then discusses innovations in both practice and service delivery related to adoptions. Two innovations in adoption practice, the emergence of attachment theory/therapy and the family therapy movement, which has changed the focus from individual to the small group, that is, the family, level are presented. Three service delivery innovations are discussed, including the increased use of computer technologies in adoption; increase in interdisciplinary involvement to meet the unique needs of the growing number of medically fragile, international, and other special-needs children; and a focus on adoption and child welfare system reforms, including an increase in public-private partnerships in adoption. In discussing these innovations, Groza shows how they differ from past work and discusses implications for practice, service delivery, education, and policy. Implications for future research are also presented.

In the child welfare field, there has been a growing concern with the increasing number of children in out of home placement. In chapter 5, Julia H. Littell and John R. Schuerman focus on a major service delivery innovation in child welfare, namely, the provision of intensive in-home services aimed at keeping families together and preventing the out-of-home placement of children. Though these programs have been widely adopted throughout the country and have been seen by political leaders as an answer to the problem of growing child welfare costs, over time family preservation programs continue to be modified to address the needs of specific subpopulations and findings from research. The chapter begins with an overview of vulnerable children served by the child welfare system and then discusses the functioning of this system and issues in child welfare practice as the context for understanding and evaluating intensive in home service. The intensive in-home service delivery model is then discussed, with attention to both theory and practice issues. The authors critically review the empirical evidence concerning the effectiveness of this popular intervention, challenging some assumptions and offering some important cautions. The authors present carefully considered implications for practice, policy, and future research in this area.

In the final chapter of this section, Raymond P. Lorion, Anne E. Brodsky, and Michelle Cooley-Quille discuss a major public health issue of growing attention and concern, namely, the extent of urban violence and the effects of the exposure of children and adolescents to this violence. The chapter begins with an extensive discussion and review of the literature concerning the nature, extent, and effects of pervasive community violence on children and adolescents. The authors then present a framework by which interventions can be categorized and organized, followed by a review of the literature concerning current knowledge of some of the more successful intervention programs that have been developed to address this problem and utilizing Gordon's classification of preventive interventions into universal, selected, indicated, and useful. The authors identify gaps in knowledge and offer suggestions for future work in this area, focusing on our need to understand the contextual nature of urban violence. Thus, in treating the child or adolescent, interventions must also address family, neighborhood, school, and community contexts. This will require changes in graduate education so that exogenous factors and ecological principles are understood and considered.

Part III, *Innovations in Practice and Service Delivery with Adults*, contains four chapters that focus on innovations with persons with severe mental illness, mental retardation, or alcohol problems or who are homeless. The emphasis on community-based care for adults with serious mental illness has led to a search for effective programs that can prevent the revolving-door syndrome of persons going back and forth between the community and the hospital, a problem too often associated with the early failures of deinstitutionalization. In chapter 7, Phyllis Solomon discusses one such effort, Assertive Community Treatment (ACT), an intensive case management program whose roots go back to a program developed more than twenty years ago in Madison, Wisconsin. Solomon begins with a discussion of the subpopulations of adults with serious mental illness, including those with a coexisting substance abuse disorder, those who are homeless and mentally ill, and those involved with the criminal justice system. This discussion is followed by a presentation of the theoretical underpinnings of intensive case management and a review of the precursors of this innovation. Solomon then discusses the ACT model. She provides evidence of its effectiveness and discusses adaptations that have been developed over time to address the needs of specific subpopulations and to extend its domain to areas not previously focused upon, such as the involvement of family caregivers, and efforts to increase the employment of persons with serious mental illness. Solomon then addresses an extremely important issue, namely, the degree to which the ACT model, which was developed through research service demonstration projects, has been implemented in actual case management practice. In other words, how diffused has the innovation become? The chapter ends with implications for practice, service delivery, policy, education, and research.

In chapter 8, David Braddock discusses service delivery innovations that have been developed in working with persons who have mental retardation. After discussing the definition, etiology, and prevalence of mental retardation, Braddock presents a brief historical overview of mental retardation services. In contrast to Solomon's approach of focusing on a specific intervention, Braddock provides an overview of major service delivery innovations in the mental retardation field, first discussing the expansion of community-based living for persons with mental retardation, a trend not unsimilar to the mental health field. He then discusses the emergence of supported community living and related innovations, offering empirical support, where available, for the effectiveness of the cited innovations. The reader will note, in this discussion, the similarity to a number of the themes and issues discussed by Solomon in the preceding chapter. Braddock also discusses service delivery innovations for an important subpopulation of those with mental retardation, namely, persons who also have behavioral disorders. Implications for service delivery, policy, and education are presented to conclude the chapter.

In chapter 9, Allen Zweben and Susan Rose focus attention on an important but underrecognized component of the alcohol-abusing population—individuals who may not be alcoholics or alcohol-dependent clients but who have mild to moderate alcohol difficulties or who are nondependent alcohol clients. The chapter discusses the treatment needs of this population, with focus on brief intervention as an alternative model for treating alcohol problems. The rationale for this model, together with its task components, are presented. The chapter critically reviews empirical evidence of its effectiveness and presents recommendations for future research. Material is also presented concerning how health care practitioners can use this brief intervention technology with at-risk individuals. Implications for service delivery, practice, and education are delineated.

In chapter 10, the final chapter of this section, Judith A. B. Lee discusses innovation in practice and service delivery with homeless persons. The chapter begins with an identification of the characteristics of the homeless population and a brief discussion of practice and service delivery issues. The chapter then discusses a number of service delivery innovations that have been developed to help address the needs of this population, including enriched service emergency shelters, transitional living facilities, and permanent housing with services. A major focus of this chapter is the presentation by the author of her innovative practice with homeless populations, with an emphasis on interventions that empower persons who are homeless. She presents the theoretical underpinnings for this work and then illustrates the empowerment approach by providing examples of empowerment group work, political activities, and individual- and family-oriented empowerment practice at a program for homeless and formerly homeless women, children, and men in Hartford, Connecticut. Case examples are liberally used to highlight the application of this work. Implications for future policy, practice, and research are presented.

Part IV, *Innovations in Practice and Service Delivery with the Elderly*, contains three chapters. One focuses on innovations in institutional care, while the other two focus on innovative interventions with Alzheimer's patients and family caregivers, respectively. There has been an emphasis in developing alternatives to institutional care of the elderly, as has been the case with other populations. Nonetheless, nursing home care is an important and necessary component for subpopulations of the elderly. In chapter 11, Eva and Boaz Kahana and Heidi T. Chirayath offer their unique perspective on innovations in institutional care for the elderly. The chapter begins with a brief discussion of goals and intervention approaches in nursing homes and then presents the results of a comprehensive literature review of institutional innovations. This discussion is enhanced by the use of a framework developed by the authors for categorizing and organizing innovative interventions in institutional care. The framework discusses interventions that address three types of goals—resident focused, staff related, and family—focused with interventions being organized around the target/locus of intervention—patient, physical environment, social environment, staff organization, family, or community. In the final part of the chapter, the authors move beyond a discussion of existing innovations and develop their own conceptual framework for what they identify as "patient-responsive" care in nursing homes, which they hope can serve as a guide for future initiatives as well as to identify areas that have been neglected and require attention.

Alzheimer's disease is a form of dementia that involves gradual and progressive deterioration in functioning. Millions of Americans currently have Alzheimer's disease and related disorders, and this figure is expected to grow rapidly unless research advances are made that can help prevent this disease. In chapter 12, Cameron J. Camp and Jeanne M. Mattern challenge the assumption that the maintenance of existing abilities should be the goal of interventions with Alzheimer's disease (AD) patients. Rather, they suggest that interventions are possible that can improve levels of functioning. The chapter begins with an overview of Alzheimer's disease, including its stages and risk factors. The authors then turn their attention to rehabilitation as an innovative approach to the management of AD. Innovative interventions presented include: spaced-retrieval, focused on individuals with AD; question-asking reading, an intervention for small groups of persons with AD; and an Intergenerational Montessori-based program for dyads of persons with AD and preschool children. For each of these three innovative interventions, the authors discuss the background of the intervention, its theoretical basis, the characteristics of the intervention, and the implementation of the intervention, including data concerning its effectiveness. Implications for research, policy, education, and practice are presented.

Alzheimer's disease, like other chronic illnesses, affects not only the person with the disease but the person's family as well. Given the nature of Alzheimer's disease, caregiving by family members can be very burdensome. In the final chapter of the volume, David Coon, Richard Schulz, Marcia Ory, and the REACH Study Group present intervention approaches for family caregivers of persons with Alzheimer's disease. The material presented in this chapter stems from innovative interventions being developed and tested by a new multisite family caregiver intervention research program known as Research for Enhancing Alzheimer's Caregiver Health (REACH), which is supported by federal funding. The chapter presents information about five types of caregiver interventions—individual information and support, group support and family systems, psychoeducational and skill-based, home-based environmental, and enhanced technology systems—that are being tested in different configurations in sites throughout the country by the REACH program. There is extensive presentation of the theoretical and empirical underpinnings of the interventions, together with descriptive information about the intervention itself. A major strength of the REACH project is its use of the same standardized instruments across treatment sites to measure the effects of these interventions. The strategies developed by the project to develop these measures are presented. The chapter concludes with a discussion of future directions in caregiver intervention research and service delivery.

David E. Biegel and Arthur Blum
December 1997

REFERENCES

Blum, A. (1994). *Innovations in practice and service delivery: A framework for analysis* (unpublished manuscript). Cleveland: Center on Practice Innovations, Mandel School of Applied Social Sciences, Case Western Reserve University.

Pinderhughes, E. (1995). Direct practice overview. In R. Edwards (Ed.), *Encyclopedia of social work* (pp. 740–751). Washington, DC: National Association of Social Workers.

Part I

Theory and Conceptual Framework

1

Theories of Practice with Vulnerable Populations

FRANCIS J. TURNER

Professors Biegel and Blum have charted a difficult yet essential journey in this volume, which looks at innovations in practice and service across the lifespan with a particular focus on vulnerable populations. Blum (1994) has identified a number of variables that need to be examined in assessing the degree to which various programs, strategies, services, and interventions are innovative. Among the many variables that need to be considered in this search, an essential one is that of theory. As Blum (1994) points out, there are two aspects to the question of theory. First, we need to consider what theories provide the rationale for direct practice interventions. The second, related question is, "To what degree is there consistency among the theories utilized to explain the problem, establish outcome goals, and designate the intervention approach to be utilized to achieve the goals?" (p. 29).

An Overview

The overall purpose of this chapter is to examine four factors related to the challenge of how to best tap the contemporary theoretical richness available to the human service practitioner in working with vulnerable populations. First, in addition to a traditional understanding of theory, the implications of viewing theory from a political and sociological perspective are examined. This is followed by a discussion of the implications of our current diversity of theory and how this can be viewed and used as a resource for practice. Third, an approach to comparing theories in order to apply them in a differentially useful manner is addressed, followed by a discussion of the staggering research challenges facing the human services as we seek to make our theories more effectively and responsible with these populations.

Theory: A Multidimensional Concept

One of the difficulties in discussing theory is that it is one of those concepts that everyone seems to understand. It is a term used by everyone, and is used in day-to-day professional conversation. In this generalized usage, a commonalty of understanding is presumed. Yet, in fact, it is a term that has a variety of meanings and usage for different people. To make this question more complex, for some colleagues the idea of theory has a pejorative connotation suggesting that the term reflects unreality, imprecision, and distancing from real practice challenges. This then makes what could be, or should be, a fairly straightforward discussion diffuse and imprecise.

The present volume has a highly pragmatic thrust, one that seeks to ensure that what we as professionals are doing with and to the various groups of clients we serve is ethical, responsible, and, as far as possible, effective within the limits of current knowledge. Thus, it is important that we be clear as to our perception of the term "theory" and how it is to be used in this chapter (Turner, 1995).

Our definition, like this volume, is a pragmatic one. Theory as used here refers to the general term we use to describe an *identifiable interconnected cluster of concepts that have been or are capable of being empirically verified*. The goal of the conceptual cluster is to attempt to explain some aspect of the "person-in-situation" reality with which we deal to provide us with a basis on which we take those actions for which we are prepared to be professionally responsible. Thus, for this discussion, theory has among its many functions two principal ones: first, to explain some relevant parts of the reality confronting us in practice, and, second, to give direction as to how to respond appropriately and helpfully to presenting situations, whether individual or societal realities.

Most readers would probably agree with this operational concept of theory. However, what makes this discussion challenging is that, in the interinfluencing, multisystemic world in which we practice, each of our theories, in addition to being an explanatory tool, also has a history, a sociology, a value base, a status base, and a political identity.

The interaction of these factors creates an important challenge for us in the human service professions. At different times in our history and for different individuals and different segments of our professions, theory in general, and some theories in particular, have been viewed and treated as closed systemic quasi-dogmas that are inherently superior to others.

As quasi-dogmas they have been taught and indeed practiced as "the truth," "the explanation," "the all-encompassing search light on realty," "the last word on the understanding of various phenomena and behaviors." When this occurs, the impact of a particular theory becomes highly restricted, its limitations too often overlooked, and, interestingly for those not of the "faith," their potential to help is minimized. In such a climate, clients and situations have been made to fit theory rather than the reverse. A related outcome of a perception of a closed-mind view of theory is that professions then become internally divided along doctrinaire lines. This division, in turn, can carry over into schools, agencies, clinics, and individuals. Such divisions create "believers" and "heretics." This, in turn, leads to the waging of "holy wars."

When theories do not remain open, dynamic, changing, developing, and expanding systems, the qualities of all living systems, then the research needed to continually test theory is minimized. In such a milieu, the limitations of a theory become overlooked or perhaps not even recognized. The greatest losers in such conceptual joustings are the clients. They are either deprived of richness that particular thought systems might bring or are inappropriately served from a theoretical base that may not fit their needs and aspirations and that may not reflect where they are in a particular moment of their lives. They are also deprived of the richness that comes to practice when knowledge and its application are continuously being rigorously tested and refined, as ought to be a hallmark of every theory.

This is a succinct overview of an aspect of theory that is frequently overlooked in discussions about the differential efficacy of one theory in relation to another as applied to particular client populations. However, it is a concept that needs to be always before us as we seek to view theory in as neutral and objective way as possible, well aware of the personal blinders that lead us to prefer some theories to others because they fit us but, often, not the client.

Theories also have sociopolitical attributes that need to be carefully understood as we examine their place in practice. In the history of professions, we have seen and continue to see that, at various times and in various places, some theories are more "in fashion" and, indeed, more "politically correct" than others. If such a changing popularity is not taken to extremes, it is not all bad (Specht, 1990). A differential professional popularity for some theories compared to others might help bring less well-known theories or newly emerging theories to the fore so that their efficacy is made more broadly available to clients and groups.

When a theory is highly regarded within the professions, we frequently see that practitioners are eager to expand its use and to experiment with new applications to diverse client groups. These often result in more effective ways to serve some people and to expand the conceptual base of the system. However, "political correctness" can also become highly restrictive, so that programs and services become bound to a particular orientation to the exclusion of others. Clearly, we are not talking about situations where one theory is viewed as more powerful than another because it has been demonstrated to be more effective than some other systems in particular situations.

The Present

The factors I have discussed are of particular importance when one attempts to assess the current situation of theory and theories and how they connect to disadvantaged groups. We have come a long way from the earlier theoretical bifurcation of social work into the functional and the diagnostic schools. This division affected social work particularly but carried over into other human service professions. Although there are still traces of this split, one that clearly had all of the intersystemic, interinstitutional, intercurricular, and interpersonal marks of a true schism, its intensity has lessened. For a variety of exciting reasons, we are much more open to diversity. One of the reasons for this is the growing understanding of the essential responsibility to continuously test knowledge. As well, we are pushed to find new ways to respond by the seeming endless development of new and larger challenges for service with which the human service professions are faced. In the past forty years, we have witnessed a movement from a search for a unitary theoretical base of practice to a situation where we have a multitude of theories, which now number at least thirty (Turner, 1996).

Each of these theories views the human condition from a different point of view. Each brings us an enriched perspective on the potential of individual groups and systems to change. Each offers us unique strategies to differentially effect change in some facet of the person-in-situation. Each aspires to an expansion of its own body of knowledge, strengths, and potential for helping. Each is committed to the responsibility to identify its limitations. The challenge for us now is to come to terms with this diversity in an operationally effective manner.

Several things have happened to focus the challenge in a healthy searching manner that fosters growth and minimizes conflict. Among the most important are these:

1. The concept of theory as dogma has greatly diminished. For this we should be grateful. Certainly there are and will continue to be rivalries between theories, between schools, among those who teach theories, and between persons who espouse different theories. But, for the most part, these now appear to be the type of rivalries and challenges that promote growth and change rather than foster wall-building and exclusivity.
2. There is a growing acceptance that there need not be, indeed, given the complexity of our service mandate, that there cannot be a single truth, a single all-encompassing theory. Like practitioners in most fields of the human condition, we are learning that, as our knowledge advances, the challenge of effective intervention becomes more complex. So, too, there emerges a greater possibility for different ways of understanding reality. A corollary of this, of course, is that, as we understand more about the human-societal condition, we also become aware of the need to continually expand our repertoire of interventions.
3. There appears to be significant movement toward the concept of theory as an open system of searching and testing rather than a closed body of thought to be handed down unchanged and untouchable.
4. Following on this concept of permeable boundaries between systems, so, too, there need to be permeable boundaries between professions. No profession or societal body owns a body of knowledge. If a group of monks in Tibet can teach social workers how to help persons better get in touch with themselves in a helping way through mediation, this is to be espoused. If a group of Chilean mothers can teach social planners in a large Canadian city how to effect political change, this, too, is to be

welcomed in a manner of respect and appreciation. In the past decade, we have seen a much greater comfort with the idea that knowledge is where you find it and that no one person or group owns knowledge. This has exciting potential for our work with diverse groups.

5. The one change that perhaps is the most encouraging, at least for this author, is the growing understanding that, as individual learners and practitioners, we are capable of dealing with considerable complexity and plurality. We do so in our own lives. Our clients do so on a daily basis. We are intellectually capable of dealing with the concept of a multiplicity of theories. Each theory gives us an enriched understanding of the practice world we face. Each should expand our range of ways to intervene and seek desired change. Each should also caution us as to the limitations of our knowledge and the risk of making things much worse, rather than better, for our clients, whether individuals, dyads, families, groups, or communities.

6. We have come to accept that, as practitioners, we are capable not only of massive theoretical diversity but of an extensive expansion of our methodologies and techniques. We are far from the day when many would practice in only one modality or with only one client age or type of problem. Now, in entering any of the human services, we are aware and accept that we must have a broad range of competencies and intervention strategies.

As we struggle with the reality of an ever broadening range of theories rather than a coalescence of systems, an important question for deliberation is, why? Why is it that we have moved dramatically to a position of diversity with little apparent interest in a search for a general, all-encompassing theory? Why the multitude of theories? What do new theories try to address that others did not? What shortcomings of older theories do new theories try to remedy (Merton, 1957)?

Putting aside any ego issues involved in the process of developing a theory with which a person's name might be attached, what other factors have led to the expansion of our theoretical base? There appear to be four principal ones.

1. *New theories have evolved because those that existed were seen to be too focused on a particular aspect of the human condition to fully address the realities of the many vulnerable populations in society.* We were, and indeed still are, enriched by theories such as psychoanalysis with all its derivations. Such theories have helped us to understand the critical way in which a person's early history and early significant relationships can and do affect current functioning. However, as practitioners in the human services, we have long been aware that other significant events, systems, and realities also restrict the ability of persons to achieve their potential. Thus, other conceptual systems have been required to broaden our understanding of the human condition and to expand our ability to intervene more efficiently and effectively.

2. *New theories have evolved because many existing thought systems were seen to be overly focused on inner pathology and failed to fully address the many positive and growth-enhancing factors of the human condition in interaction with society.* In no way disparaging such theories as ego psychology, which greatly enriches our understanding of the way in which healthy development is slowed, flawed, or derailed, practitioners have long been aware that this theory was not enough. Frequently we need to do more than help persons understand what has happened to them during their developmental odyssey. In our practices, we need other views of the person-in-situations and other strategies of intervention to deal directly with the healthy parts of our clients and to use their abilities to help them make more effective and efficient use of themselves.

3. *New theories have evolved because some theories were seen as too person-oriented to fully respond to the reality of people's lives as they and their significant others interact with society and its structures and groups.* Hence the strong interest in and need for models and theories of practice such as systems theory and the life model. Both of these systems are conceptual constructs that take us beyond people and their dynamic lives to help us better understand their functioning, interactions, and interinfluences, and the impacts of the complex societal and environmental structures and realities with which they live. As these theories emerged and took their place in the repertoire of practitioners, they did not take anything away from the richness that more inner-psychic theories give us. Rather, as with all useful theories, they help us to understand more inclusively and, thus, more comprehensively the reality of the lives of vulnerable persons and groups.

4. *New theories have evolved because there was and is a need for models to help us understand how persons function in and come to terms with various components of reality to optimize their potentials and to tap effectively their environments to better cope, function, and achieve their goals.* Over the decades, we have seen a cluster of theories that target discrete aspects of the human condition. Examples of these are behavior strategies, task, problem and cognitive approaches, and crisis interventions. Each of these addresses a specific aspect of the potential of people to face and deal with life in its many manifestations.

This discussion touches only lightly on the variety of causal factors that has led to our present abundance of theories. It is presented to identify some of the factors that have shaped this multifaceted process. In summary, each new system attempts to look at some facet of the person-in-situation realities addressed by the human service professions that has been untouched or too lightly touched or too narrowly focused.

It would be misleading to imply that this development has been a smoothly evolutionary one that moved from the inner person outward, or from more general theories to those that are more specific. Even now, highly generic theories are emerging that look at such factors as the spiritual nature of humans, the meaning of life, and the complexities of gender. Other theories will continue to emerge that are also highly focused on specific aspects of the human condition. The process of theory development is complex and uneven, influenced by economic, political, historic, ideological, sociological, and charismatic factors.

As we ponder this exciting process of theory development and practice innovations stemming from them, it is important to recognize that such developments are not to be viewed as a process of developing substitutes for preexisting systems. New theories emerge to fill limitations or gaps in existing systems and to conceptualize new insights about the evolving human-societal conditions.

As we become increasingly aware of and less naive about the complexities of the realities with which we deal, we see the need to expand and enrich our theoretical repertoire. We do this in a way that avoids our throwing out the past. Rather we need to see that new perceptions and new formulations only add to the "corpus sapientiae." They do not detract from it. Each new theory, as it has emerged and found its place in the helping professions, represents efforts to expand and deepen our knowledge of persons, families, and groups and how they interact with the frequently grim realities of society.

The Case for Specialization

Before we apply these ideas to disadvantaged groups, a brief discussion of the case for specialization in theory and practice is needed. In the history and the sociology of professions there can often be observed the Hegelean tendency to move from one extreme to the other. In social work, for example, as in other professions, for several decades the prevailing wisdom held "one person, one theory, one method." As I discussed, we now appear to have moved from this position. But we must hope that this is not a movement that will take us to the other extreme, which eschews any concept of specialization and argues that everyone must practice in all methods from a pantheoretical base; hence, everyone must be a generalist. It is this author's position that as we seek to greatly expand and diversify our breadth of knowledge, skill, and technique, we must understand, support, and maintain a strong commitment to the need for specialists in all theories.

Just as we need persons who are multiskilled, so, too, do we need persons who concentrate on advancing each skill, each technique, each theory, to its possible limits. That is, we need specialists. But this needs to arise from a conceptual commitment to the diversity of which we have been speaking. Thus, for example, we need to have persons who take a theory such as gestalt, and a method such as family treatment, and a specific client group such as abused women, and become as knowledgeable about the potential for good of this theory and this method for these clients, and, of equal importance, of their limitation for helping and their potential for harm. A concomitant component of this search for optimum expertise is to feed this knowledge back to the practice arm of the professions so that all may benefit from it.

At all events, we must avoid the heresy of dichotomization and understand how the generalist and the specialist need each other and how each mutually enhances the other's competencies for the ultimate good of our clients and patients (Siporin, 1989).

Theoretical Diversity and Vulnerable Persons and Populations

By now the reader will know that the thesis of this chapter is that each and every one of our available practice theories, when used appropriately, selectively, accurately, and ethically, can be of benefit to some persons and groups, including any or all of our vulnerable groups. Of equal importance, it is also posited that each of these theories can cause hurt to individuals and populations when used inappropriately. We do not believe that any one theory or cluster of theories "in se" is more appropriate for vulnerable groups than any other. What we posit is that all have potential for helping when used skillfully and selectively.

Our range of available theories is broad. Their potential is rich in the extreme. The possibilities for an almost unlimited range of helping strategies is immense. Never have we had such a rich array of theoretical diversity, which presents us with an almost unlimited range of possible strategies for helping. Some examples:

- *Crisis* theory, when appropriately used, can help with the immediate and debilitating psychic impact of the many overwhelming situations met by disadvantaged people. As we learn more about the hitherto unrecognized events and their repercussions, such as leaving people feeling totally overwhelmed, the applications for crisis work is expanding.

- *Empowerment* theory can give us an understanding of how persons and groups can be assisted in taking effective action on their own behalf. It is an approach used with many vulnerable groups who have been helped to find strengths, abilities, and confidence in themselves to address some of the disempowering aspects of their lives. It is a system that makes special use of the power of groups as agents of self-help.

- *Systems* theory teaches us to understand, and make positively operative, the complexities and interfaces of the many systems in which individuals and groups function, whether physical, environmental, political, or economic. Although it does not necessarily provide needed resources, this theory can help persons better understand and become more able to maneuver and less limited by the impact of social situations.

- *Psychosocial* theory helps us and our clients broaden our understanding of persons and their development and their interaction with life's situations and to plan strategies that meet clients' values, wishes, and abilities and to help locate or create resources to enhance their autonomy. Again, in this theory, there is a strong thrust to helping persons learn to function in an autonomous manner and take charge of their own destinies. Although this theory has its own unique identity, it incorporates into its understanding of persons and their development the insights of attachment theory and object relations theory.

- *Task-centered* theory is a highly focused approach to specific problems in which emphasis is given to structured and concrete strategies that are within the client's ability and perception of acceptable outcomes. Many of the vulnerable clients we meet in practice have very little skill in dealing with the problems they face on a day-to-day basis. As they become more task-skilled, they are able to move to deal with other problem-producing situations and find acceptable solutions to them.

- *Meditation* can help persons find a growth-enhancing serenity amid turmoil and confusion, the reality of many disadvantaged clients. Among its many advantages are its ability to help persons cope with the physiological impact of their deprived or limited life situations in a manner that permits them to function more autonomously.

- *Aboriginal* theory teaches us how clients and societal groups can heal and help their hurting members in a way that benefits all. Although the theory is an outgrowth of the centuries-old knowledge of our First Nations People, we are learning how this theory can assist many other societal groups to become tremendously powerful agents of support and change for each other.

- *Existential* theory is an approach that is gaining considerable strength in the human service professions. Based on a philosophical understanding of the human condition, it is a powerful way to assist persons to find meaning and dignity in the depths of adversity and to free themselves from a perception of enforced servitude. It has been shown to be highly useful to assist persons to shift their image of themselves and to move to a much more self-actualizing stance.

- *Narrative* theory is emerging as one of the major therapeutic approaches of the 1990s. It is an approach that helps clients focus on the ways that they have constructed their histories in their own minds and used these histories as the bases for limiting their sense of power and ability to change. It is a format of intervention that is particularly useful in helping persons or families who have developed highly constricted negative self-images, such as abusing families that view themselves as powerless to change these self-images and take control of their lives.

This list could be continued through each of our thirty or so practice theories. The examples are presented to show how each of our theories can be useful, indeed, essential, in particular situations. The critical point is that each new theoretical understanding of the "person-in-society" situation and the intervention strategies that emerge from the theory provide us with knowledge and skills as to how to help and how to avoid or limit hurt.

Treatment then becomes a question of understanding the client, what he or she wishes, how the client wants to get there, and how one can best help the client achieve his or her goals.

In looking at this spectrum of theories, we require a threefold perspective: (1) what is unique about each of these systems that will give me as the therapist some specific knowledge and understanding of the client and situation; (2) how does my understanding of the client and situation fit with the client's view and perception of the world and how it functions; (3) how do various theoretical systems interlock in a manner that best fits the client and the situation? That is, we need to continually ask ourselves how each system is similar to some and all other systems and how each system is unique. Our ongoing professional responsibility is to make judgments for which we are prepared to take responsibility based on what theory tells us will help the client.

Later in this volume, different groups of clients will be examined and innovations in responding to them will be discussed. These discussions will be built on what current knowledge tells us is at the cutting edge of knowledge. Here we will see how our understanding of these societal groups has grown from an expanding conceptual base that enriches our practice.

An Analytical Framework

Thus far the content of this chapter has been hortative and descriptive. More is needed! As we continue our dialogue on how to improve the richness of theoretical knowledge now available to us in an increasingly effective manner, we need to have a way of comparing theories. It is not enough to be acquainted with the spectrum of practice theories available to us. We must also have a way of comparing and assessing their differential use. We need to know how theories are similar, how they are different, and how they interlock. One of the difficulties in comparing programs, services, agencies, techniques, and, of course, theories, is imprecise terminology. In other words, how do we avoid the problem of "apples, oranges, and fruit salad"?

From this salad perspective, there are three major challenges in comparing theories and their effect on service: (1) Some theories use similar terminology to describe different things. The use of the term "diagnosis" is an example. At this time we have several different theories that speak of the importance or unimportance of this concept but that use the term in a theory-specific manner. (2) Some theories use different terminology to describe similar things. For example, all theories have a concept of the helping relationship but utilize a range of terminology and ideas to describe it. Thus, in existential theory, the relationship is called "the encounter," a term frequently misunderstood by persons who do not know the theory. (3) Some theories have unique concepts and terminology. These need to be understood if one is to understand the theory. For example, in systems theory the terms "equifinality" and "multifinality" are proper to it and are concepts not found in other theories. Nevertheless, they are concepts useful in understanding aspects of other theories.

The question of how to develop a system to aid us and our colleagues to compare different theories has been a vexing one. The approach that has been taken has been to start from a position that presumes some structural commonality between systems. In so doing, we attempt to identify the questions that every theory has to address if it is to be useful in understanding different presenting situations. Although still in a development state thus far, this approach appears to have some utility.

It has been observed that each theory has to formulate and describe concepts in the following areas:

1. *General attributes.* This item addresses a theory's origins, its connection to other theories, its level of integration, and its empirical base.
2. *Therapeutic attributes.* This variable examines the therapeutic process including judgments on the importance of items such as gender and culture. It also assesses the importance of significant environments and the nature of the helping relationship.
3. *Value bases.* This aspect of the comparison paradigm considers theories from the perspective of differing value bases such as time and activity.
4. *Perception of person.* This attribute deals with concepts such as free will, rationality, heredity, environment, ability to change, and the nature of functioning and change in a manner that permits comparisons between theories.
5. *Nature of the therapeutic process.* Each theory is assessed on a series of variables related to treatment. Some of the items considered here are the goals of intervention, the concept of history, diagnosis, techniques for working with client systems, the role of goal setting, and the range of change agents and techniques that are available.
6. *Therapist skills.* In this phase of the comparison, such things as self-awareness, required knowledge and skills, the function of supervision, and the specifics of training are explored.
7. *Applications.* Under this variable, levels of application, importance of various methodologies, specificity of target, client types, and known limitations are examined.

For each of these variables, common terminology has been developed for each item and subitem, thus permitting comparisons on a common ground. If testing of this formulation proves successful, it should permit us to match a theoretical orientation to specific needs, wishes, abilities, and situations of clients, whether individuals or groups.

Using an abridged form of this matrix Table 1.1 shows how three theories currently available as a basis of working with persons from various vulnerable groups can be looked at in a comparative manner. This type of comparison provides an opportunity to differentially compare these theories from the perspective of its potential in a particular situation to meet the needs of particular clients. This table is a highly abridged application of a project in which twenty-eight theories currently extant in human service practice have been compared, along a list of fifty-two variables (Turner, 1997).

In looking at the variables for three different approaches to practice, there are a variety of ways in which one of the three could have a better goodness of fit with some clients more than others, be attractive to some clients, or frighten

TABLE 1.1

A Comparison of Three Practice Theories of Import in Working
with Disadvantaged Groups by Ten Selected Attributes

Variable	Cognitive Theory	Existential Theory	Task Centered Theory
Related to which other theories	Communication Constructivism Existentism	Client-centered Cognitive Gestalt	Problem solving
Nature of the helping relationship	A reality-based educational relationship	A reality based trusting interchange between equals which is open and safe	A caring relationship that stresses client and practitioners avoidance of hidden agendas
Nature of the therapeutic process	To change patterns of irrational thinking	To promote understanding, to enhance choice and responsibility Emphasis on heightened awareness	To help clients specify self-perceived problems and to develop and implement tasks to resolve them
Value orientation in regard to time	Present Future Past	Present Future Past	Present Future Past
Value orientation in regard to human activity	Doing Being = Being in Becoming	Being in Becoming Doing Being	Doing Being in Becoming Being
Value orientation in regard to human relationships	Individual Group Family	Family Group Individual	Individual Family Group
Importance of heredity over environment	Both of equal importance	Environment is more influential than heredity	Both of equal importance
Importance of self-awareness for the practitioner	Moderately important	Strongly important	Moderately important
Principle applications of theory	Low-, middle-, and high-functioning clients	Well-motivated, resistant, and ambivalent persons Groups with common interests Alienated, confused persons	Clients whose problems can be resolved by their own actions Clients with sufficient cognitive competence to collaborate in treatment Clients not primarily interested in self-examination.

Adapted from Social Work Theory Chart, F. J. Turner, 1996.

some away. For example, a client seeking a relationship with a professional with the expectation that the practitioner would function in a teacher-expert role, as in cognitive therapy, might well find the trusting, mutually open style of an existential therapist to be quite threatening and intrusive.

From the perspective of value differences, we will meet clients who are very past-oriented and view much of their lives and condition as stemming from past events. Such a person may well want to focus on history to better understand who he or she is in the present. If he or she finds that the helping person is very present- or future-oriented, there will be a poor fit between the helping person and the client and a perception that little positive is going to occur in the process. On the other hand, if the client wants to deal with the here and now and the therapist wants to look at the past, they are also on a collision course right from the beginning of a process.

It is probably the case that many clients who have been considered resistant or unmotivated in treatment were in fact reflecting a different perception of the helping process. Since they didn't fit the therapist's view, they could not engage in a useful dialogue and instead terminated. Our research has shown that all theories have a perception of time, seeing the past, the present, or the future as primary. Frequently, practitioners are insensitive to their own value preferences about time and how this impacts on their practice.

Another important variable along which theories differ is that of the differential perception of the nature of preferred human activity. For some persons, and thus for some theories, the primary activity value is placed on "doing," on actions, on getting things done, on solving problems, on carrying out tasks. Other persons and other theories stress the concept of "being." That is, life in all its aspects is to be experienced. In applying this viewpoint to a helping situation, the expectation is that the process will be an emotive one, not a cognitive or action-oriented one. The relationship is to be trusting and open and exploring, rather that action based. Again, we find situations where there is an enabling goodness of fit between clients, the goal of the process, and the theoretical orientation of the helping person and situations where there are marked divergences that can create situations of confusion on the client's part and a felt failure to be understood and helped.

One further value issue of considerable import for the differential use of theories relates to the theory's perception of the relative importance of an individual focus over groups and both of these over family. Clearly, if a theory is group oriented, and so are the practitioner and the clients, this bodes well for the process. But there are situations where, for example, the practitioner strongly favors a family orientation and the client prefers either individual or group.

There are, of course, many combinations of these and other values that can be envisaged. The examples simply suggest how complex the picture is when one is commited to finding the best theoretical fit between client and practice. In addition to these few variables, there are many other factors related to such things as perceived best length of contact, specificity of goals, use of contracts, perception of human nature, and importance of the environment.

The number of profiles of treatment is vast if one thinks about the range of combinations that can exist among persons and within theories. As yet, we do not know how to best make use of this concept of fitting theory to client. Nor do we know how important each factor is for effective intervention. However, if there is validity to the idea that some theories are a better fit for some clients than others, just as some theories are a better fit for some therapists than others, we need to ask and attempt to ascertain how important this is. We need also to challenge severely the often noted practice of practitioners choosing to make use only of the theories to which they are most attracted. It is our view that we have a responsibility to have our approach fit the client, rather than trying to get the client to fit our theoretical positions (Kluckhohn & Murray, 1953). One of the essential underlying tenets of the form of comparison presented in Table 1.1 is that much more attention needs to be given to matching the theory to fit the client, rather than applying a particular theoretical preference to the client.

Perhaps much more important, we should pay more attention to processes that allow the client to make this choice. It may well be that if clients were presented with options, they could and would make a more efficacious choice of the conceptual base of the intervention than the therapist could. Even though we think that helping a client understand the impact of past history on present functioning would be most helpful, the client may think that learning some problem-solving skills is more important. A former supervisor of mine used to say, "If a client wants bread and we provide insight therapy, we have failed her, but if a client wants insight therapy and we give her bread, we have also failed her just as badly."

We are now in a position of being theory-rich, a dramatic change from our days of being theory-poor. The challenge now is what to do with these emerging innovations to enrich our practice for particular individuals and groups of clients.

Some Research Questions

We are not yet in a position to state with confidence that some theories are more relevant for some vulnerable persons and populations than others. The concept of vulnerability is much too complex a term and too diffuse a variable at this juncture to make precise correlations between theory and outcomes related to some aspect of vulnerability (Reid, 1984). However, this is not to be viewed as a statement of cynicism or despair. It is rather a recognition of the immense spectrum of complex research challenges facing us. We cannot shy away from these challenges because of their immensity or difficulty. Rather, we must examine them as a whole and begin to identify and operationalize the range of research questions in a manner that advances our knowledge.

The driving question is how the strategic use of particular bodies of practice theory can be most effectively used in particular situations to advance the human and societal condition. As our body of knowledge expands, we become more aware of the intricacies and multidimensionality of the factors that lead to vulnerability. We are also humbled by the understanding that our knowledge base is not going to expand by dramatic breakthroughs. Rather, we will advance in very small steps stemming from many thousands of well-designed projects that together will help us find better and more effective ways of helping the vulnerable members of society.

As we struggle with these gaps in our knowledge, we remain well aware that only rarely can we make linear relationships between the use of a particular aspect of a theory and a specific outcome. Over and over again, we need to be reminded of two principles from systems theory, mentioned earlier: *multifinality* and *equifinality.* Multifinality tells us that similar inputs into a situation can have differing outputs or results. Equifinality is the converse of this; it says that different inputs into situations can have similar outputs. This, of course, makes the research challenge even greater. The implications of these two dicta caution us against a position that attempts to prescribe in a particular instance which theory is to be used to achieve a particular outcome. The principle of equifinality also alerts us in an optimistic way to the fact that, in many situations we meet in practice, there are probably several different theoretical orientations that will lead us to attain the same outcome. That is, if we can presume a common base of commitment to understanding human behavior in interaction with societal and natural systems and can presume a commitment to human concern and a desire to help, then it appears that there is much more in common between and among our treasure house of theories than one might expect on first consideration. The power of the helping relationship, the ability to intervene in systems, the recognition of hurt, and the respect for identity all result in the humbling awareness that many persons are helped to achieve similar goals by persons with a variety of theoretical orientations, some even operating from a nontheory basis. Undoubtedly, there are factors basic and common to any helping process that clearly supersede what is specific to any particular theory.

For example, I may practice from a strong psychosocial base and you, my colleague, from a strong cognitive base and yet help my client, Mrs. M., achieve both a strong sense of self and ability to function in a much more empowered way so that she greatly restricts the extent to which she is vulnerable.

Similarly, we may both practice from a well-grounded gestalt base and use similar strategies in our interventions yet have very different impacts on clients. In one instance, you may help a client achieve a much enhanced image of self that is highly satisfying and empowering, while I may have helped a client to make decisions that result in major changes in his or her life. Our theoretical orientations are strong and similar, yet result in different ways of functioning in our interventions. Thus, in no way is there as yet a direct cause and effect relationship between use of theory and a particular outcome.

But it would be wrong to use these two concepts as a rationale for shirking our efforts to tap the richness of our theoretical base to better respond to vulnerable persons and populations through the rigors of research, to avoid a search for identifiable differences of outcome. This we can do with confidence that each of the thirty or more theories have been shown to be effective in some practice situations (Thomlison, 1984). We have moved from the earlier position of arguing the efficacy of a particular theory out of charisma and enthusiastic loyalty. Our task is to move this body of accumulating knowledge forward (Turner, 1996).

A critical question underlying this chapter is the relationship between theory and practice. At this point in our history, it is strongly held and consistently taught that theory and practice are inextricably interrelated. This is believed almost as an article of faith. However, when the question is asked about the basis of this strong conviction, we find that the direct evidence is very sparse. When we then move to asking how we might begin to address this question, we are faced with a series of research questions, each of which is answerable. But we cannot answer them in any unilinear manner. To answer each requires myriad smaller but critical projects.

As we move forward, therefore, some of the questions that need to be addressed are as follows: (1) What theories do people *believe* they use in practice, both in general and in specific instances? This is important because for some practitioners it may be that it is believed commitment to a particular theoretical base that gives them confidence in their practice, even though they may in fact not have a full understanding of the theory.

However, as mentioned earlier, since theories have both a fashion quality and a political correctness quality, a different yet important question also needs to be tested: (2) What theories do people *say* they use in particular practice situations? This is important, for it may be that what people say about their theoretical base and what they believe that base to be are quite different.

To examine this question further, we need to ascertain the extent to which people in fact know the theory they state or believe they are using. Thus, a third question is: Do practitioners have sufficient knowledge of those theory bases with which they are identified to use them responsibly in practice? That is, is it enough to believe in a theory to use it effectively, or is it also necessary to know the theory? This is not a frivolous question. We know that being convinced about the efficacy of an intervention sometimes makes it effective.

Once we are able to identify the theoretical framework from which practitioners function, a further challenge is to attempt to identify whether different theoretical bases do indeed lead to different patterns of intervention. That is: (4) Is it possible to conclude from which theoretical base people are functioning by examining their plans and their styles for intervention in particular cases? Thus, in observing practitioners, could the theory base or bases that are driving the intervention be ascertained, and, if so, is it indeed the framework they believe they are using?

If we could show that different practitioners' theoretical orientations did indeed lead to different patterns of intervention, a further research challenge would be to ask: (5) Are there different outcomes when different practice strategies based on different theories are employed?

This, of course, then leads to a further set of questions, which can be summarized as follows: (6) If there are different outcomes, are they patterned so that some profiles of intervention are more likely to lead to a particular desired outcome than others? It is not our place here to attempt to describe how these questions could be tested except to state that each of them in our opinion is operational and to urge that researchers address more attention to them than we have to the present.

Truly these are daunting questions, but they are not insurmountable. What is needed is a strong commitment to answering the more general questions of the relationship between practice theory and desired outcome in cases and how these are patterned so that different populations of clients can be better served. The challenge for us remains the same as that question put by Kendall and Butcher (1982): "What intervention conducted by what therapist, with what clients, to resolve what psychosocial dysfunction, produces what effects?"

Some Theoretical Challenges

As we struggle with these many challenges to knowledge building in seeking to serve more sensitively and responsibly those many persons and groups in our society who are vulnerable to the deprivations, hurts, rejections, and wounds of uncaring or rejecting societies, we need not be pessimistic. One of the exciting components of the rapid expansion of new theoretical systems in our professions is that there have emerged from the dedicated, concerned, and determined striving of colleagues ways to respond to the biopsychosocial needs of the many vulnerable persons we meet (Curnock & Hardicker, 1979).

Certainly, there is an understandable rivalry between systems. However, it is this author's view that in the past decade there has been a dramatic opening up of theoretical diversity in two ways. The first is the realization that every theory has its limitations. Thus, over and over again, we see the proponents of theory not only arguing for the advantages of a particular system but also stressing its limitations and potential for harm if improperly used. Second, inherent in this value can also be seen an expansion of the concept of the interconnection and interlocking components of theory. As we move to an understanding of theory as an open, dynamic system, there is much more thrust to the search for interconnectedness and permeability of boundaries than to the wish for exclusivity and compliance.

Accompanying this twofold maturation of our theoretical base, or perhaps as a result of it, there has also been a dramatic, indeed almost unprecedented, increase in the quantity and quality of the research bases of all of our theoretical models. Clearly, some of these bases are richer than others. It is not our place here to rank or differentially evaluate them. It is evident that such bases are expanding. Each month we see material published that indicates how particular theories have been utilized with discrete bodies of clients to achieve particular goals. Overall, the evidence is that people and groups are helped by our interventions (Rubens, 1985). Overall, we are much more open to a quest for expanded knowledge. As stated earlier, knowledge is where we find it. There are no sources that by definition are superior to others. The tests for knowledge in the human services are: Is it ethical? Does it help? And what are the known risks and limitations?

In my own country, Canada, we are finally ready to learn from our First Nations People much about skills in healing and in community action that have broad application/knowledge we have long ignored. Feminist theory has helped us look at many aspects of our earlier practice models that were not helpful, indeed, were harmful. Task-centered theory has given us a strongly demonstrated set of strategies and tools that is broadly effective. Each theory has given us something of use for all peoples in various situations. Each of our spectrum of theories has much to offer. Each has some elements of specificity that limit its overall utility.

The skill of the contemporary practitioner and the challenge for the field is to learn how to differentially draw from the spectrum of practice theories we are privileged to have and put together a profile of intervention that best suits the situations of various vulnerable individuals, dyads, families, groups and communities (Mishne, 1993).

As we move ahead in this direction, we must continually be aware that knowledge must be ever tested and, thus, be ready to accept that today's certainty may have to yield to tomorrow's data that give us new understandings of the human condition. Always, we are seeking to find ways to respond to that vast array of groups in our society that for a plethora of reasons and causes are vulnerable.

REFERENCES

Blum, A. B. (1994). *Innovation in practice and service delivery: A framework for analysis* (unpublished manuscript). Cleveland: Center for Practice Innovations, Case Western Reserve University.

Curnock, L., & Hardiker, S. P. (1979). *Towards practice theory.* London: Routledge and Keagan.

Kendall, P. C., & Butcher, J. N. (Eds.). (1972). *Handbook of research methods in clinical psychology.* New York: John Wiley & Sons.

Kluckhohn, C., & Murray, H. A. (Eds.). (1953). *Personality in nature, society and culture.* New York: Knopf.

Merton, R. K. (1957). *Social theory and social structure.* Glencoe, IL: Free Press.

Mishne, J. M. (1993). *The evolution and application of clinical theory.* New York: Free Press.

Reid, W. J. (1984). Treatment of choice or choice of treatment: An essay review. *Social Work Research and Abstracts,* 20(2), 33–38.

Ruben, A. (1985). Practice effectiveness: More grounds for optimism. *Social Service Review,* 63(3), 474–480.

Siporin, M. (1989). Metamodels, models and basics: An essay review. *Social Service Review,* 63(3), 474–480

Specht, H. (1990). Social work and popular psychotherapies. *Social Service Review, 64*(3), 345–357.

Thomlison, R. J. (1984). Something works: Evidence from practice effectiveness studies. *Social Work, 29* (Jan.–Feb.), 51–56.

Turner, F. J. (1995). Social work practice: Theoretical base. In R. Edwards (Ed.), *Encyclopedia of social work* (19th ed. Vol. III, pp. 2258–2265). Washington, DC: NASW.

Turner, F. J., (1996). *Social work treatment* (4th ed.). New York: Free Press.

Turner, F. J. (1997). *Social work theories and models* (chart comparing 27 theories by fifty variables). Toronto: F. J. Turner.

2

Fostering Innovation in Organizations and Creating Innovative Organizations

A Synthesis of Empirical Research

JACK ROTHMAN

JOANN DAMRON-RODRIGUEZ

Human service organizations increasingly face issues of change and innovation: whether and how to do things differently and better. Change may be required in order to provide more effective and resource efficient services, increase client satisfaction, improve staff morale, or computerize information systems. The Information Age and the era of the global economy have accelerated the rate of organizational change dramatically (Schwartz, 1992). Innovation is especially pertinent under certain environmental or internal circumstances that affect the organization. When there is an abundance of resources, this allows for the funding to try out new things. When resources are scarce or diminishing, there is pressure to adapt in order to apply resources to the best effect and to survive.

The 1960s and early 1970s were characterized by a high resource climate, the 1980s by a demand for accountability for the use of allocated resources, and the 1990s by a constricting climate. Approaching the year 2000, service providers encounter an environment that demands accelerated response to change, measurement of outcomes, and continuous improvement. Professionals at the end of the century have been discouraged about the possibility of innovation when, indeed, the times both permit and demand change. When faced with budget cuts, organizations can simply carry on in the same established way on a smaller scale, or take creative actions that optimize those potentials that exist in the situation.

Serving vulnerable clients and organizational innovation are closely related. The provision of services to vulnerable populations requires an understanding of the particular characteristics of these clients and the climate surrounding intervention on their behalf. This practice involves clients whose disabilities are severe and long term and whose needs are rather diverse and broad in scope. They require not only individualized direct practice assistance but also numerous connections to external resources that provide community support.

The clients often have skill and coping deficiencies, lack information, and have low self-esteem. An organization that serves this group has to be adaptive and innovative because the external environment it interacts with is varied and complex. In addition, client needs may involve services including health care, housing, psychological support, employment, transport, and income maintenance. These considerations suggest an organizational atmosphere of flexibility, with an emphasis on individualizing service and interacting sensitively with the community service system. Because of the fluidity and variability needed to respond to vulnerability, the service pattern is emergent and typical of organizations described as innovative.

Chapter Orientation: Methodology and Theory

This chapter is based on comprehensive synthesis of empirical research from 1960 to 1997 on organizational change and innovation. The senior author previously consolidated a wide range of research findings on social change and drew intervention implications from the consensus of the findings (Rothman, 1974). The present work reflects an updating and reformulation of these materials and includes research from 1980 to 1997 that meshes with the purposes of this book. Consistent with the perspective of this volume, data was gathered from a broad spectrum of disciplines. The computerized databases included Educational Resources Information Center (ERIC), Psychlit, Social Work Research and Abstracts (SWAB), Business Periodicals Index (BPI), and Medline.

The methodology, called systematic research synthesis, has been described in detail elsewhere (Rothman, Damron-Rodriguez, & Shenassa, 1994). It involves the retrieval, codification, and integration of empirical knowledge and is essentially the methodology for this chapter. Systematic research synthesis uses structured protocols to provide a conceptual rather than statistical meta-analysis of empirical findings in a given content area. This form of data synthesis aims to aid in practice and policy development. The purpose in this synthesis is to produce prescriptive guidelines for both bringing about innovation in organizations and developing organizations that are responsive and creative.

The theoretical foundation for understanding organizational innovation lies in the general systems paradigm as it has developed into more specific perspectives, including diffusion (Rogers, 1983; Zaltman, Duncan, & Holbeck, 1984) and contingency theory (Kaluzny & Hernandez, 1983). Diffusion is the process by which an innovation is communicated to a social system over time (Rogers, 1983). Innovation in this chapter refers to the adoption by an organization of an idea, practice, or product that is perceived as new. The focus is on organizational rather than individual creativity and innovation. The innovation process is delineated in this chapter through defining the organizational characteristics that foster and create change. Diffusion theory is a relevant framework from which to analyze innovations in service delivery for vulnerable populations because, in contrast to the static conceptions of organizations that characterize functional theories (Parsons, 1956), this systems approach recognizes the mutable nature of organizations (Bertalanffy, 1968; Miller, 1978). The two distinctive characteristics of organizations are that (a) they are created to attain specific goals through the collective efforts of their members, and (b) their structure specifies their operation (Zaltman, Duncan, & Holbeck, 1973). Organizations as systems have structural characteristics, including size, auspices, centrality, and formality, that influence their patterns of innovation adoption. These characteristics will be used to describe variables in the innovation process that are empirically related to innovation in organizations. Currently, human service organizations are engaged in the dynamic of structural change as well as reevaluation of goals.

Contemporary diffusion theory emphasizes the important role of the organizational environment and interorganizational linkages (Fennell & Warnecke, 1988). Resource dependence posits that no single organization can generate all the resources it needs for survival. Federal, state, and local governments, as well as communities of consumers, are important environmental elements for agencies that serve vulnerable populations.

Contingency theory (Kaluzny & Hernandez, 1983) adds further to our understanding of the findings of the research synthesis because of its emphasis on the environment. The basic premise of contingency theory is that organizational performance depends upon the contingent nature of environmental and technological constraints and the organizational structures developed to match those constraints.

> Contingency theory is based on three assumptions: (1) There is no one best way to organize to achieve maximum performance; (2) different ways of organizing are not always equally effective; and (3) the most effective organizational plan depends upon the environment in which the organization exists. In short, good matching (strategic contingency) leads to good performance. (Fennell & Warnecke, 1988, p. 18)

Human service agencies must employ this strategic decision-making process in order to apply this research synthesis for organizational change. An organization's characteristics must be explained in relationship to its service goals and its delivery system environment. Strategic decision-making can foster innovation in organizations as well as create innovative organizations.

This chapter is organized in two parts: organizational factors, which focuses on structural considerations in innovation, and the dynamics of innovation, which emphasizes process considerations. Among the organizational factors we include external linkages, goals, organizational size, professional composition, leadership, and the task environment. Dynamic elements include the previous experience of the organization regarding innovation, the degree of discontent with things as they are, the type of innovation, communication, and contact among actors in the process, innovation initiators, and implementation follow-through. The analysis assumes the existence of an individual or agency that acts as the catalyst for innovation. The change agent who takes professional responsibility for getting the innovation process under way may be internal or external to the organization.

Organization Factors in Innovation

EXTERNAL EXCHANGE RELATIONSHIPS AND FUNDING

Organizations may reduce possible environmental controls and maximize their autonomy by avoiding a dependency relationship with a single funding source (philanthropic agency, foundation, governmental bureau, client or member fees) and forming exchange relationships with many and diverse units of their task environment that can provide needed resources (Alter, 1990; Alter & Hage, 1993; Bailey & Koney, 1995; Galaskiewicz, 1985; Lang & Lockhart, 1990). The Assembly Democratic Economic Prosperity Team (1992) issued a report that asserts "traditional ways no longer suffice in today's complex global economy. . . . The organizational unit that offers the most hope for meeting these challenges and at the same time achieving its own goals is the interorganizational collaborative" (cited in Dreher, 1996, p. 132). These interorganizational collaboratives as described by Bailey and Koney (1996) may take several forms, including a for-profit company (Kanter, 1989); a nonprofit community-based consortium (Kanter, 1989), or a social change coalition (Mizrahi & Rosenthal, 1992).

The more external resource units can be dealt with separately, the greater the level of autonomy the service provider enjoys. The difficulty in using multiple resources is that the organization must expend a relatively high percentage of its energy in cultivating, administering, and maintaining inputs from many different organizations, which can be time consuming and can detract from other activities (Alter, 1990; Emery & Mamerow, 1986). Numerous reporting forms and evaluation mechanisms are examples of possible complications in coping with multiple resource units. Computerized data management systems may alleviate some aspects of this duplication of effort.

Organizations with many linkages to external influences (as demonstrated by the number of collaborative projects with other organizations) tend to be more innovative (Alter & Hage, 1993; Armstrong, 1982; Kaplan, 1986; Kanter, 1983, 1988). Stated another way, the innovativeness of an organization is associated with the degree to which its boundaries are open (Alter & Hage, 1993). From a system's perspective, organizations function best with relatively open boundaries. This research synthesis confirms the dysfunctional nature of relatively closed organizations in the current resource environment.

Interorganizational collaboration is exemplified when independent agencies work together for specific purposes and tangible outcomes while maintaining their own autonomy (Abramson & Rosenthal, 1995). An example of a relatively closed system that has changed to having more open boundaries and innovating to form successful interorganizational collaboratives is the Veterans Health Administration. Serving homeless veterans, the VA Medical Center in West Los Angeles formed partnerships with the Salvation Army and other nonprofit community organizations to share resources, including unused VA buildings, in order to provide better access to both housing and services for vulnerable veterans. A change agent or administrator wishing to emphasize innovative organizational characteristics might develop interrelationships with other organizations. This could include having meetings on program issues of mutual concern, engaging in collaborative training, preparing joint grant proposals or program initiatives, and sharing expertise.

GOALS

An organization's dominant goals reflect the influences of the most powerful individuals or groups in the system and their vested interests. Several researchers (Cohn & Turyn, 1984; Fennel, 1984; Fennell & Warnecke, 1988) define power in terms of access to resources both internal and external to the organization. Thus, to influence the change process, individuals and groups that control the required resources must be targeted. For example, physicians and hospitals with the most influence and the greatest access to resources and hospital staff were targeted to adopt new cancer treatment standards (Fennell & Warnecke, 1988).

Change agents who wish to modify organizational goals may approach this task by shifting the division of power in the organization, by either increasing the power of those groups within the organization that hold goals compatible with theirs (such as promoting a staff union) or introducing into the organization new groups that have goals compatible with theirs ("stacking the board"). One of the purposes of introducing grassroots paraprofessionals into human-service organizations was to change the organizations' goals through the infiltration of new social groups with different norms and goals. New models of community-based care, in contrast to institutional care, not only encourage but frequently mandate the involvement of community members as stakeholders in program development (Health Resources and Services Administration, 1991; Schietinger, Coburn, & Levi, 1995). Caregivers of the frail elderly and residents of community facilities are important consumer representatives in community-based program planning, and funding sources evaluate proposals in part based on the level of consumer representation they incorporate.

The nature of an organization's goals may have direct impact on its structure and leadership patterns (Hoffman & Roman, 1984; Meyer & Goes, 1988). Multiple leadership is most likely to appear in organizations with a wide range of goals. Agencies that serve vulnerable populations are likely to have multiple goals that reflect the varying needs of the population. A wide range of goals facilitates adaptation and change in organizations. An organization that has a wide range of goals and that must satisfy an external constituency will tend to decentralize, exhibit a strong concern for membership involvement, and emphasize internal communication, all of which foster a climate conducive to innovation (Lang & Lockhart, 1990). Area Agencies on Aging (AAA) increasingly have shifted goals toward service to the frail elderly in their homes while they maintain services for well older adults in senior centers. The breadth of goals for AAA includes coordinating and advocating for transportation, nutrition, information and referral, socialization, home repair, case management, and health services for older adults. Multiple goals imply diversity and complexity, including the use of variety of skills, talents, and outlooks—all of which are conducive to innovation. The structure of the AAA system is very decentralized and requires diverse service arrangements with varied providers. However, beyond a given point, pursuing a plethora of goals can result in overextension and fragmentation. This again is exemplified in the AAA, for which the funding is limited but the mandate and goals are comprehensive. A change agent can work toward broadening the range of goals as a means to encourage greater flexibility, democratize a target system, develop new or expanded leadership, and generally strengthen the innovation tendencies of an organization.

Organizations that expend much effort on legitimation goals per se (gaining funding and public approval for organizational existence) often exhibit a low level of planning or action outputs (Alter, 1990). Concentrating on maintenance leaves the organization with diminished energy for program development and service innovation. Concern with the survival of the organization may damage its ability to act proactively and creatively. Therefore, an organization needs to maintain a proper balance between maintenance and growth goals (Cameron & Zammuto, 1983). In business and industry this is differentiated in terms of the current market and future demand. In a study of innovative corporations, those that dedicated a significant portion of their resources to future markets were more innovative and successful (Kanter, Koa, & Wiersema, 1997). Scott (1967), in a study of services for the blind, found that, while the majority of the blind were elderly, the majority of services were oriented toward children because this group had greater appeal and facilitated the fund-raising potential of the agencies. Population-based service analysis and projection can aid agencies avoid being mired in a maintenance mentality not related to current and, most important, future demands for service.

There is a need for organizations to define their outcome objectives clearly (such as providing housing for clients or reducing their use of drugs). The goals of case management programs vary by population served and influence the timing and outcomes of the service delivered (Damron-Rodriguez, 1993). Understanding the difference between acute and chronic disabilities of the chronically mentally ill and the functionally impaired elderly generates differences in case management goals. Thus, defining goals related to the targeted population will increase the likelihood of achieving the desired intervention outcomes adaptively.

ORGANIZATIONAL SIZE

The effects of size on organizational structure and function represent one of the most thoroughly studied issues in organizational innovativeness (Damanpour & Evan, 1984; Kim, 1980; Kimberly & Evanisko, 1981; Meyer & Goes, 1988; Van de Ven & Rogers, 1988). Yet organizational size alone does not appear to have a consistent relationship with innovativeness (Herbig, 1994). Instead, size is important for innovation depending on other variables (richness of resources, organizational slack, number of professionals, and centralization) that interact with it (Herbig, 1994).

Large organizations generally have more rules and procedures for routine operations (Kagona, 1983). However, the change agent should refrain from drawing the popular conclusion that larger organizations are necessarily more bureaucratic and therefore may not be flexible and democratic (Daft, 1982; Ostroff & Smith, 1992). Size does not lead to the presence of all bureaucratic features in organizations. Instead, Herbig (1994) concludes, from an international study of innovation, that it is the culture of the organization that begets creativity. Large organizations may be run as democratically as small ones and, indeed, often are. Role definitions may be quite loose and broad in large organizations, depending on tasks and functions. Division of labor is likewise more dependent on the nature of the task and the product than necessarily or automatically a function of the size of the organization (Damanpour & Evan, 1984; Nord & Tucker, 1987). An organization may have a dual form for purposes of innovation, which allows it to maintain a small team that operates within the larger organization in order to address the multifaceted requirements of both initiating and implementing an innovation (Chandler & Ingrassia, 1991; Cole, 1985; Damanpour, 1988).

Large organizations tend to have available more organizational slack (uncommitted resources), which can be applied to innovative programs. When organizational size is associated with organizational slack, large organizations will be more innovative than smaller ones (Kimberly & Evanisko, 1981). Large organizations can afford to employ more and higher-level professionals, who, as we will soon see, may serve as an innovative force (Damanpour & Evan, 1984). When organizational size is directly related to the number of professionals employed, a larger organization may be more innovative, as we discuss later. However, smaller organizations sometimes devote their resources to fewer and smaller nontraditional programs but implement them more intensively and comprehensively, and with greater dedication, than do larger organizations (Ettlie, 1980; Kagona, 1983).

A decline in environmental resources generally decreases organizational innovation and change (Cameron, 1984; Cameron & Zammuto, 1983; Chaffee, 1984). The era of fiscal constraint growing out of the desire to balance the national budget has led to a reduction in federal funding for human services (Nathan, 1996). Organizational responses to environmental scarcity often take the form of closing channels of communication, tightening rules, and centralizing decision making in order to protect the core of the organization (Cameron, Whetten, & Kim, 1987; Yasai-Ardekan, 1989). Expansion of resources reduces the need for protection and often results in the growth of the organization, less rigidity, and more innovation (Cameron, Whetten, & Kim, 1987; Cole, 1985). However, certain innovations may take place in response to scarcity, such as the creation of new job market programs and other service innovations that occurred in Massachusetts from 1975 to 1986 (Dukakis & Kanter, 1988). Certainly, new programs and approaches in welfare are related to recessionary periods combined with increased need, as well as to shifts in political ideology.

A change agent who wants to design innovative organizations should not be concerned with the size of the organization per se. One must gauge the balance among various size-related factors, some of which are conducive to innovation and some of which are detrimental at different stages of the innovation process. Small innovation groups within large organizations are an option. It is useful to work toward creating resources to be used for innovation, which can be accomplished by marshaling a greater overall volume of resources, scaling programs to a level that does not absorb all resources, or setting aside specially designated development funds in the budget.

PROFESSIONALIZATION

Professionalization and organizational structure are related. For example, increased professionalization is associated with a decentralized authority structure, which means more authority is vested in staff at middle and lower echelons (Cohn & Turyn, 1984; Ostroff & Smith, 1992). Accordingly, increased professionalization leads to fewer rules, less standardization, and less job codification—the professionals themselves define their roles in a somewhat autonomous fashion (Daft, 1982). Other correlates of increased professionalization include the use of diverse and less routine technologies (Ostroff & Smith, 1992) and increased organizational complexity, defined as having more functional units, and a greater range of disciplinary diversity within the organization (Abramson & Rosenthal, 1995; Kanter, 1988). With more professionals on staff, organizations typically establish a broader range of linkages with external organizations (Johnson, 1994) and adopt new programs and novel solutions to organizational problems (Sanburn, 1983). However, increased professionalization, which results in a diversified staff, may lead to interprofessional rivalry over resources, to stalemate, and to the establishment within the organization of bargaining mechanisms for conflict resolution (Alter, 1990; Patti, 1980). Professionalization offers a high potential for innovation but also carries the seeds of conflict.

It follows from our discussion that professionals and activists who want to establish creative organizations or to increase the potential innovativeness of a system (decentralization, fewer rules, more external links, novel programs) should do one or more of the following: (1) hire more professionals; (2) increase the number of occupational specialties within the organization; (3) encourage and facilitate staff participation in extraorganizational professional activities; (4) increase the amount of formal and informal training required of employees; (5) encourage external professional inputs; (6) employ supervisors who are professionally stimulating. It seems reasonable that these actions, which raise the professional level of organizations, will improve services to vulnerable populations who need competent and varied professional inputs.

At the same time, procedures need to be established for communicating among professional specializations, agreeing on common goals, and adjudicating disagreements. This assumes the qualification of "all things being equal." The team approach is a growing form of organizational management and health care delivery that is a model of professionals working together for a common goal (Katzenbach & Smith, 1993). Interdisciplinary teams are used to address the multiple needs of functionally impaired populations (Rubenstein, Sui, & Wieland, 1989; Saltz, 1994). A growing body of literature describes the roles, conflict resolution strategies, and coordination functions of interdisciplinary teams. Interdisciplinary teams of professionals can provide effective and creative care plans for vulnerable populations because their needs transcend any one discipline. The need to synthesize and reconfigure professional services within the team is a force for innovation. However, some professionals, disciplines, and interdisciplinary teams are not innovative or open to the environment but remain insular and protective of their privileges and the status quo.

There are, however, services that paraprofessionals or volunteers may perform that enhance professional care. These include friendly visiting to the isolated elderly and offering "big brother" services to inner-city youth. In these cases, paraprofessionals are an important adjunct to professional services, not a substitute. With the current trend toward "downsizing" and "right sizing" organizations, there has been a move to deprofessionalize certain roles. Nurses in New York ran an ad in the *New York Times* asking patients to ask, "Is the person serving you a *real* nurse?" Public departments of social services, particularly adult protective services, may have low levels of professional staff and may be expected to be less innovative because of this. The efforts to deprofessionalize must be examined over the long term for their consequences for organizational responsiveness to change and innovation. However, grassroots nonprofessional workers and citizens represent a potentially important source of organizational innovation, particularly with respect to making organizations more responsive to the needs of lower-income or less powerful populations (Mizrahi & Rosenthal, 1992). A dynamic for change is greater when persons who represent the perspective of the client population served are given a voice.

Change agents who are external to an organizational system and who wish to introduce innovation in as little time as possible should seek out those units of the organization that display the characteristics discussed in this section. They can also introduce professional persons from the outside, thereby "opening up" the agency through external inputs. This may take considerably longer than working with change potential within the existing system.

LEADERSHIP AND PARTICIPATION

A key issue in organizational change is the role of leadership and group participation (Dubnicki, 1991). Participation is of two general types—policy participation, in which members contribute to substantive decisions concerning goals, and implementation participation, in which they formulate a means of enacting prior decisions. Most of the studies that were reviewed concern implementation participation, and, indeed, most of the professional work in organizational development is in this mode.

Broad participation, which we ordinarily view favorably in terms of innovation, in actuality under some circumstances stimulates change and under other circumstances impedes change (Knoke, 1990). Research indicates that a high degree of centralization (control of decision making at the top) ordinarily works against innovativeness. A related organizational characteristic, formalization (the existence of established rules and procedures), also generally inhibits change (Resnick, 1980). However, a highly centralized system (police or fire departments come to mind, or Social Security) with an executive committed to innovation, can have strong change potential (Magill & Roger, 1981). An example is the case of the successful fluoridation of water in American cities, where the critical factor was the presence of a centralized and determined decision-making authority represented by a city manager or mayor. Implementing school desegregation by school superintendents is another example. In a public welfare department providing child welfare services, top down innovation might work; in a small voluntary agency serving battered women, the input of staff and clients would likely be a strong impetus for change.

The attitude of staff is not necessarily associated with innovativeness (see the discussion of worker satisfaction). Lower-level workers have greater potential than their middle-level, more conservative supervisors to formulate novel decisions (Patti, 1980; Sanborn, 1983). The change agent under conducive circumstances can increase the innovativeness of an organization by appropriately activating and increasing the participation of its employees in decision making (Kanter, 1983; Resnick, 1980). When the chief executive of a centralized organization (such as agencies that administer public assistance) is innovative, and the change agent has access to him or her, it may be effective instead to work through the chief executive. Once the executive has adopted the innovation in principle, it can be rapidly transmitted, since high centralization facilitates the downward flow of information and policy. The change agent should realize, however, that the degree of implementation may be low in such situations, since adoption requiring actions by others may be superficial and unstable.

Some innovations may require significant participation by employees or members, particularly if the tasks are nonroutine or cannot be monitored, such as providing clinical services. Increasingly, management and production teams are viewed as the vehicle for change and increased performance (Katzenbach & Smith, 1993). The team approach is required whenever collective work is needed for real-time integration of multiple skills, experience, and judgments. For example, teams are often used in case management programs for many vulnerable populations, including the chronically mentally ill, the developmentally disabled, and the functionally limited elderly. Curriculum innovations frequently require a forum of participation from students, faculty, and affiliated agencies (Carmon, Hauber, & Chase, 1992; Rothman, 1987). For example, innovation is facilitated by team brainstorming. High performance organizations have found "Work Out" sessions or "jamming" to be powerful means to generate creative ideas a portion of which lead to real innovation (Kanter, Koa, & Wiersema, 1997).

THE TASK ENVIRONMENT

The exchange system of an organization is its task environment. The task environment interactions involve the organization in "strategic choices" about how to respond to and influence its environment (Kanter, 1988).

Organizational systems that operate in a task environment of high certainty and regularity tend to have more pronounced bureaucratic or "machine system" features—high centralization and formalization. This relationship is associated with efficiency of operation. Conversely, when the task environment is uncertain and unpredictable, less pronounced bureaucratic features are typical and desirable (Yasai-Ardekani, 1989).

In a situation that calls for high centralization, technically oriented leadership is required. Increased centralization may require technical equipment, forms, and routines that may take a good deal of planning and administrative know-how. A decentralized structure may require a different type of leadership—individuals who are more attuned to human relations, more willing to share decision making, and capable of providing charismatic as opposed to purely formal leadership. In the decentralized organization, it may be necessary to put in place special mechanisms of coordination (such as case conferences in child welfare or interdepartmental committees in large, complex geriatric programs) in order to maintain a reasonable level of stability in the organization (Ostroff & Smith, 1992).

This generalization is based on a study of organizations across the board and at a specific time. However, it is useful to recognize that organizations are often transformed as they develop over time, and an organization that starts out with an erratic task environment may, as it matures, become powerful enough to gain control and create environmental stability (Lang & Lockhart, 1990). An example is the airline industry in the United States. During the time of deregulation, the industry created patterned interorganizational linkages in its environment in order to foster industry stability. Organizations sometimes move in the opposite direction; economic and political conditions can change in such a way that disturbs the ecology of the organization. The effect of devolution, or the shift from federal to state responsibility for decisions related to entitlement programs that has occurred during the Clinton administration, has had a significant destabilizing effect on the human services system.

Recognizing that some circumstances call for a level of centralization does not assume that *extreme* centralization is effective. It is necessary to make judgments concerning the appropriate degree of centralization. Income maintenance agencies can probably tolerate a greater degree of centralization than can settlement houses or grassroots social action organizations. Let us take Social Security as an example. This organization is effective to the degree that it functions in a precise, reliable, repetitive way. Checks to recipients must be processed, mailed, and delivered monthly to the elderly in such a way that clients can make daily living plans and financial commitments based on predictability. A fixed structure of personnel and procedure needs to be in place to guarantee such regularity.

Organizations that want to develop a more flexible structure, which is conducive to innovation, might consider diversifying their task environment. External change agents who want to induce such change might consider introducing abrupt or unexpected elements into the task environment, as social action groups do through demonstrations, work stoppages, and the like.

JOB SATISFACTION

Centralization is often correlated with job dissatisfaction and work alienation (Patti, 1980). Staff participation in the system (as measured by control over the method and order of performance and ability to try one's own ideas and to utilize one's skills independently) tends to increase satisfaction and identification with the organization (Daft, 1982; Kim, 1980). Such job satisfaction and identification may or may not be a force for innovation. Satisfied workers with a strong identification with the organization and with special privileges or prerogatives can be a force for keeping things as they are (Resnick, 1980).

An organization that wishes to prevent alienation from work and to encourage amiable relationships should decrease the degree of hierarchy in the organization. This can be done by permitting decisions to be made at lower levels or consulting staff on decisions made by top administrators and by giving staff members a degree of independence in their activities (Kanter, 1983). In *New Work Habits for a Radically Changing World* Prichett (1996) urges employees to act like they are in business for themselves. Management strategies currently emphasize "enabling" staff to problem solve and make decisions themselves to improve services. This should help increase job satisfaction and hypothetically aid in retention of staff—which can serve to increase effectiveness and efficiency. It may also increase organizational innovation, but it also can have a variable effect on propensity for change.

Dynamics of Innovation

The structure of an organization can affect its propensity to innovate. But innovation is essentially a process involving precursors, stages, and key actors. We refer to such fluid forces as the dynamics of innovation and illustrate their role in inducing change.

PREVIOUS EXPERIENCE

The innovativeness of an organizational system is directly related to its *previous experience with innovations* and is inversely related to its previous negative experience. Target systems (organizations, neighborhoods, or communities that a change agent, internal or external, wishes to motivate to do things differently) that have previously experienced successful innovations are more innovative than those that have not; target systems that have previously experienced unsuccessful innovations become even less innovative (Kimberly & Evanisko, 1981; Leonard-Barton, 1988). Innovative organizations are more comfortable taking risks with new ways of doing things even if the result is not the expected outcome. The knowledge gained by trying something new becomes part of the organizational knowledge bank and contributes to better service over time (Kanter, Kao, & Wiersema, 1997).

The change agent who wishes to maximize innovativeness should approach systems that have had positive experiences with innovations, particularly if these past innovations were similar to the present one. Appropriate service organizations (or subunits) might be selected. In order to facilitate the eventual adoption of a major innovation, the change agent may want to promote more attractive or simpler innovations first, perhaps something more familiar

(Van de Ven & Rogers, 1988). For example, rather than introducing a full case management program for the mentally ill, one might start with training to strengthen the referral aspects of the existing clinical program. This is already an aspect of clinical service and might be viewed by practitioners as helping to lessen their felt service pressure. This incremental strategy may be particularly useful in cases where the key innovation would seem too risky or radical if it were introduced without prior experience. Finally, the change agent should be cautiously analytical when introducing innovations to avoid possible unfavorable conditions (such as moving too quickly or with little information), which could lead to failure and engender a negative attitude toward innovation in general. The development of assisted living as an alternative to nursing homes and an innovative form of residential housing has occurred incrementally in many settings. Some consider assisted living "just good board and care." Other ventures have developed significantly new models, in terms of both architecture and service. All outcomes to an intervention should be processed as contributing to the change process.

DISCONTENT AND ADVANTAGE OF INNOVATION

The innovativeness of a target system is directly related to the extent to which that system *feels a need for change. Discontented target systems* generally are more innovative than contented ones (Tushman & Nadler, 1986). The change agent who wishes to maximize the rate of adoption of an innovation should concentrate on those organizations that have expressed discontent in one way or another and are therefore more predisposed to favor change. Building agency coalitions to integrate services for children was motivated by recognition of the negative impact of service fragmentation (Armstrong, 1982).

Heightening existing discontent is another possible tactic. Benchmarking with more a successful organization can increase the desire for change. Benchmarking is a technique used in Total Quality Management (TQM) to measure performance against a "gold standard" of the most successful organization (Berwick, 1989). Newspaper and media coverage of service delivery inadequacies may increase motivation for improvement as well as attention to consumer service surveys that point out service deficiencies. Starkey (1985) describes the "desperation" innovation, which occurs when, due to system failures and their recognition, the system must do something quickly. The welfare reform of the mid-1990s could be a cautionary case in point.

The rate of adoption of an innovation is related to people's perception of its *relative advantages* compared to other innovations or the status quo (U.S. General Accounting Office, 1981). The advantages need to be communicated in clear, measurable, and impactful ways. A crisis situation (such as an economic downturn, policy shifts, political upheaval, turnover in leadership, or natural disaster) may provide an opportunity to emphasize the relative advantage of an innovation (Kaluzny & Hernandez, 1983). Rapid shifts in the organization of health care from fee-for-service to managed care have created new models of service delivery. Innovations in managed care for high-risk populations are emerging as health maintenance organizations (HMOs) are transformed into social health maintenance organizations (SHMOs) with distinctive features targeted to different populations.

During a crisis, the relative advantage of an innovation may be increased as the disadvantages of continuing the status quo become dramatically apparent. Vice President Al Gore's campaign to "reinvent government," as well as shifts to managed care, has presented the Veterans Administration health services with a challenge for change. VA medical centers are moving to decrease hospital care and increase community care options. In addition, the organizational structure is changing to combine health care resources into VA Integrated Service Networks (VISNs). Change agents need to be alert in order to capitalize on such "unfreezing" occurrences.

TYPES OF INNOVATIONS

Different types of innovations, whether technical or administrative, are associated with different types of conditions and organizations (Kanter, 1988; Kimberly & Evanisko, 1981; Nord & Tucker, 1987). Change agents must consider the type of innovation in order to facilitate the appropriate organizational characteristics to enhance its diffusion and implementation. Technical innovation (e.g., using cognitive therapy for certain psychiatric disorders) is generally facilitated by low levels of formalization, decentralization in decision making, and a high degree of employee professionalism (Damanpour, 1988; Damanpour & Evan, 1984; Meyer & Goes, 1988). Administrative innovation (e.g., using computerized systems for data management) is characterized by higher levels of formalization, concentrated power, and lower levels of professionalism (Fennel, 1984). Environmental factors affect technological or administrative innovations differentially (Damanpour, 1988). Technological innovations are more frequent in conditions of plenty (think of Office of Economic Opportunity program approaches), in contrast to administrative innovations (e.g., cutting back on midlevel managers or line staff), which frequently take place even in times of scarce resources (Kimberly & Evanisko, 1981; Van de Ven & Rogers, 1988).

Innovations vary by the degree of change they impart to a system (Ettlie, 1980; Kagona, 1983). The degree of change also relates to organizational structure. Incremental innovations or small changes (e.g., a new reporting form) are more likely in more formalized, centralized organizations; more radical innovations (e.g., high-technology home care) are more likely in organizations that are more decentralized yet complex (Cohn & Turyn, 1984; Damanpour, 1988; Nord & Tucker, 1987).

COMMUNICATION AND CONTACT

Strategic elements are involved in communication processes used in promoting innovations and in the key actors that are brought into the process. We discuss these in turn.

The rate of adoption of an innovation is related to the amount of *positive direct contact* with the target system. Innovations that are successfully experienced have a higher adoption rate than innovations that are interpreted to the target system (Hoffman & Roman, 1984; Kimberly & Evanisko, 1981; Leonard-Barton, 1988). In order to maximize the adoption rate of an innovation, the change agent may promote it in such a way that it can be pilot tested by a limited portion of a large system, which can then demonstrate its success to the rest of the organization (Magill & Rogers, 1981). The utilization of demonstration projects that clearly show that the innovation works and has good results is a frequently used method that employs this principle (Bailey & Koney, 1995a; Ettlie, 1980; Kagona, 1983). Medicare waiver projects are frequently used to demonstrate the effectiveness of new models. Hospice care for the terminally ill was first provided as a waiver program in select sites and now is an alternative form of terminal care throughout the nation. Community-based consortia have been developed as models (Bailey & Koney, 1995b) and are now replacing hospital-based care.

The rate of adoption of an innovation is also related to its communicability (Rogers, 1983). Innovations that can be explained or demonstrated with ease have a higher adoption rate than those that are difficult to explain or demonstrate (Boutwell, 1994; Chaffee, 1983; Hoffman & Roman, 1984). In order to maximize the adoption of an innovation, the change agent should attempt to formulate it in a simple and direct form. Practice guidelines disseminated by the Health Services Research Administration (HSRA) are clearly stated prescriptive statements for physicians and related health professionals. The practice guidelines are based on empirical research and formulated by expert panels and aim to increase best practices in care for specific medical conditions and to ensure equitable care across settings and localities.

The language of the communication message is also quite obviously related to its communicability. Generally, the closer the communication to the target's language or vernacular, the better. Similarly, compatibility with the values of a subculture may facilitate the communication of information about an innovation. Thus, the change agent should attempt to reach a subculture through its own communication channels (i.e., former addicts, former clients). The alternative—attempting to change existing norms, values, and customs—is indeed a formidable undertaking.

Oral communication should be supplemented by visual aids or feedback loops to ensure that target groups grasp the information that is provided to them. Quality management and assurance methodologies variously referred to as Total Quality Management (TQM) and Continuous Quality Management (CQM) provide multiple techniques for visual presentation and feedback. Fish boning, decision trees, and Gantt charts present data related to organizational change (Berwick, 1989). The visual techniques can present the reasons for change as well as the impact of the innovation.

INNOVATION ACTORS

The rate of adoption of an innovation increases when the target system receives *peer support* in favor of adoption. The rate of adoption of an innovation is also facilitated by a consensus of goals among peers within the target system (when the innovation is compatible with those goals) (Cohn & Turyn, 1984; Fennell, 1984; Kimberly & Evanisko, 1981). The change agent can attempt to gain peer support around a target individual or group he or she wishes to influence toward adoption of an innovation, such as social workers in an agency, citizens in a neighborhood, or physicians in a health care system (Fennell, 1984; Fennell & Warnecke, 1988; Kimberly & Evanisko, 1981). An example of this interpersonal network approach to the diffusion of innovations can be seen in the dissemination of cancer treatments among physicians. Change agents from the National Cancer Institute built support within small groups of physicians and then built larger networks within hospitals (Fennell & Warnecke, 1988). Arriving at a peer consensus regarding the innovation and making it publicly explicit speeds adoption. Persons should be encouraged to seek advice from others with similar characteristics when those others are likely to be supportive. Alternatively, the change agent might seek out a segment of influential peers and urge them to advocate the innovation with the target population.

Certain individuals of a target system are more influential in expediting the diffusion and adoption process (Rogers, 1983; Zaltman, Duncan, & Holbeck, 1984). The rate of adoption of an innovation is directly related to the extent to which these "opinion leaders" promote it (Fennell & Warnecke, 1988; Kanter, 1983; Kimberly & Evanisko, 1981; Staw, 1984).

In order to maximize personal influence in favor of an innovation, the change agent should identify the target system's opinion leaders with respect to the *relevant issue area* (a professional matter, technical issue, political question) and enlist their support in favor of adoption (Fennell, 1984). This is exemplified in the diffusion of new cancer treatments (Fennell & Warnecke, 1988). One can usually best identify opinion leaders by asking people to whom they go for advice and information about an idea. Opinion leaders are not necessarily individuals with a history of being innovative. If, however, for a given issue or program they can be motivated to either innovate or encourage others to innovate, their influence on the adoption process can be significant. Opinion leaders are usually found among the somewhat better-educated, more cosmopolitan, higher social-status segments of a larger population. They are likely to have higher rates of social participation. In an agency, supervisors, program directors, or union representatives are likely candidates for this designation.

IMPLEMENTATION FOLLOW-THROUGH

Mere initiation of an innovation does not assure its implementation (Ettlie, 1980; Nord & Tucker, 1987). The organizational characteristics related to the initiation of an innovation vary from those related to implementation (Hoffman & Roman, 1984; Kagona, 1983). Low degrees of formalization and centralization have been found to be associated with more rapid progress at the initiation stage of innovation, although this is not necessarily the case at the implementation phase (Daft, 1982; Kim, 1980). This is also consistent with the conceptualization of organic and mechanistic organizations as related to high and low degrees of innovation, respectively. Organic organizational features that encourage broad participation in decision making may facilitate initiation of an innovation (for example, new health service approaches in free clinics), while well-developed mechanistic characteristics of centralization and formalization can facilitate the implementation of innovations (Ostroff & Smith, 1992) (e.g., use of a token economy in a large state mental hospital). The targeted stage of innovation must be identified in order to foster the appropriate organizational characteristics (Damanpour, 1988; Ettlie, 1980; Leonard-Barton, 1988; Meyer & Goes, 1988).

Both intra- and extraorganizational actors may offer resistance to the implementation of the innovation (Kimberly & Evanisko, 1981; Knoke, 1990; Meyer & Goes, 1988; Tushman & Nadler, 1986). Resistance to the implementation of an innovation may come from line staff, such as teachers who oppose educational reform (Sanborn, 1983); other organizations intimately involved with the innovation, for example, AMA opposition to medical reforms (Lang & Lockhart, 1990; Mizrahi & Rosenthal, 1992); or the consumers of a target system that the innovation is intended to serve, for example, older adults, as represented by the American Assciation of Retired Persons (AARP), who rejected catastrophic health care coverage (Kaluzny & Hernandez, 1983; Roberts & DeGennaro, 1986; Schietinger, Coburn, & Levi, 1995). Also, the charismatic leadership needed to institute an innovative idea or program is often different from the stable, technical leadership needed to carry it out. Planning must involve an analysis of both the decision to innovate and the process of expediting new social programs that have been authorized.

Conclusion

This discussion has revealed some of the complexities and nuances involved in inducing organizational change. It has identified a range of variables to be considered and interrelated in the process of initiating innovation. Beyond that, it has brought forward some concrete strategies that offer promising and productive guidelines for those who seek to promote innovation in organizational contexts. Using a contingency theory framework, there is no one best way to foster organizational innovation. However, there are better ways, and the innovative human service organization must strategically plan to effectively and creatively match its organizational structure and process to service environment demands.

This presentation has attempted to demonstrate the utility of applying existing empirical knowledge in the development of strategies of planned change. The approach involves a research utilization methodology that the senior author has evolved over a period of some twenty years (Rothman, 1974, 1980a, 1980b) and that has been refined as systematic research synthesis (Rothman, Damron-Rodriquez, & Shenassa, 1994). This is not to say that other sources of knowledge cannot accomplish such objectives, or that this one has overriding superiority. Practice knowledge may be advanced by codifying practice wisdom, observing practice in action, analyzing occurrences of successful practice, and in other ways.

We have outlined a variety of approaches to innovation based on existing research. Many of these initiatives appear to be promising, but the research is incomplete, sometimes contradictory, and there are gaps. Implementation needs to be exploratory and cautionary, as with social practice in general. Much of the research on innovation has been conducted within the market economy; more research on innovation in public and not for profit service organizations is needed. Human service organizations are increasingly held accountable for documenting the success of their interventions. Systematic demonstration of the outcomes of service interventions to vulnerable populations can form a foundation knowledge on health and human service innovation. This can strengthen the leadership role of providers in not only responding to change but creating new systems of care.

Innovation is more than a technical matter; it brings about outcomes that are infused with values. Although the current environment in the human services puts a certain stress on efficiency and cost containment, questions of quality and service effectiveness require continuing attention and vigilance, especially for vulnerable clients who suffer severely in coping with the hardships of life. From a professional standpoint, innovation is more than change as such; it is change for the better in terms of enhancing the life chances of clients for whom we take responsibility. We have not discussed the value dimensions of innovation in this presentation on methods of innovation but want to insist, before closing, that it is a background factor that readers need to consciously factor into the process.

REFERENCES

Abramson, J. S., & Rosenthal, B. (1995). Interdisciplinary and interorganizational collaboration. In R. L. Edwards (Ed. In Chief), *Encyclopedia of social work* (19th ed., Vol. 2, pp. 1479–1489). Washington, DC: NASW Press.

Alter, C. (1990). An exploratory study of conflict and coordination in interorganizational service delivery systems. *Academy of Management Review, 33*, 478–502.

Alter, C., & Hage, J. (1993). *Organizations working together*. Newbury Park, CA: Sage Publications.

Armstrong, R. F. (1982). Using agency coalitions to integrate services for children. *Social Work in Education, 4*(3), 59–68.

Bailey, D., & Koney, K. M. (1995a). Community-based consortium: One model for creation and development. *Journal of Community Practice, 2*(1), 21–42.

Bailey, D., & Koney, K. M. (1995b). An integrative framework for the evaluation of community-based consortia. *Evaluation and Community Practice, 18*, 245–252.

Bailey, D., & Koney, K. M. (1996). Interorganizational community-based collaboration. *Social Work, 41*(6), 600–611.

Barg, F. K., McCorkle, R., Robinson, K., Yasko, J. M., Jepson, C., & McKeehan, K. M. (1992). Gaps and contract: Evaluating the diffusion of new information. Part I. A description of the strategy. *Cancer Nursing, 15*(6), 401–405.

Benson, J. K. (1975). The interorganizational network as a political economy. *Administrative Science Quarterly, 20*(1), 229–249.

Bertalanffy, L. Von (1968). *General systems theory*. New York: George Braziller.

Berwick, D. M. (1989). Continuous improvement as an ideal in health care. *New England Journal of Medicine, 320,* 53–56.

Boutwell, W. B. (1994). Theory-based approaches for improving biomedical communications. *Journal of Biocommunication, 21*(1), 2–6.

Cameron, K. S. (1984). Organizational adaption and higher education. *Journal of Higher Education, 54,* 359–380.

Cameron, K. S., Whetten, D. A., & Kim, M. U. (1987). Organizational dysfunctions of decline. *Academy of Management Journal, 30,* 126–138.

Cameron, K. S., & Zammuto, R. F. (1983). Matching managerial strategies to conditions of decline. *Human Resource Management, 22,* 359–375.

Carmon, M., Hauber, R. P., & Chase, L. (1992). From anxiety to action. *Nursing and Health Care 13*(7), 364–368.

Chaffee, E. E. (1984). Successful strategic management in small private colleges. *Journal of Higher Education, 55,* 212–241.

Chandler, C., & Ingrassia P. (1991, April 11). Just as U.S. firms try Japanese management, Honda is centralizing. *Wall Street Journal,* A1.

Clark, P., & Starkey, K. (1988). *Organizational transitions and innovation-design.* New York: Pinter Publishers.

Cohn, S. F., & Turyn, R. M. (1984, November). Organizational structure, decision-making procedures, and the adoption of innovations. *IEEE Transactions on engineering management, EM31,* 154–161.

Cole, R. E. (1985). The macropolitics of organizational change: A comparative analysis of the spread of small group activities. *Administrative Science Quarterly, 30*(4), 560–585.

Daft, R. L. (1982). Bureaucratic versus non-bureaucratic structure and the process of innovation and change. *Research in the Sociology of Organizations, 1,* 129–166.

Damanpour, F. (1988). Innovation type, radicalness, and the adoption process. *Communication Research, 15*(5), 545–567.

Damanpour, F., & Evan, W. M. (1984). Organizational innovation and performance: The problem of "organizational lag." *Administrative Science Quarterly, 29*(3), 392–402.

Damron-Rodriguez, J. (1993). Case management in two long-term care populations: A synthesis of research. *Journal of Case Management, 2*(4), 125–129.

Damron-Rodriguez, J., Wallace, S., & Kington, R. (1994). Service utilization and minority elderly: Appropriateness, accessibility and acceptability. *Gerontology & Geriatrics Education, 15*(1), 45–63.

Dreher, D. (1996). *The Tao of personal leadership.* New York: Harper Collins.

Dubnicki, C. (1991). Building high-performance management teams. *Healthcare Forum Journal,* May–June, 19–24.

Dukakis, M. S., & Kanter, R. M. (1988). *Creating the future: The Massachusetts comeback and its promise for America.* New York: Summit Books.

Emery, K. J., & Mamerow, D. C. (1986). Making services integration work at the local level: The partnership in Dayton, Ohio. *New England Journal of Human Services, 6*(2), 12–15.

Ettlie, J. E. (1980). Adequacy of stage models for decisions on adoption of innovation. *Psychological Reports, 46*(3), 991–995.

Fennell, M. L. (1984). Synergy, influence, and information in the adoption of administrative innovations. *Academy of Management Journal, 28,* 113–117.

Fennell, M. L., & Warnecke, R. B. (1988). *The diffusion of medical innovations: An applied network analysis.* New York: Plenum.

Galaskiewicz, J. (1985). Interorganizational relations. *American Sociological Services, 11,* 281- 304.

Health Resources and Services Administration. (1991, May). *Guidance for the Healthy Start Program.* Rockville, MD: U.S. Department of Health and Human Services.

Herbig, P. A. (1994). *The innovation magic.* Westport, CT: Quorum Books.

Hoffman, E., & Roman, P. M. (1984). Information diffusion in the implementation of innovation process. *Communication Research, 11*(1), 117–140.

Johnson, A. K. (1994). Linking professionalism and community organization: A scholar/ advocate approach. *Journal of Community Practice, 1*(2), 65–86.

Kagona, T. (1983). An evolutionary view of organizational adoption. Working paper, Kobe University.

Kaluzny, A. D., & Hernandez, S. R. (1983). Managing change in health care organizations. *Medical Care Review, 40,* 16–203.

Kanter, R. M. (1983). *The change masters.* New York: Simon & Schuster.

Kanter, R. M. (1988). Three tiers for innovative research. *Communication Research, 15*(8), 509–523.

Kanter, R. M. (1989). *When giants learn to dance.* New York: Simon & Schuster.

Kanter, R. M., Kao, J., & Wiersema, F. (1997). *Innovation.* New York: HarperBusiness.

Kaplan, M. (1986). Cooperation and coalition development among neighborhood organizations: A case study. *Journal of Voluntary Action Research, 15*(4), 22–24.

Katzenbach, J. R., & Smith, D. K. (1993). *The wisdom of teams.* New York: HarperBusiness.

Kim, L. (1980). Organizational innovation and structure. *Journal of Business Research, 8,* 225–245.

Kimberly, J. R., & Evanisko, M. J. (1981). Organizational innovation: The influence of individual, organizational, and contextual factors on hospital adoption of technological and administrative innovations. *Academy of Management Journal, 24*(4), 689–713.

Knoke, D. (1990). *Organizing for collection action: The political economics of associations.* New York: Aldine de Gruyter.

Lang, J. R., & Lockhart, D. E. (1990). Increased environmental uncertainty and changes in board linkage patterns. *Academy of Management Journal, 33*(1), 106–128.

Leonard-Barton, D. (1988). Implementation characteristics of organizational innovations: Limits and opportunities for management strategies. *Communication Research, 15*(5), 603–631.

Magill, K. P., & Rogers, E. M. (1981). Federally sponsored demonstrations of technological innovations. *Knowledge, 3,* 23–42.

Meyer, A. D., & Goes, J. B. (1988). Organizational assimilation of innovations: A multilevel contextual analysis. *Academy of Management Journal, 31*(4), 897–923.

Miller, J. G. (1978). *Living systems.* New York: McGraw-Hill.

Mizrahi, T., & Rosenthal, B. (1992). Managing dynamic tensions in social change coalitions. In T. Mizrahi & J. D. Morrison (Eds.), *Community organizing and social administration: Advances, trends, and emerging principles* (pp. 11–40). New York: Haworth Press.

Mulford, C. L. (1984). *Interorganizational relations: Implications for community development* (Vol. IV). New York: Human Sciences Press.

Nathan, R. P. (1996). The "devolution revolution": An overview. In *Rockefeller Institute Bulletin, Symposium on Federation* (pp. 5–13). Albany: State University of New York, Nelson A. Rockefeller Institute of Government.

Nord, W. R., & Tucker, S. (1987). *Implementing routine and radical innovations.* Lexington, MA: Lexington Books.

Ostroff, F., & Smith, D. (1992). The horizontal organization. *McKinsey Quarterly, 1*, 148–168.

Parsons, T. (1956). *The social system.* New York: Free Press.

Patti, R. J. (1980). Organizational resistance and change: The view from below. In H. Resnick & R. Patti (Eds.), *Change from within: Humanizing social welfare organizations* (pp. 114–131). Philadelphia: Temple University Press.

Peterson, G. B. (1995, April). *A block grant approach to welfare reform.* (Welfare Reform Brief No. 1). Washington, DC: Urban Institute.

Pritchett, P. (1996). *New work habits for a radically changing world.* Dallas, TX: Pritchett & Associates.

Resnick, H. (1980). Effecting internal change in human service organizations. In H. Resnick & R. Patti (Eds.), *Change from within: Humanizing social welfare organizations* (pp. 186–199). Philadelphia: Temple University Press.

Roberts-DeGennaro, M. (1986). Factors contributing to coalition maintenance. *Journal of Sociology and Social Welfare, 13*, 248–264.

Rogers, E. (1983). *Diffusion of innovations.* New York: Free Press.

Rothman, J. (1974). *Planning and organizing for social change.* New York: Columbia University Press.

Rothman, J. (1980a). *Using research in organizations.* Beverly Hills, CA: Sage Publications.

Rothman, J. (1980b). *Social R&D: Research development in the human services.* Englewood Cliffs, NJ: Prentice-Hall.

Rothman, J. (1987). Disseminating curriculum innovations among schools of social work. In M. P. Keenan (Ed.), *The chronically mentally ill in rural areas: Model curricula for social work education* (pp. 205–211). Washington, DC: Council on Social Work Education.

Rothman, J., Damron-Rodriguez, J. A., & Shenassa, E. (1994). Systematic research synthesis—conceptual integration methods of meta-analysis. In J. Rothman & E. J. Thomas (Eds.), *Intervention research: Design and development for human service* (pp. 133–163). New York: Haworth Press.

Rothman, J., Erlich, J. L, & Teresa, J. G. (1976). *Promoting innovation and change in organizations and communities: A planning manual.* New York: John Wiley & Sons.

Rubenstein, L. V., Sui, A. L., & Wieland, J. D. (1989). Comprehensive geriatric assessment: Understanding its efficacy. *Aging Clinical and Experimental Research, 1*(2), 87–98.

Saltz, C. (1994). *Guide to interdisciplinary practice in rehabilitation settings.* New York: American Association of Physical Therapy.

Sanborn, L. O. (1983). *Worker innovation: A model and empirical test.* University of Houston. Dissertation Abstracts International 44(3-B): 944.

Schietinger, H., Coburn, J., & Levi, J. (1995). Community planning for HIV prevention: Findings from the first year. *AIDS & Public Policy Journal, 10*(3), 140–147.

Schwartz, R. M. (Ed.) (1992). *Managing organizational transitions in a global economy.* Los Angeles: Institute of Industrial Relations, University of California.

Scott, R. A. (1967). The selection of clients by social welfare agencies: The case of the blind. *Social Problems, 14*, 248–257.

Starkey, K. P. (1985). The lengthening hour-time and the demise of psychoanalysis as therapy. *Social Science and Medicine, 20*(9), 939–943.

Staw, B. M. (1984). Organizational behavior: A review of reformulation of the field's outcome variables. *Annual Review of Psychology, 35*, 627–666.

Stocking, B. (1985). *Initiative and inertia. Case studies in the NHS.* London: Nuffield Provincial Hospitals Trust.

Tushman, M., & Nadler, D. (1986). Organizing for innovation. *California Management Review, 28*, 74–92.

U.S. General Accounting Office. (1981). *Small businesses are more active as inventors than as innovators in the innovation process* (Report PAD-82-19). Washington, DC: Author.

Van de Ven, A. H., & Rogers, E. M. (1988). Innovations and organizations: Critical perspectives. *Communication Research, 15*(5), 632–651.

Yasai-Ardekani, M. (1989). Effects of environmental scarcity and munificence on the relationship of context to organizational structure. *Academy of Management Journal, March*, 131–156.

Zaltman, G., Duncan, R., & Holbeck, J. (1984). *Innovations & organizations* (1st ed., 1973). Malabar, FL: Robert E. Kreiger.

Part II

Innovations in Practice and Service Delivery with Children and Adolescents

3

Innovations for High-Risk Infants

LYNN T. SINGER
SONIA MINNES
ROBERT E. ARENDT

Multiple historical perspectives have shaped the development of a national policy for infants conceptualized as developmentally vulnerable or high risk, culminating in the 1986 passage of the Education for All Handicapped Children Amendments (Public Law 99-457). This statute calls for "statewide, comprehensive, coordinated, multidisciplinary, interagency" programs of early intervention services for all handicapped infants and their families (Sec. 671) and provides authorization for facilitated development of comprehensive early intervention programs for infants and toddlers with developmental delays or disabilities. The establishment of infancy and preschool early intervention programs as targeted national and state goals is, in itself, a recent, major innovation in service delivery for practice with vulnerable populations, as infants had been largely ignored in mental health and educational policies and practices apart from general pediatric health and growth issues.

The prior success of the Head Start Program and the Mental Retardation Centers initiated in the 1960s, combined with the results of decades of developmental research, provided impetus for a downward age extension of educational interventions. Several landmark longitudinal studies that followed cohorts of infants from birth to beyond school age, including the Collaborative Perinatal Project from the National Institute of Neurological Diseases and Blindness (Broman, Nichols, & Kennedy, 1975) and the Kauai studies from Hawaii (Werner, Bierman, & French, 1971), highlighted the importance of the caregiving environment to the eventual developmental competence of the child. These studies encouraged

Preparation of this paper was supported by Grants R01-DA07957 and R29-DA07358 from the National Institute on Drug Abuse, Grant MCJ-390592 and 390715 from the Bureau of Maternal and Child Health, and Grant RR00080 from the General Clinical Research Center.

hope that early intervention efforts could recalibrate the developmental trajectories of at-risk infancy populations, particularly those with sensory-motor and cognitive disabilities or from impoverished environments. While actualization of the mandates of PL 99-457 remains a challenge, early intervention efforts are benefiting from a number of advances, including an array of innovative infant assessment instruments derived from decades of research (Bayley, 1993; Porges, 1988; Singer & Fagan, 1984; Zeskind & Lester, 1981), advances in molecular biology and brain imagery that demonstrate the vulnerability and malleability of the infant brain (Chugani, Phelps, & Mazziotta, 1987), and the establishment of new training programs for clinicians specifically geared to infancy populations (Klein & Campbell, 1990).

Both vulnerability and risk imply a developmental perspective, such that over time there is a higher than average probability that negative outcomes or adverse consequences will accrue. The term "risk" suggests a stronger emphasis on the possibility that the "risk factor" may lay in the environment. The classification of risk conditions in infancy was introduced by Tjossem (1976) and included three categories: (1) *established diagnosis*, in which early developmental disabilities are related to a diagnosable medical condition, such as Down Syndrome; (2) *biological vulnerability*, referring to children with perinatal conditions associated with higher rates of negative developmental sequelae, such as prematurity; and (3) *environmentally at risk*, designating children whose early life experiences are limited by nutritional, economic, and social deficits.

This chapter presents an overview of current intervention efforts relevant for caregivers of several groups of high-risk infants in whom vulnerability is determined from known or presumed biological or physical conditions: (a) infants born after fetal exposure to maternal substance abuse, particularly cocaine and alcohol; (b) those with chronic illnesses diagnosable in infancy, such as bronchopulmonary dysplasia and human immunodeficiency virus (AIDS); and (c) the growing population of preterm infants with low and very low birthweight, recognizing that these categories may also be disproportionately caused by or exacerbated by the environmental risk conditions.

Intrauterine Drug Exposure—Prevalence and Effects

Alcohol, marijuana, and cocaine are widely used by women of childbearing years of all racial, social class, and ethnic groups. A study in Florida revealed that use of illegal drugs by pregnant women varied little between public and private health practices (Chasnoff, Landress, & Barrett, 1990). As a consequence, an alarmingly high percentage of prenatally drug exposed infants are born each year at risk for medical, developmental, and psychological problems requiring specialized interventions.

FETAL ALCOHOL SYNDROME (FAS)

An average of 62% of women between the ages of 18 and 34 report drinking alcohol in the past month (USDHHS, 1996), raising concerns about the prevalence of heavy drinking during pregnancy (Institute of Medicine, 1996). Data from the 1995 Household Survey indicate that 2.99% of pregnant women, ages 15–44 years, binge drank during the month prior to the survey (USDHHS, 1996). FAS rates of the most complete studies estimate 0.5 to 3 cases per 1,000 births (Institute of Medicine, 1996). The rates of fetal alcohol exposure, leading to the broader diagnosis of alcohol-related birth defects (ARBDs) or alcohol-related neurodevelopmental disorders (ARNDs), are believed to be much higher than FAS (Institute of Medicine, 1996). Native Americans have the highest FAS rate, almost 2.97 per 1000 births (Chavez, Cordero, & Becerra, 1988); African Americans have the second highest rate, 0.6 cases per 1000, followed by Caucasian and Hispanic populations. Asian populations have the lowest rate, with 0.03 cases per 1000.

FAS is characterized by slow growth before and after birth, below-average mental, motor, and social abilities, and a consistent pattern of minor physiological anomalies of the face, heart, and limbs (Aase, 1994). Often, nonspecific abnormalities occur or predictable facial abnormalities change as the infant matures, making it difficult to detect FAS. Since many clinicians are reluctant to stigmatize the mother or infant, FAS is frequently undiagnosed.

ILLICIT DRUG USE

Marijuana

In 1994 and 1995, 40,000 pregnant women (15–44 years old) reported smoking marijuana during the month prior to the surgery (USDHHS, 1996), including between 4 and 8.7% of women between the ages of 18 and 34. Similar percentages of black and white individuals use marijuana (4.7–5.9%), while the use among Asians and Hispanics (3.9–2.8%) is considerably lower. Relatively little is known about the effects of fetal marijuana exposure on child outcome. Fried, O'Connell, and Watkinson (1992) followed children prenatally exposed to marijuana, cigarettes, and alcohol for a period of from 60 to 72 months and found that lower cognitive and receptive language scores were associated with prenatal cigarette, but not marijuana, exposure, while observations at 48 months revealed associations between marijuana use and cognitive outcomes (Fried & Watkinson, 1990). Day et al. (1994) found no significant effects of marijuana use during any trimester of pregnancy on composite scores of an intelligence test, although there were significant negative effects of marijuana on short-term memory. When environmental effects were controlled, children exposed prenatally to marijuana had lower IQs than nonexposed children. To date, no consistent pattern of abnormalities has been documented among prenatally marijuana exposed infants (Day & Richardson, 1991).

Cocaine

Lifetime cocaine use is reported by 9.3% of women ages 15–44 who are not pregnant and have no children and by 2.3% of pregnant women within the same age category (USDHHS, 1996). Before the advent of crack cocaine in the late 1980s, cocaine was used primarily by Caucasian, middle-class, educated women.

Currently, crack cocaine is used with much greater frequency by minority individuals of low socioeconomic status (SES), especially African American and Hispanic women, compared to Caucasian women (USDHHS, 1996). According to the 1995 Household Survey (USDHHS, 1996), more than 1 million women between the ages of 15 and 44 reported having used cocaine in the past year, and 0.4% reported use during the prior month.

Cocaine use during the childbearing years is of particular concern because it has led to an alarmingly high number of prenatally cocaine-exposed infants born each year who are at risk for complicated medical, developmental, and psychological problems requiring specialized interventions. Prevalence rates for prenatal cocaine exposure range from 1% to 30% in some urban minority populations (Woods, Behnke, Eyler, Conlon, & Wobie, 1995). Estimates are largely based on research among low-SES women who receive care at teaching hospitals that serve indigent and high-risk cases. Research on cocaine-using pregnant women indicates that they also have higher rates of alcohol, tobacco, and marijuana use than do noncocaine-using women of similar race and social class (Singer et al., 1995).

Maternal cocaine use during pregnancy has been associated with complications including preterm birth, precipitous labor, abruptio placentae, poor prenatal nutrition (Bingol, Fuchs, Diaz, & Stone, 1987; Chasnoff, Burns, & Burns, 1987; Evans & Gillogley, 1991; Singer, Arendt, Song, Warshawshy, & Kliegman, 1994; Slutsker, 1992), and sexually transmitted diseases (STDs) (USDHHS, 1993). While no consistent pattern of adverse developmental or medical effects has been identified, some children suffer moderate to severe central nervous system (CNS) effects (Azuma & Chasnoff, 1993; Dominiquez, Vila-Coro, Slopis, & Bohan, 1991; Little & Snell, 1991), developmental delays including mental, motor, behavioral and social problems, and attention problems (Arendt, Singer, Angelopoulos, Bass, & Mascia, 1994; Griffith, Azuma, & Chasnoff, 1994; Hurt et al., 1995; Schneidner & Chasnoff, 1987; Singer, Arendt, Farkas, Minnes, Huang, & Yamashita, 1997). However, much of the research concerning developmental outcomes of prenatal cocaine exposure has been flawed because of poorly controlled studies that did not consider postnatal factors, such as poverty, maternal psychosocial status, or early intervention (Singer, Arendt, & Minnes, 1993).

Opiates

Historically, opiate epidemics have occurred after cocaine epidemics subsided. Therefore, hospitals have begun to monitor for in utero opiate exposure. A neonatal abstinence syndrome affects 60–80% of opiate exposed infants. An early study (Wilson, Desmond, & Verniaud, 1973) found that half of infants observed for a year or longer had behavioral disturbances such as hyperactivity, brief attention span, and temper outbursts.

In a study of opiate-exposed children, the relationship between prenatal exposure and neurobehavioral outcomes at age two was reported most harmful within the group from the most disadvantaged homes. Disruptions in interactions between methadone-maintained mothers and their children at 4 and 24 months were also related to maternal psychological problems (Hans, Bernstein, & Hensen, 1990). By school age, methadone-exposed children are reported to have a greater incidence of disruptive behavior and attention deficit-hyperactivity disorders (Hans, 1996). These studies highlight the importance of environmental factors, particularly the caregiving relationship, to later behavioral difficulties in drug-exposed children.

ISSUES IN PRACTICE

The recent call for innovations in practice for drug-exposed infants (Kandall, 1993) may be linked to the rise in the number of infants born exposed to cocaine. Crack cocaine's cycle of addiction (Gold, 1992) and association with greater use of other drugs (Singer et al., 1995) has alarmed medical professionals, human service workers, policymakers, and educators and has led to a focus on identifying the problems of maternal drug users and their infants.

The most obvious evidence of need for innovative practice comes from the overburdened foster care system. From 1977 to 1991, referrals to Child Protective Services grew from 838,000 to 2.7 million in the United States (Daro & McCurdy, 1992). In most cities, infants are removed from the care of cocaine-using mothers and placed with relatives or with foster care parents. In many cases, mothers give birth to several infants successively while addicted to cocaine. Guidelines for providing prenatal care for pregnant, addicted women have been proposed by the medical community (USDHHS, 1993). These include monitoring the change in patterns of drug exposure in the newborn population, providing preventive counseling to promote abstinence from drug use during pregnancy, reducing barriers to treatment access, and staying abreast of new information concerning the developmental outcomes of cocaine-exposed infants.

Follow-up and aftercare have been the most open areas for innovation. Many environmental factors exacerbate the effects of drug exposure, including poverty, poor nutrition, inadequate or lack of prenatal health care, sexually transmitted diseases, domestic violence, child abuse or neglect, alcohol and other drug abuse within the family, homelessness, unemployment, incarceration, low educational achievement, poor parenting skills, and discrimination based on race, gender, or culture (USDHHS, 1993). Two main components of aftercare are early intervention and psychosocial services for infants and their families. Early interventions counter biological disadvantages of drug-exposed infants, while psychosocial interventions promote stability and nurturance in the home environment.

Follow-up medical intervention requires that the infant receive more than the standard level of care, with earlier and more frequent surveillance. Medical staff should be supplemented with a child development specialist and a social worker to help to reduce barriers to service and referrals for therapies (Arendt, Minnes, & Singer, 1996).

The goals of psychosocial services for drug-exposed infants and their families include providing racially and culturally sensitive services to the infant and family through outreach. The services are directed to the mother and indirectly influence infant outcome. Maternal health services such as postpartum care, infant care training, reproductive health services, counseling, and testing for HIV also indirectly affect the child's environment. Mental health services for the mother, including psychological evaluations and counseling, assessment for sexual abuse and associated post-traumatic stress disorder, and training in the areas of interpersonal skills, self-sufficiency, and relationships, are also valuable components of psychosocial services (Tracy & Farkas, 1994). Parental education, vocational services, child care services, transportation, parenting skills, outreach and legal assistance have all been suggested for integration into psychosocial aftercare for drug-exposed infants (Farkas, Doucette, & White, 1992).

Drug-exposed infants subsequently placed in foster care also require specialized services, including specially trained case managers and foster parents. Foster parents need ongoing training regarding their attitudes toward, and the special needs of, drug-exposed infants.

Although systematic investigations of interventions for infants with FAS have not been completed, evidence from reports of parents, teachers, and support groups indicates that strategies that focus directly on remediating neurodevelopmental impairments can affect intelligence and behavior. The basic strategies include restructuring the child's environment to remove barriers to progress, teaching a child how to learn, and maintaining a consistent environment (Weiner & Morse, 1994).

INTERVENTIONS

Model medical based innovations have been developed to address the needs of drug-exposed and other high-risk infants (see Carmichael-Olson & Burgess, 1997). The rationale for such services, or "one-stop shopping," is based on three goals: preventing future births of substance abused infants; assisting addicted mothers in enhancing their parenting skills and thus promoting family preservation; and identifying, screening, and referring infants to specialized interventions. Innovative programs in the United States include Families First in Detroit, The Family Center in Philadelphia, Operation PAR (Perinatal Awareness), Womens and Infants Clinic in Boston, and the Center for the Advancement of Mothers and Children (CAMAC) in Cleveland. The Women and Infants Clinic, begun at Boston City Hospital in the late 1980s (Kaplan-Sanoff & Lieb, 1995), was a pioneering clinic that recruited women from the newborn nursery whose babies tested positive for cocaine. Infants received intensive pediatric care and weekly developmental group and play therapies as needed. Mothers received drug treatment through individual and group counseling, relapse prevention, weekly urine screening, and 12-step groups. An effort was made to enhance parenting skills through parent support groups and mother-child groups. The CAMAC uses the "high-risk," hospital-based model of care to identify cocaine-exposed infants who have a greater than average probability of encountering obstacles that make healthy development difficult (Arendt, Minnes, Diffenbacher, Davis, & Nagusky, 1991). Strategies for intervention target the whole family, recognizing that the health or psychological problems of one family member influence all members. The interdisciplinary approach offers well-child care, social work services, developmental follow-up, and outreach services offered by the home visitor project. While specific outcome data are not available, children in need of early intervention services were identified early, referred promptly, and supported by the home visitors.

Although few data exist comparing effectiveness of these "one-stop" shopping programs, few researchers doubt that they are superior to noncoordinated intervention efforts. The programs are believed to be superior because they incorporate the ten protective factors for families involved with substance abuse that have been identified through research (Carmichael-Olsen & Burgess, 1997), including (1) appropriate diagnosis of child and family problems, (2) nonjudgmental professional attitudes, (3) realistic expectations, (4) prenatal drug treatment, (5) an improvement in "goodness of fit" between caregiver and child, (6) availability of responsive and safe home care, (7) support for caregivers, (8) use of a primary agent for service, (9) culturally relevant education, and (10) an effective transition between caregiving environments.

Home visitation has been demonstrated to affect long-term outcome of maternal factors that are related to high-risk infant outcome (Kitzman et al., 1997; Olds et al., 1997; Olds, Henderson, Chamberlin, & Tatelbaum, 1986). In these studies, women visited by nurses prior to their infants' births were perpetrators of child abuse and neglect less and had fewer subsequent births and fewer behavioral impairments due to use of drugs and alcohol. Their children had fewer hospitalizations and injuries during the first two years after delivery.

Another home visitation project was evaluated by Marcenko and Spense (1994) for improvements in the home environment, reduced drug use, social support, psychological symptom improvement, and service satisfaction of at-risk families. Modeled after work by Olds and colleagues (1986), the project used specially trained home visitors, a social worker, an indigenous home visitor, and a nurse who were from the same community as the target families, had positive parenting experiences, and were trained to be sensitive to the needs of the family. The home visitor's role was to provide peer support, assist in identification of services needed, and provide home based health education and parent training. Home visitors were community women with positive parenting experience and who understood the needs of the families. Intensive training in nutrition, family violence, substance abuse, child development, relationship building, and interviewing skills was given to home visitors, who modeled appropriate parenting and helped families to overcome barriers by helping them complete forms and accompanying them to appointments. Social workers assessed the psychosocial needs of families and developed and implemented plans to address their needs. They intervened in a different way than home visitors by assessing psychosocial family needs such as drug treatment and housing and implementing plans to address the needs. Nurses were responsible for coordination of health care services, child developmental assessments, family planning, and health education. Services were provided from the first prenatal care visit until the child's first birthday. Women were interviewed at baseline and then six months later for substance abuse, child protective service involvement, home environment, service use and satisfaction, social support, psychological functioning, and self-esteem. Standardized measures indicated that, after ten months of intervention, women in the home visitation project reported increased social support, greater access to services, and decreased psychological distress. However, the intervention was not successful at reducing child out-of-home placement, perhaps because home visitors had greater opportunity to help families identify a family member who could assume temporary responsibility for a child in need of care.

In addition to intervention programs that target the child, prevention of maternal drug abuse is a specific goal of some programs. The Perinatal 20 Treatment Research Demonstration Program of the National Institute on Drug Abuse includes the evaluation of 20 treatment programs for pregnant drug users begun in 1989 and 1990. Each targets treatment of pregnant and postpartum women and comprises an integrated system of services or a specific targeted clinical intervention delivered with a continuum of care. This unique collaborative research effort has led to advances in research methodology (NIDA Research Monograph 166, 1996), identified barriers to treatment, outlined retention techniques, and highlighted the importance of gender sensitive interventions (Lewis, Haller, Branch, & Ingersoll, 1996).

Pediatric HIV and AIDS

DEFINING POPULATION

Reported HIV/AIDS cases in 1995 surpassed the half-million mark, severely impacting national health (CDC, 1995). As AIDS has become the third leading cause of death among women ages 25–44 (CDC, 1995), the epidemic has spread to infants who acquire the virus prenatally. In 1995, of children reported with AIDS, 84% were black or Hispanic, a rate 16 and 6 times higher, respectively, than that for white children (CDC, 1995). A recent decline in the number of pediatric AIDS cases is thought to be due to improved clinical management of women and children, a decline in the number of infected women giving birth, and changes in surveillance patterns.

Children at risk due to prenatal drug exposure overlap with children at risk due to maternal human immunodeficiency virus (HIV). Seventy-five percent of infants exposed to HIV in utero have mothers who are intravenous drug users (Brazoziunas, Roizen, Kohrman, & Smith, 1994). In addition, there is overlap for both groups in the environmental risks associated with drug abuse and HIV exposure from the detrimental effects of poverty, poor nutrition, inconsistent caregiving situations, stigmatization, and social isolation. One possible social difference for the infants born to HIV-infected women is loss of a parent due to maternal death.

HIV attacks T lymphocytes, resulting in progressive and irreversible immunosuppression (Armstrong, Seidel, & Swales, 1993) and subsequent opportunistic infections and neoplasms (Fauci, 1988). When HIV is acquired in infancy, the child's normal developmental progression is interrupted, affecting developmental functioning in two ways. HIV infection can affect the central nervous system (CNS) indirectly by opportunistic infection or directly by attack of CNS tissue. Findings of neuropsychological impairment and behavioral deficits in infants with HIV have shown that infants have an unpredictable course, making early intervention a critical issue. Social and behavioral problems have also been reported in perinatally infected children as they enter preschool (Seidel, 1991). It is not clear, however, if the emotional and behavioral problems observed are related to compromised frontal cortex, basal ganglia, and connecting structures in the CNS or whether multiple environmental stressors may be the cause. Behavioral problems probably result from a combination of both environmental and physiological causes.

ISSUES IN PRACTICE

An infant with HIV requires a complex set of interventions that address medical, psychosocial, and educational components. Earlier identification (prenatally) of children at risk for HIV and use of antiviral agents such as AZT may have resulted in extended periods of survival and quality of life (Armstrong, Seidel, & Swales, 1993). Relatively little is known about the psychological effects of HIV. Adjustment reactions, depression, attachment issues, and behavioral problems are thought to affect HIV-infected children and their families. Counseling for parents and other family members as well as support groups are recommended interventions. Again, although little is known about the effects of early interventions for HIV-infected infants, early interventions are recommended in order to help infants maintain the highest level of functioning possible and to improve their quality of life. Most affected infants require multifaceted interventions, including occupational, physical, and speech and language therapy, that extend beyond direct treatment of the child to working with parents to improve the child's self-care and motor control and to provide adaptive equipment and stimulation of the child in the home. The issues that affect the efficacy of the service include the age at which the child is referred and parental involvement (Rossetti, 1993). All children of HIV-positive parents should be considered at developmental risk, as it has been shown that uninfected infants of HIV-positive mothers also show significant delays (Brazoziunas, Roizen, Kohrman, & Smith, 1994).

INTERVENTIONS

Comprehensive care includes prevention of pediatric HIV/AIDS, integrated medical care, developmental and educational services, psychosocial support, including mental health assessment, and basic legal and financial support. Bruder (1995) outlined a service framework for the development and implementation of service systems for children with HIV and AIDS, the focus of which is to provide services that integrate educational intervention services with special health care needs within community-based placements. This is a challenging concept that requires that the services be respectful of the families and children they serve while providing privacy and autonomy in decision making.

According to D. Beck and colleagues (personal communication, May 26, 1997), medical interventions related to HIV-infected children now occur prenatally and postnatally and involve prophylactic antiviral agents given to the mother during the second and third trimesters and at the time of delivery. The use of antiviral agents continues into the early months after the child's birth and then continues only if the infant is infected. This change in procedure has greatly reduced the incidence in transmission of HIV prenatally from about 20% to 7–8%.

The major issue with administering this successful treatment is compliance on the mother's part with the prenatal regime and aggressive follow-up care required by the infant. Given that women infected with HIV also have multiple life stressors, such as living in poverty or having a drug dependence problem, extensive medical-based social work intervention is necessary.

Comprehensive, innovative hospital service programs are also based on the one-stop-shopping idea and may include combined pediatric and adult care for HIV, on-site legal counseling, referrals for nursing, referrals to special Head Start programs, and an OB liaison. Evaluation and outcome studies of innovative hospital-based programs are not available, although they are believed to increase compliance with medical and psychosocial intervention.

An ecosystemic approach to intervention, similar to the one proposed for treatment of prenatally drug-exposed infants, was proposed by Walker (1991). This hospital-based intervention program advocates community-designed, -based and -directed intervention that is family-centered and integrated. This model grew out of a pediatric AIDS program in an inner-city hospital that utilizes family case conferences that emphasize (1) creating a supportive atmosphere for family and staff, (2) helping staff to view each family as a living system of which death is a part, (3) teaching staff members to create alternative narratives and positive redescription of family members, (4) helping staff members to identify family resources, (5) creating a collaborative relationship with families, and (6) eliminating redundancy of services.

Another intervention, Pediatric Life Enrichment (APPLE), in Baltimore, deals with HIV as a prevention issue (Santelli et al., 1995). This program uses street outreach and community-targeted small-media materials to increase condom use. Evaluation of this project was accomplished through a two-community time-series quasi-experimental design. Street surveys sampled approximately 500 subjects ages 17–35. Results showed postprogrammatic behavior change. Condom use at most recent sexual encounter was significantly improved in the intervention community, although other HIV prevention behaviors, such as inquiring about sexual partners' practices and STD history, rejecting sex for fear of STDs or HIV, and avoiding sex when condoms were not available, showed no change.

It is widely believed that prevention of pediatric AIDS through reduction of maternal high-risk behaviors, prenatal screening, and prophylactic medical intervention prenatally should be the focus of innovations for practice in this area.

Prematurity and Low and Very Low Birthweight

DEFINING POPULATION

Because the United States has one of the most advanced medical care systems, it has become an international leader in rescuing the lives of the very smallest infants at birth. Premature infants are those who are born before expected term date of 40 weeks' gestation, usually at less than 37 weeks. The rate of prematurity has risen almost annually for the past decade, with 1 out of 10 births now occurring prematurely (Ventura, Martin, Taffel, Matthews, & Clark, 1994).

Low-birthweight (LBW) infants (i.e., those born at less than 2,500 grams) are frequently premature and constitute approximately 7% of all births. Many infants of birth weights of 750 grams (one pound, ten ounces) and younger than 28 weeks' gestation are now able to survive. In 23 years, the number of survivors per 1,000 live births who weighed less than 1,000 grams has increased seventy-fold (Bhushan, Paneth, & Kiely, 1993). Very-low-birthweight birth (VLBW) (i.e., less than 1500 grams) has become an even more common occurrence.

Many experts believe that the overall increase in the number of children with developmental disabilities in the United States may be a result of medical and technological advances that have kept so many underweight newborns alive. Infants born at less than 1,500 grams have been shown to have a higher risk for major handicapping conditions, such as cerebral palsy and sensory deficits (Escobar, Littenberg, & Pettiti, 1991; McCormick, Brooks-Gunn, Workman-Daniel, Turner, & Peckham, 1992), as well as a higher rate of learning disabilities at school age, even when only children with normal intelligence are considered (Klein, Hack, & Breslau, 1989; Ross, Lipper, & Auld, 1991). A number of risk conditions associated with prematurity and very low birthweight have been shown to be linked to poorer outcomes, namely, documentable neurologic conditions, such as seizures, intraventricular hemorrhage ("bleeds"), and periventricular leukomalacia (Bendersky & Lewis, 1994), as well as significant respiratory problems due to the immaturity of the lungs when birth occurs before 28 weeks' gestation, such as bronchopulmonary dysplasia (Singer, Yamashita, Lilien, Collin, & Baley, 1997).

Low-income children are at higher likelihood of incurring prematurity, and consequent low and very low birthweight, with a rate of occurrence double that of children of average income (Paneth, 1995). In addition to social disadvantage, low birthweight is also related to ethnicity in the United States. African American infants are more than twice as likely to be born at low birthweight (13.6%) as white infants (5.8%), while Hispanic, Native American, and Asian Americans have rates similar to those of whites. Lifestyle behaviors, particularly cigarette smoking, alcohol and drug use, and poor maternal nutrition, are also implicated in low birthweight. Cigarette smoking is the largest known risk factor for low birthweight. It is estimated that 20% of all low birthweight births could be avoided if women did not smoke while pregnant (Chomitz, Cheung, & Lieberman, 1995).

ISSUES IN PRACTICE

Recently, there has been some recognition of the impact on the family of parenting an infant born at very low birthweight. Many of these infants are hospitalized at length at birth. After discharge, they often incur infections that require rehospitalizations, are in need of complex medical services, and may be difficult feeders (Singer, Yamashita, Lilien, Collin, & Baley, 1997). These serious problems impose multiple family stressors. Several studies suggested that mothers of VLBW babies experience significant symptoms of depression and anxiety in the perinatal period (Brooten et al., 1988; Singer, Davillier, Bruening, Hawkins, & Yamashita, 1996). In the only controlled longitudinal study, only mothers whose VLBW children had significant disabilities at two years of age continued to self-report such symptoms (Singer, Yamashita, Hawkins, Huang, & Baley, 1995).

The effects of maternal employment on child developmental outcome have been investigated for preterm groups, and the results indicate that about 55% of mothers are employed by the time the child reaches 18 months of age, independent of the risk status of the infant neonatally (Youngblut, Loveland-Cherry, & Horan, 1990). Preliminary analyses with data from a sample of 800 two-parent families with LBW or full-term preschoolers showed no effects of employment on child development or behavior scores (Youngblut, Singer, Madigan, Swegart, & Rodgers, 1997). For both groups, inconsistency between maternal actual and desired employment was related to lower mental-processing scores and more internalizing and externalizing behavior problems and was more important than whether the mother was employed. As numerous barriers to accessing children exist for mothers of preterm infants with chronic illnesses and disabilities, and as economic pressures push more parents into the workplace, continued assessment of the factors related to maternal employment and outcomes for preterm infants is needed.

The shift in definition away from a "medical model," with its emphasis on disease entities, to a service delivery model, with an emphasis on supports, has brought to the fore several issues relevant for preschool children (Luckasson, Schalock, Snell, & Spitalnik, 1996). Predicting long-term development is extremely difficult. The process of development is resilient, and some children who are identified as "at-risk" mature and become competent adults (Werner, 1990). It is possible that minor delays in development considered by caregivers and professionals as "within normal limits" may be indicative of significant problems that will occur when greater learning demands are placed on the child at school age. Compounding the problem, the current assessment instruments that document developmental delay or risk status in comparison to same-age peers have been shown to be notoriously misleading predictors of later functioning when used prior to two years of age in both normal and at-risk infants (Fagan & Singer, 1983).

INTERVENTIONS

Neonatal intensive care (NICU) technology changes rapidly, making it difficult to evaluate how changes in care affect later outcomes. Numerous controlled, randomized clinical trials have been instituted through multicenter NICU networks for various medical protocols to evaluate outcomes (see Horbar & Lucey, 1995, for review). In addition to medical protocols, several controlled trials of behavioral and environmental interventions in the NICU have been initiated, but most of these have not yet been replicated. These studies generally have shown better outcomes for infants with trials of individualized care protocols (Als et al., 1994), regulation of bright-light exposure (Glass et al., 1985), use of waterbeds (Korner, 1986), massage (Scafidi et al., 1990), and nonnutritive sucking (Gill, Behnke, Conlon, & Anderson, 1992).

Because of the increased rates of disability among low- and very-low-birthweight cohorts, including much higher rates of special educational placement at school age (34% VLBW vs. 14% full-term) (McCormick, Gortmaker, & Sable, 1990), some early-intervention trials, both parent and infant focused, have specifically targeted this group, demonstrating some improvements in outcome (see Blair & Ramey, 1997, for review). The most comprehensive intervention to date, the Infant Health and Development Program (IHDP) (Brooks-Gunn et al., 1994), a national multisite, randomized trial, included 985 premature and low-birthweight children. This study compared an early home-visitor program, followed by attendance at a child development center and parent support groups, to standard developmental surveillance and community referral. The home-visitor program started when the baby left the hospital and continued weekly for the first year, then biweekly until the child was three years old. Attendance at a five-day-a-week, center-based educational child care program began at twelve months and extended to three years of age. The support groups, where caregivers discussed health, parenting, child development, and social support concerns, met bimonthly beginning at twelve months.

At age three years the mean IQ score for the intervention group, adjusted for birth outcomes and maternal factors, was 9.4 points higher than that for the follow-up-only group. At five-year follow-up, positive effects of the intervention on intelligence were still evident in the children with birthweights between 2,001 grams and 2,500 grams (Brooks-Gunn et al., 1994). The intervention group had a 3.7-point full-scale and a 4.2-point verbal higher mean IQ than the follow-up-only group. The intervention, therefore, appeared to have greater effects for children who were in the high range of low birthweight.

The pioneering aspects of this study, that is, the application of the randomized clinical trial to human development studies, the potential of long-term savings through the prevention of disabilities, and the ability to target those infants in greater need, as well as most likely to benefit, through both biologic and family characteristics, have set new standards for such clinical trials (Richmond, 1990). Findings from the IHDP and other studies with LBW children indicate that comprehensive interventions, begun early, are most likely to be successful. Intervention effectiveness is moderated by socioeconomic variables, such as maternal education level and biological variables, such as birthweight. Given the effectiveness of both direct, center-based intervention and home-based intervention for LBW infants, continued investigation of parent-focused programs, with an emphasis on the importance of educational and interpersonal practices in the home, offers both economic advantages and the potential to readily modify the program to accommodate individual differences. This applicability of a program to each family's needs is also likely to increase the number and intensity of appropriately stimulating exchanges between parents and infants, thereby fostering optimum development.

Implications

RESEARCH

Several high-risk-status infant groups, including drug-exposed and LBW infants and infants with HIV or AIDS, have been defined, and relevant practice-related issues and innovations have been discussed. Despite recent innovations in practice, there is an ongoing need for well-controlled evaluation studies to determine if the innovations are clinically and cost effective. For example, few well-controlled outcome studies that evaluate intervention services for drug-exposed infants and mothers exist. Intervention research in this area needs to be further developed as more specific information regarding the cause of developmental disabilities in drug exposed infants is determined. If the cause is primarily direct prenatal insult, then research emphasis should be on evaluating prevention strategies and interventions directed toward the child. If developmental outcomes are determined to be influenced by environmental factors as well, then intervention strategies should also be aimed at family variables.

Similarly, very few evaluations of novel interventions for HIV-exposed infants are available for review. Although the most efficient delivery method is yet to be determined, it is clear that infants with HIV need a unique set of complex medical and psychosocial interventions. Coordination of these medical and psychosocial services is imperative to lower costs and to provide the best quality of life for these infants. Advances in treatment with antiviral agents prenatally and early in development emphasize the importance of prenatal care. Because a high percentage of women with HIV are also drug users, there are many obstacles to adequate prenatal care. Women who use drugs frequently avoid prenatal care. Adequate drug treatment programs for pregnant drug users are few, although their services would advance prevention of HIV transmission through reduction of drug use.

Because research dealing with at-risk infants covers a period in the lifespan when numerous maturational changes are occurring, research must be done longitudinally. Some of the difficulties in conducting longitudinal research include subject attrition, practice effects, changes in social/cultural practices, and a need for different analytic approaches (Applebaum & McCall, 1983; Singer, 1997). Examples of techniques to maintain subject cohorts can be found in a study done in Cleveland with cocaine-exposed infants (Singer, Arendt, Farkas, Minnes, Huang, & Yamashita, 1997). Methods include providing transportation, either cab fare or money for gas and parking fees; giving gift certificates for a local supermarket chain upon completion of each assessment; offering the caregiver a Polaroid picture of the child at the visits; and presenting the child a small toy. Because many of the families move or their phones are disconnected, it is important to obtain phone numbers for family, friends, and relatives who could be alternative points of contact. One technique for verifying mailing addresses is to send birth cards with an offer of a children's book or a gift certificate if the caregiver will mail back an enclosed postcard updating address information.

POLICY

Recent recognition of high-risk infants as a distinct service delivery population has occurred during a period of rapid changes in American society, particularly during cataclysmic shifts in the health care delivery systems. In a 1994 report, the Carnegie Corporation of New York reiterated the consensus of child developmental experts who identified several essential factors that potentially influence children's early growth and development. These included a dependable nuclear family, a supportive extended family and community, education for parenthood, a perception of hope for the future, and predictability about the adult environment (Hamburg, 1994). Recent societal changes have made attainment of these requirements more difficult.

More than half of all mothers with children under three years of age now work outside the home (Galinsky, Bond, & Friedman, 1993). Since 1950, the percentage of children living in single-parent, female-headed households has tripled. Twenty-five percent of all children now live in one-parent households. Day care needs have also accelerated. Now that empirical research has shown the importance of quality child care for infants (NICHD Early Child Care Research Network, 1996), the need has become more critical. Yet, most available care is substandard and potentially harmful (Whitebook, Phillips, & Howes, 1989).

In the provision of services for high-risk infants, the health care delivery system is a critical nexus, as it is the only institutional system with which all infants must intersect. A recent report noted numerous problems in serving the health care needs of infants and young children (Center for the Future of Children, 1995). Access to care is limited and unwieldy, as it is tied to income, insurance, employment status, and geographic location, with many underserved areas and a maldistribution of pediatricians, obstetricians, social workers, and child psychologists. Despite the proliferation of managed health care systems, incentives remain for technology-intensive, high-cost care at the expense of case finding, prevention, outreach, and support programs. Attempts to control costs through managed care are likely to limit access to expensive health care needed by the high-risk infant groups we have described. Managed care plans are limiting access to the habilitation services needed by infants at risk, such as speech, occupational, and physical therapies (Center for the Future of Children, 1995).

Realization of the goals of PL 99-457 for early intervention for all handicapped and at-risk infants will require adaptation to this new American social and medical landscape. Shonkoff and Meisels (1990) have summarized some of the major critical challenges to public policy imposed by the new law, which requires that each state define which infants and children will qualify for services for developmental delay or as "at-risk" children; develop criteria and procedures for a family assessment; develop a lead agency for the state for service provision; and facilitate the transition of children and families from early intervention programs to appropriate preschool services. A significant challenge will be the need for cooperation and integration across traditional disciplinary boundaries of the social work, psychological, medical, nursing, and special educational fields.

There is considerable overlap among most attempts to categorize at-risk/handicapped infant groups, making determination of the coordinating discipline for services difficult. A typical infant in need of intervention has multiple problems and risk factors (e.g., a preterm, cocaine-exposed infant with developmental delay who is on public support). Current bureaucratic intradisciplinary service systems are problematic (to whom should the infant and family be referred, and how will services be reimbursed?). Coordination of services across the multiple agencies needed for intervention remains a major hurdle for families and professionals.

A final challenge iterated by Shonkoff and Meisels (1990) is the need for the field of early intervention to redefine the relationships of professionals to parents in their mutually necessary efforts to ameliorate the infant's risk condition. As parent advocacy has been a generative force behind many of the legislative changes that have driven the advances made in the special educational and early intervention fields, and as legislative "due process" now allows parents to challenge professional recommendations, this new era of parent "empowerment" will require shifts and accommodations in the balance of power between parents and professionals.

There is a need to coordinate intervention at all levels of functioning. When the responsibility for a child's development is spread across various service providers, only the primary caregiver is responsible for the coordination of services. The Family Service Plan or the Individualized Education Plan, now mandated by law, is multidisciplinary, and the parent or guardian, as part of the team, provides informed consent and preeminent guidance. Often, however, the caregiver is in a poor position to make decisions, having little information or resources. Educating and providing support to the caregiver becomes a critical aspect of intervention. This support appears to be one of the chief factors in successful programs. Successful programs also provide a continuum of services, from total inclusion in a typical classroom to highly specialized and intensive treatment, and allow families and professionals to select the most appropriate service for each child, avoiding the "one size fits all" approach.

It is likely, given current trends in poverty rates, climbing drug use, and technological medical advances that allow increased survival of infants, that the prevalence rates of high-risk infants will continue to increase. Recent federal recognition of the needs for identification and intervention for this group poses great challenges for the delivery of services to these infants and their families. Meeting these challenges, however, raises great hope for the amelioration of later disorders and a reduction in the societal burden.

REFERENCES

Aase, J. M. (1994). Clinical recognition of FAS: Difficulties of detection and diagnosis. *Alcohol Health and Research World*, *18*, 5–9.

Als, H., Lawhon, G., Duffy, F. H., McAnulty, G. B., Gibes-Grossman, R., & Blickman, J. G. (1994). Individualized developmental care for the very low birthweight preterm infant. *Journal of the American Medical Association*, *272*(11), 853–858.

Applebaum, M. I., & McCall, R. B. (1983). Design and analysis in developmental psychology. In P. H. Mussen (Ed.), *Handbook of child psychology* (4th ed., Vol. 1, pp. 415–476). New York: John Wiley & Sons.

Arendt, R., Minnes, S., Diffenbacher, N., Davis, G., & Nagusky, H. (1991). Cocaine exposed infants and their mothers: An interdisciplinary model of service and research. *Child, Youth, and Family Services Quarterly*, *14*, 2–4.

Arendt, R., Singer, L., Angelopoulos, J., Bass, O., & Mascia. (1994). Sensory-motor development in four-month-old, cocaine-exposed infants. *Infant Behavior and Development*, *35*, 18A.

Arendt, R. E., Minnes, S., & Singer, L. T. (1996). Fetal cocaine exposure: Neurologic effects and sensory motor delay. *Physical and Occupational Therapy in Pediatrics*, *16*, 129–144.

Armstrong, F. D., Seidel, J. F. D., & Swales, T. P. (1993). Pediatric HIV infection: A neuropsychological and educational challenge. *Journal of Hearing Disabilities*, *26*, 92–103.

Azuma, S., & Chasnoff, I. (1993). Outcome of children prenatally exposed to cocaine and other drugs: A path analysis of 3-year data. *Pediatrics*, *92*, 396–402.

Bayley, N. (1993). *Bayley Scales of Infant Development* (2nd ed.). San Antonio, TX: Psychological Corp.

Bendersky, M., & Lewis, M. (1994). Environmental risk, medical risk, and cognition. *Developmental Psychology*, *30*, 484–494.

Bhushan, V., Paneth, N., & Kiely, J. L. (1993). Impact of improved survival of very-low-birthweight infants on recent secular trends in the prevalence of cerebral palsy. *Pediatrics*, *91*, 1094–1100.

Bingol, N., Fuchs, M., Diaz, V., & Stone, P. K. (1987). Teratogenicity of cocaine in humans. *Journal of Pediatrics*, *110*, 93–96.

Blair, C., & Ramey, C. T. (1997). Early intervention for low-birth-weight infants and the path to second-generation research. In M. J. Guralnick (Ed.), *The effectiveness of early intervention* (pp. 77–97). Baltimore: Paul H. Brookes.

Brazoziunas, D. M., Roizen, N. J., Kohrman, A. F., & Smith, D. K. (1994). Children of HIV-positive parents: Implications for intervention. *Psychosocial Rehabilitation Journal*, *17*, 145–149.

Broman, S., Nichols, P. L., & Kennedy, W. (1975). *Preschool IQ: Prenatal and early developmental correlates*. Hillsdale, NJ: Lawrence Erlbaum.

Brooks-Gunn, J., McCarton, C. M., Casey, P. H., McCormick, M. C., Bauer, C. R., Bernbaum, J. C., Tyson, J., Swanson, M., Bennett, R., Scott, D. T., Torascia, J., & Meinert, C. L. (1994). Early intervention in low-birthweight premature infants. *Journal of the American Medical Association*, *272*, 1257–1262.

Brooten, D., Gennaro, S., Brown, L., Britts, P., Gibbons, A., Babenwill-Sachs, S., & Kumar, S. (1988). Anxiety, depression, and hostility in mothers of preterm infants. *Nursing Research*, *37*, 213–216.

Bruder, M. D. (1995). The challenge of pediatric AIDS: A framework for early childhood special education. *Topics in Early Childhood Special Education*, *15*, 83–99.

Carmichael-Olson, H., & Burgess, D. M. (1997). Early intervention for children prenatally exposed to alcohol and other drugs. In M. J. Guralnick (Ed.), *The effectiveness of early intervention* (pp. 109–145). Baltimore: Paul H. Brookes.

Center for the Future of Children. (1995). Low birthweight: Analysis and recommendations. In P. Shiono & R. Behrman (Eds.), *The future of children: Low birthweight*, (Vol. 5, pp. 4–18). Los Angeles: Author.

Centers for Disease Control and Prevention. (1995). *HIV/AIDS surveillance report 7* (no. 2). Washington, DC: U.S. Department of Health and Human Services.

Chasnoff, I., Landress, H. J., & Barrett, M. E. (1990). The prevalence of illicit drug or alcohol use during pregnancy and discrepancies in mandatory reporting in Pinellas County, Florida. *New England Journal of Medicine, 322,* 1202–1206.

Chasnoff, I. J., Burns, K. A., & Burns, W. J. (1987). Cocaine use in pregnancy: Perinatal morbidity and mortality. *Neurotoxicology and Teratology, 9,* 291–293.

Chavez, G. F., Cordero, J. F., & Becerra, J. E. (1988). Leading major congenital malformations among minority groups in the United States, 1981–1986. *Morbidity and Mortality Weekly Report, 37,* 17–24.

Chomitz, V. R., Cheung, L., & Lieberman, E. (1995). The role of lifestyle in preventing low birth weight. In P. Shiono & R. Behrman (Eds.), *The future of children: Low birthweight* (Vol. 5, pp. 121–138). Los Angeles: Center for the Future of Children.

Chugani, H., Phelps, M. E., & Mazziotta, J. C. (1987). Positron emission tomography study of human brain function development. *Annals of Neurology, 22*(4), 495.

Daro, D., & McCurdy, K. (1992). *Current trends in child abuse reporting and fatalities: The results of the 1991 annual fifty-state survey* (No. 808). Chicago: National Committee for Prevention of Child Abuse.

Day, N. L., & Richardson, G. A. (1991). Prenatal marijuana use: Epidemiology, methodologic issues, and infant outcome. *Chemical Dependency and Pregnancy, 18,* 77–91.

Day, N. L., Richardson, G. A., Goldschmidt, L., Robles, N., Taylor, P. M., Stoffer, D. S., Cornelius, M. D., & Geve, D. D. (1994). The effect of prenatal marijuana exposure on the cognitive development of offspring at age three. *Neurotoxicology and Teratology, 16,* 169–175.

Dominiquez, R., Vila-Coro, A. A., Slopis, J., & Bohan, T. P. (1991). Brain and ocular abnormalities in infants with in utero exposure to cocaine and other street drugs. *American Journal of Diseases in Children, 145,* 688–695.

Escobar, G. H., Littenberg, B., & Pettiti, D. B. (1991). Outcome among surviving very low birthweight infants: A meta-analysis. *Archives of Diseases in Children, 66,* 204–211.

Evans, A., & Gillogley, K. (1991). Drug use in pregnancy: Obstetric perspectives. *Clinics in Perinatology, 18,* 23–31.

Fagan, J. F., & Singer, L. T. (1983). Infant recognition memory as a measure of intelligence. In L. P. Lipsitt (Ed.), *Advances in infancy research* (Vol. 2, pp. 31–78). Norwalk, NJ: Ablex Publishing.

Farkas, K. J., Doucette, M. G., & White, W. (1992). Addressing perinatal addiction: A comprehensive hospital based model. *Substance Abuse, 13,* 1–22.

Fauci, A. S. (1988). The human immunodeficiency virus: Infectivity and mechanisms for pathogenesis. *Science, 239,* 617–622.

Fried, P., & Watkinson, B. (1990). 12- and 24-month neurobehavioral follow-up of children prenatally exposed to marijuana, cigarettes, and alcohol. *Neurotoxicology and Teratology, 11,* 49–58.

Fried, P. A., O'Connell, C. M., & Watkinson, B. (1992). 60- and 72-month follow-up of children prenatally exposed to marijuana, cigarettes, and alcohol: Cognitive and language assessment. *Developmental and Behavioral Pediatrics, 13,* 383–391.

Galinsky, E., Bond, J. T., & Friedman, D. E. (1993). *The changing American workforce: Highlights of the national study*. New York: Families and Work Institute.

Gill, N. E., Behnke, M., Conlon, M., & Anderson, G. C. (1992). Non-nutritive sucking modulates behavioral state for preterm infants before feeding. *Scandinavian Journal of Caring Sciences*, 6, 3–7.

Glass, P., Avery, G. B., Subramanian, K. S., Keys, M. P., Sostek, A. M., & Friendly, D. S. (1985). Effect of bright light in the hospital nursery on the incidence of retinopathy of prematurity. *New England Journal of Medicine*, 313(7), 401–404.

Gold, M. (1992). Cocaine and crack: Clinical aspects. In J. Lowinson, P. Ruiz, & R. Milliman (Eds.), *Substance abuse: A comprehensive textbook* (pp. 205–221). Baltimore: Williams & Wilkins.

Griffith, D., Azuma, S., & Chasnoff, I. (1994). Three-year outcome of children exposed prenatally to drugs. *Journal of the American Academy of Child and Adolescent Psychiatry*, 33, 20–27.

Hamburg, D. (1994). *Starting points: The report of the Carnegie task force on meeting the needs of young children*. New York: Carnegie Corp.

Hans, S., Bernstein, V., & Hensen, L. (1990). Interaction between drug-using mothers and toddlers. *Infant Behavior and Development*, 13, 190.

Hans, S. L. (1996). Prenatal drug exposure: Behavioral functioning in late childhood and adolescence. In C. L. Wetherington, V. L. Smeriglio, & L. P. Finnegan (Eds.), *Behavioral studies of drug-exposed offspring: Methodological issues in human and animal research* (NIDA Research Monograph 164, NIH Publication No. 96-4105, pp. 261–276). Rockville, MD: National Institutes of Health.

Horbar, J., & Lucey J. (1995). Evaluation of neonatal intensive care technologies. In P. Shiono & R. Behrman (Eds.), *The future of children: Low birthweight* (Vol. 5, pp. 139–161). Los Angeles: Center for the Future of Children.

Hurt, H., Brodsky, N. L., Betancourt, L., Braitman, L. E., Malmud, E., & Giannetta, J. (1995). Cocaine-exposed children: Follow-up through 30 months. *Developmental and Behavioral Pediatrics*, 16, 29–35.

Institute of Medicine. (1996). *Fetal Alcohol Syndrome: Diagnosis, epidemiology, prevention, and treatment*. Washington, DC: National Academy Press.

Kandall, S. R. (1993). Improving treatment for drug exposed infants. Rockville, MD: U.S. Department of Health and Human Services.

Kaplan-Sanoff, M., & Lieb, S. A. (1995). Model intervention programs for mothers and children impacted by substance abuse. *School Psychology Review*, 24, 186–199.

Kitzman, H., Olds, D. L., Henderson, C. P., Hanks, C., Cole, R., Tatebaum, R., Mc-Connochle, K. M., Sidora, K., Luckey, D. W., Shaver, D., Englehardt, K., James, D. B., & Barnard, K. (1997). Effects of prenatal and infancy home visitation by nurses on pregnancy outcomes, childhood injuries and repeated childbearing: A randomized controlled trial. *Journal of the American Medical Association*, 278(8), 644–652.

Klein, N., & Campbell, P. (1990). Preparing personnel to serve at-risk and disabled infants, toddlers, and preschoolers. In S. Meisels and J. Shonkoff (Eds.), *Handbook of early childhood intervention* (pp. 679–699). Cambridge: Cambridge University Press.

Klein, N. K., Hack, M., & Breslau, N. (1989). Children who were very low birth weight: Developmental and academic achievement at nine years of age. *Journal of Developmental Behavior in Pediatrics*, 10, 32–37.

Korner, A. F. (1986). The use of waterbeds in the care of preterm infants. *Journal of Perinatology*, 6(2), 142–147.

Lewis, R. A., Haller, D. L., Branch, D., & Ingersoll, K. S. (1996). *Retention issues involving drug-abusing women in treatment research* (NIDA Research Monograph 166, 110–122). Rockville, MD: National Institutes of Health.

Little, B. B., & Snell, L. M. (1991). Brain growth among fetuses exposed to cocaine in utero. *Obstetrics and Gynecology, 77*, 361–364.

Luckasson, R., Schalock, R. L., Snell, M. E., & Spitalnik, D. M. (1996). The 1992 AAMR definition: Issues for preschool children. *Mental Retardation, 34*, 247–253.

Marcenko, M. O., & Spense, M. (1994). Home visitation services for at-risk pregnant and postpartum women: A randomized trial. *American Journal of Orthopsychiatry, 65*, 468–478.

McCormick, M., Gortmaker, S., & Sable, A. M. (1990). Very low birthweight children: Behavior problems and school difficulty in a national sample. *Journal of Pediatrics, 117*, 687–693.

McCormick, M. C., Brooks-Gunn, J., Workman-Daniel, K., Turner, J., & Peckham, G. J. (1992). The health and developmental status of very low birthweight children at school age. *Journal of the American Medical Association, 267*, 2204–2208.

National Institute on Drug Abuse (1996). *Treatment for drug-exposed women and their children: Advances in research methodology* (NIDA Research Monograph 166). Rockville, MD: U.S. Department of Health and Human Services.

NICHD Early Child Care Research Network (1996). Characteristics of infant child care: Factors contributing to positive caregiving. *Early Childhood Research Quarterly, 11*, 269–306.

Olds, D. L., Eckenrode, J., Henderson, C. R., Kitzman, H., Powers, J., Cole, R., Sidora, K., Morris, P., Pettitt, L. M., & Luckey, D. (1997). Long-term effects of home visitation on maternal life course and child abuse and neglect: Fifteen-year follow-up of a randomized trial. *Journal of the American Medical Association, 278*(8), 637–643.

Olds, D. L., Henderson, C. R., Chamberlin, R., & Tatelbaum, R. (1986). Preventing child abuse and neglect: A randomized trial of nurse home visitation. *Pediatrics, 78*, 65–78.

Paneth, N. (1995). The problem of low birthweight. In P. Shiono & R. Behrman, (Eds.), *The future of children: Low birthweight* (Vol. 5, pp. 19–34). Los Angeles: Center for the Future of Children.

Porges, S. W. (1988). Neonatal vagal tone: Diagnostic and prognostic implications. In P. M. Vietze & H. G. Vaughan (Eds.), *Early identification of infants with disabilities* (pp. 147–159). Philadelphia: Grune and Stratton.

Richmond, J. (1990). Low birthweight infants: Can we enhance their development? *Journal of the American Medical Association, 263*, 3069–3070.

Ross, G., Lipper, E., & Auld, P. (1991). Educational status and school-related abilities of very low birthweight premature children. *Pediatrics, 88*, 1125–1134.

Rossetti, L. M. (1993). Enhancing early intervention services to infants/toddlers and their families. *Journal of Childhood Communication Disorders, 15*, 1–6.

Santelli, J. S., Celentano, D., Rozsenich, C., Crump, A. D., Davis, N. M. V., Polacsek, M., Augustyn, M., Rolf, J., McAlister, A. L., & Burwell, L. (1995). Interim outcomes for a community-based program to prevent perinatal HIV transmission. *AIDS Education and Prevention, 7*, 221–231.

Scafidi, F. A., Field, T. M., Schanberg, S. M., Bauer, C. R., Tucci, D., Roberts, J., Morrow, C., & Kuhn, C. M. (1990). Massage stimulates growth in preterm infants: A replication. *Infant Behavior and Development, 13*, 167–188.

Schneidner, J., & Chasnoff, I. (1987). Motor assessment of cocaine-exposed infants. *Pediatric Research, 21*, 184A.

Seidel, J. F. (1991). The development of a comprehensive pediatric HIV developmental service program. In A. Rudigier (Ed.), *Technical report on developmental disabilities and*

HIV infection (No. 7, pp. 1–4). Silver Springs, MD: American Association of University Affiliated Programs.

Shonkoff, J., & Meisels, S. (1990). Early childhood intervention: The evolution of a concept. In S. Meisels & J. Shonkoff (Eds.), *Handbook of early childhood intervention* (pp. 3–32). Cambridge: Cambridge University Press.

Singer, L., Arendt, R., Farkas, K., Minnes, S., Huang, J., & Yamashita, T. (1997). The relationship of prenatal cocaine exposure and maternal postpartum psychological distress to child developmental outcome. *Development and Psychopathology, 9,* 473–489.

Singer, L., Arendt, R., & Minnes, S. (1993). Neurodevelopmental effects of cocaine. In M. C. Walsh-Sukys & R. M. Kliegman (Eds.), *Clinics in perinatology: Vol. 20(1). Current controversies in perinatal care II* (pp. 245–262). Philadelphia: W. B. Saunders.

Singer, L., Arendt, R., Minnes, S., Farkas, K., Yamashita, T., & Kliegman, R. (1995). Increased psychological distress in post partum, cocaine-using mothers. *Journal of Substance Abuse, 7,* 165–174.

Singer, L., Davillier, M., Bruening, P., Hawkins, S., & Yamashita, S. (1996). Social support, psychological distress, and parenting strains in mothers of very low birth weight infants. *Family Relations, 45,* 342–350.

Singer, L., Yamashita, T., Hawkins, S., Huang, J., & Baley, J. (1995). Psychological distress resolves by two years for mothers of VLBW, but not BPD, infants. *Pediatric Research, 38,* 273A.

Singer, L. T. (1997). Methodological considerations in longitudinal studies of infant risk. In J. Dobbing (Ed.), *Developing brain and behavior: The role of lipids in infant formula* (pp. 210–230). London: Academic Press.

Singer, L. T., Arendt, R., Song, L. Y., Warshawsky, E., & Kliegman, R. (1994). Direct and indirect interaction of cocaine with childbirth outcomes. *Archives of Pediatric and Adolescent Medicine, 148,* 959–964.

Singer, L. T., & Fagan, J. F. (1984). The cognitive development of the failure-to-thrive infant: A three-year longitudinal study. *Journal of Pediatric Psychology, 9,* 363–384.

Singer, L. T., Yamashita, T. S., Lilien, L., Collin, M., & Baley, J. (1997). A longitudinal study of outcomes of infants with very low birthweight and bronchopulmonary dysplasia. *Pediatrics, 100,* 987–993.

Slutsker, L. (1992). Risks associated with cocaine use during pregnancy. *Obstetrics and Gynecology, 79,* 778–789.

Tjossem, T. D. (Ed.). (1976). *Intervention strategies for high-risk infants and young children.* Baltimore: University Park Press.

Tracy, E. M., & Farkas, K. J. (1994). Preparing practitioners for child welfare practice with substance-abusing families. *Child Welfare League of America, 73*(1), 57–68.

U.S. Department of Health and Human Services. (1993). *Improving treatment for drug exposed infants—Treatment Improvement Protocol (TIP) Series 5.* Rockville, MD: Author.

U.S. Department of Health and Human Services. (1996). *Preliminary estimates from the 1995 National Household Survey on Drug Abuse* (Report #18). Rockville, MD: Mental Health Services Administration.

Ventura, S. J., Martin, J. A., Taffel, S., Matthews, T., & Clarke, S. (1994). *Advance report of final fatality statistics, 1992* (43, suppl.). Hyattsville, MD: National Center for Health Statistics.

Walker, G. (1991). Pediatric AIDS: Toward an ecosystemic treatment model. *Family Systems Medicine, 9,* 211–227.

Weiner, L., & Morse, B. A. (1994). Intervention and the child with FAS. *Alcohol Health and Research Word, 18,* 67–72.

Werner, E., Bierman, J. M., & French, F. E. (1971). *The children of Kauai: A longitudinal study from the prenatal period to age ten.* Honolulu: University of Hawaii Press.

Werner, E. E. (1990). Protective factors and individual resilience. In S. J. Meisels & J. P. Shonoff (Eds.), *Handbook of early childhood intervention.* Cambridge: Cambridge University Press.

Whitebook, M., Phillips, D., & Howes, C. (1989). *Who cares? Child care teachers and the quality of care in America: National child care staffing study.* Oakland, CA: Child Care Employee Project.

Wilson, G. S., Desmond, M. M., & Verniaud, W. M. (1973, October). Early development of infants of heroin-addicted mothers. *American Journal of the Diseases of Children, 126,* 457–462.

Woods, N., Behnke, M., Eyler, F. D., Conlon, M., & Wobie, K. (1995). Cocaine use among pregnant women: Socioeconomic, obstetrical, and psychological issues. In M. Lewis & M. Bendersky (Eds.), *Mothers, babies, and cocaine* (pp. 305–309). Hillsdale, NJ: Lawrence Erlbaum.

Youngblut, J. M., Loveland-Cherry, C. J., & Horan, M. (1990). Factors related to maternal employment status following the premature birth of an infant. *Nursing Research, 39,* 237–240.

Youngblut, J. M., Singer, L. T., Madigan, E. A., Swegart, L. A., & Rodgers, W. L. (1997). Maternal employment and parent child relationships in single parent families of LBW preschoolers. *Psychology of Women Quarterly, 21,* 247–263.

Zeskind, P. S., & Lester, B. M. (1981). Analysis of cry features in newborns with differential fetal growth. *Child Development, 52,* 207–212.

4

Innovations in Adoption

VICTOR GROZA

Adoption is a unique experience, in that it is both a legal event and a lifelong experience. It is estimated that 2% to 5% of American households include adopted children (Bachrach, 1986; Bachrach, Adams, Sambrano, & London, 1989; Moorman & Hernandez, 1989; Stolley, 1993) and that more than 100,000 adoptions occur each year (Stolley, 1993). While adoption has been practiced for centuries, there have been significant changes since the mid-1970s. A major change is the increase in stepparent adoptions as a result of the increase in the number of stepfamilies. In addition, general adoption practices have changed from finding infants for infertile couples (i.e., parent-centered adoption practice) to finding adoptive families who can meet the needs of older or special-needs children (i.e., child-centered adoption practice). Children with special needs include those who (1) are older at placement (usually five or older), (2) have physical, developmental, emotional, behavioral, or mental disabilities, (3) are minority or mixed racial children, (4) have histories of abuse or neglect, or (5) are members of sibling groups. Children who have none of these characteristics but who are older when they become available for adoption (usually school age and up), are also thought of as having special needs. This chapter outlines the different populations of adoptees in the United States, discusses their unique needs and vulnerabilities, and reviews and evaluates recent innovations, addressing the implications for policy, practice, and research.

The Population of Adoptees

The groups that constitute the population of adoptees have undergone major shifts in the past two decades. One group of adoptees, representing the biggest shift in adoption populations, consists of those who live with one birth parent and are subsequently adopted by that parent's spouse, who is not otherwise related to the child (a stepparent adoption). In most states, stepparent adoptions are the most common form of adoption (Barth, 1992), reflecting the general societal trend of stepfamilies replacing nuclear families as the dominant form of family life in the United States. Usually, stepparent adoptions involve stepfathers adopting a stepchild. This type of adoption has been classified as a related adoption and makes up about half of all adoptions in the United States (Stolley, 1993).

A second group of adoptees consists of healthy infants, who are placed predominantly with middle- and upper-middle-class families. About one-third of unrelated domestic adoptions are arranged independently (Stolley, 1993), meaning that children are placed directly in adoptive families without agencies acting as intermediaries. Usually, in independent adoptions, the primary intermediaries are attorneys. Infant adoptions account for 15% to 20% of adoptions (Barth, 1992; Stolley, 1993).

A third group consists of foreign-born children who are adopted into the United States. It was only after World War II that international adoptions developed. Barth (1992) estimates that about 10% of placements are international adoptions, while Stolley (1993) suggests that international adoptions are about 16% of all unrelated domestic adoptions. Before 1990, most international adoptees came from Asia or South America, primarily from Korea and Colombia. In 1990, the fall of communism added new children to the population of those adopted internationally. There was a steady decrease in the number of children adopted from Asia and an increase in adoptions from Europe. European adoptions, particularly in 1990 and 1991, involved predominantly children from Romania. By 1992, Romanian adoptions ranked second to those involving children from the republics of the former Soviet Union. In 1995, there was an increase in the number of children arriving from Asia, predominantly from China, as a result of increased flexibility in adoption regulations in China.

A fourth group consists of the minority children who enter foster care as infants or toddlers but who grow older while in foster care because the system has not successfully implemented permanency plans or developed adoption plans and resources. According to a study by Schwartz, Ortega, Guo, and Fishman (1994), a significant proportion of minority infants does not achieve permanent placements within four years of initial placements in child welfare systems. In other words, minority infants who come to the attention of the public welfare system have lower permanent placement rates than white infants. When minority children are adopted, they are usually adopted by their foster families. Each year, about 60% of all adoptions of children in child welfare systems are foster-adopt arrangements. While only about 8% of adoptive placements are transracial (Stolley, 1993), practice wisdom suggests that significant proportions of such adoptions are foster-to-adopt placements (excluding international transracial and transcultural placements).

Some minority children have avoided child welfare systems altogether and are placed in kinship care. They are subsequently adopted by relatives or extended family members who have been serving as their caregivers, formally or informally. Small groups of minority children may enter child welfare systems but then be placed successfully in kinship care. While kin are typically thought of as people related by blood or by marriage, for many families people considered to be kin are chosen by the family and are not related either by blood or by marriage. Kinship arrangements have increased substantially since the early 1990s. While the vast majority of these arrangements do not result in adoption, for some minority children the path to permanency and adoption is through kinship care. Since they are not tracked separately and the system of reporting on adoption is based on estimates and voluntary reporting, kinship adoptions typically are included as related or relative adoptions.

A fifth group includes children who have physical or developmental disabilities, who may or may not be infants when they become available for adoption. This group includes children who are mentally retarded, children with congenital birth defects such as spina bifida, technology-dependent children, children with HIV, and children who suffer effects from prenatal exposure to alcohol and other drugs. There are no accurate estimates of the number of mentally retarded or technology-dependent children who become available for adoption each year. Technology-dependent children are children who rely on machines to assist with routine biological functioning, such as breathing or eating, and who would die without the artificial means (i.e., life support or life-sustaining machines). Estimates of the number of infants born with exposure to illegal drugs each year range from 30,000 (Besharov, 1989) to 375,000 (Schneider, Griffith, & Chasnoff, 1989), with 150,000 probably being the best estimate (Gomly & Shiono, 1991). In 1993, the Centers for Disease Control (CDC) reported more than 4,000 cases of pediatric AIDS in children less than 13 years of age, which represents about 2% of the AIDS population (CDC, 1992). For every child with AIDS, three to five children are infected with HIV (Novick, 1989; Oleske, 1987). Extrapolating from the 1993 reports from the CDC, this implies that from 12,000 to 20,000 children are infected with HIV. Gwinn, Pappaioanou, and George (1991) estimate that up to 80,000 women of childbearing age may currently be infected with HIV. This means that from 1,500 to 2,100 babies may be born with HIV in the United States each year. In addition, with the advances in medical care technology, an increasing number of children born prematurely, as well as the increasing number of those born with complicated health problems, are being kept alive and functioning through sophisticated medical equipment. While most of these children remain with their birth families, an increasing number have become available for adoption. Only since 1980 has an emphasis been placed on finding adoption resources for these children.

The sixth group is made up of older children, who are often victims of abuse or neglect and have spent considerable time in child welfare systems. In the recent past, children became involved in child welfare systems due to parental neglect. In the past decade, an increasing number of children have entered care because of physical and/or sexual abuse. About 44% of child maltreatment reports were confirmed as neglect, 24% were confirmed as physical abuse, and 15% were confirmed as sexual abuse (National Center on Child Abuse and Neglect, 1993). The number of reports of child maltreatment more than doubled from 1970 to 1980 (American Humane Association, 1988), with sexual abuse reports rising at a faster rate than other types of maltreatments (Lie & McMurtry, 1991).

The seventh and final group is composed of children who are members of sibling groups. Sibling groups often enter child welfare systems because one or more were abused or neglected. Most children grow up with siblings. In the child population in the United States, it is estimated that more than 80% of children belong to sibling groups and 60% have at least two siblings. The amount of time siblings spend with each other, in their early years, is often greater than the amount they spend with their parents. The sibling relationship is complex and lasts for a lifetime, longer than most marriages and parent-child relationships (Dunn, 1985; Pfouts, 1976). A critical issue in child welfare systems is siblings in care. Studies suggest that 93% of children in foster care have either full, half, or stepsiblings (Timberlake & Hamlin, 1982), and 30% to 85% of children enter foster care with their siblings (Wedge & Mantle, 1991). Only recently has a concerted effort been made in policy and practice to keep siblings together or reunite those whom child welfare systems have separated. More often than not, one or more of the siblings has special needs.

Many of the groups we have identified can be characterized as special-needs adoptees. In the United States, children are considered as having special needs if they (1) are older at placement (usually five or older), (2) have physical, developmental, emotional, behavioral, or mental disabilities, (3) are minority or mixed-race children, (4) have histories of abuse or neglect, or (5) are members of sibling groups. These children are usually eligible for federal and state adoption subsidies. The use of the term "special needs" is problematic for several reasons. First, some infants who are placed with middle-class families do not show evidence of special needs at placement but develop these needs later in life. Often, because they were placed privately (i.e., independently) and were not classified as special-needs children at placement, there is minimal support from public and private agencies. Second, while similarities exist among these groups of adoptees, and some overlap in their service needs (for example, sibling groups often contain one or more children with a history of abuse), there are also many differences among the groups. Service needs and clinical issues are different depending on the children's needs and histories. Each of these groups of children represents different challenges to the service delivery system. Their needs are unique and agencies must address them as such, rather than treat the entire population as one group. Third, many international adoptees have special needs as a result of spending their formative years in institutional settings. However, there are explicit and implicit barriers, in public policy and in service delivery, to including these children and their families as part of a plan for service delivery for special-needs adopted children.

Service Needs of Different Subgroups of Adoptees

For the most part, adoption has been a very successful social arrangement. There are several ways to assess the success of adoption. One method is to examine the negative consequences that are unique to the adoption experience. Disruption, which means the removal of the child from the adoptive placement prior to finalization, occurs in some placements. However, in the vast majority of cases the adoption does not disrupt. The most common estimate is that about 15% of adoptions disrupt (Barth & Berry 1988), which means that most (85%) adoptions remain intact. Even with the higher rate of disruptions for older, special needs children (Barth & Berry, 1988; Groze, 1986; Kagan & Reid, 1986; Rosenthal, Schmidt, & Conner, 1988), research on adoption disruption suggests that the majority of adoptive placements make it to legalization.

A second problem unique to adoption is dissolutions, which is a legal process in which adoptive parents petition the courts to end their parental rights after adoptions have been finalized. There are few studies that address dissolutions; many studies place disruptions and dissolutions in the same category. The best estimate is that fewer than 2% of adoptive placements dissolve after finalization (Barth, 1988; Rosenthal et al., 1988; Schaffer & Lindstrom, 1990).

In addition to exploring problems unique to the adoption experience, researchers examine success by analyzing postlegal adoption outcomes. Several studies report that adoption outcomes are overwhelmingly positive. Kadushin and Martin (1988), in a review of 24 studies of infant adoptions, suggest that 66% of adoptions are successful, 18% are partially successful, and only about 16% are problematic. Rosenthal and Groze (1992), in their follow-up of 800 families who adopted older and special needs children, reported parent-child relations to be overwhelmingly positive. Seventy-five percent of parents were very or mostly positive about the impact of adoption on their families. In a subsequent longitudinal study of families who adopted older and special needs children, Groze (1996) found that 78% of parents reported their adoptions to be very or mostly positive in year one, and 69% felt the same way by year four of the study. Only 8% of the children resulted in out-of-home placements in the course of four years. Longitudinal studies of transracial adoptions (Simon & Altstein, 1977, 1981, 1987; Simon, Altstein, & Melli, 1994), as well as at least one cross-sectional study of minority children in minority families (Rosenthal, Groze, Curiel, & Westcott, 1991), report that transracial adoptions and inracial adoptions of minority children by minority families are very successful; children prosper and families are very positive about the adoptions. Finally, results from adoption studies of international adoptees (Harvey, 1983; Kim, Hong, & Kim, 1979; Rathbun, DiVirgilio, & Waldfogel, 1958; Rathbun, McLaughlan, Bennett, & Garland, 1965), a review of adoption studies of children adopted internationally (Tizard, 1991), and recent reports about children from Romania (Groze & Ileana, 1996) are also quite positive. Most children fare well in their adoptive families, and service needs for these children and families are not profound.

While there is much cause for optimism in adoption, there are also some areas of concern. Several studies suggest that adopted children are overrepresented in mental health services (Brinich & Brinich, 1982; McRoy, Grotevant, & Zurcher, 1988) and may have more behavior problems than the general population (Verhulst, Althaus, & Bieman, 1990). Rosenthal and Groze (1992) found that about one-third of families who adopted older and special-needs children participated in therapy for their children, and about one-fourth participated in family therapy after placement. Thus, while, overall, adoptions are decidedly positive, there is some indication that a significant proportion of adoptees may require mental health or other therapeutic interventions. While disruption and dissolution are uncommon, it is important to gain an understanding of these problems so that services and programs can be developed to reduce their incidence.

Adoptees are a vulnerable population, due, in part, to the uniqueness of the social arrangement, the community's response to the arrangement, issues that emerge in families as they integrate a new person into the system, and the vulnerabilities that children bring to the arrangement because of their genetic dispositions, prenatal treatments, and preplacement histories. Table 4.1 outlines the needs and service delivery issues for the different subgroups of adoptees.

It is apparent, from reviewing the summaries presented in Table 4.1 and from the preceding discussion, that there are areas of need that overlap as well as areas that are unique to each subsample of adoptees. There has been little, if any, attempt to provide a paradigm for understanding the needs of adoptees. In addition, there is no integrated, coordinated, or adoption-sensitive service system designed to meet similar as well as different needs of various groups of adoptees. With more than 5% of children affected by adoption issues, there is a need to conceptualize these issues more critically, as well as to make improvements and innovations in the adoption service system in order to better meet the needs of children and families affected by adoption.

Recent Innovations in Practice and Service Delivery

While the practice of adoption has been around for centuries, the placement of older and special needs children, stepparent adoptions, and international adoptions are fairly new developments. Several recent practice innovations have had an effect on adoption, including the emergence of attachment theory/ therapy for better understanding adopted children and the family therapy movement, which has moved the focus away from the individual and toward the family. In service delivery, there have been at least three recent innovations. One is the increase in the use of computer technologies. Computer technological innovations affect how management information systems are developed and used to both monitor and influence policy decisions. In addition, there has been a dramatic increase in the use of the Internet for adoption education, recruitment, and postplacement support. A second innovation, which has been fostered by the increasing numbers of medically fragile international and other special needs children, is the interdisciplinary focus on meeting the unique needs of these children and their families. A third innovation, funded by the Federal Adoption Opportunities Program at the Children's Bureau and by private foundations such as the Kellogg Foundation and the Dave Thomas (Wendy's) Foundation for Adoption, focuses on adoption system and child welfare system reforms, including an increase in public-private partnerships in adoption.

ATTACHMENT THEORY/THERAPY

While attachment theory has been very popular since the 1960s, informing research and practice with infants and toddlers (Bowlby, 1969, 1973, 1988; Main, Kaplan, & Cassidy, 1985; Main & Weston, 1981; Waters & Deane, 1985), it is only recently that some adoption researchers and writers have begun to examine the applicability of attachment theory to adoption dynamics (Groze, 1996; Groze &

TABLE 4.1

Outline of Population of Adoptees, Areas of Vulnerability, and Service Needs

Population of Adoptees	Needs of the specific population (areas of vulnerability)	Services
Stepparent adoptions	• assistance in "blending" as a family • loyalty conflicts over absent birth parent	• individual and family therapy as needed
Healthy infants in middle-class families	• entry into school identifies some child as having special educational needs • adolescence seems to be a partciularly vulnerable period • parents struggle when child does not meet their expectations	• support groups for children and families • individual and family therapy as needed • educational support services • parent classes and family therapy as needed
International adoptees	• many suffer delays as a result of institutionalization at critical periods in their development • institutionalization causes health, educational, and developmental difficulties	• comprehensive health and developmental assessments at placement • special education • occupational therapy • early-intervention programs • speech therapy • complicated medical care
Minority children in the child welfare system	• most likely to end up in transracial placements • most will be adopted by their foster family	• support for development of cultural identity • support for families as they move from foster to adoptive status • economic and social support for kinship placements
Children with physical or developmental disabilities	• have complicated health or developmental needs in every day life • have special educational needs	• special education • occupational therapy • physical therapy • speech therapy • complicated medical care
Victims of abuse or neglect	• many have attachment and behavior difficulties with many being diagnosed with hyperactivity • some have special educational needs because of either emotional and behavioral problems or learning disabilities	• special education • individual, group, and family therapy • expressive therapies (art, music, occupational) • residential treatment
Sibling groups	• some sibling groups have difficulty knowing appropriate boundaries and behavior with each other • many have same needs as children who have been victims of abuse or neglect	• sibling and family therapy • many have same service needs as children who were victims of abuse or neglect

Rosenthal, 1993; Johnson & Fein, 1991; Keck & Kupecky, 1995; McRoy, Grotevant, & Zurcher, 1988). However, there have been no empirical studies that tested the propositions of this theory as they apply to older, adopted children. Attachment theory posits that the ability to establish and maintain effective relationships is influenced by the quality of children's early relationships with a primary caregiver or caregivers (Bowlby, 1969, 1988; Crittenden, 1985; Tavecchio & Van Ijzendoorn, 1987). Within the context of this primary relationship, children begin to construct an image of themselves as well as their caregivers and transfer this understanding to other relationships and to their understanding of the world (Bowlby, 1969, 1988). If caregivers are responsive to the children's needs, the children learn to be confident that their needs will be met and that they will be comforted in times of distress. Through this process and over time, children will develop a secure emotional bond to their parents. Adequate attachments have a positive effect on children's behavior and children behave in ways that are congruent with parental values and expectations.

The attachment process is reciprocal. As children become attached to their parents, the parents respond with increased attachment to the children. Essentially, with a secure attachment, parents and children are likely to be attuned to each other—mutually sensitive and responsive to each other's needs. This type of relationship facilitates children's identification with adults, which, in turn, results in behavior that is more congruent with the parental value system as well as the development of mutual affectional and emotional ties to each other (Bowlby, 1969, 1988).

Problems occur when there is a disruption in the attachment process (Bowlby, 1969, 1988). A disruption in the parent/child relationship occurs when the primary caregiver is either unresponsive or unavailable to meet the child's needs. Two obvious situations where this may occur involve abuse or neglect and cases of institutional deprivation. A disruption occurs when the response to the child is hurtful, such as physical, sexual, or emotional abuse. Children who are institutionalized at early ages (including for prolonged hospitalization), often become listless and blank after attempts to get their needs met in a consistent and timely manner are ignored. Disruptions that are less obvious can also occur. With infant adoptees, issues involving disrupted relations are often denied because the abandonment or relinquishment happened so early in the child's life. Recently, the "primal wound theory" (Verrier, 1993) was introduced. According to this theory, separation of a child from the birth mother results in a separation trauma, that is, a fundamental loss of the birth bond that will resonate throughout an adoptee's life. Verrier believes that the younger the child at the time of separation from the birth mother, the greater the trauma. Some adoption specialists feel that adoptees placed as infants struggle with attachment issues, even more so than older children who have had the benefit of an earlier experience of bonding, because the birth bond was disrupted while the child was at a preverbal stage. Attachment difficulties develop because children have no words to express what has happened to them, yet experience the loss and separation from their birth mothers. For children adopted by a stepparent, often the attachment issue is the quality of the relationship with the nonrelated parent. Also, children in stepparent adoptions may experience loyalty conflicts when they feel strong attachment to the present stepparent as well as a continuing attachment to the absent birth parent. Thus, attachment issues may be problematic for all the subgroups of adoptees.

Early attachment difficulties may be reinforced further by later life experiences. Difficulties can become more pronounced as a result of the separation that occurs when the child is removed from the biological home and placed in foster care (Iglehart, 1993; Yancey, 1992). Even if placement out of the home is voluntary, as is often the case in kinship arrangements or in the case of a divorce where a parent leaves the home, leaving or changing familiar settings can be traumatic. Children often do not differentiate what is good and what is bad for them; they differentiate only what is familiar and what is unfamiliar.

The attachment difficulties that can develop from problems in early relationships include insecure attachment, anxious-avoidant attachment, and a pattern of attachment that blends insecure and avoidant styles. Furthermore, multiple moves may exacerbate attachment problems; multiple moves contribute to deleterious outcomes for the child throughout all developmental stages (Kotsopoulos et al., 1993). Thus, not only does the initial move place the child at risk, subsequent and frequent moves also place the child at risk for later difficulties.

Ultimately, adults who were emotionally deprived or who experienced other types of relationship trauma as infants or children may have difficulty developing "healthy," effective relationships. These individuals are more likely to remain isolated or to engage in behaviors that elicit supportive responses from others without having to invest emotionally. Whether or not these individuals, throughout their teen years and into adulthood, display overt delinquent (acting out) behaviors or withdrawal, they remain lonely and isolated (Hodges & Tizard, 1989; Jaffee & Fanshel, 1970).

While these early experiences can have a profound effect throughout people's lives, there is ample evidence that people can recover from early negative or traumatic incidents. A stable, nurturing environment may have an ameliorating effect on poor attachment experiences early in life (Fanshel, 1992; Feigelman, 1997; Lahti, 1982; Triseliotis, 1984). The belief is that adjustment to adoption, while affected by the quality of preplacement or preadoptive relationships, can be positively affected over time and a person's cognitive representation of the world and relationship can be positively influenced by exposure to positive, continuous, committed relationships. The more stable and long term (or permanent) the placement, the greater the opportunity for the individual to develop a sense of belonging and to work toward resolving early attachment issues. Following this line of reasoning, the resolution of early issues likely contributes to better outcomes for the individual throughout the various developmental life stages that lead to adulthood and old age. Thus, later positive experiences can have a profound effect on counteracting early negative experiences.

The advent of attachment theory as a way to understand the needs of all subgroups of adoptees is a recent innovation. The research conducted in this area has been primarily conceptual. Most of the writing offers clinical or anecdotal evidence about how attachment theory applies to specific subgroups of adoptees,

such as older children (Keck & Kupecky, 1995), children with preadoptive histories of sexual abuse (Smith & Howard, 1994), or international adoptees (Tizard,
1991). Empirical research has focused on methods of measuring attachment in
older and special-needs children (Groze & Rosenthal, 1993), although there is an
inadequate consensus about measurement and methodologies. Little has been
done to show how interventions developed from the theory have been effective
in increasing attachment and decreasing attachment problems. In addition,
because of a lack of set definitions and accurate diagnoses, some current treatment programs for children with attachment difficulties present questionable
validity and utility. Some therapies are highly experimental and unusual, such
as rage induction techniques or holding techniques (Anderson, 1986; Cline, 1979,
1981; Welch, 1988). One technique involves holding children against their will
until they are in a rage and then comforting them as a vehicle for promoting
attachment. The belief that the most opportune time for building a connection
or attachment is after children experience stress and begin to relax. The relaxation
process makes them vulnerable to building a connection. These techniques are
clinically based, not empirically based; that is, in carefully constructed research
studies, the more intrusive techniques have not been shown to be effective.
Several states have started discussions in their legislature about outlawing
practices such as rage induction therapies. While there is no evidence to indicate
that it is ineffective, more research is needed if it is going to be a viable strategy
for interventions to help children who have attachment difficulties.

Historically, while attachment has been discussed as an issue in adoption,
there has been little attempt to draw from the theoretical and empirical literature
for birth families and to integrate it into adoption practice. Recent innovations
allow the adoption community to better understand, describe, and begin the
process of exploring ways to intervene in problematic attachments. In the past,
the emphasis would have been on child behavior without a concommitant effort
to understand the dynamics of attachment or the relationship of attachment to
family functioning or child behavior and vice versa. Little effort was spent on
trying to help children understand their past relationships in order to promote
more positive relations in adoptive families and extended family systems. Thus,
attachment theory and related therapies have helped shape adoption practice
and provided a useful framework for assessing and understanding one of the
many issues faced in adoptive families.

FAMILY-CENTERED OR FAMILY-BASED ADOPTION PRACTICE

The family therapy movement of the 1960s and social work's unique person-
in-environment approach have been major influences in the development of a
family-centered or family-based approach to adoption practice.

The family-centered or family-based perspective has moved adoption practice away from a child-only focus on intervention. Instead of viewing the child
as "ill" or "pathological," behavior is examined in the context of the family system's capacity for dealing with the unique challenges the child brings to family
functioning. Thus, while not precluding child-specific intervention strategies,

this approach focuses on strengthening and supporting families in being able to manage and deal with their children. It is an approach that focuses less on blame (i.e., the child is or has a problem) and more on solutions and strengths (i.e., how can we assist the family in managing the child or changing its expectations of the adoptive relationship?). In traditional interventions, the child was the focus of intervention and attempts were made to improve the child's "fit" into the family by changing the child. In a family approach, the focus of intervention is on the family and helping the family change to accommodate the child as well as better manage the child. This approach tries to help families understand their children's behavior in the context of their preadoptive histories as well as to change the family's expectations about the attachment relationship.

A family-based perspective recognizes that it is important to strengthen and work collaboratively with the informal helping resources that are already a part of the life of many adoptive families. This approach is also more culturally sensitive, because it focuses on the family's natural social networks. The use of this perspective includes evaluating the strengths and limitations of a family's social environment and the impact that environment has on the family. Intervention may then focus on strengthening current sources of support, increasing the supports and resources to the families, and working to develop resources for families and children.

A family-based perspective in adoption puts the family in control of deciding who helps them master a difficulty or a problem. This viewpoint recognizes that the family is the most critical part of the child's life. It recognizes that, while service providers and social workers weave in and out of the adopted child's life, the family is permanent. Using this approach, it becomes important to rely on family members for their perceptions of issues and include them in selecting the services to be provided. This perspective requires the social worker to work as a partner with the family.

Recent research and practice in adoption have highlighted that successful adoption depends less on the child who enters the family and more on the family as a complex social system. There are several stressors that put families at-risk of adoption instability. These problems include high parental expectations (Partridge, Hornby, & McDonald, 1986; Rosenthal, Schmidt, & Conner, 1988; USRE, 1985), family rigidity (Boneh, 1979; Cohen, 1984), and inadequate support systems (Groze, 1996; Rosenthal & Groze, 1992). High parental expectations can develop for the "dream" or "fantasy" child. Imbued with popular myths about adoptees (Sandmaier, 1988), parents develop dreams and expectations about the children they adopt. Socioeconomic status can reinforce these dreams and expectations, with middle- and upper-class families holding rigid, high aspirations for their children. Often, parents imagine that their children will be loving, happy "orphans," willing and grateful to be adopted. In professional career families, there may be implicit or explicit expectations that the child will pursue a similar career path. Clearly, with many special-needs children being adopted who have severe emotional and behavioral problems as well as an array of significant learning difficulties, these expectations will not be congruent with reality.

Rigid families have reduced capabilities to change their expectations or deal with the stress of integrating adopted children into their families, which places adoptive placements at greater risk for negative adoption outcomes (Boneh, 1979; Cohen, 1984). To accomplish family integration, the adoptive family and the family system that the adopted child brings to the family must change to develop a third system, much like the experiences of blended families (Carter & McGoldrick, 1988). One of the most significant tasks, related to those discussed in the previous section, is for family members to understand the attachment behaviors and expectations of one another to allow for mutual understanding and the process of integrating different histories of relationships into a new way of relating. When a family system is too rigid, the tasks associated with integration become problematic.

Involvement with formal (e.g., professional service providers) and informal support systems (e.g., adoptive parent support groups) can provide more energy to the adoptive family system. Social support can strengthen the family and can buffer family stress; it is often viewed as a significant factor in promoting success in adoption (Barth & Berry, 1988; Nelson, 1985; Partridge, Hornby, & McDonald, 1986). Social support allows families to take advantage of the concrete, emotional, and informational foundation they need in parenting children with special needs.

As with attachment theory/therapy, little research has been conducted that compares outcomes for the traditional child-centered approach to those achieved by the family-centered approach. The books and articles that highlight this model, in terms of intervention, use case studies to evaluate this practice (e.g., Bourguignon & Watson, 1987; Hartman, 1984; Katz, 1986; Reitz & Watson, 1992; Rosenberg, 1992). As is the case with many innovations in adoption, limited research has been conducted, although this perspective is the major influence in contemporary adoption practice.

TECHNOLOGICAL INNOVATIONS

Computers in general, and the Internet specifically, have radically reshaped adoption since 1990. The increase in the use of computer technologies has allowed both large public agencies and small private and public agencies to better track the children in their systems. These management information systems have been developed and used to monitor the impact of policy decisions as well as to generate data that can inform the process of developing better child welfare policies and practices.

The Internet has exploded since 1995 as a source of adoption education, recruitment, and postplacement support. There are sites on the Internet that give information about all the subgroups of adoptees listed in Table 4.1. These information sites include abstracts of research studies as well as parent and practitioner newsletters and reports about the different groups of adopted children, advice to families, a listing of services by geographic area that children and families might find helpful, and a list of agencies that provide support and services to families and/or children. "Chat rooms" or discussion forums have been set up for parents considering adoption and for parents who have adoption-related questions. Some sites also have chat rooms for adoptees. Public and private agencies, as well as individuals, have Web sites that advertise their services and children available for adoption. Requests for additional information and application forms are available over the Internet, both for general and for child-specific recruitment. Families can charge some fees to their credit cards and complete the first steps in the adoption process on-line, sending additional paperwork at a later date. Research and policy forums have been created on bulletin boards around the country, some open to the public and others accessed through invitation only. These forums are also used to promote grassroots advocacy whenever adoption issues emerge in the media, in state legislatures, or in federal legislation and policy making. Both adoption researchers and practitioners participate in these forums.

The Internet will continue to play a role in adoption, although the scope and depth of its influence are unknown, since it is a relatively new innovation in adoption. Technology will continue to shape practice environments, perhaps in ways that are not imaginable. At this point, the adoption services delivered through technological interventions represent value-added informal services to supplement traditional informal and formal services.

INTERDISCIPLINARY INTERVENTIONS

Many children who are adopted have complicated life histories before they enter their adoptive families. Many older children are veterans of the child welfare system, which they entered because of parental neglect, physical abuse, or sexual abuse. Often, they have endured multiple moves and suffer from emotional and behavioral problems. Children born to mothers affected by substance abuse or HIV are often medically fragile; both their prenatal care and the complicated health and development issues these children face early in life make caring for them very difficult. Finally, international adoptees have often spent extended periods of time in orphanages or other institutions prior to adoption. Institutional care does not give children the physical and social stimulation necessary for healthy development and affects their ability to make smooth transitions from one developmental stage to another throughout their lives. These three subgroups of adoptees require, and benefit from, multidisciplinary intervention.

Although communities have treatment, support, and adoption services available to families, often these services are not coordinated, and few practitioners are experienced in or knowledgeable about the combination of special-needs adoption and the array of child welfare, mental health, educational, medical, and therapeutic services. Interdisciplinary approaches, such as the PARTNERS Program (Groze & Gruenewald, 1991), create a specially trained team of professionals who represent a cross-section of the community. The PARTNERS team includes those professionals and agencies critical to adoption, treatment, and community adjustment, comprising representatives of the department of human services, education, mental health, medicine, child psychiatry and social work.

For these teams to function effectively in communities, members of the team must understand the unique aspects of adoption; the best mechanism in building a multidisciplinary team that is knowledgeable about adoption is through joint training in adoption theory, practice, and programming.

Since this approach is relatively new, these teams are not in widespread use, and limited research has been conducted to evaluate their effectiveness and efficiency. Often, a team approach is emphasized at the two existing international adoption health clinics (one in Minnesota and one in Massachusetts). In two demonstrations of this interdisciplinary team concept for older and special needs adopted children, both based on outpatient services delivered by community-based agencies, the team met monthly to review case evaluations and quarterly to provide an oversight function for the program's operation and purposes (see Groze, Basista, & Persse, 1993; Groze, Young, & Corcran-Rumppe, 1991). Results from these two federal demonstration projects indicate that most families were referred for mental health and counseling services rather than support services, health care, or educational services. The issues that most frequently led families to pursue services were concerns about the children's behavior and problems of attachment. Interventions that were most helpful in working with adoptive families included constructing and reviewing placement genograms (a graphic tool to diagram children's placement histories) about the children in order to understand current functionings in the context of their preadoptive histories, normalizing the experiences of family members as part of the struggle of adoptive family life, reframing some of the difficulties as issues around separation, grief, and loss, and helping families use parenting skills appropriate to their children's level of development.

At service termination, families' perceptions of children's behavior and parent-child relations improved. It was clear to the staff in the project that children's behavior rarely dramatically changed; often, however, changing the families' expectations and normalizing their experiences as well as helping them understand the reasons their children were misbehaving helped families to change their perceptions of their children's behavior. This was also the case with parent-child relations; normalizing their experiences with their children's attachment difficulties and helping them understand the reasons for their children's attachment difficulties helped families to change their expectations of attachment relationships. Families evaluated positively the services they received, and, even in those families where the child was placed out-of-home for treatment, family connections to the child were strengthened and preserved (see Groze, Basista, & Persse, 1993; Groze, Young, & Corcran-Rumppe, 1991). The interdisciplinary approach is relatively new and, while not widespread, may be an innovation that will expand over time to other communities and for other populations of adopted children.

SYSTEM REFORM AND RENOVATION

Several major initiatives related to adoption system reform have been initiated in several communities throughout the country. The Kellogg Foundation has funded the adoption system reform initiative, and grants have been provided by the Children's Bureau, Adoption Opportunities, Department of Health and Human Services.

The Kellogg Foundation, as part of its Families for Kids initiative, has funded more than 20 sites throughout the United States to accomplish five system change goals. These goals include: (1) the development of a coordinated single assessment process; (2) assurance that children in foster care will have single, stable foster placements within their communities until permanence; (3) improved permanency for all children to tackle the problem of "foster care drift"; (4) system change to allow all families in contact with the child welfare system to have the community-based support and assistance they need to strengthen their abilities to function; and, (5) the provision of one caseworker or casework team that will work with families or children throughout the implementation of their permanency plans.

These system change efforts were funded in 1995 for a period of three years. Quantitative results are not yet available. However, preliminary data based on anecdotes and interviews suggest a renewed recognition that the backlog of children waiting for permanency must be a priority. To this end, there have been increased explorations of different options for permanency, including promoting and supporting kinship care, as well as guardianship. There is a renewed effort to promote public-private partnerships, focusing on children and permanency and trying to remove intra-agency conflict that undermines the focus on children, as well as increasing intra-agency collaboration and coordination on behalf of waiting children. Ongoing meetings, joint training opportunities, and written commitments or contracts have been developed to foster better public-private partnerships. These efforts have focused on not only public and private social service agencies but also the relationship between social agencies and the courts. Judges, attorneys, and guardians ad litem have participated in Kellogg-sponsored forums and training about how to work together more effectively.

The Dave Thomas Foundation plans to sponsor adoption training for judges and attorneys so that these professionals can better understand the many issues faced by the children and their families as well as the social service systems that serve them. The policy/system barriers in fost-adopt arrangements are being explored and removed on a case-by-case basis; many of these policy barriers deal with financial and service system arrangements. Historically, financial subsidies and services are reduced when families make commitments to adopt their foster children. This policy creates huge disincentives for families to move from foster to adoptive status. Legislative changes have begun to remedy this difficulty, and public child welfare agencies are learning how to negotiate subsidy and service arrangements that allow children to move into permanent adoption arrangements.

Also, the Kellogg projects have focused on using marketing principles in adoption practice. Reports using geodemography (taking demographic information and mapping the information by neighborhoods, cities, regions, or states) have been generated, summarizing market information about communities and adoptive families in order to assist projects in developing recruitment strategies targeted to family configurations that are underrepresented in their areas. For example, in a report by the LIDA Group (1997), single-parent families and middle-class families are suggested for recruitment in certain counties in Ohio. These counties are color-coded to show where single-parent and middle-class families cluster. The report also provides a profile of the interest and activities of these families that can be used to develop recruitment strategies. A case in point: in one community where single-parent families were targeted, one of the activities that such families frequently engaged in was participation in a health club. Thus, one strategy for recruitment was to advertise in local health clubs for single parents to adopt waiting special-needs children.

The use of marketing concepts in adoption practice is innovative; many adoption practitioners have little to no training or experience in communications and marketing. As these principles become integrated into adoption practice, the expectation is that they will contribute to adoption service and system reform.

Adoption Opportunity grants, developed by the Children's Bureau, Department of Health and Human Services, have supplemented the efforts of private foundations. For more than a decade, the federal government has solicited proposals from the public and private sectors to develop, implement, and evaluate innovative practices and programs in adoption recruitment, preparation, placement, or postlegal (postfinalization) activities in both public and private agencies. These projects have focused on decreasing barriers to minority recruitment, increasing the placement of older minority children, preparing children in residential treatment for adoption, increasing adoptive placements of foster children in permanent custody, and strengthening adoptive families after legal finalization (postlegal projects). Federal funding has been awarded for projects in the public and the private sectors for almost every state. Unfortunately, the information gathered from these projects is not centrally located. Evaluation reports are not widely distributed, leading to replication of unsuccessful programs or activities as well as a pattern of "reinventing the wheel" at different sites. In addition, few of the innovations developed by these projects appear in the research literature. Thus, while the projects funded by Adoption Opportunity lead to system changes in specific locations, the opportunity for wider system impact is lost because evaluations are not widely distributed and fail to appear in journals and periodicals.

Implications for Practice, Service Delivery, Policy, Education, and Research

Adoption, while most often a successful social arrangement, is also a complicated social structure. It continues to be a changing practice—whether due to changes in family structure, which has resulted in increased stepparent adoptions, or changes in the populations of children who enter families through adoption, such as the increase in medically fragile children, or changes in the paradigms, such as attachment theory or family-centered practice; or changing technology, that determine how adoption is practiced.

Attachment theory offers much hope for a better understanding of many issues in adoption. Techniques to help children overcome attachment difficulties and promote positive attachment in adoptive families need to be developed and tested. At the same time, techniques to help families learn different methods of intervening in attachment difficulties also need to be developed. Standardized methods of assessing attachment in children would help practitioners to better understand attachment problems. Better assessment techniques could assist in matching a child's pattern of attachment with family patterns or family expectations about attachment. In addition to these practice areas, research to test hypotheses derived from attachment theory needs to be carried out for the different populations of adoptees. There is a need for outcome research that explores how the therapies evolving from attachment theory affect adopted children, their families, and their lives together.

The family-centered approach and the use of interdisciplinary teams have implications for service delivery. Family-centered adoption practice is consistent with many social work principles, including the strengths perspective, empowerment, and the ecological framework. However, the integration of a family-centered framework is not uniform in the service delivery system. Many public welfare systems, because of the emphasis on rescuing children from abuse or neglect, have not embraced a family-centered approach in delivering services. Also, many programs that serve children who live out of the home, such as those in residential treatment centers and group care facilities, do not have a family-centered orientation. To help implement this approach, a significant increase in training and technical support for staff who currently work in this area is needed. In addition, graduate programs that deal with various aspects of adoption must help their students understand the family-centered approach and integrate it into their practices.

An interdisciplinary approach to adopted children and their families is difficult to develop and maintain. At the same time, an interdisciplinary model of service delivery may offer the best hope for an integrated, holistic response that would not only strengthen and preserve adoptive families but would maximize the opportunity for growth and development of children and families. In addition to the turf issues for each discipline, the many demands on their time make it difficult for professionals to commit to working collaboratively. An additional part of the problem is that few training programs teach professionals how to collaborate and cooperate across disciplines, nor do they provide training opportunities for multidiscipline teamwork. Interdisciplinary team approaches require major shifts in professional relations and systems of care. Graduate and professional programs in the helping professions must assist their students to learn the skills to work as an interdisciplinary team. Continuing education programs for professionals already working in the field also need to focus on ways to promote interdisciplinary collaboration.

Other service delivery issues emerge from the growth of technological innovations in adoption services. There are policy issues around standards of practice and the regulation of practice. One policy issue is the standards of practice that apply or need to be developed in order to have some assurance about the quality of services provided over the Internet. Even the standards developed by such groups as the Child Welfare League of America have yet to develop guidelines for this new way of delivering services. A related policy issue is credentialing and the regulation of practice. Each state has its own standards and guidelines for licensing the professionals in that state. There are no real guidelines for delivering services via the Internet if the practitioner resides and is licensed in one state but provides services to a consumer in another state. The issues around standards and regulation are very complicated. On the one hand, we want to be able to use technology on behalf of children who are waiting for permanent families through adoption, as well as strengthen and support families through every mechanism possible who have made the commitment to adopt. On the other hand, we have to make sure the process and services delivered are consistent with standards that we apply in a traditional manner of delivering services.

It is also important to recognize that access to and use of the Internet is class based. The service is accessible and used most often by middle-class and upper-middle-class families. The dilemma is that there is a clear and consistent relationship among incomes, social class, and adoption outcomes: as income increases, negative outcomes increase. That is, higher-income families seem to have more difficulties changing their expectations about adopted children or adoptive relationships, which results in higher risk for problems (see Groze, 1996; Rosenthal & Groze, 1992). Thus, the bias among middle- and upper-middle-class families in favor of using technological innovations may not recruit the families who will be the most successful with adopted children but will probably provide some service to the families at greater risk for adoption difficulties. It also means that recruitment and support for working-class and poor families must continue to be provided through traditional means.

The effects of this new technology on increasing the placement of waiting children and the stability of adoptions are not known. Nor is it known whether these vehicles will result in a group of families more knowledgeable about adoption issues and more willing to use advocacy. It is clear, however, that technology has and will continue to shape adoption practice and will have implications for policy development and service delivery. Students who earn degrees from graduate and professional schools in the helping professions must be technologically literate, able to use the advances in computer hardware and software to improve the services they deliver. Professionals already working in the field will have to participate in training and continuing education programs to develop the skills necessary to survive and thrive in the computer age.

Finally, as attempts are made to reform the adoption system, the issue of fees and the costs of adoption need to be reexamined. There are several reasons for regulating expenses in the adoption process. First, compromises are made in agency decision making and in the quality of services given to parents before and after adoption. Such compromises include the information given to prospective adoptive families when children become a commodity in a market economy and families are seen as consumers. In addition, compromises occur in several other ways. Professionals experience a conflict of interest when they are paid only when placements are made. They may not gather information about the health, development, and living conditions of children or may ignore it in order to facilitate a placement. Once the agency receives funds from the adoptive family, it may be inclined to approve the family for adoption even if it has reservations about the appropriateness of the family. Thus, there is an implicit understanding that the family will be approved as an adoptive family after money changes hands. If the family is unwilling to participate in preparation activities, the agency may not force the issue because it is competing for market share in the adoption market. If the family feels that preparation activities are an additional hassle to the adoption process, it may choose an agency that will give it less of a hassle. Thus, when adoption as a practice becomes a business enterprise, it loses focus and integrity.

Second, there is wide variation in the cost of adoptions at different agencies or through different individuals in the same state. In 1994, the costs ranged from $8,000 to $50,000. While the exact reason for this discrepancy is not known, professionals should be concerned that it exists. The more desperate the family, which often means the older the adoptive family, single or couple, and the longer it has waited to adopt, the higher the costs. The evidence suggests that federal oversight into costs and regulation of fees for adoptions may be warranted.

Third, when a family pays a fee for an adoption, the emphasis becomes finding "a child for a family" (parent-centered), rather than "a family for a child" (child-centered). Contemporary adoption practice has moved to a child-centered model because it is in the best interest of the child. The fee-for-service arrangement undermines this philosophy and results in inferior adoption practices. Children and families will benefit from regulating the costs associated with adoption. The regulation of adoption financing remains an advocacy issue for social workers.

REFERENCES

American Humane Association. (1998). *Highlights of Official Child Abuse & Neglect Reporting-1986*. Denver, CO: Author.

Anderson, J. (1986). Holding therapy: A way of helping unattached children. In P. F. Grabe (Ed.), *Adoption resources for mental health professionals* (pp. 62–69). Mercer, PA: Mental Health Adoption Therapy Project.

Bachrach, C. A. (1986). Adoptive plans, adopted children, and adoptive mothers. *Journal of Marriage and the Family, 48*(2), 243–253.

Bachrach, C. A., Adams, P. F., Sambrano, S., & London, K. A. (1989). *Advance data: Adoption in the 1980s. Advance data from vital and health statistics, no 181.* Hyattsville, MD: National Center for Health Statistics.

Barth, R. (1988). Disruption in older child adoptions. *Public Welfare, 6*(1), 323–329.

Barth, R. P. (1992). Adoption. In P. J. Pecora, J. K. Whittaker, A. N. Maluccio with R. P. Barth, & R. D. Plotnick (Eds.), *The child welfare challenge: Policy, practice, and research* (pp. 361–400). New York: Aldine De Gruyter.

Barth, R. P., & Berry, M. (1988). *Adoption and disruption: Rates, risks, and response.* New York: Aldine De Gruyter.

Besharov, D. (1989). The children of crack: Will we protect them? *Public Welfare, 47*(4), 6–11.

Boneh, C. (1979). *Disruptions in adoptive placements: A research study.* Boston: Massachusetts Department of Public Welfare.

Bourguignon, F. P., & Watson, K. W. (1987). *After adopton: A manual for professionals working with adoptive families.* Springfield, IL: Illinois Department of Children and Family Services.

Bowlby, J. (1969). *Attachment and loss: Attachment.* New York: Basic Books.

Bowlby, J. (1973). *Attachment and loss: Separation, anxiety and anger.* New York: Basic Books.

Bowlby, J. (1988). *A secure base: Clinical applications of attachment theory.* London: Tavistock.

Brinich, P. M., & Brinich, E. B. (1982). Adoption and adaptation. *Journal of Nervous and Mental Disease, 170,* 489–493.

Carter, B., & McGoldrick, M. (1988). Overview: The changing family life cycle—a framework for family therapy. In B. Carter & M. McGoldrick (Eds.), *The changing family life cycle* (2nd ed., pp. 3–28). New York: Gardner Press.

Centers for Disease Control. (1992, Jan.). *HIV/AIDS Surveillance Report,* pp. 1–22. Washington, DC: U.S. Department of Health and Human Services.

Cline, F. (1979). *Understanding and treating the severely disturbed child.* Evergreen, CO: Evergreen Consultants in Human Behavior.

Cline, F. (1981). *Understanding and treating difficult children and their parents.* Evergreen, CO: Evergreen Consultants in Human Behavior.

Cohen, J. S. (1984). Adoption breakdown with older children. In P. Sachder (Ed.), *Adoption: Current issues and trends.* (pp. 129–138). Toronto: Butterwork.

Crittenden, P. M. (1985). Maltreated infants: Vulnerability and resilience. *Journal of Child Psychology and Pyschiatry, 26*(1), 85–96.

Dunn, J. (1985). *Sisters and brothers.* Cambridge, MA: Harvard University Press.

Fanshel, D. (1979). *Computerized information for child welfare: Foster children and their foster parents.* New York: Columbia University School of Social Work.

Fanshel, D. (1992). Foster care as a two-tiered system. *Children and Youth Services Review, 14,* 49–60.

Feigelman, W. (1997). Adopted adults: Comparisons with persons raised in coventional families. *Marriage and Family Review, 25*(3/4), 199–223.

Gomly, D. S., & Shiono, P. H. (1991). Estimating the number of substance-exposed children. *The Future of Children, 1*(1), 17–25.

Groze, V. (1986). Special needs adoption. *Children and Youth Services Review, 8,* 81–91.

Groze, V. (1996). *Successful adoptive families: A longitudinal study of special needs adoption.* Westport, CT: Greenwood Publishing.

Groze, V., Basista, M., & Persse, L. (1993). *Strengthening resources and decreasing stressors in adoption families: The post-legal special needs adoption family preservation treatment team project.* Prepared with the Family Resources in Davenport, Iowa, for the Department of Health and Human Services, Adoption Opportunities Program, Washington, DC.

Groze, V., & Gruenewald, A. (1991). PARTNERS: A model program for special needs adoptive families in stress. *Child Welfare, 70*(5), 581–589.

Groze, V., & Ileana, D. (1996). A follow-up study of adopted children from Romania. *Child and Adolescent Social Work Journal, 13*(6), 541–565.

Groze, V., & Rosenthal, J. (1993). Attachment theory and the adoption of children with special needs. *Social Work Research and Abstracts, 29*(2), 513.

Groze, V., Young, J., & Corcran-Rumppe, K. (1991). *Post adoption resources for training, networking and evaluation services (PARTNERS): Working with special-needs adoptive families in stress*. Prepared with Four Oaks, Inc., Cedar Rapids, Iowa, for the Department of Health and Human Services, Adoption Opportunities, Washington, DC.

Gwinn, M., Pappaioanou, M., & George, J. R. (1991). Prevalence of HIV infection in child-bearing women in the United States: Surveillance using newborn blood samples. *Journal of the American Medical Association, 265*, 1704–1708.

Hartman, A. (1984). *Working with adoptive families beyond placement*. New York: Child Welfare League.

Harvey, I. J. (1983). Adoption of Vietnamese children: An Australian study. *Australian Journal of Social Issues, 18*(1), 55–69.

Hodges, J., & Tizard, B. (1989). Social and family relationships of institutional adolescents. *Journal of Child Psychology and Psychiatry, 30*(1), 77–97.

Iglehart, A. P. (1993). Adolescents in foster care: Predicting behavioral maladjustment. *Child and Adolescent Social Work Journal, 10*(6), 521–532.

Jaffee, B., & Fanshel, D. (1970). *How they fared in adoption: A follow-up study* (Studies of the Child Welfare League of America). New York: Columbia University Press.

Johnson, D., & Fein, E. (1991). The concept of attachment: Applications to adoption. *Children and Youth Services Review, 13*(5/6), 397–412.

Kadushin, A., & Martin, J. (1988). *Child welfare services* (4th ed.). New York: Macmillan.

Kagan, R. M., & Reid, W. J. (1986). Critical factors in the adoption of emotionally disturbed youth. *Child Welfare, 65*, 63–74.

Katz, L. (1986). Parental stress and factors for success in older-child adoption. *Child Welfare 65*, 569–578.

Keck, G. C., & Kupecky, R. M. (1995). *Adopting the hurt kid: Hope for families with special-needs kids*. Colorado Springs, CO: Pinon Press.

Kim, S. P., Hong, S., & Kim, B. S. (1979). Adoption of Korean children by New York area couples: A preliminary study. *Child Welfare, 57*(7), 419–427.

Kotsopoulos, S., Walker, S., Copping, W., Cote, A., & Stavrakaki, C. (1993). A psychiatric follow-up study of adoptees. *Canadian Journal of Psychiatry, 38*, 391–396.

Lahti, J. (1982 Dec.). A follow-up study of foster children in permanent placements. *Social Service Review 56*(4), 556–571.

LIDA Group. (1997). *Consumer ID: Report for Ohio families for kids*. Wichita, KS: Author.

Lie, G., & McMurtry, S. L. (1991). Foster care for sexually abused children: A comparative study. *Child Abuse and Neglect, 15*, 111–121.

Main, M., Kaplan, N., & Cassidy, J. (1985). Security in infancy, childhood, and adulthood: A move to the level of representation. In I. Bretherton & E. Waters (Eds.), *Growing points of attachment theory and research* (pp. 66–104). Monographs of the Society for Research in Child Development, 50(1-2, Serial No. 209). Chicago: University of Chicago Press.

Main, M., & Weston, D. (1981). The quality of the toddler's relationship to mother and to father: Related to conflict behavior and the readiness to establish new relationships. *Child Development, 52*, 932–940.

McRoy, R. G., Grotevant, H., & Zurcher, S. (1988). *Emotional disturbance in adopted adolescents*. New York: Praeger.

Moorman, J. E., & Hernandez, D. J. (1989). Married-couple families with step, adopted, and biological children. *Demography, 26*(2), 267–277.

National Center on Child Abuse and Neglect (NCCAN). (1993). *National Child Abuse and Neglect Data System, Working Paper 2*. Gaithersburg, MD: Author.

Nelson, K. A. (1985). *On the frontier of adoption: A study of special-needs adoptive families.* New York: Child Welfare League of America.

Novick, B. E. (1989). Pediatric AIDS: A medical overview. In J. M. Seibert & R. A. Olson (Eds.), *Children, adolescents, and AIDS* (pp. 1–23). Lincoln: University of Nebraska Press.

Oleske, J. (1987). Natural history of HIV infection II. In B. K. Silverman & A. Waddell (Eds.), *Report of the surgeon general's workshop on children with HIV infection and their families* (pp. 24–25). DHHS Publication No. HRS-D-MS87-1. Washington, DC: U.S. Government Printing Office.

Partridge S., Hornby, H., & McDonald, T. (1986). *Legacies of loss, visions of gain: An inside look at adoption disruptions.* Portland: University of Southern Maine, Human Services Development Institute.

Pfouts, J. H. (1976). The sibling relationship: A forgotten dimension. *Social Work, 21*(3), 200–203.

Rathbun, C., DiVirgilio, L., & Waldfogel, S. (1958). The restitutive process in children following radical separation from family and culture. *American Journal of Orthopsychiatry, 27*, 408–415.

Rathbun, C., McLaughlan, H., Bennett, O., & Garland, J. A. (1965). Later adjustment of children following radical separation from family and culture. *American Journal of Orthopsychiatry, 35*, 604–609.

Reitz, M., & Watson, K. W. (1992). *Adoption and the family system.* New York: Guilford Press.

Rosenberg, E. (1992). *The adoption life cycle.* New York: Free Press.

Rosenthal, J. A., Groze, V., Curiel, H., & Westcott, P. A. (1991). Transracial and inracial adoption of special needs children. *Journal of Multicultural Social Work, 3*(1), 13–32.

Rosenthal, J. A., & Groze, V. G. (1992). *Special-needs adoption: A study of intact families.* New York: Praeger.

Rosenthal, J. A., Schmidt, D., & Conner, J. (1988). Predictors of special-needs adoption disruption: An exploratory study. *Children and Youth Services Review, 10*, 101–117.

Sandmaier, M. (1988). *When love is not enough.* Washington, DC: Child Welfare League of America.

Schaffer, J., & Lindstrom, C. (1990). Brief solution-focused therapy with adoptive families. In D. M. Brodzinsky & M. D. Schechter (Eds.), *The psychology of adoption* (pp. 253–272). New York: Oxford University Press.

Schneider, J., Griffith, D., & Chasnoff, I. J. (1989). Infants exposed to cocaine in utero: Implications for developmental assessment and intervention. *Infants and Young Children, 2*(1), 25–36.

Schwartz, I., Ortega, R., Guo, S., & Fishman, G. (1994, Sept.). Infants in nonpermanent placement. *Social Service Review*, 405–416.

Simon, R. J., & Altstein, H. (1977). *Transracial adoption.* New York: John Wiley & Sons.

Simon, R. J., & Altstein, H. (1981). *Transracial adoption: A follow-up.* Lexington, MA: Lexington Books.

Simon, R. J., & Altstein, H. (1987). *Transracial adoptees and their families: A study of identity and commitment.* New York: Praeger.

Simon, R. J., Altstein, H., & Melli, M. S. (1994). *The case for transracial adoption.* Washington, DC: American University Press.

Smith, S. L., & Howard, J. A. (1994). The impact of previous sexual abuse on children's adjustment in adoptive placement. *Social Work, 39*(5), 491–501.

Stolley, K. S. (1993). Statistics on adoption in the United States. In I. Schulman (Ed.), *The future of children* (pp. 26–42). Los Altos, CA: Center for the Future of Children.

Tavecchio, L. W. C., & Van Ijzendoorn, M. H. (1987). *Attachment in social networks: Contributions to the Bowlby-Ainsworth attachment theory.* New York: Elsevier Science.

Timberlake, E. M., & Hamlin, E. R. (1982). The sibling group: A neglected dimension of placement. *Child Welfare, 61*(8), 545–552.

Tizard, B. (1991). Intercountry adoption: A review of the evidence. *Journal of Child Psychology and Psychiatry, 32*(5), 743–756.

Triseliotis, J. (1984). Identity and security in adoption and long-term fostering. *Early Child Development and Care, 15,* 149–170.

Urban Systems Research & Engineering. (1985). *Evaluation of State activities with regard to adoption disruption.* Washington, DC: Urban Research and Engineering.

Verhulst, F. C., Althaus, M., & Bieman, H. J. M. V. (1990). Problem behavior in international adoptees: I. An epidemiological study. *Journal of the American Academy of Child and Adolescent Psychiatry, 29*(1), 94–111.

Verrier, N. (1993). *The primal wound: Understanding the adopted child.* Baltimore: Gateway Press.

Waters, E., & Deane, K. E. (1985). Defining and assessing individual differences in attachment relationships: Q-methodology and the organization of behavior in infancy and early childhood. In I. Bretherton & E. Waters (Eds.), *Growing points of attachment theory and research* (pp. 41–65). Monographs of the Society for Research in Child Development, 50(1-2, Serial No. 209). Chicago: University of Chicago Press.

Wedge, P., & Mantle, G. (1991). *Sibling groups and social work.* Brookfield: Avebury Press.

Welch, M. (1988). *Holding time.* New York: Century.

Yancey, A. K. (1992). Identity formation and social maladaption in foster adolescents. *Adolescence, 27*(108), 817–829.

Yarrow, L. J., & Goodwin, M. S. (1973). The immediate impact of separation: Reactions of infants to a change in mother figure. In L. J. Stone, H. T. Smith, & L. B. Murphy (Eds.), *The competent infant: Research and commentary* (pp. 1032–1040). New York: Basic Books.

5

Innovations in Child Welfare

Preventing Out-of-Home Placement
of Abused and Neglected Children

JULIA H. LITTELL

JOHN R. SCHUERMAN

In the past fifty years, there has been increasing concern about the abuse and neglect of children. The response of society to serious maltreatment of children by parents has been to remove the children from the family, usually placing them in foster care, sometimes in institutions or other substitute care arrangements. The result has been a dramatic increase in the numbers of children in foster care. In this chapter, we focus on the major service innovation in child welfare in recent times: intensive, in-home services aimed at preserving families of maltreated children. Family preservation is a policy goal, based on a set of principles underlying child welfare practice, as well as a model of service delivery (Henggeler, Melton, Smith, Schoenwald, & Hanley, 1993; Wells & Tracy, 1996).

To put this service innovation in context, we begin with a discussion of child abuse and neglect, the functioning of the child welfare system, and underlying principles of child welfare practice. We touch on the social movement aspects of family preservation but focus on it as a method of service delivery. We consider features of the current service environment that are likely to impinge on family preservation practice and suggest directions for practice, policy, and further research.

Clients of the Child Welfare System

Until the middle of the twentieth century, the field of child welfare was concerned with dependent children, that is, orphans and half-orphans and children of parents who were unable to care for them because of disability or severe poverty. In the past thirty years, child abuse and neglect have become the focus of the public child welfare system, particularly after the "discovery" of the "battered child syndrome" in the 1960s (Kempe, Silverman, Steele, Droegemueller, &

Silver, 1962). In many jurisdictions today, abused and neglected children make up the vast majority of the cases.

Child abuse and neglect have occurred since the beginning of civilization, but the definition of child maltreatment as a social problem and organized responses to it are fairly recent. The labeling of certain acts of commission or omission as abusive or neglectful is largely determined by cultural, professional, and individual values (Giovannoni, 1989; Giovannoni & Becerra, 1979; Sternberg, 1993). In the federal Child Abuse Prevention and Treatment Act of 1974, child maltreatment was defined as the "physical or mental injury, sexual abuse, negligent treatment, or maltreatment of a child under the age of eighteen by a person who is responsible for the child's welfare under circumstances which would indicate that the child's health or welfare is harmed or threatened thereby." Definitions of abuse and neglect have gradually been expanded in the past thirty years from actual physical harm to conditions that are not easily defined: risk of physical harm, inadequate supervision, medical neglect, and educational neglect. Legal definitions vary from state to state (e.g., some states include emotional harm as a form of child maltreatment, while others do not); most are vague. State statutes are interpreted in different ways by judicial, medical, and social service professionals (Giovannoni, 1989).

Child maltreatment is considered to be a widespread problem in the United States, caused by a confluence of individual, family, and environmental factors (Belsky, 1980; Cicchetti & Carlson, 1989; Garbarino, 1977). No longer considered the result of a single factor, such as parental psychopathology, "child maltreatment is thought to occur when multiple risk factors outweigh multiple protective factors" (Wells & Tracy, 1996, p. 673). Risk factors include parental substance abuse and other mental health disorders, domestic violence, social isolation, poverty and unemployment, children's handicapping conditions, neighborhood characteristics, situational stressors, and cultural norms regarding violence and corporal punishment. Protective factors include parents' understanding of children's developmental tasks, communication and coping skills, and availability of material resources and emotional support. Risk and protective factors also appear to vary with the child's age, developmental stage, and type of maltreatment (Wells & Tracy, 1996).

While abuse and neglect of children occur in all socioeconomic and ethnic groups, poor families, African Americans, teenage parents, and single-parent female-headed families are disproportionately represented among those reported for child maltreatment. Relationships between child maltreatment and poverty, race, and gender have been the subject of considerable debate. Several factors contribute to the overrepresentation of poor families in the child welfare system. First, conditions related to extreme poverty—such as the lack of adequate food, clothing, shelter, and medical care—are defined as child neglect in many states. Second, families who are receiving public assistance and other public benefits are subject to increased scrutiny by the state. Finally, poverty and its concomitants—poor housing, inadequate medical care, and lack of access to supportive social institutions—often lead to despair and frustration, which may in turn lead to abusive or neglectful behavior.

The effects of substance abuse, particularly abuse of crack cocaine, on the child welfare caseload have been profound. Caseworkers report that parental substance abuse is one of the most serious problems encountered by child welfare agencies today. Estimates of the prevalence of parental substance abuse in child protection cases range from 13% to 70% (Magura & Laudet, 1996). A national sample survey found that 24% of indicated reports involved a caretaker who abused alcohol, and 18% involved illicit drug use on the part of a caretaker (Westat, 1992). Parental substance abuse can affect children in many ways, by depleting the family's emotional and financial resources. Of great concern has been the recent increase in prenatal exposure to drugs, such as crack cocaine. There is considerable confusion about what to do about these infants, fueled in part by lack of understanding of the long-term effects of in utero exposure to cocaine and evidence that young children exhibit a great range of responses to such exposure. There is little consensus as to whether prenatal exposure to drugs constitutes abuse or neglect and whether or under what conditions these children should be removed from their families.

Many families in the child welfare system face multiple, often chronic problems in living. Maternal depression is thought to be common, and other affective disorders and personality disorders are present in some cases. The problems faced by families in this system include deficits in knowledge and skill, physical or learning disabilities, HIV and AIDS, and other serious and chronic health conditions. Each of these issues poses unique difficulties for family preservation and child welfare workers.

Functioning of the Child Welfare System

Expanded definitions of child maltreatment, along with increased public awareness of this phenomenon, have led to dramatic increases in reports of abuse and neglect. The Child Abuse Prevention and Treatment Act of 1974 (PL 93-247) required states to establish statewide systems for documenting and investigating reports. Approximately 1.2 million children were reported for abuse or neglect in 1980 (National Center on Child Abuse and Neglect, 1993). Following sharp increases in reports in the mid-1980s (annual increases were approximately 17% in 1983 and 1984), the annual rate of increase slowed to about 6% in the early 1990s. In 1990, state child protective services agencies received reports of maltreatment involving 2.6 million children, and in 1994 there were over 2.9 million reports (National Center on Child Abuse and Neglect, 1996).

State guidelines for determining whether child maltreatment has occurred are ambiguous. As a result, workers are able to consider the circumstances and facts of each case individually, but there is considerable inconsistency in how they make decisions (Rossi, Schuerman, & Budde, 1996) and a lack of due process. The determination that child abuse or neglect has occurred is often hampered by its private nature; evidence for it is often indirect (Ammerman & Hersen, 1990).

About 38% of the 1994 reports were either substantiated or indicated, resulting in the identification of more than 1 million victims of child abuse or neglect in

48 states, an increase of almost 27% over 1990 figures (National Center on Child Abuse and Neglect, 1996). (This is an underestimate of the actual incidence of child maltreatment because many of these events are not reported.) More than half (53%) of the victims were neglected, 26% were physically abused, 14% were sexually abused, and 5% were victims of emotional maltreatment. Almost 80% of the perpetrators were parents; another 10% were other relatives (National Center on Child Abuse and Neglect, 1996).

When maltreatment is detected, child welfare staff have several options. When the situation is not considered serious enough to warrant further action, usually because the child is not thought to be at risk of further harm, cases are simply closed. In fewer than 20% of the substantiated cases nationwide, the child is considered to be at great risk of further harm and is removed from the home and placed in foster care or another form of substitute care. The majority of substantiated cases of maltreatment are neither closed nor placed but are opened in the child welfare system, where they will be monitored and may receive some in-home services or referrals for counseling.

Burgeoning caseloads have been of great concern to child welfare workers and administrators. The foster care caseload increased by about 60% from the beginning of 1985 through the end of 1992 (from 273,000 to 442,000 nationwide), although the annual rate of increase declined from a high of 13% in fiscal year 1988 to 3% in 1992 (American Public Welfare Association, 1989–1993). Increased reliance on approved kinship care accounts for a substantial proportion of the increase in placement rates. Between 1987 and 1989, the period of most rapid caseload growth, the number of formal placements with kin increased by 63% in New York City and 24% in the Chicago area (Cook County) (Wulczyn & Goerge, 1992). Children in approved kinship care tend to remain in these placements longer than children in regular foster care, which contributes further to the size of the caseload at a given point in time. Recent evidence suggests that, at least in some jurisdictions, the number of new placements is now declining (Goerge, Wulczyn, & Harden, undated).[1]

Issues in Child Welfare Policy and Practice

Since the late nineteenth century, child welfare policy and practice have been dominated by the principle of *the best interests of the child*. Exactly what constitutes a child's best interests and how we might achieve them have been thought of in various ways in the intervening years (Goldstein, Solnit, Goldstein, & Freud, 1996). The history of child welfare has been marked by a series of pendulum swings between preferences for in-home and out-of-home care of children (Lindsey, 1994).

---

[1]In New York state, foster care admissions peaked in 1989 (at 29,000 placements), with substantial declines since then (to 18,000 in 1993). In California, admissions reached an all-time high in 1989, dropped in 1990 and 1991, then increased slightly in 1992 and 1993. Foster care entries in Michigan peaked in 1991, were down in 1992 and back up a bit in 1993. Illinois and Texas have shown continued increases (Goerge, Wulczyn, & Harden, undated).

For centuries prior to the mid-1800s, family relationships were governed by the notion of children as their fathers' chattel. The English concept of *parens patriae* was developed to allow the King (the state) to protect children from abuse, neglect, and exploitation by their guardians (Blackstone, 1793). In the late nineteenth century and in the early twentieth century, the authority of the state in matters of the family increased. The result is a tension between the assertion of the state's interest in the protection of children, on the one hand, and the protection of individual liberties and the integrity and privacy of the family, on the other. That tension is a central feature of debates on child welfare policy today.

In the United States today, nonintrusiveness of the state in family life is asserted as a basic value. However, the reporting of child maltreatment is encouraged and all states require professionals to report suspected abuse and neglect. Some states extend mandatory reporting to all citizens. As a result, many families are caught up in intrusive investigations of maltreatment that result in insufficient evidence to warrant further state intervention.[2]

As to what to do once the state has intervened, current child welfare policy in the United States implements the principle of best interests of the child through what may be thought of as three subprinciples: reasonable efforts, permanency planning, and least restrictive alternative. The Adoption Assistance and Child Welfare Act of 1980 (PL 96-272) requires that states exert reasonable efforts to prevent out-of-home placement of children and to reunify families after children have been separated from their parents. However, "reasonable efforts" has not been defined, either in law or regulation, so the specification of what is meant is largely left to the states and local judges. The idea of reasonable efforts is based on the notion of the specialness of the original parent-child bond and a wish to maintain that relationship in most, or nearly all, cases. Support for the original bond is claimed to be found in the work of Bowlby and other research on mother-child interaction (Bowlby, 1952, 1969–1973, 1988).

The principle of permanency planning grows out of concern with the length of time that some children spend in foster care and with the problem of foster care "bounce," the fact that children in foster care often experience multiple place-ments. As we have noted elsewhere, it is curious that the principle is put in terms of "permanency planning," rather than simply "permanency," thereby seeming to put more emphasis on process than on results (Schuerman, Rzepnicki, & Littell, 1994, p. 7). Permanency planning is implemented through a hierarchy of placement options. From most to least desirable they are: placement with natural parents, adoption, placement with relatives, placement with nonrelatives, and various forms of group and institutional care (the exact order of these options may vary, depending on the locality or theorist expounding them). In the vast majority of cases, the goal is keep the child at home or to return home a child who has been placed out of the home.

---

[2]About two-thirds of the cases that are investigated are "unfounded," which means that there is not enough evidence to conclude that maltreatment occurred.

The principle of least restrictive alternative is less often discussed and invoked than the other principles. That may be because it is now taken for granted as basic to the relationship between the state and its citizens. It arises out of strong American traditions of limiting state interference in our lives and was first implemented in the context of adult mental health care (limiting commitments to psychiatric institutions). The principle of least restrictive alternative can be thought of as supporting the placement hierarchy cited earlier.

The Family Preservation Movement

In the 1980s, the principle of best interests and the subprinciples of reasonable efforts, permanency planning, and least restrictive alternative came to be expressed in the development of family preservation policies and programs. The interests of children were thought to be best served by maintaining them in their birth families, whenever possible. Emphasis was placed on helping parents provide adequate care for their children, rather than on removing children from their homes. This approach appeared to resolve the tension between the state's interest in protecting children and respect for family integrity, although the involvement with the families that is required to effect family preservation is sometimes quite intensive. The approach also promised to reduce foster care costs. Hence, at least when it was introduced, family preservation appealed to liberals because it provided help to the disadvantaged and to conservatives because of the potential savings of tax funds.

The family preservation movement in child welfare has been fueled by several assumptions. It has been argued that the child welfare system is biased toward placing children in out-of-home care (Forsythe, 1992). This bias is thought to derive from overemphasis on child protection and distortions in the funding of child welfare services. Federal matching funds are available for foster care and other out-of-home placements, but the states receive relatively little federal money for preventive or supportive services for intact families. The bulk of resources in public child welfare agencies is concentrated in investigations and placements. It has been argued that the problems that lead to child maltreatment and out-of-home placement could be resolved in ways other than placement and that the system lacks the financial incentives and the organizational structures to support alternative interventions. A related argument is that a large number of placements are unnecessary—and that unnecessary placements are detrimental to children. Finally, it is assumed that many placements can be prevented by providing direct services to families.

The family preservation movement was advanced by optimistic early reports of program effectiveness and zealous efforts on the part of the Edna McConnell Clark Foundation (and, to a lesser extent, the Annie E. Casey Foundation) to promote family preservation services nationwide (Adams, 1994). In most states, family preservation is synonymous with placement prevention (although that was not the intent of the federal Adoption Assistance and Child Welfare Act of 1980), and there have been relatively few efforts to apply family preservation efforts to the reunification of families with children already in substitute care. Here, we focus on placement prevention efforts.

Family Preservation Services

By the mid-1980s, there were a handful of innovative programs that provided home-based services aimed at preventing out-of-home placements.[3] Most notable was the Homebuilders program, developed in the mid-1970s by David Haapala and Jill Kinney, founders of the Behavioral Sciences Institute of Tacoma, Washington (for a description, see Kinney, Haapala, & Booth, 1991). In the past decade, family preservation programs have been established in most states. These programs represent a significant departure from traditional child welfare services in that workers have extensive contact with family members in their homes over a brief period of time.[4]

The following standards for intensive family preservation services were developed by the Child Welfare League of America (1989) (the League refers to these as "family-centered crisis services"):

- Services are *family-centered*, aimed at enhancing family functioning as a whole so that the child can remain in the home safely (as opposed to focusing on the child). Workers often involve family members in goal setting and treatment planning.

- Services are *home-based*, that is, much of the contact between family preservation workers and clients occurs in the family's home, where workers are able to observe and help correct conditions that may pose risks to children. Traditional office-based counseling sessions are rare, although families may receive these and other services through referrals.

- Services are *crisis-oriented*, taking advantage of the dynamics of crisis to bring about rapid change. As such, services are initiated immediately after referral (usually within 24 hours).

- Services are *intensive* (average of 8 to 10 hours of face-to-face contact with family members during the first week) and available 24 hours a day, seven days a week. Related to the principles of intensity and availability, caseloads are small (2 to 6 families per full-time worker).

---

[3]The roots of family preservation services can be found in the friendly visitor movement of the late nineteenth century and in several demonstration projects of the 1950s and 1960s, such as the St. Paul Family-Centered Project (Birt, 1956; Horejsi, 1981).

[4]Ordinarily, intact families are assigned a caseworker who monitors the home situation through phone calls and monthly visits and, in some cases, makes referrals for counseling or support services. Family preservation work is much more intensive and involves a wider array of services. In Illinois, for example, family preservation cases received a median of 70.3 hours of face-to-face contact with workers in the first 90 days after referral, compared with 2.5 hours for regular services cases (Schuerman, Rzepnicki, & Littell, 1994). Half of the Illinois family preservation cases received 4 or more different types of concrete services, while two-thirds (68%) of regular services cases received none.

- Services are *time-limited* (4 to 12 weeks in duration) and focus on a limited set of goals.

- Programs include a mix of concrete and clinical services. *Concrete services* include financial assistance, food, clothing, shelter, and transportation. *Clinical services* include individual and family counseling, parent education, skills training, and supportive services.

- Services are *community-focused*, including advocacy and case management efforts to forge and improve linkages between families and other formal and informal resources in the community. Referrals are made for specialized services, such as substance abuse treatment and home health care, and for long-term counseling and support.

These hallmarks are thought of as ideals or guidelines, but there is some deviation from them in practice. For example, the duration of intensive in-home services is often extended beyond 12 weeks and, in spite of the emphasis on family-centered service, treatment is usually directed toward one parent or primary caregiver (usually the mother).

There is considerable variation within and between programs in the amounts, intensity, duration, and mixture of concrete and clinical services provided to families. Most states have developed guidelines regarding the duration and intensity of services. Some have altered these aspects of services after their initial experiences. An analysis of 38 family preservation programs in 20 states indicated that half (19) had adopted or adapted the intensive 4- to 6-week model developed by Homebuilders, 4 programs had 8-week time limits, 10 provided services for 3 to 4 months, 4 were 8 to 12 months in duration, and one program had time limits that varied (National Evaluation of Family Preservation Services, 1995).[5] Short-term programs tend to have lower caseloads and thus offer more intensive service to families than long-term family preservation programs.

Much has been made about the lack of fidelity to established program models (such as Homebuilders)—or "model drift"—that occurred as family preservation programs proliferated in child welfare. We will return to this issue.

CASES REFERRED

Family preservation programs are intended to serve families at "imminent risk" of placement. But, not all placement cases are considered appropriate; there must be confidence that the child's safety can be ensured while the child is left in the home. It is conceded there are some placements that cannot be prevented (these include cases of abandonment and those in which the risks of further harm to children are too high). There is no uniform definition of "imminent risk" of placement (Tracy, 1991). Some programs specify a time frame within

---

[5]At least 8 programs allowed services to be extended beyond the predetermined time-limit in special cases. The authors noted that the 4 long-term programs were implemented in states that also had short-term, more intensive family preservation programs.

which placement is expected to occur in the absence of family preservation services (time frames range from 24 hours to several months). Risk of placement is usually determined by the referring worker (in some states a screening or risk assessment instrument is used to support decision making), but the predictive validity of judgments of risk is weak (Lyons, Doueck, & Wodarski, 1996; Wald & Woolverton, 1990). Further, there is some evidence that family preservation services are not viewed as an alternative to placement by referring workers. Budde (1995) found that protective services workers rarely considered family preservation services as an alternative in cases in which they took custody—and they rarely considered placement as an alternative in the cases they referred to family preservation service.

Referrals to family preservation services are usually made during or after the investigation of a report of child abuse or neglect. Families are often thought to be in crisis at the time of referral. The crisis may have been precipitated by events leading up to the maltreatment, the incident of maltreatment itself, the child protective services investigation, or the threat of removal of a child. It is not clear, however, that families always perceive the events leading to referral as a crisis. Further, many workers believe that families do not need to be in crisis to benefit from these services (Barth, 1990).

Another referral criterion in most programs is that at least one family member (usually a parent or other caregiver) must be willing to participate in the program. In many cases, this simply means that clients have agreed to allow a worker to make frequent in-home visits.

The characteristics and needs of family preservation cases are not markedly different from those of other clients in the child welfare caseload as a whole. They are mostly poor, single-parent, female-headed families, and racial and ethnic minorities are overrepresented. Many clients lack adequate housing and other resources required to meet the basic needs of children. Substance abuse, mental illness, and knowledge and skill deficits are common. Some programs have narrowed their intake to families with specific presenting problems (e.g., substance abuse), but most tend to be broad in focus, serving a very heterogeneous population. Within these programs, services must be tailored to meet specific family needs.

THEORETICAL FOUNDATIONS

Family preservation work draws on several theoretical bases: crisis intervention theory, family systems theory, social learning theory, and ecological theory (Barth, 1990). Attachment theory and functional theory are also thought to be applicable (Grigsby, 1993). Although programs vary in their adherence to different theoretical bases and service delivery models, they share a common set of beliefs and values that guides service provision. Of course, the most fundamental belief is that, "in most cases, it is best for children to grow up with their natural families" (Kinney, Haapala, Booth, & Leavitt, 1990, p. 32). Other beliefs are that most parents want to be good parents; workers should focus on family strengths; clients should be viewed as colleagues, as partners in change;

and services should not foster dependency but should empower families by helping them develop the ability to solve their own problems and advocate for themselves. Change is thought to occur through the helping relationship, the instillation of hope, problem solving, skills building, and resource provision.

PRACTICE ISSUES

Family preservation work requires considerable flexibility and availability on the part of practitioners. For this reason, most states have chosen to provide family preservation services through contracts with private agencies. Family preservation workers need to be able to engage family members quickly, often in the face of considerable resistance, and utilize a wide range of knowledge and skills. Some programs use teams, pairing caseworkers with paraprofessional aides or assigning specialists to certain cases. Treatment follows the common phases of social work practice: intake, engagement and assessment, goal setting and service planning, service delivery, and termination.

Aftercare planning often involves attempts to link family members to other resources in the community in advance of the termination of family preservation services. When intensive services end, cases are usually turned back to public agency caseworkers, who monitor some cases and close others. The dearth of resources in the public child welfare, public aid, and mental health systems and gaps in community resources have produced sharp discontinuities in care, particularly for poor families. There has been a notable lack of follow-up in many family preservation cases. In response, there has been pressure to extend the length of intensive services (Schuerman, Rzepnicki, Littell, & Budde, 1992).

The paucity of services and supports for families in the child welfare system has led many caseworkers to view family preservation work as a vehicle for achieving other objectives (Littell, Schuerman, Rzepnicki, Howard, & Budde, 1993). Intensive in-home services produce more thorough assessments of family problems than protective services investigations can—and may promote better service planning. In some cases, in-home assessments conducted by family preservation workers have provided documentation that out-of-home placement is necessary. Thus, family preservation services have served as extensions of child protective services investigations (to some extent this is inevitable, since family preservation workers must be concerned about child protection). Family preservation services have also been used to meet pressing family needs (e.g., for emotional support or material aid), even when these needs would not have led to out-of-home placement of children. This accretion of goals, spurred by street-level bureaucrats' attempts to stretch a limited set of services across an expanding pool of cases, has fueled controversy and confusion about the aims of these programs.

EVALUATION OF FAMILY PRESERVATION SERVICES

Evidence of the effectiveness of family preservation programs is mixed (Pecora, 1991; Rossi, 1991; Rossi, 1992; Schuerman, Rzepnicki, & Littell, 1994; Wells & Biegel, 1991). Early studies of families served in the Homebuilders program found that 73% to 91% remained intact for at least one year after referral (Kinney, Haapala, & Booth, 1991). Based on the assumption that all of these families would have had a child placed in out-of-home care had they not received intensive services, these percentages were thought of as "success rates." These findings—and related estimates of the savings in foster care costs that might be achieved—fueled optimism about the efficacy of family preservation services. However, these studies did not include control or comparison groups that would show what would have happened in the absence of family preservation services. Some early studies employed overflow or matching designs, but questions can be raised about the comparability of groups in those investigations (Littell, 1995). Hence, we focus here on the results of controlled experiments.

Prior to 1986, seven randomized experiments compared the effects of family preservation services with those of regular child welfare services. Of these, three found statistically significant reductions in placement in favor of the treatment group (Halper & Jones, 1981; Jones, Neuman, & Shyne, 1976; Lyle & Nelson, 1983), and four found that the family preservation program did not result in significant reductions in placement rates (Hennepin County Community Services Department, 1980; Nebraska Department of Public Welfare, 1981; Szykula & Fleischman, 1985; Willems & DeRubeis, 1981). Sample sizes were small, and some of the interventions differed from current family preservation practice (e.g., caseworkers in the project described by Jones et al. [1976] carried caseloads of 10 families, and services lasted approximately 14 months).

In the late 1980s, larger experiments were launched in California, New Jersey, and Illinois. McDonald and Associates' (1990) study of California's AB 1562 In-home Care Demonstration Project involved random assignment of 304 cases to in-home services or regular child welfare services in five counties. Placement occurred between two and eight months after random assignment in 20% of the control cases and 25% of the experimental group (a nonsignificant difference). The New Jersey experiment (Feldman, 1991) compared family preservation services, modeled after Homebuilders, with regular child welfare services in four counties. A total of 150 cases were randomly assigned to family preservation programs, but 33 were excluded because they did not meet the eligibility criteria, the caregiver refused to participate in the program, or a child was removed from the home within the first three days; apparently no control cases were excluded. Data are available on 117 experimental and 97 control cases. The effects of excluding some cases from the family preservation group on the comparability of the groups are not known, but it is likely that the excluded cases experienced placement more often than those that remained in the experimental group; this could have lowered the risk of placement in that group relative to the control group. At one year after termination, placement had occurred in 57% of the cases in the control group and 43% of those in the experimental group (a statistically significant difference). In the Illinois study (Schuerman, Rzepnicki, & Littell, 1994), 1564 families were randomly assigned to family preservation or regular child welfare services in 6 sites over a 2-year period. At a year after random assignment, placement had occurred in 21% of control cases and 27% of family preservation cases (a statistically significant difference that disappeared after controlling for variations in case characteristics).

It is important to note that, in almost all of the experiments, fewer than 20% of the control group cases experienced placement within 60 days after random assignment.[6] Since placement rates in a control group are estimates of the risk of placement for both groups in the absence of family preservation services, this means that *services were generally not delivered to the target group* of families at "imminent risk of placement." When the risk of placement is low to begin with, it is unlikely that programs will demonstrate placement prevention effects.

Several studies examined program effects on the recurrence of child abuse and neglect. As with placement, rates of maltreatment in both the experimental and control groups in these studies were low. Two studies (Jones, 1985; McDonald & Associates, 1990) found no significant differences between experimental and control groups. The Illinois program produced a statistically significant, but small, increase in the risk of subsequent maltreatment (Schuerman, Rzepnicki, & Littell, 1994). It may be that intensive, in-home treatments have a surveillance effect, increasing the reporting of maltreatment and the likelihood of placement in some cases.

Measures of child and family functioning were employed in several experiments. Results indicate that modest improvements were found in some areas for the treatment groups, but these tended to be short-lived (see Feldman, 1991; McCroskey & Meezan, 1997; Schuerman, Rzepnicki, & Littell, 1994).

Available evidence sheds little light on whether family preservation services have differential effects for different kinds of families.[7] Features of services that are often considered among the hallmarks of family preservation—brevity, intensity, and the provision of an array of concrete and specialized services—do not appear to be correlated with outcomes once case characteristics are taken into account (Schuerman, Rzepnicki, & Littell, 1994; Littell, 1997).

---

[6]At 6 weeks after random assignment, placement had occurred in 16.5% of control cases in New Jersey; at about 10 weeks, the figure was 26.8% (Feldman, 1991). Thirteen percent of children in the California control group and about 10% of families in the Illinois control group had experienced placement within 60 days of random assignment (McDonald & Associates, 1990; Schuerman, Rzepnicki, & Littell, 1994). Family-level data on placements at 60 days are not available for California.

[7]Most research on this topic ignores the fact that there are significant relationships between case characteristics and outcomes in the *absence* of these services (Schuerman, Rzepnicki, & Littell, 1994, p. 41). Three experimental studies have addressed this issue. Szykula and Fleischman (1985) found that placement prevention efforts were less successful with "difficult" cases (i.e., those with chronic child abuse and neglect or other major problems, such as employment, transportation, and housing). Family preservation services appeared to reduce the risk of placement for single-parent families in the New Jersey study (Feldman, 1991), although intensive services were associated with an increase in placement among single-adult households in Illinois (Schuerman, Rzepnicki, & Littell, 1994).

Finally, there is little evidence that family preservation programs save money. Obviously, if placements aren't prevented, there are no savings in foster care costs.

The Current Situation

It is important to distinguish family preservation as a movement from family preservation as services. As we have seen, family preservation services appear to have had, at most, limited success in the prevention of placement of children in substitute care. Other benefits also appear to be limited and probably short-lived. As a movement, family preservation may have had more success, although it is difficult to prove conclusively. The precept that we should avoid placement of children whenever possible seems to be well accepted in the field (although some workers argue that has always been the case).

The federal government has finally begun to provide some small monetary support for the development of family preservation services (the 1980 Act requiring reasonable efforts included no funds to the states for these efforts). In 1993, as part of the annual Omnibus Budget Reconciliation Act, Congress appropriated nearly one billion dollars to the states for beginning or enhancing family support and family preservation programs. This amount is not large since it is spread over five years and fifty states; the hope is that it will encourage new investment in these programs. States have considerable discretion in allocation of these funds, and, at this writing, it appears that the majority of these funds will be used for family support rather than family preservation per se.

In recent years, a number of jurisdictions have seen the development of a substantial backlash against family preservation. Usually, the backlash has focused on the family preservation movement, that is, on the value of preserving families. States are criticized for putting families, rather than children, first. Critics make use of well-publicized tragedies in which children known to the child welfare system have been killed or severely hurt, attributing such incidents to the policy of family preservation. Some suggest that it does not make sense to try to preserve these families, since they are not really families; giving birth to a child does not a family make, and some parents display no evidence of desire to parent properly.

Further threatening to erode the gains that have been made in the past decade in the development of family preservation programs is the adoption in 1996 of welfare "reform," the Personal Responsibility and Work Opportunity Reconciliation Act (PL 104-193). There will be direct effects on the support of family preservation programs due to funding reductions in and new demands on the Social Services Block Grant, used by many states for child protection services. A number of states also use funds from the Emergency Assistance Program (Title IV-A) for family preservation services. These funds are now folded into the block grant, which includes funds that formerly went to Aid to Families with Dependent Children, so family preservation programs must compete with income maintenance functions. More broadly, the reduction in welfare provision and restrictions on receipt of welfare will likely cause an increase in levels of family and child poverty, resulting in increased demands on the child welfare system.

New initiatives are now capturing the imagination of child welfare policy-makers. Two of these new ideas are the devolution of responsibility to communities and the use in child welfare of the concept of managed care.

Moving responsibility to communities avoids the use of monolithic state power and the dependence on large, unresponsive bureaucracies. The idea is that communities are in the best position to understand the problems of families and to marshal the resources necessary to help them. Devolution to communities is usually accompanied by an attempt to defuse the adversarial quality of many child welfare encounters, replacing a policing function with a therapeutic one. As in the case of family preservation, the approach is dependent on a belief in the desire of parents to learn to relate positively with their children. It is also dependent on a faith that communities, with help, can build institutions capable of dealing with serious family problems. Devolution of responsibility is likely to result in considerable variation among localities in the way child welfare problems are addressed. It is also likely to result in varying degrees of success, with some communities functioning quite well and others less successfully. Perhaps the most prominent effort at community involvement in child welfare is a project conducted by the Edna McConnell Clark Foundation, in which efforts are being made to implement "dual track" responses to allegations of child maltreatment: Communities will be given responsibility to provide support in lower-risk cases, while public child welfare agencies serve high-risk cases.

Managed care is now sweeping the social services, having been imported from the field of medical care. As applied in child welfare, the idea has many meanings. One approach focuses on financing mechanisms, such as capitation schemes. For example, New York City has tried a system under which private child welfare agencies responsible for children in foster care are given a flat amount of money to provide care for a certain number of children over a particular period of time. The amount of money is determined by historical experience with the length of time children are in care. Thus, there is an incentive to save money by quickly reunifying children with their parents, thereby avoiding foster care costs. Other forms of managed care involve the specification and pricing of packages of services for particular groups of cases defined in terms of their problems or needs. Still another form of the idea emphasizes putting responsibility for dealing with a particular family in the hands of a single case manager, who determines the services to be provided, usually with some limits or guidelines on allowable cost. A primary interest in managed care schemes is the reduction of cost, so efficiency is of central concern. It remains to be seen whether efficiency and service quality can both be achieved.

Implications for Practice, Policy, and Further Research

Many lessons can be drawn from the family preservation movement and the implementation of intensive in-home services in child welfare. Chief among them is that the fundamental assumptions upon which service innovations are based ought to be carefully scrutinized. A central assumption has been that intensive in-home services are an alternative to out-of-home placement for many cases of child abuse and neglect. Embedded in this idea are certain views of the nature of a social problem (child maltreatment) and society's responses to it (the functioning of the child welfare system). Recent experience with family preservation services provides a basis for reexamining these views and raises questions about the targeting, delivery, and outcomes of these services.

TARGETING

As mentioned earlier, findings of experimental studies indicate that family preservation programs are not serving many of the cases for which they were intended, that is, families of children who would experience placement in the absence of these services. Because of this targeting problem, programs cannot meet the placement prevention objective. Similar problems have been encountered in targeting prevention efforts in other fields, for example, in prevention of nursing home admissions (Weissert, 1988, 1991) and in diversion of juvenile offenders (Polk, 1984; Spergel & Hartnett, 1990).

What are the reasons for the targeting problem? First, the "imminent risk of placement" criterion is ambiguous and is not consistently used in referral decisions. Lack of agreement among experts and workers about which cases are appropriate for family preservation indicates that there are considerable variations in the thresholds for placement and referral decisions (Rossi, Schuerman, & Budde, 1996). Second, there are no adequate estimates of the number of placements that could be prevented with intensive services. It is possible that the size of the target group has been overestimated, leaving many openings for other kinds of cases in family preservation programs. These openings have been filled with families who have many pressing needs but are not candidates for placement. Given the paucity of services available in child welfare, family preservation programs are an attractive alternative for nonplacement cases.

Efforts are under way in several places to improve targeting by getting the "right" kinds of cases (those truly at risk of placement) into family preservation programs. Evidence from randomized experiments (specifically, placement rates of control cases) will be needed to determine whether or to what extent these efforts succeed. (The present authors are involved in one such study, as part of a national evaluation of family preservation services mandated by the Omnibus Budget Reconciliation Act of 1993 and conducted by Westat, Inc., Chapin Hall Center for Children, and James Bell and Associates.)

It may prove to be quite difficult to shift referral decisions in the "right" direction. Budde's (1995) interviews with referring workers indicate that, when custody was taken, this was almost always viewed as the only option, due to the seriousness of the case, the unavailability of caretakers, or the caretaker's unwillingness to engage in efforts to retain custody. Budde suggests that the availability of family preservation services has not been sufficient to change the decision frame, which is basically a choice between placement and no placement. Further research is needed to understand referral decisions within the larger context of available options for child welfare cases and the individual and contextual (organizational, community) factors that affect decision making.

SERVICE DELIVERY

Much has been made about various models of intensive family preservation services and the extent of adherence to them in practice. Wide attempts to replicate the Homebuilders model have been particularly instructive in this regard. In many sites, central aspects of this model have been modified: The duration of services has been lengthened, some programs have moved to using teams instead of single therapists, and elements of other approaches (e.g., family systems techniques) have been incorporated (Adams, 1994). The lack of consistency within and between programs has caused considerable concern in some quarters. Yet, modifications are often required to tailor services to particular client and community needs. For instance, workers' concerns about their own safety make the Homebuilders single-therapist model untenable in some neighborhoods. While the tendency to extend the duration of family preservation services in many locations may be evidence of "model drift," it is also a direct response to the needs of many families. There is need for better descriptive information about service delivery in current family preservation programs and further investigation of the reasons for deviation from well-known models.

Several controlled studies have shown that substantial increases in the intensity and amounts of services—key features of family preservation programs—do not produce dramatic results. (More is not always better.) Given that there is no convincing evidence of the superiority of one approach over another, arguments for strict adherence to any one model are not compelling. Efficacy studies of the Homebuilders model are long overdue. In the absence of this information, models such as Homebuilders are best thought of as useful heuristic devices, in that they provide a philosophical base and many useful guidelines for practice. Once there is solid evidence that a particular model is more effective than others under certain circumstances, then the issue of fidelity to a specific type of treatment becomes relevant; that type of evidence does not currently exist in relation to child welfare cases. In the interim, thoughtful experimentation in practice ought to be encouraged and closely studied.

Current ecological models of the etiology of child abuse and neglect suggest that the personality and psychological well-being of the parent, characteristics of the child, and contextual sources of stress and support all contribute to maltreatment (Belsky & Vondra, 1989). Thus, several types and levels of intervention may be needed in these cases. The "multisystems" approach, which appears to be common in family preservation work, provides a loose framework for intervention at the individual, family, and community levels. Formative and summative evaluations of various multisystems interventions in child welfare are needed.

In child welfare and mental health, there are many schools of thought about how to bring about change in abusive and neglectful families. But the relationships between specific theories (including crisis intervention theory, social learning theory, and family systems theory) and family preservation practice are not always clear. The process of change is not well understood and is hampered by the fact that many of these parents are resistant to treatment. There is need for more dialog on these issues across disciplines and treatment settings and among practitioners (at all levels) in child welfare, mental health, addictions, and other related fields. Studies of important aspects of service delivery and the processes of change are needed; issues include the engagement of involuntary clients, the development of helping relationships between clients and workers, and the fit between family problems and the frequency, intensity, and types of treatment provided.

PROGRAM GOALS AND OUTCOMES

Experience with family preservation programs raises questions about how to think about program success and failure. In early studies, placements were considered program "failures." Elsewhere, we have discussed conceptual problems in the emphasis on placement as an outcome (Schuerman, Rzepnicki, & Littell, 1991). At the case level, when placement occurs, it is almost always thought to be in the child's best interest; yet, in the aggregate, placements are viewed as something to be avoided. This conflict between clinical and policy goals in some cases muddies the interpretation of placement as an outcome. As in the past, there are differing views about what constitutes the best interests of children, but, clearly, placement prevention is not always in a child's best interest. We think it will be more productive to focus on the goals of removing risks to children (child protection) and achieving continuity of care (permanency).

Extant knowledge about the causes of child abuse and neglect and the conditions in which many of these families live leads to the conclusion that there will be no easy answers or quick fixes for these problems.[8] If short-term family preservation programs have any tangible benefits at all, these benefits will be modest. Although intensive, the programs are too short term to effect significant improvement in the serious problems facing families who are about to have their children taken away. Nor can the programs make much headway in battling the effects of the depleted environments many of these families face. Until recently, this perspective has been lacking in much of the research and rhetoric in this area. Evaluation research should include multiple outcome measures, including proximal measures that reflect realistic objectives articulated by program staff.

Family preservation services have clearly fallen short of meeting their primary objective: the prevention of many out-of-home placements. As a result, some observers have suggested that these programs should abandon the placement prevention objective and be put to other uses (Wells & Tracy, 1996). Specifically,

---

[8]In a review of results of 89 treatment programs, Cohn and Daro (1987) found that one-third or more of parents maltreated their children during intensive treatment and more than half were thought to be likely to maltreat their children following termination.

intensive family preservation programs provide the opportunity to assess comprehensively the needs of individual maltreated children and the needs of their parents; to confront parents' pressing problems relating to food, shelter, safety, and disability; and to begin to teach . . . behavioral alternatives to abuse and neglect. . . . (Wells & Tracy, 1996, p. 682)

With more interdisciplinary staffing patterns, these programs could serve an important "gateway" function (Wells & Tracy, 1996). The need for careful assessment may fit well within various managed care schemes, but we suspect that there will be pressures to restrict the long-term treatments and follow-up needed by many of these families. This approach also raises new questions for policy and evaluation research. To what extent does intensive in-home assessment lead to "better" treatment decisions? And what kinds of gains can be expected in the assessment phase?

CONTEXTUAL ISSUES

There are reciprocal relationships between service innovations and the larger social systems in which they operate. The systemic effects of family preservation services are often thought of as broad acceptance of the placement prevention objective and adoption of certain features of services associated with this approach. Ironically, pressures from other parts of the child welfare system—particularly the need for services for nonplacement cases—have been so great that family preservation programs have been unable to meet their central objective. There has also been pressure to alter basic features of family preservation services (e.g., brevity) in order to fill other gaps in services. Given the depleted environment in which family preservation services were implemented, it is no surprise that these resources were quickly absorbed and put to use for many purposes in the child welfare system.

Innovations in service delivery are, at best, only partial solutions to social problems. "Services cannot alter the social conditions that produce or exacerbate, and ultimately reproduce, individual and family problems" (Halpern, 1990, p. 647). Family preservation has not become a panacea for the disarray in the child welfare system, but we believe that it does have a part to play in a comprehensive set of services. Intensive, short-term, crisis-oriented services can benefit some families, helping them to deal with problems that brought them to the attention of the state—and may help the state determine how to best serve these families in the future.

Service innovations can serve as a distraction from other aspects of the system that need attention. As the family preservation movement swept the field of child welfare in the past decade, little attention has been paid to improvements needed in foster care and other forms of substitute care, family reunification, and aftercare services. Little headway has been made in the development of effective linkages among child welfare, health, mental health, and educational services. If we are to consider the best interests of children seriously, there must be continuity of care as children move from in-home to out-of-home treatment (and back again) and greater reliance on specialists in the mental health and health care fields.

Finally, there is need for empirical research on the reciprocal relationships among social movements, service innovations, and the larger social systems (organizational, community, and political contexts) in which they are embedded. The effectiveness of family preservation services may depend on the presence of certain resources in communities, in the child welfare system, and in other service delivery systems.

REFERENCES

Adams, P. (1994). Marketing social change: The case of family preservation. *Children and Youth Services Review, 16*, 417–431.

American Public Welfare Association, Voluntary Cooperative Information System. (1989–1993). *VCIS research notes*. Washington, DC: Author.

Ammerman, R. T., & Hersen, M. (1990). Research in child abuse and neglect: Current status and an agenda for the future. In R. T. Ammerman & M. Hersen (Eds.), *Children at risk: An evaluation of factors contributing to child abuse and neglect* (pp. 3–19). New York: Plenum.

Barth, R. P. (1990). Theories guiding home-based intensive family preservation services. In J. K. Whittaker, J. Kinney, E. M. Tracy, & C. Booth (Eds.), *Reaching high-risk families: Intensive family preservation* (pp. 89–112). New York: Aldine de Gruyter.

Belsky, J. (1980). Child maltreatment: An ecological integration. *American Psychologist, 35*, 320–335.

Belsky, J., & Vondra, J. (1989). Lessons from child abuse: The determinants of parenting. In D. Cicchetti & V. Carlson (Eds.), *Child maltreatment: Theory and research on the causes and consequences of child abuse and neglect* (pp. 153–202). Cambridge: Cambridge University Press.

Birt, C. (1956). The family-centered project of St. Paul. *Social Work, 1*, 41–47.

Blackstone, Sir William. (1793). *Commentaries on the laws of England. Book I, Of parent and child*. Excerpted in G. Abbott (1938), *The child and the state* (Vol. 1). Chicago: University of Chicago Press.

Bowlby, J. (1952). *Maternal care and mental health*. Geneva: World Health Organization.

Bowlby, J. (1969–73). *Attachment and loss* (2 vols.). London: Hogarth Press.

Bowlby, J. (1988). *A secure base: Parent-child attachment and healthy human development*. New York: Basic Books.

Budde, S. (1995). *Understanding the targeting problem in family preservation services: A study of child protection decision making*. Ph.D. dissertation, School of Social Service Administration, University of Chicago.

Child Welfare League of America. (1989). *Standards for services to strengthen and preserve families with children*. Washington, DC: Author.

Cicchetti, D., & Carlson, V. (Eds.). (1989). *Child maltreatment: Theory and research on the causes and consequences of child abuse and neglect*. Cambridge: Cambridge University Press.

Cohn, A. H., & Daro, D. (1987). Is treatment too late?: What ten years of evaluative research tells us. *Child Abuse and Neglect, 11*, 433- 442.

Feldman, L. H. (1991). *Assessing the effectiveness of family preservation services in New Jersey within an ecological context*. Trenton: New Jersey Division of Youth and Family Services, Bureau of Research, Evaluation, and Quality Assurance.

Forsythe, P. (1992). Homebuilders and family preservation. *Children and Youth Services Review, 14*, 37–47.

Garbarino, J. (1977). The human ecology of child maltreatment: A conceptual model for research. *Journal of Marriage and the Family, 39*, 721–732.

Gelles, R. J. (1973). Child abuse as psychopathology: A sociological critique and reformulation. *American Journal of Orthopsychiatry, 43*, 611–621.

Giovannoni, J. (1989). Definitional issues in child maltreatment. In D. Cicchetti & V. Carlson (Eds.), *Child maltreatment: Theory and research on the causes and consequences of child abuse and neglect* (pp. 3–37). Cambridge: Cambridge University Press.

Giovannoni, J. M., & Becerra, R. M. (1979). *Defining child abuse*. New York: Free Press.

Goerge, R. M., Wulczyn, F. H., & Harden, A. W. (Undated). An update from the multistate foster care data archive: Foster care dynamics 1983–1993. Chicago: Chapin Hall Center for Children at the University of Chicago.

Goldstein, J., Solnit, A., Goldstein, S., & Freud, A. (1996). *The best interests of the child*. New York: Free Press.

Grigsby, R. K. (1993). Theories that guide intensive family preservation services: A second look. In E. S. Morton & R. K. Grigsby (Eds.), *Advancing family preservation practice*. Newbury Park, CA: Sage Publications.

Halper, G., & Jones, M. A. (1981). *Serving families at risk of dissolution: Public preventive services in New York City*. New York: Human Resources Administration, Special Services for Children.

Halpern, R. (1990). Fragile families, fragile solutions: An essay review. *Social Service Review, 64*, 637–648.

Henggeler, S. W., Melton, G. B., Smith, L. A., Schoenwald, S. K., & Hanley, J. H. (1993). Family preservation using multisystemic treatment: Long-term follow-up to a clinical trial with serious juvenile offenders. *Journal of Child and Family Studies, 2*, 283–293.

Hennepin County Community Services Department. (1980). *Family study project: Demonstration and research in intensive services to families*. Minneapolis: Author.

Horejsi, C. R. (1981). The St. Paul Family-Centered Project revisited: Exploring an old gold mine. In M. Bryce and J. C. Lloyd (Eds.), *Treating families in the home: An alternative to placement*. Springfield, IL: Charles C. Thomas.

Jones, M. A. (1985). *A second chance for families, five years later: Follow-up of a program to prevent foster care*. New York: Child Welfare League of America.

Jones, M. A., Neuman, R., & Shyne, A. W. (1976). *A second chance for families: Evaluation of a program to reduce foster care*. New York: Child Welfare League of America.

Kempe, C. H., Silverman, F. M., Steele, B. F., Droegemueller, W., & Silver, H. K. (1962). The battered child syndrome. *Journal of the American Medical Association, 181*, 17–24.

Kinney, J., Haapala, D., & Booth, C. (1991). *Keeping families together: The Homebuilders model*. New York: Aldine de Gruyter.

Kinney, J., Haapala, D., Booth, C., & Leavitt, S. (1990). The Homebuilders model. In J. K. Whittaker, J. Kinney, E. M. Tracy & C. Booth (Eds.), *Reaching high-risk families: Intensive family preservation in human services* (pp. 31–64). Hawthorne, NY: Aldine de Gruyter.

Lindsey, D. (1994). Family preservation and child protection: Striking a balance. *Children and Youth Services Review, 16*, 279–294.

Littell, J. H. (1995). Evidence or assertions? The outcomes of family preservation services. *Social Service Review, 69*, 338–351.

Littell, J. H. (1997). Effects of the duration, intensity, and breadth of family preservation services: A new analysis of data from the Illinois Family First experiment. *Children and Youth Services Review, 19*, 19–39.

Littell, J. H., Schuerman, J. R., Rzepnicki, T. L., Howard, J., & Budde, S. (1993). Shifting objectives in family preservation programs. In E. S. Morton & R. K. Grigsby (Eds.), *Advancing family preservation practice* (pp. 99–116). Newbury Park, CA: Sage Publications.

Lyle, C. G., & Nelson, J. (1983). *Home based vs. traditional child protection services: A study of the home based services demonstration project in the Ramsey County Community Human Services Department* (unpublished paper). St Paul, MN: Ramsey County Community Human Services Department.

Lyons, P., Doueck, H. J., & Wodarski, J. S. (1996). Risk assessment for child protective services: A review of the empirical literature on instrument performance. *Social Work Research, 20*, 143–155.

Magura, S., & Laudet, A. B. (1996). Parental substance abuse and child maltreatment: Review and implications for intervention. *Children and Youth Services Review, 81*, 193–220.

McCroskey, J., & Meezan, W. (1997). *Family preservation and family functioning.* Washington, DC: Child Welfare League of America.

McDonald, W. R., & Associates. (1990). *Evaluation of AB 1562 in-home care demonstration projects: Final report.* Sacramento, CA: Author.

National Center on Child Abuse and Neglect. (1993). *National Child Abuse and Neglect Data System (NCANDS).* Working Paper 2, 1991 Summary Data Component. Washington, DC: U.S. Government Printing Office.

National Center on Child Abuse and Neglect. (1996). *Child maltreatment 1994: Reports from the States to the National Center on Child Abuse and Neglect.* Washington, DC: U.S. Government Printing Office.

National Evaluation of Family Preservation Services. (1995). *A review of family preservation and family reunification programs.* Paper submitted to the U.S. Dept. of Health and Human Services Assistant Secretary for Planning and Evaluation by Westat, Inc. in association with James Bell Associates, Inc., and the Chapin Hall Center for Children at the University of Chicago.

Nebraska Department of Public Welfare. (1981). *Final report: Intensive services to families at-risk project.* Omaha, NB: Author.

Pecora, P. J. (1991). Family-based and intensive family preservation services: A select literature review. In M. W. Fraser, P. J. Pecora, & D. A. Haapala (Eds.), *Families in crisis: The impact of intensive family preservation services* (pp. 17–47). Hawthorne, NY: Aldine de Gruyter.

Polk, K. (1984). Juvenile diversion: A look at the record. *Crime and Delinquency, 30*, 648–659.

Rossi, P. H. (1991). *Evaluating family preservation programs: A report to the Edna McConnell Clark Foundation.* New York: Edna McConnell Clark Foundation.

Rossi, P. H. (1992). Assessing family preservation programs. *Children and Youth Services Review, 14*, 77–97.

Rossi, P. H., Schuerman, J., & Budde, S. (1996). *Understanding child maltreatment decisions and those who make them.* Chicago: Chapin Hall Center for Children at the University of Chicago.

Schuerman, J. R., Rzepnicki, T. L., & Littell, J. H. (1991). From Chicago to Little Egypt: Lessons from an evaluation of a large-scale child welfare family preservation program. In K. Wells & D. E. Biegel (Eds.), *Family preservation services: Research and evaluation* (pp. 187–206). Newbury Park, CA: Sage Publications.

Schuerman, J. R., Rzepnicki, T. L., & Littell, J. H. (1994). *Putting families first: An experiment in family preservation.* Hawthorne, NY: Aldine de Gruyter.

Schuerman, J. R., Rzepnicki, T. L., Littell, J. H., & Budde, S. (1992). Implementation issues. *Children and Youth Services Review, 14,* 193–206.

Spergel, I. A., & Hartnett, M. A. (1990). *Evaluation of the Illinois Department of Children and Family Services (DCFS) Comprehensive Community Based Youth Service System (CCBYS).* Chicago: Chapin Hall Center for Children at the University of Chicago.

Sternberg, K. J. (1993). Child maltreatment: Implications for policy from cross-cultural research. In D. Cicchetti & S. L. Toth (Eds.), *Child abuse, child development and social policy* (pp. 191–211). Norwood, NJ: Ablex Publishing Company.

Szykula, S. A., & Fleischman, M. J. (1985). Reducing out-of-home placements of abused children: Two controlled field studies. *Child Abuse and Neglect, 9,* 277–283.

Tracy, E. M. (1991). Defining the target population for family preservation services. In K. Wells & D. E. Biegel (Eds.), *Family preservation services: Research and evaluation* (pp. 138–158). Newbury Park, CA: Sage Publications.

Wald, M. S., & Woolverton, M. (1990). Risk assessment: The Emperor's new clothes? *Child Welfare, 69,* 483–511.

Weissert, W. G. (1988). The National Channeling Demonstration: What we knew, know now, and still need to know. *Health Services Research, 23,* 175–187.

Weissert, W. G. (1991, Summer). A new policy agenda for home care. *Health Affairs,* 67–77.

Wells, K., & Biegel, D. E. (1991). Conclusion. In K. Wells & D. E. Biegel (Eds.), *Family preservation services: Research and evaluation* (pp. 241–250). Newbury Park, CA: Sage Publications.

Wells, K., & Tracy, E. (1996). Reorienting family preservation services to public child welfare practice. *Child Welfare, 76,* 667–692.

Westat Inc. (1992). Report on child maltreatment in substance abusing families. Washington, DC: Author.

Willems, D. N., & DeRubeis, R. (1981). *The effectiveness of intensive preventive services for families with abused, neglected, or disturbed children: Hudson County Project final report.* Trenton: Bureau of Research, New Jersey Division of Youth and Family Services.

Wulczyn, F. H., & Goerge, R. M. (1992). Foster care in New York and Illinois: The challenge of rapid change. *Social Service Review, 66,* 278- 294.

6

Exposure to Urban Violence
A Framework for Conceptualizing Risky Settings

RAYMOND P. LORION

ANNE E. BRODSKY

MICHELE COOLEY-QUILLE

This chapter presents urban violence as a significant risk to the nation's mental and public health. We believe that the threat of urban violence includes both the impacts of isolated events and the cumulative emotional and behavioral consequences of a series of actual or potential encounters with violence. We postulate that awareness of this threat represents a measurable characteristic of environments that, in interaction with individual characteristics, can have long-term emotional, cognitive, and physiological consequences. In this chapter, we argue that the nation's mental health services must respond proactively to this threat consistent with the ongoing evolution of those services toward a merger of mental health and public health.

A significant marker event in this evolution occurred in 1942. Nearly 500 deaths resulted from a tragic fire at the Coconut Grove nightclub in Boston. Survivors presented emotional and physical symptoms that for some were part of the natural mourning process and for others were potential catalysts for serious and long-term disruption to functioning. By responding immediately, Lindemann (1944) and his colleagues appeared to serve the needs of both groups. Their efforts enabled many survivors to cope with the consequences of the trauma and some to avoid long-term emotional problems. Their crisis-oriented response opened an important chapter in mental health. From these efforts (Lindemann, 1944) evolved grief theory and counseling, crisis intervention, preventive psychiatry (Caplan, 1964), and the contemporary prevention movement (Mrazek & Haggerty, 1994).

This proactive response to trauma moved mental health services from their predominantly reactive stance (e.g., diagnosis and treatment of established disorder) and shifted attention toward the identification of risk and causal factors, etiological processes, and alternative response options. It also challenged long-held assumptions about several aspects of mental health interventions: (a) providers (e.g., clergy or neighbors as well as psychiatrists and psychologists); (b) duration (e.g., time-limited services); (c) goals (e.g., the reinforcement of coping rather than the removal of symptoms); and (d) timing (i.e., prior to or early in the evolution of symptoms) (Slaikeu, 1990). It also focused attention on the influence of situational factors on immediate and long-term emotional functioning and on the opportunities such events and situations offered for the avoidance of emotional and behavioral disorders (Bloom, 1984; Levine & Perkins, 1997).

The Public Health Implications of Urban Violence

Conceptualizing urban violence in contextual rather than event-specific terms represents a shift in perspective for the behavioral sciences. Criminologists (e.g., Elliot, Hamberg, & Williams, 1998), sociologists (e.g., Levine & Rosich, 1996), psychologists (e.g., American Psychological Association, 1993), and other social scientists (e.g., Singer, Anglin, Song, & Lunghofer, 1995) typically describe community violence in terms of the occurrence of events or behaviors intended to cause injury, harm, or death to another. Summaries of such events, available in national and local crime statistics (e.g., Uniform Crime Report [UCR] rates), inform one about some characteristics (e.g., age, race, gender) of the victims and the perpetrators of community violence. Other archival sources (e.g., emergency room and trauma center records) reflect associated levels of morbidity and mortality. Other data (e.g., local and state health and welfare services budgets) document the resources invested in attempts to avoid or mitigate such events.

These data do not, however, convey the qualitative experience of those who encounter such events where they live, work, and play. Exposure to pervasive community violence (PCV) represents a serious environmental toxin that can contaminate intra- and interindividual functioning (Elliot, Williams, & Hamberg, 1998; Levine & Rosich, 1996). For whom is PCV a risk? The dose effects of exposure to urban violence are not well understood. To assume that the residents of major urban settings generally and of violent communities specifically are the only ones vulnerable underestimates PCV's toxic potential. Assuming that someone living or working in a neighborhood marked by random shootings and widespread gang violence occurs is vulnerable to emotional and behavioral disorders seems reasonable. But what of those who travel through such settings and those who learn about such violence in their schools or through the media? In an otherwise quiet and safe neighborhood, does a single act of violence have a lesser, similar, or greater impact on its inhabitants' psychological status than one more act in a generally violent setting?

Studies of urban violence must consider as well as complement studies of the etiology and effects of exposure to violence within intimate settings. Such forms of violence include spousal and child abuse, elder abuse, and abuse occurring within dating relationships (Strauss & Gelles, 1992). The reciprocal influence of PCV and violence within intimate settings needs careful study since each appears likely to increase in the presence of the other. Moreover, we assume that exposure to violence across multiple settings (e.g., both at home and in the community) can have particularly toxic effects.

From this perspective, exposure to urban violence is clearly a public health problem. In this chapter, violence refers to the act as well as to the consequences of the intentional use—or threat of the use—of force to cause intentional injury, harm, or death to another. The qualifier "intentional" excludes from consideration unintended or accidental acts of violence. For PCV, the consequences of violent acts refer to the rippling health and mental health effects experienced by (a) individuals directly victimized by an act or threat of violence; (b) individuals indirectly victimized because of their status as a bystander, witness, acquaintance, or loved one of a victim of an act or threat of violence; and (c) individuals indirectly victimized by their awareness of, and anxiety about, the occurrence of acts or threats of violence within settings they occupy or might occupy, regardless of their actuarial risk of being victimized.

PCV's impacts on the morbidity and mortality of the nation's citizens, especially its youth, appear truly staggering. As summarized by Hamburg (1998):

> The costs to both health and society of the devastation of violence are immense. . . . The total medical cost of all violence that occurred in the United States was $13.5 billion in 1992, including $10.5 billion that resulted from interpersonal violence such as murder, rape, assault, robbery, drunk driving, and arson. To these figures we must add the costs of years of potential life lost and the psychological trauma that results from intentional injuries. (p. 37)

Focusing on PCV's impact on those who learn and teach in the nation's schools reveals a similarly disturbing picture (Lorion, 1998). Within schools, acts of violence range from verbal hassling to abuse; from poking and pushing others (mostly, but not exclusively, students) as one moves down a hallway to knocking them over; from verbal threats to acts of assault and even homicide; from vandalism to robbery to rape. As described by Beland (1996):

> In schools, teachers find themselves spending increasing amounts of time attending to students' disruptive and angry outbursts, interpersonal conflicts, and off-task behavior, or worse. Every day, approximately 100,000 children are assaulted at school, 5000 teachers are threatened with physical assault, and 200 are actually attacked. (Geiger, 1993, p. 209)

Mental health service providers represent another professional group that confronts directly the victims and perpetrators of violence. Little, however, is known of the emotional impact of such encounters on these and other human service workers. As with any other public health problem, designing and implementing an appropriate response depends on the capacity to assess its presence, consequences, and stability within a community. For that reason, preliminary work on measuring PCV is addressed next.

MEASURING PCV

In the past decade, measures of PCV exposure have focused mainly on school-age youth. Work by Richters and associates (Lorion & Saltzman, 1993; Martinez & Richters, 1993; Osofsky, Wewers, Hahn, & Fick, 1993; Richters & Martinez, 1993) catalyzed much of this effort. Applying a common measure across diverse populations and settings produced scientific evidence to support public concerns about children's PCV exposure and its consequences. In Richters's work, PCV exposure is measured with the "Survey of Children's Exposure to Community Violence" (Richters & Saltzman, 1990). Instructed explicitly *not* to include media exposure (i.e., what was seen or heard on radio or television, or in movies), respondents indicate along a five-point Likert scale (from 0 = "never" to 4 = "a lot of the time") the frequency with which they have been victimized by, heard about, or witnessed violent events or violence-related activities (e.g., shooting, stabbing, mugging, seeing a dead body).

Extending the work of Richters and associates, Singer, Anglin, Song, and Lunghofer (1994, 1995) designed the "Recent Exposure to Physical Violence" and the "Past Exposure to Violence" surveys to measure adolescent exposure during the past year and lifetime, respectively. The acts of violence surveyed by Singer et al. include threats, slapping/hitting/punching, beatings, knife attacks, and shootings. Separate reports for each (other than knife attacks and shootings) were obtained for home, school, and neighborhood. Respondents were also asked how often they had witnessed someone else victimized at each of these sites. Two additional items inquired about respondents' having been "made to do a sexual act" or having witnessed someone else "being made to do a sexual act." Using a variation of Singer's measure, Saltzman (1995) documented the independent contribution of PCV exposure to adolescents' involvement in antisocial and delinquent behaviors separate from peer and familial contributors to such disorders.

Other researchers have devised comparable measures for a range of populations. Jenkins and her associates (Bell, Hildreth, Jenkins, Levi, & Carter, 1988; Jenkins, 1993; Jenkins & Thompson, 1986), for example, studied African American children's encounters with violence (Bell & Jenkins, 1993). Using related measures, Jenkins and her colleagues obtained information about school-aged youths' exposure in terms of (a) knowing someone who was a victim of violence; (b) having witnessed *in real life* violent events; (c) having been a victim of a violent incident; and (d) having perpetrated a violent act. Cooley-Quille, Turner, and Beidel (1995a) developed the 32-item "Children's Report of Exposure to Violence" (CREV) for youth ages 9 to 18. The CREV defines community violence as deliberate acts intended to cause physical harm to a person or persons in the community. The CREV assesses frequency of lifetime exposure to various types of community violence (i.e., media, hearsay, directly witnessed, directly victimized events) across three categories of victims (i.e., strangers, familiar persons, and self). Violent situations considered include being chased or threatened, beaten up, robbed or mugged, shot, stabbed, or killed.

ESTIMATES OF PCV EXPOSURE

Apfel and Simon (1996) described a violent community as a setting in "which every child has witnessed or expects to witness violence and has been or expects to be violated" (pp. 4–5). The levels of PCV exposure obtained across multiple urban surveys do not quite meet that universal standard.[1] Estimates of *direct* victimization levels derived from reports by elementary school children ranged from as high as 47% for being threatened with physical harm (Martinez & Richters, 1993) to 37% for living in a home that had been broken into (Richters & Martinez, 1993) to 31% for being pressured into involvement in the drug trade (Saltzman, 1992) to 22% for sexual assault (Martinez & Richters, 1993) to less than 5% for other forms of physical violence. Estimates of *indirect* victimization resulting from witnessing, hearing about, or knowing someone who has been victimized come closer to Apfel and Simon's description. Up to 40% of children assessed had seen a dead body (Osofsky et al., 1993). Most (74%) of the children in Martinez and Richters's (1993) study had witnessed an arrest or an accident involving serious injury; high percentages had witnessed drug use (69%) and the use of an illegal weapon (58%). Approximately 4 of 5 children surveyed had witnessed some form of violence during the past year (e.g., Bell & Jenkins, 1993).

PSYCHOLOGICAL CONSEQUENCES OF PCV

Additional epidemiological studies (Lilienfeld & Lilienfeld, 1980) must be conducted if we are to understand the links among PCV exposure, physical health, and mental health. Available findings (e.g., Singer et al., 1994) suggest that PCV's impacts accumulate over time, have synergistic effects across func-tional modalities, and can have lasting health-related consequences for those exposed. Surveys have, in fact, confirmed PCV's toxicity. Saltzman (1992), for example, observed significantly higher levels of generalized emotional distress in fifth- and sixth-grade respondents in the upper quartile of PCV exposure. This pattern was found by Richters and Martinez (1993), Martinez and Richters (1993), Osofsky et al. (1993), and Bell and Jenkins (1993). Across these studies, children with PCV exposure reported affective and vegetative signs of depres-sion and indices of stress-related disorders. Cooley-Quille, Turner, and Beidel (1995b) found that youth exposed to high levels of PCV are more likely to show impaired social relationships and increased general activity and restlessness, as well as to externalize behavior disturbances. Summarizing reported findings, Singer et al. (1994) argued that evidence supports a link between PCV exposure and increased aggression, conduct disorder, and running away. In their view, witnessing is more related than direct victimization to the adoption of a defensive stance in which anticipatory violence predominates over reactive violence. In

[1] Work in progress by Singer and his colleagues (personal communication, April 1997) suggests that PCV is limited in neither its occurrence nor its contagion to urban settings. These investigators are beginning to obtain epidemiological data about the extent, nature, and consequences of exposure to violence as experienced by youth in suburban and rural settings.

effect, convinced of their risk for harm, youth strike the first blow to gain some advantage in the face of a perceived threat (Singer et al., 1994). PCV exposure has also been associated with decreases in self-esteem and social competence. Saltzman (1995) observed that PCV exposure is a significant predictor of involvement in antisocial and violent acts independent of peer, familial, and other recognized predictors. Furthermore, self-reported fears, worrying, and affiliation with deviant peers were associated with the risk of starting to carry a lethal weapon (Arria, Borges, & Anthony, 1997). Rubinetti (1996) reports that PCV exposure appears most strongly related to involvement in violent activities in youth with decreased levels of empathy, hopefulness, and self-esteem.

As noted, we have yet to apply these measures to assess adults' exposure in PCV-marked communities and the consequences of such exposure on their emotional and behavioral functioning. Presumably, PCV exposure has comparable impacts on the health and mental health of parents/caregivers, educators, mental health providers, and the other adults residing and working in affected communities. Whether such epidemiological surveys must be completed before interventions can be designed and applied is debatable.

Knowledge of the extent to which PCV's toxicity has spread throughout a community and its residents does, however, seem necessary for targeting interventions (e.g., should the focus be on youth or on their caregivers?) and for determining the human resources locally available to deliver the intervention. If, for example, teachers or parents are to buffer the effects of children's exposure, it may first be necessary to mitigate the effects of exposure on parents' and teachers' emotional functioning. Slaikeu (1990) notes the importance of recognizing that local human service providers are themselves impacted by local tragedies and thus may be unavailable or limited in their capacity to assist with crisis intervention efforts. One must wonder how this effect extends to mental health providers whose clients include substantial proportions of PCV victims and perpetrators.

PCV'S TOXIC POTENTIAL

We expect that systematic inquiry will reveal the insidiously negative and widespread consequences of exposure to PCV. A program of research is being designed to examine whether and how PCV exposure relates to the development and operation of cognitive functions such as arousal, memory, concentration, abstract reasoning, vigilance, and emotional reactivity (e.g., Pynoos & Nader, 1989). Available findings confirm that exposure relates to psychological functions such as affective lability, empathy, depression, anxiety, hopelessness, and impulse control (e.g., APA, 1993; Levine & Rosich, 1996; Lorion & Saltzman, 1993; Martinez & Richters, 1993; Rubinetti, 1996; Saltzman, 1995). Extrapolating findings from research on stress and post-traumatic stress disorder (PTSD), (Slaikeu, 1990) to the study and control of PCV, it is reasonable to assume that PCV exposure compromises physiological processes such as digestion, growth rates, sleep-wake cycles, dream patterns, as well as patterns of alcohol, tobacco, and other drug use. Indeed, children exposed to PCV, directly or indirectly, have exhibited symptoms of PTSD, including reexperiencing the events (e.g., having intrusive thoughts and nightmares, worrying about their own safety and that of loved ones); avoidance and numbing (e.g., feeling estranged from others, demonstrating constricted affect, a sense of foreshortened future, and anhedonia); and heightened physiological arousal (e.g., exhibiting hypervigilance, attention and concentration difficulty, exaggerated startle responses, nervousness, irritability) (Arria, Borges, & Anthony, 1997; Fitzpatrick & Boldizar, 1993; Jenkins, 1993; Raia, Pedersen, & Dana, 1995). It is evident that this pathogen has serious implications for the physical health, stamina, and coping ability of a community's residents.

CONFRONTING AN ENVIRONMENTAL TOXIN

Based on findings reported thus far, PCV's toxicity appears confirmed, at least for youth. Understanding how contamination occurs represents an important challenge for social and mental health scientists. We speculate that individual acts of violence become so commonplace, and awareness of that pattern so widespread, that PCV becomes a defining and toxic characteristic of settings. Thus, the setting and the expectations and behaviors of those within the setting become linked, and violence becomes an expected and seemingly accepted part of interactions that occur within that setting.

This process, in fact, defines Barker's (1968) concept of a "behavior setting" (Schoggen, 1989). Insight into the emergence of a "behavior setting" effect may be provided by revisiting the concept of "miasma" as an early (and generally dismissed) explanation for epidemics (Lilienfeld & Lilienfeld, 1980). In the early 1700s, "miasma theory" was offered as an alternative to "germ theory," the proposition that the contagion of disease occurred through the passage of living organisms from one individual to another. As a negative quality of a setting (i.e., "something in the air"), miasma referred to an unspecified aspect of a setting that made its inhabitants vulnerable to disease. That intangible quality may have been inhaled, absorbed, or otherwise ingested. Generally, however, it was assumed that the setting simply reduced resistance to disease. Whatever its processes, miasma theory hypothesized that one's presence in certain environments threatened one's physical health.

Applied to PCV, the miasma (i.e., the "something") may involve inhabitants' assumptions, attitudes, and expectations about their vulnerability to physical harm. In turn, these factors influence residents' interpretation of the threatening quality of events and the decision to respond aggressively to those events. Thus, PCV's miasma refers to a *psychological* quality of a setting.

In our view, Barker's (1968; Schoggen, 1989) concept of a "behavior setting" offers a more contemporary version of miasma. In Barker's view, certain settings characteristically "pull for" behaviors regardless of who enters the community. To adapt to these environments, people conform behaviorally to the sensed demands of the setting. The development of suspicious, anxious, avoidant, and aggressive characteristics may be functional in settings dominated by PCV. Further complicating the concepts of miasma and behavior settings is the difficulty encountered in efforts to change characteristics developed over a lifetime.

Responding to PCV's Mental Health Impacts

In spite of the recency of attention to PCV's extent and consequences, many interventions have been designed and tried (Tolan & Guerra, 1994). Most represent grassroots, local attempts to "do something" in the face of an overwhelming problem. Applying what is known about crisis intervention (e.g., Slaikeu, 1990), most attempt to treat the emotional and behavioral consequences of exposure. Some attempt to reduce exposure and to prevent its sequelae. Unfortunately, little objective evidence confirms the value of these efforts. Nevertheless, what has been learned from these efforts does provide insights into intervention strategies that hold promise for reducing PCV's emotional and behavioral sequelae through the application of preventive interventions.

Earlier, Price (1983; Price & Lorion, 1989) explained that, under ideal circumstances, preventive interventions evolve logically through a four-step sequence, beginning with analysis of the problem through the diffusion of a proven intervention. Price's (1983) "prevention research process" described the evolution of preventive interventions as an incremental sequence of four stages of activity. Stage I, careful problem analysis, leads to documentation of the presence or absence of the pathogen. The components of this stage include the capacity to define epidemiologically vulnerable segments of the population and to identify factors that increase (i.e., risk factors) or reduce (i.e., protective factors) that vulnerability. Information gained at this stage provides insights into those points along the etiological chain potentially responsive to intervention.

At this point, important progress has been made in the design of measures and the assessment of PCV's effects and consequences for youth. As noted, that work needs to be extended to other segments of the population (e.g., parents, teachers, mental health providers) and to settings diverse in terms of their assumed levels of PCV (e.g., suburban and rural communities).

Problem analysis (Stage I) informs innovation design (Stage II). Stage II efforts seek to determine those contributors to the pathogen's formation and influence that are amenable to intervention and to translate that knowledge into specific intervention procedures. Stage III, field trial, moves from intervention design to the systematic assessment of efficacy under relatively controlled conditions. This stage includes both formative (i.e., process) and summative (i.e., outcome) evaluations of the intervention's components and measurable effects under field conditions.

Answers to two basic questions are sought at Stage III. First, what specific activities define an intervention's application? In effect, what is done, by whom, when and under what conditions? Second, what are the intervention's measurable positive and negative effects? Preventive interventions frequently involve the application of interventions at one point in development (e.g., at preschool or during the transition from elementary school to middle school) to reduce a problem expected to appear later in development (e.g., substance involvement, adolescent pregnancy).

For that reason, analyses of preventive outcomes distinguish between proximal and distal effects (Price, 1983). By definition, proximal outcomes represent short-term gains, indicating that a normative rather than a pathogenic developmental trajectory is operative (Lorion, Price, & Eaton, 1989). Relative to the effects of pervasive community violence on students, proximal effects might include improvements in attendance rates, increases in students' on-task and attentional performance, acceleration of learning rates, associated increases in standardized tests performance, and reductions in the number of required disciplinary actions. Ultimately, changes in such parameters should lead to proximal effects such as reductions in students' (a) experience of stress-related symptoms; (b) involvement in antisocial and delinquent behaviors; and (c) failure to achieve career and life goals.

Stage IV, innovation diffusion, focuses on documentation of intervention effectiveness (Shadish, 1990) when implemented under real-life circumstances without the artificial controls of a controlled field trial. Under such "noisy" conditions, one can assess the adaptability and the viability of an intervention and determine the limits of its application across settings, populations, and levels of funding. Often circumvented in the rush to disseminate "promising" interventions, the steps required for innovation diffusion provide confirmation of an intervention's potential for achieving its stated goals with its intended population. Avoiding this stage leads to the present situation regarding the prevention of violence and its sequelae in schools, in which limited resources are invested in untested and unproven strategies.

ORGANIZING PCV INTERVENTION DEVELOPMENT

As noted, knowledge of the nature, extent, and sequelae of youths' PCV exposure is presently limited. Figure 6.1 outlines major categories of information on which substantive preventive interventions could be established. Step 1 focuses on the field's need to arrive at a common definition of the pathogen, that is, PCV exposure. Based on that definition, Step 2 calls for development of procedures for determining the nature and extent of individual exposure. Ideally, such procedures will derive from a theory of the problem. Thus far, most such procedures have involved self-report measures, few of which have documented psychometric properties. Perhaps archival records such as reports of the activities of police, fire departments, and other emergency services (e.g., ambulance calls), which can be obtained at less expense and effort than individual self-reports, can serve as acceptable proxies for targeting contaminated settings.

Assuming that the field agrees on a set of measures, Step 3 involves documentation of the pathogen's impacts across a range of functioning. Whether distinct impacts can be documented in each modality, in both the short (i.e., proximal) and the long term (i.e., distal), is an empirical question. Given the pathogen's pervasive quality, it is reasonable to assume that its effects extend beyond the youth to be targeted by a school- or community-based preventive intervention. For that reason, Step 4 focuses on examining the "spread of effects." Findings from this stage of the work are likely to identify both (a) the resources (e.g., teachers, parents, gatekeepers) that may be available for the intervention

Step 1. Operationalizing the Pathogen's Influence Through:
  • direct exposure
  • indirect exposure
Step 2. Documenting the Pathogen's Reach Via:
  • self-report/rating measures of exposure to PCV
  • proxy/archival measures of exposure to PCV
Step 3. Documenting the Pathogen's Impacts in Terms of Its:
  • biological effects (proximal/distal)
  • cognitive effects (proximal/distal)
  • emotional effects (proximal/distal)
  • behavioral effects (proximal/distal)
Step 4. Documenting the Pathogen's Spread of Effects to:
  • parents/parenting
  • teachers/teaching
  • gatekeepers/gatekeeping
Step 5. Opportunities for Preventive Interventions in:
  • single settings (e.g., schools, homes)
  • multiple settings (e.g., schools, home, neighborhood)
Step 6. Opportunities for Preventive Interventions Through:
  • changes in knowledge, attitudes, and behavior
  • setting procedures and policies
  • collaborations across settings

Figure I   A Sequence for Understanding the Pathogenic Qualities of Student Exposure to Pervasive Community Violence (PCV)

to reduce the pathogen's effect on youth and/or (b) those individuals beyond youth who need to be served by an intervention.

Step 5 focuses on clarification of the processes by which the preventive intervention mitigates the pathogen's influence. In effect, Step 5 involves development of a theory of the solution. Alternatives in Figure 6.1 include alterations in youth's knowledge, attitudes, and behaviors as they relate to recognizing and responding to threatening situations, in the procedures and policies of the settings in which vulnerability occurs, and in the degree to which collaborations in procedures and programs occurs across settings. These options represent merely a few of the strategies that may be developed to assist youth to avoid or cope effectively with exposure to violent settings and events.

Finally, Step 6 examines the feasibility of implementing efficacy trials across the settings in which youth are exposed to violence or may be available for an intervention responsive to such exposure. In addition to schools and homes, such interventions may be located in community centers, playgrounds, housing projects, or local churches. Moreover, the relative merits of single- and multisetting interventions need to be determined.

Initial Steps in the Prevention and Treatment of PCV

Treatment and interventions in the area of youth and violence have suffered from what Blum (1994) describes as the absence of clear linkages across an array of involved service delivery systems, organizations, and service settings. Violence prevention programs for youth, for example, have developed within service delivery systems as diverse as schools, mental health clinics, recreation centers, and juvenile justice settings. Typically, there is little if any contact across or within these systems. In searching for innovative approaches to violence prevention programs, Blum (1994) offers the identification of a "common component" as a useful organizing device. In seeking such a components across interventions, one needs to appreciate that the meaning of each intervention for those who provide and those who receive it (regardless of the commonality of their stated objectives) is affected greatly by its host system.

Because we view treatment and prevention efforts as steps along a continuum of service delivery, we find Gordon's (1983) differentiation of preventive interventions into universal, selected, and indicated useful. This typology helps us to understand the interaction of system, client, and intervention for both preventive and treatment activities. Gordon's categories are as follows:

- *Universal interventions* are designed for and provided to all members of a targeted population (e.g., youth) regardless of risk. Universal efforts tend to be inexpensive in terms of cost per individual reached, broad in their reach, and minimally iatrogenic. Chlorination of water, the "Just Say No" campaign against drug use, and public service announcements in which celebrities encourage children to remain in school are examples of universal interventions.

- *Selected interventions* are designed for distinct segments of a population on the basis of epidemiologically known risks. Examples include malaria shots for those who travel to locations in which the disease is prevalent and conflict mediation programs in schools known to have high levels of gang activity or youth violence.

- *Indicated interventions* are designed for those who present individually confirmed risk for the outcome to be avoided. An indicated intervention to prevent depression, for example, would be provided to individuals who screen positive for subclinical signs of affective difficulties. Mammographic screening for women with a family history of breast cancer represents an initial stage of an indicated intervention. If the screen is positive, treatment of the malignancy in its early stages is initiated.

Preventive efforts can interrupt the worsening of a condition and avert negative outcomes that might be related to an existing, subclinical condition. Once clinical criteria have been met, however, treatment rather than prevention is necessary (Mrazek & Haggerty, 1994). This distinction has implications for the design, targeting, and evaluation of the intervention (Lorion, Price, & Eaton, 1989). Given the early stages in the development of programmatic responses to PCV exposure, it is essential that both prevention and early treatment efforts be pursued. As noted, the physical and mental health implications of such exposure are sufficiently serious that no avenue should be ignored at this point.

DIVERSITY OF SERVICE SETTINGS

The contextual nature of PCV argues for the placement of interventions to reduce its effects across multiple settings. Responding to this pathogen requires that mental health professionals move out into their communities. Schools and recreation centers, for example, may be ideal sites for providing universal preventive interventions. Examples of community centers that sponsor general violence prevention programs are the Police Athletic Leagues (PAL) Centers and the South Baltimore Youth Center (Baker, Pollack, & Kohn, 1995). Schools provide educational services that are in many ways relevant to violence prevention. Options range from including in the curriculum opportunities for students to gain health-related knowledge (e.g., medical and social consequences of aggressive behavior and substance use), strategies for conflict resolution, the provision of youth support groups, and the long-terms benefit of upward social mobility through an education (Walker, Goodwin, & Warren, 1992).

Health clinics may be involved in indicated interventions. An interesting example of this involves community efforts to reduce risks for lead poisoning. This is based on Needleman's (1990) hypothesis that "some of the disorder behaviors of those who commit violent crimes result from disordered brain function and that much of this disorder is provoked by lead exposure" (Walker et al., 1992, p. 492). Other steps of such a preventive program might include early lead screening and diagnostic evaluation of children. Community mental health centers may provide violence prevention programs to reduce the negative effects of violence exposure in groups at increased risk (selected intervention), to short-circuit the traumatic consequences of exposure to a traumatically violent event, or to treat victims exposed to violence (indicated interventions).

By contrast, because of the close association of adjudicated juvenile crime and violence (Tolan & Guerra, 1994), the juvenile justice system typically relies on indicated prevention strategies. This system has the most contact with youth at individual risk for engaging in violent acts (e.g., as members of a gang) or who already have acted in violent ways and thus risk involvement in more serious and potentially lethal acts. In some cases, the juvenile justice system applies efforts to divert at-risk youth to treatment services in the hopes of avoiding formal adjudication. Depending on whether youth are chosen because a sibling has been incarcerated or because of their involvement in antisocial behavior, this is a selective or an indicated intervention. In some cases, correctional agencies intervene to reduce crime and violence by programs such as vocational training, education, counseling, casework, and clinical services (Walker et al., 1992). Unfortunately, little evidence exists regarding their effectiveness.

THE NEED FOR PROBLEM CLARIFICATION

In considering intervention alternatives, Blum (1994) notes that his review of services and program makes evident the need for a clear definition of the participant population and problem definition. As noted, the association between juvenile crime and violent behavior raises the possibility of confounds in the description and definition of client populations, as well as in the design and evaluation of many antiviolence programs (Tolan & Guerra, 1994). Blum (1994) also correctly points out that evaluations of systems and services suffer from the failure to appreciate that similarly named components may not actually be similar. Such definitional confusion further complicates attempts to compare interventions across systems and programs. This warning certainly applies to the examination of violence prevention efforts. In fact, confusion arises around the very definition of violence.

In an attempt to reduce the latter problem, Tolan and Guerra (1994) offer a useful typology of violence. They describe four distinct types of violence:

1. *Situational violence* refers to acts that are prompted by factors such as heat waves, violence, availability of weapons, frustration over unavoidable accidents, or setting- or occasion-specific occurrences.
2. *Relational violence* refers to acts arising from interpersonal disputes among known individuals.
3. *Predatory violence* refers to acts that are perpetrated intentionally for gain.
4. *Psychopathological violence* represents a relatively rare form marked by repetitive and extreme violence reflecting an underlying pathological condition.

Were this typology to be broadly adopted, the meanings and implications of types of violence targeted by interventions should be clarified. Unfortunately, program evaluations rarely define intended participants and types of violence targeted. A notable exception are programs aimed specifically at forms of domestic violence such as child or spouse abuse. It must also be noted that violence prevention programs have generally been marked by methodologically weak or nonexistent evaluations.

In their review of such programs, Tolan and Guerra (1994) identified few programs that had been rigorously tested. In fact, they report an almost inverse relationship between the popularity and broad application of programs and the methodological quality of their evaluation (Tolan & Guerra, 1994). Despite these limitations, Tolan and Guerra have compiled two useful reviews of violence prevention programs aimed at adolescents (Tolan & Guerra, 1994; Guerra, Tolan, & Hammond, 1994). Examination of these reports offers a good overview of the strengths and weaknesses of existing violence intervention alternatives.

Review of Extant Innovative Programs

In this section we describe examples of the more successful programs, organized by type of intervention.

I. UNIVERSAL INTERVENTION

A promising school based program not described in the reviews of Tolan et al. (1994) and Guerra et al. (1994) is the Johns Hopkins University's Prevention

Research Center longitudinal study of approximately 2000 first graders who participated in a universal intervention called the Good Behavior Game. This classroom- based intervention promoted group cooperation, encouragement, and collective reward and punishment based on the capacity of all members of the group to follow classroom rules, including those limiting aggressive behavior. Outcomes years after the intervention reveal reductions in aggressive behavior as rated by teachers and students. Such reductions are particularly noticeable for boys at points of major life change, such as the entrance to middle school. A substantial number of aggressive boys involved in the intervention show a distinct decrease in the trajectory of the aggressive behavior compared with controls boys, whose aggression increases at this transition (Kellam, Rebok, Mayer, Ialongo, & Kalodner, 1994).

Universal interventions at the societal level also include efforts to reduce the effects of exposure to media violence. Some studies have shown reductions in subsequent violence when children watch nonviolent programming and participate in discussions about the fantasy world of TV (Eron, 1986). Although there appear to be few lasting effects to such programs, two natural experiments were highlighted by Tolan and Guerra as indicating that reductions in media violence may impact the occurrence of violent events. In a remote town in Canada, violent acts increased when television reception was introduced in the former case; in many South African communities, violent acts increased when reception was restored. Although the difficulty of conducting such interventions is evident given the pervasiveness of media violence, these findings suggest that this avenue merits attention.

Further evidence of the potential impact of interventions at the policy or societal level is found in comparisons of the rates of violence and death from handguns in two matched cities, one with a handgun ban and one without. In this natural experiment, rates differed greatly, with much lower rates in the city without easy access to handguns. (Sloan, Rivera, Reay, Ferris, Path, & Kellerman, 1991).

II. SELECTED INTERVENTION

Tolan and Guerra (1994) conclude that interventions targeted to family processes are among the most successful in curbing youth violence. Work by Patterson and his colleagues at the Oregon Social Learning Center (e.g., Patterson, 1982, 1986; Patterson, Chamberlain, & Reid, 1992; Patterson & Reid, 1973) exemplifies these strategies. Their intervention is designed to decrease child antisocial behavior by decreasing negative and coercive parenting styles. Importantly, their approach has also provided insight into the relationship of violence focusing on the role of violence within single-mother and low-income families (Patterson, DeBaryshe, & Ramsey, 1989; Wahler & Dumas, 1989). Tolan and Guerra (1994) note that successful family interventions typically combine behavioral parent training with interventions aimed at improving family relationships.

III. INDICATED INTERVENTION

Feldman's (1992) evaluation of the St. Louis Experiment provides a useful example of a program that appeared to be unsuccessful yet had embedded within it an effective intervention technique. The overall evaluation of this program found that, while a behavior modification treatment intervention had better outcomes than a guided group interaction (designed to increase prosocial behavior and norms through changed peer interaction) in changing the behavior of boys with antisocial characteristics, its effects did not differ from those observed in the minimal treatment group. The finding of importance for this peer group-based intervention is that groups composed of a mix of prosocial and delinquent youths displayed less antisocial behavior at follow-up than did groups with only delinquent youth. Greene's (1993) work supports this conclusion. Of additional importance was the finding that, while the delinquent youth were apparently changed by their association with the prosocial youth, the reverse did not occur. Guerra, Tolan, and Hammond (1994) report, however, that juvenile diversion programs do not appear to reduce the likelihood of subsequent criminal or violent behavior.

Although evidence is limited, Tolan and Guerra suggest that promising school-based interventions for at-risk youth provide continuity and structure for students by using alternative classrooms and increased parental involvement (e.g., Bry, 1982; Gottfredson, 1987). Hammond and Yung's (1991) Positive Adolescent Choices Training (PACT) represents another promising approach. This program is designed for at-risk African American youth. PACT uses cognitive-behavioral group training in combination with a series of videotapes that teach skills in giving and receiving negative feedback and negotiation. Results showed that middle schoolers receiving 20 one-hour weekly sessions were less likely than controls to be referred to juvenile court during the three years following the intervention, and less likely to be charged with violent offenses.

IV. TREATMENT

Comprehensive treatment programs appear most successful when designed to reduce the reoccurrence of violence. Guerra and Slaby's (1990) research exemplifies this approach. Their study examined the random assignment of juvenile offenders incarcerated for violent crimes to a cognitive-behavioral intervention that included training in social problem-solving skills, enhanced perspective taking increased self-control, and an effort to change beliefs and attitudes toward violence. Intervention participants had reduced staff ratings on aggression compared to the attention-control or nontreatment group (Tolan & Guerra, 1994). Tolan and Guerra find little evidence that residential treatment programs are effective in treating and preventing further violent behavior over the long term.

Implications

This overview offers bases for hope tempered with evidence that much remains to be learned if PCV's effects are to be mitigated by the efforts of mental health service providers. Few available interventions are specific about the forms of violence for which they are relevant, the societal contexts in which the youth, families, schools, and communities function, the systems in which the interventions are operating, and the specific conditions under which specific interventions are applicable. What the evidence shows is that some program components hold promise, especially comprehensive interventions that involve prosocial adults and peers and include changes in the family and environment setting. There is also evidence that attention to the developmental timing and measurement of proximal and distal outcomes is important. Few of these interventions, however, directly address the setting level antecedents and consequences of PCV.

The issue of setting-level changes deserves careful attention. Interventions to treat or prevent youth violence may not be sufficient in a violent or nonsupportive family, neighborhood, school, or community. If Barker's (1968) concept of "behavior settings" is relevant to understanding violent communities, it is important that mental health providers look beyond the individual to understand factors that contribute to the occurrence of violence and sustain some emotional and behavioral problems in such settings. To achieve this shift in perspective requires that traditional graduate training in the mental health disciplines include consideration of exogenous factors and an understanding of ecological principles (Levine & Perkins, 1997). An element of that shift in perspective is appreciation of PCV's impact on the providers as well as recipients of human services. Just as in an airplane, where adults must care for themselves (i.e., put on their oxygen mask) before helping others, those who serve identified victims of violence may themselves need to care for their personal reactions to the inevitable exposure that accompanies the delivery of such care (Lorion, 1998). How the needs of these workers are to be identified, especially in light of their self-concepts as caring "objective professional" who is both empathic and accepting, remains to be solved.

A change in perspective for mental health service providers is necessary if they are to appreciate their risk for PCV contamination through client contact. Some may find it difficult to sustain empathy for clients who are violent or who report victimization. Some may become distant and professional in their interactions with clients as an unconscious means of protecting themselves against awareness of the harshness of the settings in which those clients must live. Others may find themselves increasingly wary as they travel within urban areas or increasingly suspicious in their encounters with residents of violent communities. Whatever the response, solving the resulting problems cannot begin until mental health providers recognize and accept their risk for PCV exposure through their contacts with and their awareness of those who live, work, and teach in violent settings.

What should be evident to readers is that the mental health and the social sciences confront significant challenges as they attempt to understand and respond to pervasive community violence and its sequelae. In our view, these challenges offer unique opportunities for these disparate scientific disciplines to appreciate the value and the necessity of approaching these problems from a truly interdisciplinary and collaborative perspective.

REFERENCES

American Psychological Association (APA), Commission on Violence and Youth. (1993). *Violence and youth: Psychology's response. Vol. I: Summary report of the American Psychological Association Commission on Violence and Youth*. Washington, DC: Author.

Apfel, R. J., & Simon, B. (Eds.). (1996) *Minefields in their hearts*. New Haven, CT: Yale University Press.

Arria, A., Borges, G., & Anthony, J. (1997). Fears and other suspected risk factors for carrying lethal weapons among urban youths in middle-school age. *Archives of Pediatrics and Adolescent Medicine, 151*, 555–560.

Baker, K., Pollack, M., & Kohn, I. (1995). Violence prevention through informal socialization: An evaluation of the South Baltimore Youth Project. *Studies on Crime and Prevention, 4*(1), 61–85.

Barker, R. G. (1968). *Ecological psychology*. Stanford, CA: Stanford University Press.

Beland, K. R. (1996). A schoolwide approach to violence prevention. In R. L. Hampton, P. Jenkins, & T. P. Gullota (Eds.), *Preventing violence in America* (pp. 209–232). Thousand Oaks, CA: Sage Publications.

Bell, C. C., Hildreth, C. J., Jenkins, E. J., Levi, D., & Carter, C. (1988). The need for victimization screening in a poor, outpatient medical population. *Journal of the National Medical Association, 80*, 853–860.

Bell, C. C., & Jenkins, E. J. (1993). Community violence and children on Chicago's southside. *Psychiatry: Interpersonal and Biological Processes, 56*, 46–54.

Bloom, B. L. (1984). *Community mental health: A general introduction*. Monterey, CA: Brooks/Cole.

Blum, A. B. (1994). *Innovation in practice and service delivery: A framework for analysis* (unpulished manuscript). Cleveland: Center for Practice Innovations, Case Western Reserve University.

Bry, B. H. (1982). Reducing the incidence of adolescent problems through preventive intervention: One- and five-year follow-up. *American Journal of Community Psychology, 10*(3), 265–276.

Caplan, G. (1964). *Principles of preventive psychiatry*. New York: Basic Books.

Cooley, M. R., Turner, S. M., & Beidel, D. C. (1995a). Assessing community violence: The Children's Report of Exposure to Violence. *Journal of the American Academy of Child and Adolescent Psychiatry, 34*, 201–208.

Cooley-Quille, M. R., Turner, S. M., & Beidel, D. C. (1995b). Emotional impact of children's exposure to community violence: A preliminary study. *Journal of the American Academy of Child and Adolescent Psychiatry, 34*, 1362–1368.

Elliott, D. S., Hamburg, B., & Williams, K. R. (Eds.) (1998). *Violence in American schools*. New York: Cambridge University Press.

Eron, L. D. (1986). Interventions to mitigate the psychological effects of media violence on aggressive behavior. *Journal of Social Issues, 42*, 155–169.

Feldman, R. A. (1992). The St. Louis experiment: Effective treatment of antisocial youths in prosocial peer groups. In J. McCord & R. Tremblay (Eds.), *Preventing antisocial behavior: Interventions from birth through adolescence* (pp. 233–252). New York: Guilford Press.

Fitzpatrick, K., & Boldizar, J. (1993). The prevalence and consequences of exposure to violence among African American youth. *Journal of the American Academy of Child and Adolescent Psychiatry, 32*, 424–430.

Geiger, K. (1993, Jan. 14). *Violence in the schools*. Statement presented at a news conference given by the president of the National Education Association, Washington, DC.

Gordon, R. (1983). An operational classification of disease prevention. *Public Health Reports*, *98*, 107–109.

Gottfredson, D. C. (1987). An evaluation of an organization development approach to reducing school disorder. *Evaluation Review*, *11* (6), 739–763.

Greene, M. B. (1993). Chronic exposure to violence and poverty: Interventions that work for youth. *Crime and Delinquency*, *39*(1), 106–124.

Guerra, N. G., & Slaby, R. G. (1990). Cognitive mediators of aggression in adolescent offenders: 2 Intervention. *Developmental Psychology*, *26*(2), 269–277.

Guerra, N. G., Tolan, P. H., & Hammond, R. (1994). Prevention and treatment of adolescent violence. In L. D. Eron, J. H. Gentry & P. Schlegel (Eds.), *Reason to hope: A psychosocial perspective on violence and youth* (pp. 383–404). Washington, DC: American Psychological Association.

Hamburg, M. (1998). Violence as a public health problem for children and youth. In D. S. Elliott, B. Hamburg, & K. R. Williams (Eds.), *Violence in American schools* (pp. 31–54). New York: Cambridge University Press.

Hammond, R., & Yung, B. (1991). *Dealin' with anger: Givin' it. Takin' it. Workin' it out: Leader's guide*. Champaign, IL: Research Press.

Jenkins, E. (1993). *Posttraumatic stress disorder symptoms of African American youth exposed to violence*. Paper presented at the meeting of the American Association of Behavior Therapy, Atlanta, GA.

Jenkins, E. J., & Thompson, B. (1986). *Children talk about violence: Preliminary findings from a survey of black elementary school children*. Paper presented at the Nineteenth Annual Convention of the Association of Black Psychologists, Oakland, CA.

Jensen, P., & Shaw, J. (1993). Children as victims of war: Current knowledge and future research needs. *Journal of the American Academy of Child and Adolescent Psychiatry*, *32*, 697–708.

Kellam, S. G., Rebok, G. W., Mayer, L. S., Ialongo, N., & Kalodner, C. R. (1994). Depressive symptoms over first grade and their response to a developmental epidemiologically-based preventive trial aimed at improving achievement. *Development and Psychopathology*, *35*(2), 259–281.

Levine, M., & Perkins, D. V. (1997). *Principles of community psychology: Perspectives and applications*. New York: Oxford University Press.

Levine, F. J., & Rosich, K. J. (1996). *Social causes of violence: Crafting a science agenda*. Washington, DC: American Sociological Association.

Lilienfeld, A. M., & Lilienfeld, D. E. (1980). *Foundations of epidemiology*. New York: Oxford University Press.

Lindemann, E. (1944). Symptomology and management of acute grief. *American Journal of Psychiatry*, *101*, 141–148.

Lorion, R. P. (1998). Exposure to urban violence: Contamination of the school environment. In D. S. Elliott, B. Hamburg, & K. R. Williams (Eds.), *Violence in American schools* (pp. 293–311). New York: Cambridge University Press.

Lorion, R. P., Price, R. H., & Eaton, W. W. (1989). The prevention of child and adolescent disorders: From theory to research. In D. Shaffer, I. Phillips, & N. B. Enzer (Eds.), *Prevention of mental disorders. Alcohol and other drug use in children and adolescents* (pp. 55–96). OSAP Prevention Monograph 2 (DHHS Publication No. ADM-89-1646). Washington, DC: U.S. Government Printing Office.

Lorion, R. P., & Saltzman, W. (1993). Children's exposure to community violence: Following a path from concern to research to action. *Psychiatry: Interpersonal and Biological Processes*, *56*, 55–65.

Martinez, P., & Richters, J. E. (1993). The NIMH Community Violence Project: II. Children's distress symptoms associated with violence exposure. *Psychiatry: Interpersonal and Biological Processes*, 56, 22–35.

Mrazek, D., & Haggerty, R. (Eds.). (1994). *Reducing risks for mental disorders: Frontiers for preventive intervention research.* Washington, DC: National Academy Press.

Osofsky, J. D., Wewers, S., Hann, D. M., & Fick, A. C. (1993). Chronic community violence: What is happening to our children? *Psychiatry: Interpersonal and Biological Processes*, 56, 36–45.

Patterson, G. R. (1982). *Coercive family processes.* Eugene, OR: Castalia.

Patterson, G. R. (1986). Performance models for antisocial boys. *American Psychologist*, 41, 432–444.

Patterson, G. R., Chamberlain, P., & Reid, J. B. (1992). A comparative evaluation of a parent training program. *Behavior Therapy*, 13, 638–650.

Patterson, G. R., DeBaryshe, B. D., & Ramsey, E. (1989). A developmental perspective on anti-social behavior. *American Psychologist*, 44 (2), 329–335.

Patterson, G. R., & Reid, J. B. (1973). Intervention for families of aggressive boys: A replication study. *Behavior Research and Therapy*, 11, 383–394.

Price, R. H. (1983). The education of a prevention psychologist. In R. D. Felner, L. Jason, J. Moritsugu, & S. S. Farber (Eds.), *Preventive psychology: Theory, research and practice in community intervention* (pp. 290–296). Elmsford, NY: Pergamon Press.

Price, R. H., & Lorion, R. P. (1989). Prevention programming as organizational reinvention: From research to implementation. In D. Shaffer, I. Phillips, & N. Enzer (Eds.), *Prevention of mental disorders, alcohol and other drug use in children and adolescents* (pp. 97–124). OSAP Prevention Monograph 2 (DHHS Publication No. ADM-89-1646). Washington, DC: U.S. Government Printing Office.

Pynoos, R. S., & Nader, K. (1989). Children's memory and proximity to violence. *Journal of the American Academy of Child and Adolescent Psychiatry*, 28 (2), 236–241.

Raia, J., Pederson, L., & Dana, J. (1995, August). *Community violence exposure and post-traumatic stress reactions.* Paper presented at the annual convention of the American Psychological Association. New York.

Richters, J. E., & Martinez, P. (1993). The NIMH Community Violence Project: I. Children as victims of and witnesses to violence. *Psychiatry: Interpersonal and Biological Processes*, 56, 7–21.

Richters, J. E., & Saltzman, W. (1990). *Survey of Exposure to Community Violence—Parent Report Version.* Unpublished measure, Child and Adolescent Disorders Research, NIMH.

Rubinetti, F. (1996). *Empathy, self-esteem, hopelessness, and belief in the legitimacy of aggression in adolescents exposed to pervasive community violence.* Unpublished doctoral dissertation. Department of Psychology, University of Maryland, College Park.

Saltzman, W. (1992). *The effect of children's exposure to violence.* Unpublished master's thesis, University of Maryland, College Park.

Saltzman, W. (1995). *Exposure to community violence and the prediction of violent antisocial behavior in a multi-ethnic sample of adolescents.* Unpublished doctoral dissertation. Department of Psychology, University of Maryland, College Park.

Sayre, J. (1994). Violence: The growing danger to children: The American case. *The Turkish Journal of Pediatrics*, 36, 49–55.

Schoggen, P. (1989). *Behavior settings: A revision and extension of Roger G. Barker's Ecological Psychology.* Stanford, CA: Stanford University Press.

Shadish, W. R. (1990). What can we learn about problems in community research by comparing it with program evaluation? In P. Tolan, C. Keys, F. Chertok, & L. Jason

(Eds.), *Researching community psychology: Issues of theory and methods* (pp. 214–223). Washington, DC: American Psychological Association.

Singer, M. I., Anglin, T. M., Song, L., & Lunghofer, L. (1994). *The mental health consequences of adolescents' exposure to violence.* Cleveland, OH: Case Western Reserve University.

Singer, M. I., Anglin, T. M., Song, L., & Lunghofer, L. (1995). Adolescents' exposure to violence and associated symptoms of psychological trauma. *Journal of the American Medical Association, 273,* 477–482.

Slaikeu, K. A. (1990). *Crisis intervention: A handbook for practice and research.* Boston: Allyn and Bacon.

Sloan, J. H., Rivera, F. P., Reay, D. T., Ferris, J. A. J., Path, M. R. C., & Kellerman, A. L. (1991). Firearm regulations and rates of suicide: A comparison of two metropolitan areas. *New England Journal of Medicine, 322*(6), 369–373.

Strauss, M. A., & Gelles, R. J. (1992). *Physical violence in American families.* New Brunswick, NJ: Transaction Books.

Tolan, P. H., & Guerra, N. G. (1994). *What works in reducing adolescent violence: An empirical review of the field.* Boulder, CO: Center for the Study and Prevention of Violence.

Wahler, R. G., & Dumas, J. E. (1989). Attentional problems in dysfunctional mother-child interactions: An interbehavioral model. *Psychological Bulletin, 105,* 116–130.

Walker, B., Goodwin, N. J., & Warren, R. C. (1992). Violence: A challenge to the public health community. *Journal of the National Medical Association, 84,* 490–496.

Innovations in Practice and Service Delivery with Adults

7

The Evolution of Service Innovations for Adults with Severe Mental Illness

PHYLLIS SOLOMON

This chapter deals with service innovations for those adults who suffer from long-lasting, persistent major mental illnesses that result in social and functional disability. Delimiting the parameters of this heterogeneous population has generally employed three dimensions: diagnosis, disability, and duration (Goldman & Mandersheid, 1987). The predominate diagnostic disorders among this population are schizophrenia, bipolar, and major depression. The concept of disability has focused on functional incapacity in various aspects of daily life, such as self-care, expressive communication, interpersonal relations, or performance of instrumental roles, such as those of homemaker or worker, and has emphasized clients' need for assistance in obtaining financial resources and establishing or maintaining a social support system and their pattern of engaging in inappropriate behavior that requires mental health or judicial system intervention (Lawn & Meyerson, 1993; Solomon & Meyerson, 1997). Definitions of duration have traditionally relied on the extent of psychiatric hospitalizations and supervised residential facilities, including nursing home placements, but recently have also included the extent of outpatient mental health treatment and emergency psychiatric service use (Goldman & Mandersheid, 1987; Special Report, 1993). Given the chronic recurring nature of these severe and persistent illnesses, emergency and crisis services are frequently required. When stabilization cannot be achieved on an outpatient basis, hospitalization becomes necessary to increase structure. For individuals to be considered severely mentally ill, they have to meet major aspects of all three criteria.

The prevalence of comorbidities is high among those with severe psychiatric disorders. These include chronic physical diseases as well as substance abuse disorders. These problems further limit the functional abilities of the population and tend to complicate the assessment and treatment of the psychiatric disorders (Attkisson et al., 1992).

Due to functional disability of the population, these individuals tend to be dependent on the government for financial and medical benefits. Only about

10–15% of the population are competitively employed (Anthony et al., 1978; Anthony & Jansen, 1984). Many of these individuals receive or are eligible for Supplemental Security Income (SSI) or Social Security Disability Income (SSDI), given their expected inability to be gainfully employed for at least a year (Solomon & Meyerson, 1997). "Compared with the general population, people with psychiatric disabilities are more likely to live in physically inadequate dwellings, to reside in high-crime neighborhoods, and to have significantly higher housing costs relative to their income" (Owen, Rutherford, Jones et al., 1996, p. 632). Regardless of the social class of origin, those with severe psychiatric disorders are of lower socioeconomic status; consequently, most of the population live in poverty.

Both genders and all ethnic groups are well represented among those who are severely mentally disabled, although they differ by diagnostic classification. For example, the prevalence of schizophrenia is equal in men and women, but major depression is greater among women (Attkisson et al., 1992). The Epidemiologic Catchment Area (ECA) study, which surveyed the mental disorders in community populations, generally found no differences between blacks and whites in prevalence rates among the major psychiatric diagnostic categories (Robins & Regier, 1991). However, there are major disparities between blacks and whites in treated populations. For example, blacks are more frequently involuntarily committed to state and county hospitals (Adebimpe, 1994). The racially based differences in treatment are attributed to clinical misinterpretations of symptom presentations of blacks and of their cultural belief systems. These factors lead to the assessment of severe psychiatric diagnoses instead of less severe ones (Jones & Gray, 1986). Given the sociodemographic characteristics of the population, there is increasing concern that service providers be culturally competent and sensitive to this diversity and that service programs receptive and appropriate to various ethnic and cultural groups be developed.

Major Subpopulations

With increasing frequency, psychiatric problems coexist with psychoactive substance disorders (Attkisson, Cook, Karno et al., 1992). Estimates are that nearly 50% of those with severe psychiatric illnesses have a co-occurring problem with substance abuse or dependency (Mueser et al., 1990; Test et al., 1989). Both the abuse and the use of drugs and alcohol further complicate the disability and compound the treatment of this population. Conventional substance abuse treatments, which often employ confrontational approaches and discourage the use of medication, tend to be ineffective for this population and may trigger an exacerbation of florid symptoms of the disorder. Furthermore, due to the dual nature of these disorders, individuals with psychiatric disorders are often discriminated against in substance abuse programs to the point of exclusion (Osher & Drake, 1996). These exclusionary policies are frequently the result of differences in eligibility as defined by various funding sources and by different orientations. There is increasing awareness of the potential for improved treatment efficacy resulting from the integration of mental health and substance abuse services (Drake, McLaughlin, Pepper, & Minkoff, 1991; Drake, Mueser, Clark, & Wallach, 1996).

Another subpopulation comprises those who are homeless and mentally ill (a substantial proportion have substance abuse problems as well). Estimates of mental illness among the homeless population range from a low of 2% to a high of 90%. But, on average, it is estimated that a third of single adults who are homeless suffer from a severe mental disorder (Johnson & Cnaan, 1995). All the attendant problems of homelessness are present to a greater extent in this population than in those who are not mentally ill. "[T]hose with severe mental disorders are more likely to have been homeless for a long time, to have limited contact with family and friends, to encounter barriers to employment, to be in poor physical health for which no treatment has been sought, and to have considerable contact with the legal system" (Attkisson et al., 1992, p. 564). However, a large proportion of homeless individuals who need mental health services are unwilling to utilize them, and only a small proportion actually receive them (Attkisson et al., 1992). Engagement and building trust with this population are necessary prerequisites to the delivery of needed services. Establishing trust usually requires that basic needs be addressed before one can deliver mental health services.

Another subgroup, which has considerable overlap with the two previous ones, is those who are involved in the criminal justice system. There is some evidence that nearly 50% of those with severe and persistent psychiatric disorders are involved with this system, and this figure may be rising (McFarland, Faulkner, Bloom et al., 1989; Mulvey, Blumstein, & Cohen, 1986; Solomon & Draine, 1993; Solomon & Draine, 1995a; Steinwachs et al., 1992). This group is difficult to serve, since it tends to be resistant to treatment and is often noncompliant with prescribed treatments. As policies de-emphasize involuntary commitment, jails and prisons are likely to be used as an alternate service system for this population (Solomon, Rogers, Draine, & Meyerson, 1995). The surveillance and coercive aspects of the criminal justice system interfere with the development of a therapeutic alliance between mental health providers and psychiatric probationers/parolees, given that providers are often mandated to report violations of stipulations. These tensions create challenges in integrating mental health services in criminal justice settings.

Conceptual Rationale for the Approach to Service Delivery

With increasing evidence from genetic and neuroscience research in the past decade, psychiatric disorders have come to be accepted as biologically based diseases that require medical interventions. However, in conjunction with these findings there has also come the recognition that psychological, social, and environmental stressors exacerbate a biological predisposition to the illness. Vulnerability models of severe psychiatric disorders integrate the biological and psychosocial factors. These vulnerability models incorporate various factors that are considered to play a central role in explaining adult psychopathology, such as stressors, psychosocial factors, or neurochemical factors (Nicholson & Neufeld, 1992; Zubin & Spring, 1977). These models explain the presence or absence of clinical symptoms as an interrelationship among three sets of factors: "inborn, often genetic, non-symptomatic predispositions or vulnerabilities; those environmental or biological stressors that may convert the latent vulnerability into overt symptoms; and those protective factors in the person, family, and community that counteract or compensate for the tendency to develop symptoms" (Wynne, 1991, p. 164). These models employ a biopsychosocial perspective that explains the onset, course, and outcome of serious mental illness as a complex interaction of biological, psychological, and environmental factors. Consequently, psychosocial interventions have been developed to complement the use of psychopharmacological agents. These psychosocial interventions serve to enhance protective factors against the recurrence, impairments, and disabilities of the disorders.

The vulnerability-stress-coping-competency model is the conceptual basis for psychiatric rehabilitation services. In this particular model, psychobiological vulnerabilities and socioenvironmental stressors are moderated in their impact on the disability or impairment by protective factors in the family, person, or community, such as social supports or psychiatric medication. Paramount among these protective factors are the coping and competencies employed by psychiatrically disabled individuals as well as others in their social environment, such as families, natural support systems, and service providers, to deal with these stressful situations. In psychiatric rehabilitation, coping and competencies are considered attributes of both the individuals themselves and their social environments. Psychiatric rehabilitation aims to habilitate and/or rehabilitate these individuals to the highest level of functioning of which they are capable with the least amount of professional assistance. In practice, psychiatric rehabilitation comprises two intervention strategies: (1) social and functional skill development, and (2) environmental resource development (Anthony & Liberman, 1986). A similar approach is the stress-coping-adaptation framework, which focuses on the need for services to enhance the individuals' coping skills in order to improve their behavioral and psychological adaptation to their illness (Hatfield, 1987). This model has been used in teaching coping strategies for this population as well as in educating their families, since the illness has a devastating and significant impact on the ill person's relatives and significant others (Solomon, 1996).

Although medication has been found to be effective in the treatment of these disorders, there has been increasing recognition of the inadequacy of traditional mental health services in providing for the total needs of this population (Hall & Mark, 1995; Lehman, Thompson, Dixon, & Scott, 1995). This limitation, coupled with the community mental health ideology that services need to be accessible, comprehensive, and coordinated, precipitated the development of the Community Support Program (CSP) at the National Institute of Mental Health (NIMH). This program developed the community support system (CSS) concept, which acknowledged that individuals with severe psychiatric disorders require a range of basic community services, specialized mental health services, and supports to function in the community at the highest possible levels (Stroul, 1993; Turner & TenHoor, 1978). Due to the diversity of functioning levels, disabilities, and sociodemographic characteristics of the severely mentally ill population and to the cyclical nature of the disorders, a broad range of services and support resources is essential to enhance their functioning and protect them from impairment and disability. At the same time, services need to ensure the safety and rights of these vulnerable individuals and to protect the community from potentially dangerous behavior due to the illness. The CSS concept delineates an array of service components to achieve these objectives, including ten essential service elements: client identification and outreach; mental health treatment; crisis response services; health and dental care; housing; income supports and entitlements; peer, family, and community supports; rehabilitation services; protection and advocacy; and case management. In other words, CSS is a model system of care for individuals with severe psychiatric disorders that contains all the essential service elements necessary to increase clients' coping behaviors and competency skills to handle socioenvironmental stressors and psychobiological vulnerability.

Case management serves as the coordinating function for the system (Stroul, 1993). It emerged as a means to compensate for the fragmentation and lack of coordination of the service system that became apparent when the mentally ill population was deinstitutionalized and evolved in response to severely mentally ill individuals' need for help in navigating a maze of organizations and delivery systems. The deinstitutionalized population, which frequently had cognitive deficits resulting from neurobiological dysfunction, was incapable of accessing this diversity of resources without assistance (Lurie, 1978; Ozarin, 1978).

The primary values of the rehabilitation and the CSP service approaches are community based to minimize disruption in recipients' lives and to include their natural support resources. The assumption is that this in situ location enhances the application of newly developed skills and increases the likelihood of clients' integration into the community. Services need to be client centered, flexible, coordinated, and personalized and to build on each individual's strengths (Stroul, 1986, 1993).

The Instigator of Current Innovations

Many of the current service innovations for this population have their roots in an innovation that was developed more than two decades ago in Madison, Wisconsin. The conceptualization of the Training in Community Living (TLC), or the Program in Assertive Community Treatment (PACT), as it later came to be called, was consistent with the rehabilitation and the CSP orientations (Stein, 1992; Stein & Test, 1980; Stroul, 1986). This program evolved from other home-based psychiatric services, such as the delivery of care by public health nurses (Stein, 1992). This model program was developed as an alternative to hospitalization. It was a comprehensive array of services that essentially transferred all the functions of the hospital to the community. The goals were to prevent unnecessary hospitalization and to develop community living skills. This program still exists and maintains its original intent.

PACT is an around-the-clock service program that is delivered by a multidisciplinary team with high staff-to-client ratios; this team is the core of the service. Individualized plans are developed based on the client's "coping-skill deficits and requirements for community living" (Stein, 1992, p. 5). The services are delivered in vivo, in clients' homes, places of work, and neighborhoods. Skills are taught to clients in the environment where they are to be applied. Assertive outreach is employed whereby clients who do not show for work or appointments are visited by staff to assist with any problem that is interfering. This approach to the provision of care increases the likelihood of keeping clients engaged with services (Stroul, 1986). In vivo service delivery accommodates the difficulty these clients have generalizing skills from a learning environment to the setting in which the skills will be used. Support for significant members of clients' social networks, including families, landlords, and community members, complements in vivo services. Medication is administered by the team psychiatrist and the medical status of clients is monitored (Stein, 1992).

In the development of this innovation, supporters faced a number of barriers because the program was under the auspices of a public psychiatric hospital. Hospital administrators were concerned about releasing staff from clinical responsibilities while they were being trained in this model of care. Concerns were also raised regarding the hospital's liability for staff transporting clients in their own cars. Administrators questioned how they could be sure staff were actually working when they were in the community and out of contact. Furthermore, staff were to be involved in unconventional activities for which they were to be paid, such as using a lunch stop in a restaurant with clients as an opportunity to teach them social skills. The innovators had to be clinically judicious, for at the time of the program's inception, community-based treatment of individuals with severe psychiatric disorders who were eligible for hospital admission was extremely controversial. The innovators were aware that all it would take was one tragedy for the program to be discontinued (Stein, 1992). The research innovators were able to obtain agreement of the hospital administration to institute the pilot program through their own "persistence, negotiation efforts, and good will" (Stein, 1992, p. 5). The administrators were reassured that the liability issue would be handled and that the team would be well supervised.

The innovators anticipated that they would encounter barriers to the dissemination of this model. The mental health community would be skeptical of the program's success, especially if this assessment was based on anecdotal evidence. Consequently, they evaluated the program with a rigorous randomized research design. Included in the research was a cost-benefit analysis, since increased cost would inevitably be raised as a concern. Family and community burden (e.g., arrests, emergency room use) were assessed, since high utilization of community facilities was already being raised as evidence of the inadequate preparation of communities to incorporate those mentally ill adults already deinstitutionalized (Stein, 1992).

The results of studies of the original PACT and its replications in Australia and Michigan found a decrease in clients' rate of hospitalization, as well as some improvement in their social adjustment and quality of life when compared to clients treated with hospitalization plus standard aftercare (Hoult et al., 1983; Mulder, 1982; Stein & Test, 1980). Furthermore, although the direct costs for this service were greater than those for the usual care, these costs were offset by increased benefits, particularly compensation from productive work (Hoult et al., 1983; Weisbrod et al., 1980). Another benefit of the program was that families were satisfied with the service, and there was no increase in their perceived burden. There was no difference in clients' rates of arrest or emergency room usage compared with those for clients who received standard care (Hoult et al., 1983; Test & Stein, 1980).

Given the program's consistency with CSP philosophy and its determined effectiveness, this model was widely disseminated by the CSP. In addition, the innovators themselves put much effort into disseminating and providing training in this new model. Even so, it took more than two decades for the model to become generally accepted. Former and current staff continue to provide training, often using the modified model, which is discussed in the next section.

The Adaptation: Assertive Community Treatment

From this initial innovation has derived a host of programs entitled Assertive Community Treatment (ACT), or in some instances Continuous Treatment Teams. The latter name has come to be employed because the teams are designed to provide continuity of care across the full range of times and settings that clients require (Drake, Teague, & Warren, 1990). An adaptation of the model was made necessary by the cost and staffing requirements of the original program, as well as the difficulty of implementing such a comprehensive intervention. These modified programs maintain many of the central elements of the original program, including a multidisciplinary team that delivers a full range of medical, psychosocial, and rehabilitation services, with emergency service availability. The team usually comprises a psychiatrist, a nurse, and case managers; generally, the staff-to-client ratio is 1 to 10 to 1 to 12. (Often the psychiatrists are available for only a limited number of hours per week.) The in vivo approach to the delivery of service also continues (Solomon, 1992; Solomon & Meyerson, 1997). Some variations of this model give more emphasis to brokering community resources, with the case manager functioning as an assertive resource coordinator (Test, 1992). Small caseloads and around-the-clock availability are primary elements of this approach, as is assertive outreach to keep clients engaged in the treatment system. These services are often reserved for the most severe of the mentally ill population, as indicated by high rates of psychiatric hospitalizations or treatment difficulties, common in, for example, the dually diagnosed or the homeless populations. Some programs have formed teams for serving special populations, such as forensic clients (Solomon & Draine, 1995a, 1995b). Like its parent, the goals of ACT remain focused on preventing hospitalization and improving the community adjustment and the quality of life of the clients.

Since this service is offered at the point of hospital discharge or to those already in the community, the issue is not hospitalization versus community care.

The concern is whether these more intensive services are cost-effective in comparison to standard care. The advocates of ACT assert that money will be saved by reducing hospitalizations and that the service will improve clients' quality of life. Regardless of the demonstrated effectiveness of PACT, the transferability of the program has been questioned, given the problems of exportating model programs generally (Bachrach, 1988; Thompson, Griffith, & Leaf, 1990). A model program that is effective in a small size city like Madison, Wisconsin, may not be effective in large urban areas or in rural ones. But without viable alternatives in the context of the spiraling costs of serving difficult clients, systems have an incentive to establish ACT teams. A number of states, including Delaware and Michigan, have established such teams. Moreover, the program has intuitive appeal, since it contains many of the service elements that are clinically observed to be essential in serving this population.

From extensive research that has been conducted on ACT programs, the ACT teams have been found to be effective in reducing hospitalization and in increasing rates of retention in community-based mental health services, whereas the psychosocial and clinical outcomes have been inconsistent and moderate at best (Bond, McGrew, & Fekete, 1995; Rapp, 1995; Scott & Dixon, 1995; Solomon, 1992). Consistent with a reduction in the length of hospitalization is improvement in housing stability (Mueser et al., 1998).

Furthermore, the research indicates that improved quality of life is often related to changes in hospitalization and housing stability (Mueser et al., 1998). The ACT results have not been very promising with regard to reducing time in jail or number of arrests (Solomon & Draine, 1995b). Although some controlled studies of ACT teams have found reductions in symptoms, most have not found statistically significant reductions (Mueser et al., 1998). The limited research that has been conducted on medication compliance has found mixed results, with two studies demonstrating improvement (Bush et al., 1990; Stein & Test, 1980), and three no change (Bond et al., 1988; Chandler et al., 1996; Solomon & Draine, 1995b). Similarly, studies that have assessed substance abuse among clients served by ACT teams have found no significant improvement in this area (Mueser et al., 1998). Only a few studies have found significant beneficial effects of the ACT program on social functioning in terms of social relationships, role function, and social support networks (Marks et al., 1994; Mulder, 1982; Test & Stein, 1980). Positive effects for vocational outcomes have been found when there has been a heavy investment in vocational interventions (Chandler et al., 1996; Test, 1992).

Although there has been no research on dismantling ACT programs to determine the effective program ingredients, there has been research on critical components of ACT as assessed by experts in the field (McGrew & Bond, 1995). Use of a team structure with shared planning and service provision, a client focus, assertive outreach, small client-staff ratio, 24-hour-7-day-a-week availability, and client involvement in treatment planning are among the 54 service and structural elements that experts of ACT programs considered to be critical for maintaining fidelity to the ACT conceptualization (McGrew & Bond,

1995). Research has found that positive outcomes of ACT have been linked to greater fidelity to the major components of the model (McGrew et al., 1994).

Research to date has found that when ACT case management is well designed, there is a cost savings. Cost savings are tied to greater fidelity to the ACT model (Bond, 1984; Bond et al., 1988). Much of these savings is attributed to reductions in hospital use (Mueser et al., 1998; Rapp, 1995). When highly structured residential programs were substituted for a reduction in hospital use, there was no cost savings for ACT (Borland et al., 1989). Consequently, when ACT programs serve the most severely disturbed clients who are the most frequent users of hospitals, the greatest cost savings occur. Mueser and his colleagues (1998) note that there is no inherent reason for community-based services to be less costly than hospital care, but these savings reflect the reimbursement procedures to hospitals in this country. However, with reforms in health care that emphasize community-based care over hospitalization, ACT programs may have a more difficult time demonstrating cost savings.

ENHANCED ACT MODELS

A number of variants of the ACT model have emerged that are focused on treating special subpopulations of those with severe psychiatric disorders or directed at specific goals for the population, such as increasing vocational outcomes. The evolution of these enhanced models was necessitated by the increasing recognition that the ACT models were not effective in improving some specific client problems, such as substance abuse. Consequently, mental health experts concluded that special efforts to address these specific problems might enhance ACT's effectiveness in achieving the desired outcomes. Given the multiplicity of needs of individuals with severe mental illness, evidence supports the necessity to provide integrated services from a diversity of perspectives and disciplines. These specialized programs employ the ACT team as a centerpiece, retaining major service elements of PACT, such as assertive outreach, in vivo treatment, a team approach, low client-to-staff ratios and 24-hour responsibility for a specified group of clients, in addition to a particular service component. Enhanced ACT programs have been developed for the dually diagnosed clients, and others have been ill directed at designated objectives, such as improved vocational outcomes and improved coping of family members.

One such enhanced ACT program, the New Hampshire program, treats the dually diagnosed substance abuse population (Drake & Noordsy, 1994). In this ACT-based program, team members focus on the integration of substance abuse and mental health services through the employment of a liaison between the two systems by cross-training clinicians in each system and by offering dual-diagnosis treatment groups (Drake, Teague, & Warren, 1990). Given that this subpopulation has a diversity of service needs that cut across a number of service delivery systems, compounded by the difficulty in engaging these clients in treatment, it was expected that assertive outreach with case management would be effective.

Another area in which the outcomes of the ACT programs were not impressive was employment, a domain of importance if the severely mentally ill population is to be integrated into the community and improve their quality of life. Targeted efforts seemed warranted to achieve positive changes in vocational outcomes. The ACT program was assumed to be a potentially effective approach, since this population requires in vivo concrete assistance in carrying out job tasks (Simmons, Selleck, Steele, & Sepetauc, 1993). This treatment orientation is consistent with supported employment, the prevailing approach to the delivery of vocational rehabilitation services for this population. Supported employment requires the integration of clients in competitive job positions with professional supports both on and off the job site (Solomon & Meyerson, 1997). This approach was developed in response to the ineffectiveness of previous vocational approaches that used segregated settings, such as job enclaves, sheltered workshops, and Fairweather Lodges. Supported employment also shifted from the train-and-place orientation, with its long prevocational training, which clients frequently found discouraging, to a place-and-train orientation. One model that has been implemented has been to add an employment specialist to an ACT team. The ACT team members provide the clinical services, and the employment specialist handles all the vocational activities. This program model has been entitled Individual Placement and Support (IPS) (Drake, McHugo, Becker et al., 1996).

Another extension of the ACT is the provision of services to families. One approach, entitled Family-Aided Assertive Community Treatment (FACT), adds the multifamily group program to the array of ACT services. This innovation is a blend of two independent interventions, ACT and Multifamily Group Therapy. Multifamily Group Therapy is one of a number of family pscyhoeducational interventions that have been adjunctive to clinical treatment of seriously mentally ill individuals that offers support, training, and education for family members. These programs acknowledge the stresses and burdens of families and their needs for coping skills to improve their quality of life and that of their relative (Solomon, 1996). The operating principles of ACT are retained in FACT, with the exception of a more gradually paced recovery concept that is derived from family psychoeducation. These groups, led by clinicians, are used to educate the families about diagnosis, course, and treatment of severe mental illness and methods for coping with the disorder. The groups function as forums for families to discuss their current problems concerning their ill relative and to engage in group problem solving and to obtain affective support from others who share similar problems, as well as from the clinicians (McFarlane, Dushay, Stastny et al., 1996).

In another approach, crisis family intervention is provided to the family. In this intervention, the team coordinates with the family during a crisis with their ill relative. This orientation to the family differs from the assumptions of the original PACT, which emphasized "constructive separation" of the client from the family. This separation was based on the premise that crisis resolution would be hindered if ill relatives interacted with their families. A number of research studies have demonstrated that collaboration with families of severely mentally ill clients produced beneficial outcomes for both the family and the client which precipitated the change in intervention (McFarlane, Dushay, Stastny et al., 1996). Another innovation has been the inclusion of a family member as additional team member to work with clients' families to educate them about the illness, provide support, and teach them coping skills (Dixon, Krauss, Kernan et al., 1995).

The motivation for each of these enhancements was that these service components or elements would improve the targeted behaviors to a greater extent than ACT alone could. The limited research to date has demonstrated this hypothesis to be generally supported (Drake, McHugo, Becker, Anthony, & Clarke, 1996; Drake, McHugo, & Noordsy, 1993; McFarlane et al., 1996). For example, the IPS model was compared to a prevocational training and brokered vocational placement. Results showed that clients in the IPS program were more likely to be competitively employed during most of the 18-month follow-up period. In addition, IPS clients who were employed worked more hours and earned more wages during follow-up. Regarding nonvocational outcomes, there were no differences between the groups (Drake, McHugo, Becker et al., 1996). Similarly, a pilot study of the New Hampshire Program found that almost two-thirds of those served achieved stable remission from alcoholism (Drake, McHugo, & Noordsy, 1993; Drake, Teague, & Warren, 1990). In a comparison of the two enhanced family interventions, McFarlane and his associates (1996) found significant reductions in rehospitalizations and symptom levels and increased participation in treatment for the family-enhanced models over the basic ACT. Families also reported a reduction in both objective and subjective burden, but otherwise there were few significant differences between the approaches.

ACT CONSUMER TEAM

One of the recent trends in the delivery of mental health services to those with severe psychiatric disorders has been services operated and delivered by consumers of mental health services themselves. The assumption is that consumers who have shared common experiences may be more empathetic and understanding of the service needs of clients and, consequently, more effective in both service engagement and provision. This approach is considered to be potentially effective with specific subpopulations such as the homeless, who may be distrustful of providers and whose culture is quite alien from that of the typical providers. In some cases, consumers have been added as members of ACT teams (Dixon, Krauss, & Lehman, 1994). In other cases the team has been completely made up of consumers. The relative efficacy of these models is yet to be tested (Paulson, 1993), although some research has been done on consumers who deliver intensive case management services. This service has been found to be as effective as the service delivered by nonconsumers (Solomon & Draine, 1995c, 1995d). There is still a great deal of resistance to having consumers deliver services because of concerns regarding their stability as well as their lack of professional training. Consequently, these services are not extensively employed.

Case Management in Practice

ACT models are in relatively widespread practice for difficult-to-serve subpopulations of those with severe psychiatric disorders. The enhanced models have largely been reserved for research service demonstration projects and are in limited general use. In actual practice, however, a number of elements of these programs, which have emerged from research interventions, have been incorporated into widespread use in serving those with severe mental disorders. Intensive case management, which incorporates a number of the features of these innovative programs, has become a common approach to serving this population. However, there is widespread variability in the characteristics of these programs (i.e., caseload size, focus on reducing hospitalization) (Scott & Dixon, 1995). These features, based on clinical experience, seem to be significant factors in producing positive client outcomes and include in vivo service delivery, 24-hour availability, assertive outreach, service coordination, high staff-to-client ratios, and continuous care with no defined termination. Intensive case management retains these aspects of ACT. Intensive case management is more appealing to administrators than the ACT model, since it seems to be less costly and is easier to implement. Intensive case managers function independently rather than as members of a team. Consequently, this approach does not require reorganization of staff, more intensive time commitment of psychiatrists and nurses (who are more costly than case managers), and daily meetings, all of which are employed in ACT programs. Case managers tend to be resistant to the shared caseload aspect of ACT teams; they prefer serving their own clients. Service providers articulate this opposition by stating that individuals with severe mental illness have difficulties in establishing relationships, and the shared caseload approach limits the client's ability to establish a therapeutic alliance with the service provider because of the need to relate to a number of individuals rather than an individual worker. Given these concerns and resistances, intensive case management is more appealing than ACT to implement on a large-scale basis.

Intensive case management relies heavily on the service environment for needed resources and services, resulting in less integration of services than is found in ACT. Since the service is dependent on the service environment, intensive case management is only as effective as the availability of resources in the community. This has engendered concern that case managers are being asked to fix an inadequate system with inappropriate resources and with limited or no authority to change the system (Stein, 1992b). While there is some evidence that intensive case management programs are effective in reducing hospitalizations and increasing service use, these programs have limited effect in producing positive clinical and social adjustment outcomes (Scott & Dixon, 1995). Some studies have found reductions in the number of hospitalizations and length of hospitalizations, while others have found no statistically significant differences. Intensive case management has had relatively poor outcomes for symptom reductions and improvements in treatment compliance but more promising outcomes in the area of instrumental role functioning (Scott & Dixon, 1995). Focusing on a specific objective seems to improve the likelihood of achieving that particular objective (Chamberlain & Rapp, 1991).

The broker model of case management, which is predominately office-based and primarily links clients to required services, is still in widespread use. The broker model is perceived as less costly than intensive case management, since caseloads are extremely high, in some instances as high as 100 or more clients per staff person. However, the research defies this assumption regarding cost; this approach tends to lead to a high rate of hospitalizations, which is a very costly service (Franklin, Solovitz, Mason et al., 1987). Intensive case management is comparable to traditional case work. It is also a more comfortable means of functioning for those mental health professionals who are used to a counseling modality of treatment, rather than a home-based service approach. But since much of the intensive case management service involves coordinating service and offering assistance in learning to carry out activities of daily living in the community, activities that more educated and trained staff, such as social workers, tend to be less interested in and somewhat resistant to, less educated staff can be employed in these positions, lowering cost. However, case management cannot be delivered without some provision of supportive counseling; consequently, clinical skills are critical for effective case management, regardless of the model employed.

These more intensive case management services have come into widespread use due to the passage of the rehabilitation option (which enables payment to psychiatric rehabilitation services) under Medicaid, which enabled these services to be reimbursed. This funding mechanism provided an incentive to shift to more intensive modalities. In addition, the passage of Public Law 99-660 in 1986 required submission of state plans detailing plans for the implementation of a total case management system by 1992 for those with serious mental illness who receive a substantial amount of public funds. This further encouraged the development of more intensive case management services (Kennedy, 1990). Intensive case management is a personalized approach to planning and delivery of services that is responsive to individual needs and incorporates cultural sensitivity in the delivery of services. Although traditional broker case management is still a dominant modality by which many adults with serious mental illness are being served, intensive case management and ACT programs are becoming more widespread. Limited funds and concerns regarding controlling costs in serving this population has resulted in a shift from clinic-based rehabilitation-oriented services such as day treatment and partial hospitalization programs to the pervasive use of case management.

The 99-660 legislation also required a plan for serving the homeless population with severe mental illness. Intensive case management is the most common method for serving this subpopulation, given their characteristics. The assertive outreach component of both intensive case management and ACT engages these individuals in the service system, and service coordination addresses the multiplicity of their problems, which requires a diversity of service systems.

In current practice, there are a few other case management models, such as clinical, rehabilitation, and strengths, but they have been researched only to a limited extent. Consequently, results concerning these models are inconclusive (Mueser et al., 1998; Scott & Dixon, 1995). Moreover, the features of the ACT model that are retained in intensive case management are generally incorporated within these models as well.

In summary, the major service elements of the original PACT and its subsequent adaptation ACT have been widely diffused among systems that serve individuals with major psychiatric disorders. Service policies for this population also frequently include a no-reject policy and have no time limit on the provision of care (although managed care is beginning to erode this), as both clinical experience and recent research has demonstrated their importance. These factors have provided evidence that the most severe of this population can benefit from intensive case management services and that, once the service is discontinued, the gains that have been made dissipate (Mueser et al., 1998). Specialized services that are promoted for this population are frequently folded into intensive case management services. For example, supported employment, by its very nature of being an in vivo service, is consistent with the primary service elements of ACT. In the provision of supported employment, the employment specialist needs to assist clients with other aspects of their lives, such as appropriate housing and health benefits, since problems in these other realms of clients' life interfere with their successful performance on the job. The original PACT program included sheltered work as a service component, but in recent years it too has moved to the provision of supported employment.

Supported housing is another service innovation promoted in the provision of care with this population (Carling, 1993). Supported housing includes in vivo supports that a person needs for maintaining independent community living in permanent housing. The degree of supports is contingent on consumer choice and need. This approach to housing is promoted in order to increase client independence, normalization, and social integration into the community, in contrast to group homes and halfway houses, which frequently increase dependency and social isolation by having clients' living arrangements be part of the mental health system. Like employment specialists, housing specialists recognize that accomplishing the objectives of clients' maintaining permanent, independent housing means assisting them in all aspects of their lives where there are problems. If these problems are left unaddressed, they may interfere with clients' retaining independent living. Again, this is a personalized approach that provides in vivo learning and 24-hour available supports with the focus on stability of independent housing.

Implications for Practice, Service Delivery, Policy, Education, and Research

Research and practice experience demonstrate that individuals with severe psychiatric disorders need at a minimum a core service component that includes the major features of ACT, such as have been implemented in intensive case management, to be effectively served. If services target specific behaviors or problems of this population without offering an integrated approach to service delivery that addresses other problems in a client's life, these other problems will impinge on the targeted behavior, resulting in limited positive change. However, there is a concern as to whether ACT and intensive case management fosters dependency through the provision of direct assistance in meeting the daily living needs of clients (Estroff, 1981). If the goal is to increase client self-sufficiency, there may need to be a greater emphasis on teaching clients social skills in order to reduce their dependency on assistance from a case manager (Mueser et al., 1998). Social skills training, cognitive rehabilitation, and other promising approaches to working with this client population may need to be considered for incorporation into intensive case management services and ACT programs (Penn & Mueser, 1996).

More attention needs to be paid to the qualifications of those delivering these services; often case managers are not professionally trained individuals (Solomon & Meyerson, 1997). In an ACT program this deficiency can be compensated for by other team members, but in intensive case management this is not the situation. More in-service clinical training is required for intensive case managers, but more clinical supervision and consultation are also essential. Effective case management cannot be delivered devoid of clinical care. For these services to be truly integrated, case managers need to have an in-depth understanding of the disorders and the medications in current use. Also, training in the functioning of interdisciplinary teams needs to be included in professional educational programs for those disciplines expected to work with this client population, which includes psychiatry, psychology, social work, and nursing. The inclusion of service enhancements requires more specially trained personnel. Training in cultural and ethnic competency is necessary to ensure that services are sensitive and responsive to all ethnic and racial groups. There are also newly emerging areas of concern for this population that will require possible incorporation of specialized services within case management, including treatment for trauma from sexual abuse, which recently has been noted as prevalent in this population (Harris, 1996).

It is yet unknown how the increasing emphasis on managed care in mental health will affect the treatment of individuals with severe and persistent psychiatric disorders generally and the current modes of service delivery for this population specifically. The emphasis on the formation of behavioral health care organizations does have the potential for integrating mental health and substance abuse services (Osher, 1996). If mental health or behavioral health care (which includes both mental health and substance abuse) is carved out from overall health benefits for those with severe disorders, allowing these services to remain under the auspice of local or state governments, it is likely that the way services are currently delivered for this population will not greatly change in the near future. If, however, they are provided by physical health care organizations and for-profit entities, it is likely that intensive case management will revert to a brokered model with a major emphasis on linkage, which was the pervasive model prior to CSP-based innovations. The emphasis of case management will be on cost control to the possible detriment of efforts to improve the quality of life of this population, for case management within managed care refers to resource control in order to contain costs (Mandersheid & Henderson, 1995). Case managers in managed care settings may have little, if any, direct contact with the clients whom they are "managing." Managed care, however, does have the potential of improving the quality of care for this population, given the focus on outcome measurement and the documentation of the efficacy of services. However, "case management must be defined as a clear clinical protocol that is replicable across a broad array of practice settings. Such operational definitions are necessary if case management is to have credibility within a managed care arrangement" (Mandersheid & Henderson, 1995, p. 9). In addition, "the field must be able to arrive at an annual cost for providing different levels of case management intensity" (Mandersheid & Henderson, 1995, p. 11).

The research to date on these service innovations offers future directions for further improvement. The clinical outcomes of these program have been modest at best. This may be attributed to the fact that the population frequently served by ACT programs includes those with severe psychiatric disorder who are most impaired but who are often symptomatically stable at program entrance. Consequently, further symptom reduction may not be feasible with this population. Detecting symptom change is further compounded by the difficulties in measuring symptoms and the variability of assessment tools used in the studies that have been undertaken (Mueser et al., 1998). There is some possibility that the enhanced innovations that focus on specific behaviors or problems may help to address clients' social functioning and symptomatic behaviors. However, there needs to be much more research in the enhancement aspects of these innovations. Also, research is required to begin to tease out the potent elements or critical ingredients in these services, identifying which service elements are effective for whom, under what circumstances. For example, questions remain unanswered concerning whether the effectiveness of the original PACT program is due to increased medication compliance. These research efforts will be able to assist in the development of protocols and outcome measures to assess the cost-effectiveness of services that are critical for managed care. Future research needs to focus on the type of qualifications and skills that are necessary for producing positive outcomes for the clients.

Families have been relatively satisfied with these innovative case management programs, in which services are often delivered in vivo. Consequently, families have frequently advocated for the expansion of ACT programs as well as intensive case management (Solomon, 1994). Prior to the establishment of these intensive models of case management, families were de facto case managers for their relatives (Intagliata, Willer, & Egri, 1986). Family advocates form a powerful lobby for effective services for their relatives. They will no doubt continue to promote further improvements in case management in order to ensure a better quality of life for themselves and their relatives.

Consumers have also advocated for and supported service innovations like intensive case management, which provides an infrastructure for competitive employment and independent living. They are opposed to services that maintain their social isolation and force them into programs that they feel do not meet their needs. They are resistant to procrustean programs that are not personalized. But a minority of seriously mentally ill individuals continue to resist ACT programs and intensive case management, as they do not like being perceived as a "case" and do not wish to be overly monitored and managed. A few have gone as far as taking out restraining orders against their case managers to stop them from being so intrusive. Efforts that focus on making the programs appealing to a wider diversity of clients are imperative.

Legislation such as 99-660 and Medicaid rehabilitation options (billable service option that can be covered by Medicaid dollars) have directly promoted intensive case management, but other legislation has been a precipitant, as well. For example, the Americans with Disability Act (ADA) and the Rehabilitation Act and its amendments have been an impetus for the provision of services, such as supported employment, that are consistent with intensive case management. It is unclear at this time whether new legislation will continue to promote case management in its current form or reform it to emphasize controlling costs of services.

Severe mental illness and its attendant problems of homelessness, substance abuse, and criminal activity are visible public health concerns. Just as in the past, when communities advocated for changes in service delivery for this population and helped to instigate the current service innovations, there is little doubt that communities will continue to advocate for an effective response from the mental health community.

Conclusion

Over the past two decades, case management has clearly emerged as the underlying concept of treatment for those with severe mental illness (Pescosolido, Wright, & Sullivan, 1995). Case management has been promoted as one of the primary means to achieving service integration without making major structural changes in the service delivery system. Case management did not evolve in a direct linear fashion from the PACT program, but this successful program offered a guidepost for the delivery of integrated services for those with severe mental illness. Development of supported housing and supported employment were precipitated by a number of factors, including a change in philosophy and beliefs regarding the capabilities of this population and the requisite service elements necessary for the treatment of these clients, as well as evidence of the lack of success of prior program models, such as sheltered workshops. These newer service innovations have heavily borrowed from the initial PACT innovation. These ACT models put the burden of service integration on case managers who often don't have the training, expertise, or power to make the necessary system reforms. At some point more structural changes may need to take place on the systems level. Possibly managed care may offer us this opportunity.

The original PACT model continues to evolve, as is evident by recent enhancements to the ACT model. Given its intuitive appeal to practitioners, ACT seems to be the centerpiece of newly developed models of care for adults with severe mental illness. For example, as existing treatments and services that have been found to be effective with other populations are thought to have potential for those with severe mental illness, it seems that these treatments, such as cognitive therapy, are considered for incorporation as enhancements to the ACT model. Similarly, as the need for specialized services for designated subpopulations of adults with severe mental illness are promoted, initial efforts are to enhance or modify ACT programs. At the same time, with an emphasis on cost containment, more stripped-down versions such as intensive case management are proliferating. Regardless of the direction that case management takes, it continues to evolve, enhanced or bare bones. The paths seem to either borrow or to emanate from this original service innovation, which was a response to the deinstitutionalization policy of more than three decades ago. The PACT service innovation has had a long-lasting impact; however, future modifications and its ability to survive within managed care are yet to be determined.

REFERENCES

Adebimpe, V. (1994). Race, racism and epidemiological surveys. *Hospital and Community Psychiatry, 45,* 27–31.

Anthony, W., Cohen, M., & Vitalo, R. (1978). The measurement of rehabilitation outcome. *Schizophrenia Bulletin, 4,* 365–383.

Anthony, W., & Jansen, M. (1984). Predicting the vocational capacity of the chronically mentally ill: Research and policy implications. *American Psychologist, 39,* 537–544.

Anthony, W., & Liberman, R. (1986). The practice of psychiatric rehabilitation: Historical, conceptual and research base. *Schizophrenia Bulletin, 12,* 542–559.

Attkisson, C., Cook, J., & Karno, M., et al. (1992). Clinical services research. *Schizophrenia Bulletin, 18,* 561–626.

Bachrach, L. (1988). On exporting and importing model programs. *Hospital and Community Psychiatry, 39,* 411–418.

Bond, G. (1984). An economic analysis of psychosocial rehabilitation. *Hospital and Community Psychiatry, 35,* 356–362.

Bond, G., McGrew, J., & Fekete, D. (1995). Assertive outreach for frequent users of psychiatric hospital: A meta-analysis. *Journal of Mental Health Administration, 22,* 4–16.

Bond, G., Miller, L., Krumwied, R., & Ward, R. (1988). Assertive case management in three CMHCs: A controlled study. *Hospital and Community Psychiatry, 39,* 411–418.

Borland, A., McRae, J., & Lycan, C. (1989). Outcomes of five years of continuous intensive case management. *Hospital and Community Psychiatry, 40,* 369–376.

Bush, C., Langford, M., Rosen, P., & Gott, W. (1990). Operation outreach: Intensive case management for severely psychiatrically disabled adults. *Hospital and Community Psychiatry, 41,* 647–649.

Carling, P. (1993). Supports and rehabilitation for housing and community living. In R. Flexer and P. Solomon (Eds.), *Psychiatric rehabilitation in practice* (pp. 99–118). Boston: Andover Medical Publishers.

Chamberlain, R., & Rapp, C. (1991). A decade of case management: A methodological review of outcome research. *Community Mental Health Journal, 27,* 171–188.

Chandler, D., Meisel, J., McGown, M., Minitz, J., & Madison, K. (1996). Client outcomes in two model capitated integrated agencies. *Psychiatric Services, 47,* 175–180.

Dixon, L., Krauss, N., Kernan, E., Lehman, A., & DeForge, B. (1995). Modifying the PACT model to serve homeless persons with severe mental illness. *Psychiatric Services, 46,* 684–688.

Dixon, L., Krauss, N., & Lehman, A. (1994). Consumers as service providers: The promise and challenge. *Community Mental Health Journal, 30,* 615–625.

Drake, R., McHugo, G., Becker, D., Anthony, W., & Clark, R. (1996). The New Hampshire Study of supported employment for people with severe mental illness. *Journal of Consulting and Clinical Psychology, 64.*

Drake, R., McHugo, D., & Noordsy, D. (1993). Treatment of alcoholism among schizophrenia outpatients: 4-year outcomes. *American Journal of Psychiatry, 150,* 328–29.

Drake, R., McLaughlin, P., Pepper, B., & Minkoff, K. (1991). Dual diagnosis of major mental illness and substance disorder: An overview. In K. Minkoff, & R. Drake (Eds.), *Dual diagnosis of major mental illness and substance disorder* (pp. 3–12). San Francisco: Jossey-Bass.

Drake, R., Mueser, K., Clark, R., & Wallach, M. (1996). The course, treatment, and outcome of substance disorder in persons with severe mental illness. *American Journal of Orthopsychiatry, 66,* 42–51.

Drake, R., & Noordsy, D. (1994). Case management for people with coexisting severe mental disorder and substance use disorder. *Psychiatric Annals, 24,* 427–431.

Drake, R., Teague, G., & Warren, S. R. (1990, June). Dual diagnosis: The New Hampshire program. *Addiction & Recovery,* 35–39.

Estroff, S. (1981). *Making it crazy: An ethnographic study of psychiatric clients in an American community.* Berkeley: University of California Press.

Franklin, J., Solowitz, B., Mason, M., Clemons, J., & Miller, G. (1987). An evaluation of case management. *American Journal of Public Health, 77,* 674–678.

Goldman, H. H., & Mandersheid, R. (1987). Epidemiology of chronic mental disorder. In W. W. Menninger & G. Hannah (Eds.), *The chronic mental patient/II* (pp. 41–63). Washington, DC: American Psychiatric Press.

Hall, L., & Mark, T. (1995). *The efficacy of schizophrenia treatment.* Arlington, VA: National Alliance for the Mentally Ill.

Harris, M. (1996). Treating sexual abuse trauma with dually diagnosed women. *Community Mental Health Journal, 32,* 371–385.

Hatfield, A. (1987). Coping and adaptation: A conceptual framework for understanding families. In A. Hatfield & H. Lefley (Eds.), *Families of the mentally ill* (pp. 60–84). New York: Guilford Press.

Hoult, J., Reynolds, I., Charbonneau-Powis, M., Weekes, P., & Briggs, J. (1983). Psychiatric hospital versus community treatment: The results of a randomised trial. *Australian and New Zealand Journal of Psychiatry, 17,* 160–167.

Intagliata, J., Willer, B., & Egri, G. (1986). Role of the family in case management of the mentally ill. *Schizophrenia Bulletin, 12,* 699–708.

Johnson, A., & Cnaan, R. (1995). Social work practice with homeless persons: State of the art. *Research on Social Work Practice, 5,* 340–382.

Jones, B., & Gray, B. (1986). Problems in diagnosing schizophrenia and affective disorders among blacks. *Hospital and Community Psychiatry, 37,* 61–65.

Kennedy, E. (1990). Community-based care for the mentally ill: Simple justice. *American Psychologist, 45,* 1238–1240.

Lawn, B., & Meyerson, A. (1993). A modern perspective on psychiatry in rehabilitation. In R. Flexer & P. Solomon (Eds.), *Psychiatric rehabilitation in practice* (pp. 31–43). Boston: Andover Medical Publishers.

Lehman, A., Thompson, Dixon, L., & Scott, J. (1995). Schizophrenia: Treatment outcomes research–editors' introduction. *Schizophrenia Bulletin, 21,* 561–566.

Lurie, N. (1978). Case management. In J. Talbott (Ed.), *The chronic patient* (pp 159–164). Washington, DC: American Psychiatric Association.

Mandersheid, R., & Henderson, M. (1995, Oct.). *Federal and state legislative and program direction for managed care: Implications for case management.* Rockville, MD: Center for Mental Health Services.

Marks, I., Connolly, J., Muijen, M., Audini, B., McNames, G., & Lawrence, R. (1994). Home-based versus hospital-based care for people with serious mental illness. *British Journal of Psychiatry, 165,* 179–194.

McFarland, B., Faulkner, L., Bloom, J., Hallaux, R., & Bray, J. (1989). Chronic mental illness and the criminal justice system. *Hospital and Community Psychiatry, 40,* 718–723.

McFarlane, W., Dushay, R., Stastny, P., Deakins, S., & Link, B. (1996). A comparison of two levels of family-aided assertive community treatment. *Psychiatric Services, 47,* 744–750.

McGrew, J., & Bond, G. (1995). Critical ingredients of Assertive Community Treatment: Judgments of experts. *Journal of Mental Health Administration, 22,* 113–125.

McGrew, J., Bond, G., Dietzen, L., & Salyers, M. (1994). Measuring the fidelity of implementation of a mental health program model. *Journal of Consulting and Clinical Psychology, 62,* 670–678.

Mueser, K., Bond, G., Drake, R., & Resnick, S. (1998). Models of community care for severe mental illness: A review of research on case management. *Schizophrenia Bulletin, 24,* 37–74.

Mueser, K., Yarnold, P., Levenson, D., & Singh, H., et al. (1990). Prevalence of substance abuse in schizophrenia: Demographic and clinical correlates. *Schizophrenia Bulletin, 16,* 31–56.

Mulder, R. (1982). *Evaluation of the Harbinger Program.* Unpublished manuscript.

Mulvey, E., Blumstein, A., & Cohen, J. (1986). Reframing the research question of mental patient criminality. *International Journal of Law and Psychiatry, 9,* 57–65.

Nicholson, I., & Neufeld, R. (1992). A dynamic vulnerability perspective on stress and schizophrenia. *American Journal of Orthopsychiatry, 62,* 117–129.

Osher, F. (1996). A vision for the future: Toward a service system responsive to those with co-occurring addictive and mental disorders. *American Journal of Orthopsychiatry, 66,* 71–76.

Osher, R., & Drake, R. (1996). Reversing a history of unmet needs: Approaches to care for persons with co-occurring addictive and mental disorders. *American Journal of Orthopsychiatry, 66,* 4–11.

Owen, C., Rutherford, V., Jones, M., et al. (1996). Housing accommodation preferences of people with psychiatric disabilities. *Psychiatric Services, 47,* 628–632.

Ozarin, L. (1978). The pros and cons of case management. In J. Talbott (Ed.), *The chronic patient* (pp. 165–170). Washington, DC: American Psychiatric Association.

Paulson, R. (1993). Comparing consumer and nonconsumer ACT team and usual care. SAMHSA Grant proposal.

Penn, D., & Mueser, K. (1996). Research on psychosocial treatment of schizophrenia. *American Journal of Psychiatry, 153,* 607–617.

Pescosolido, B., Wright, E., & Sullivan, W. (1995). Communities of care: A theoretical perspective on case management models in mental health. *Advances in Medical Sociology, 6,* 36–39.

Rapp, C. (1995). *The active ingredients of effective case management: A research synthesis.* NIMH/ National Association of Case Managers Forum.

Ridgway, P., & Zipple, A. (1990). The paradigm shift in residential services: From the linear continuum to supported housing approaches. *Psychosocial Rehabilitation Journal, 13,* 11–31.

Robins, L., & Regier, D. (Eds.). (1991). *Psychiatric disorders in America: The Epidemiologic Catchment Area study.* New York: Free Press.

Rubin, A. (1992). Is case management effective for people with serious mental illness? A research review. *Health & Social Work, 17*, 138–150.

Scott, J., & Dixon, L. (1995). Assertive community treatment and case management for schizophrenia. *Schizophrenia Bulletin, 21*, 657–668.

Simmons, T., Selleck, V., Steele, R., & Sepetauc, F. (1993). Supports and rehabilitation for employment. In R. Flexer & P. Solomon (Eds.), *Psychiatric rehabilitation in practice* (pp. 118–153). Boston: Andover Medical Publishers.

Solomon, P. (1992). The efficacy of case management services for severely mentally disabled clients. *Community Mental Health Journal, 28*, 163–180.

Solomon, P. (1994). Families' views of service delivery: An empirical assessment. In H. Lefley & M. Wasow (Eds.), *Helping families cope with mental illness* (pp. 259–274). Langhorne, PA: Harwood Academic Publishers.

Solomon, P. (1996). Moving from psychoeducation to family education of adults with serious mental illness. *Psychiatric Services, 47*, 1364–1370.

Solomon, P., & Draine, J. (1993). An assessment of gender as a factor among seriously mentally disabled case management clients. *Social Work in Health Care, 19*, 39–60.

Solomon, P., & Draine, J. (1995a). Issues in serving the forensic client. *Social Work, 40*, 25–33.

Solomon, P., & Draine, J. (1995b). One-year outcomes of a randomized trial of case management with seriously mentally ill clients leaving jail. *Evaluation Review, 19*, 256–273.

Solomon, P., & Draine, J. (1995c). One-year outcomes of a randomized trial of consumer case management. *Evaluation and Program Planning. 18*, 117–127.

Solomon, P., & Draine, J. (1995d). The efficacy of a consumer case management team: Two-year outcomes of a randomized trial. *Journal of Mental Health Administration, 22*, 135–146.

Solomon, P., & Meyerson, A. (1997). Social stabilization: Achieving satisfactory community adaptation for the disabled mentally ill. In A. Tasman, J. Kay, & J. Lieberman, (Eds.), *Psychiatry* (Vol. II). Orlando: W.B. Saunders.

Solomon, P., Rogers, R., Draine, J., & Meyerson, A. (1995). Interaction of the criminal justice system and psychiatric professional in which civil commitment standards are prohibitive. *Bulletin of the American Academy of Psychiatry and Law, 23*, 117–128.

Special Report. (1993). Health care reform for Americans with severe mental illness: Report of the National Advisory Mental Health Council. *American Journal of Psychiatry, 150*, 1447–1465.

Stein, L. (1992a). *Innovating against the current*, Research paper series 18. Madison, WI: Mental Health Research Center.

Stein, L. (1992b). On the abolishment of the case manager. *Health Affairs, 11*, 172–177.

Stein, L., & Test, M. A. (1980). Alternative to mental hospital treatment: I Conceptual model, treatment program, and clinical evaluation. *Archives of General Psychiatry, 37*, 392–397.

Steinwachs, D., Cullum, H., Dorwart, R., et al. (1992). Service systems research. *Schizophrenia Bulletin, 18*, 627–668.

Stroul, B. (1986). *Models of community support services: Approaches to helping persons with long-term mental illness*. Rockville, MD: Community Support Programs, NIMH.

Stroul, B. (1993). Rehabilitation in community support systems. In R. Flexer, & P. Solomon (Eds.), *Psychiatric rehabilitation in practice* (pp. 45–61). Boston: Andover Medical Publishers.

Test, M. A. (1992). Training in community living. In R. P. Liberman (Ed.), *Handbook of psychiatric rehabilitation* (pp. 153–170). New York: Macmillan.

Test, M. A., & Stein, L. I. (1980). Alternative to mental hospital treatment III: Social cost. *Archives of General Psychiatry, 37*, 409–412.

Test, M., Wallish, L., Allness, D., & Ripp, K. (1989). Substance use in young adults with schizophrenia disorders. *Schizophrenia Bulletin, 15*, 465–476.

Thompson, K., Griffith, E., & Leaf, P. (1990). A historical review of the Madison Model of community care. *Hospital and Community Psychiatry, 41*, 625–634.

Turner, J., & TenHoor, W. (1978). The NIMH Community Support program: Pilot approach to a needed social reform. *Schizophrenia Bulletin, 4*, 319–348.

Weisbrod, B., Test, M. A., & Stein, L. (1980). Alternative to mental hospital Treatment: II Economic benefit cost analysis. *Archives of General Psychiatry, 37*, 400–405.

Wynne, L. (1991). Systems consultation for psychosis: A biopsychosocial integration of systemic and psychoeducation approaches. In C. Eggers (Ed.), *Schizophrenia and youth: Etiology and therapeutic consequences* (pp. 158–168). Berlin: Springer-Verlag.

Zubin, J., & Spring, B. (1977). Vulnerability—a new view of schizophrenia. *Journal of Abnormal Psychology, 86*, 103–126.

8

Innovation in Mental Retardation Services

DAVID BRADDOCK

The dominant innovation in mental retardation services over the past 30 years has been the rapid growth of community services set against an equally dramatic decline in the utilization of large, state-operated residential institutions. Both the historic and the contemporary bases of this unprecedented transformation are the subject of this chapter. We begin with a discussion of the definition, etiology, and prevalence of mental retardation.

Overview of Retardation

Mental retardation refers to substantial limitations in present functioning. It is characterized by significantly subaverage intellectual functioning existing concurrently with related limitations in two or more of the following adaptive skills areas: communication, self-care, home living, social skills, community use, self-direction, health and safety, functional academics, leisure and work (American Association on Mental Retardation, 1992). The phrase "significantly subaverage intellectual functioning" is defined in terms of an IQ score of 70 to 75 or below, based on one or more individually administered tests of general intelligence. A key feature of the definition of mental retardation holds that the intellectual deficit in IQ must be accompanied by limitations in adaptive skills. The limitations in adaptive skills must be related to intellectual limitations, rather than to other factors such as cultural background.

The American Association on Mental Retardation (1992) has identified several criteria required to determine the presence of mental retardation. In addition to cultural issues, valid assessment must consider linguistic diversity and differences in communication and behavioral factors. Language spoken in the home and nonverbal communication and customs that might influence assessment results must be considered in making a valid assessment (Mercer,

The author wishes to gratefully acknowledge the assistance of the UIC doctoral students Susan Parish and Hye Jung Park and the research associates Richard Hemp and James Westrich in the preparation of this manuscript.

1973). In addition, limitations in adaptive skills must occur within the context of community environments typical of the individual's age peers. Community environments include homes, neighborhoods, schools, and businesses in which people ordinarily live, learn, work, and interact. Assessing adaptive skills also goes hand in hand with the analysis of an individual's support needs and of the environment's ability to provide such supports. Limitations in adaptive capabilities often coexist in the same individual with strengths in other adaptive skills or personal attributes. Frequently, people with mental retardation have personal strengths independent of their mental retardation. The strengths may be in social or physical capabilities or in one or more aspects of a specific adaptive skill area.

The notion of individualized supports is a key concept. With appropriate supports over a sustained period of time, the life functioning of individuals with mental retardation generally improves. "Appropriate supports" include an array of services, supportive individuals, and receptive settings that match an individual's needs. Individualized supports can be provided by the family, significant others, or service providers. The provision of appropriate and timely supports enhances adaptive functioning and successful community integration. Supports may be provided according to various levels of need—from intermittent (episodic) to pervasive (constant).

The assessment of mental retardation is referenced to the individual's chronological age and must manifest itself before the eighteenth birthday, the age when adult roles are typically assumed. It is important, however, to recognize that mental retardation is a culturally defined concept that is highly relative to the particular cultural environment in which an individual must function on a daily basis. In agrarian societies, for example, greater emphasis may be placed on physical capabilities than on purely intellectual ones. Literacy and quantitative skills are less necessary in these societies. Thus, knowledge of an individual's intellectual and adaptive capabilities and an understanding of the structure and expectations of his or her cultural environment are essential before "present functioning" can be evaluated and a diagnosis of mental retardation can be made.

ETIOLOGY

The cause of mental retardation is known in about 60–75% of cases of severe mental retardation (IQ below 50), and in about 38–55% of the cases of mild mental retardation (IQ 50–70), based on a review of thirteen studies (McLaren & Bryson, 1987). Etiology is divisible into prenatal, perinatal, and postnatal onset-causes. The most common prenatal cause of severe mental retardation is chromosomal disorders, the leading example of which is Down's syndrome. If nonsurvivors are included, 40% of severe mental retardation may be attributed to chromosomal and genetic disorders. Single-gene disorders, multifactorial/polygenic causes, and environmental factors such as the impact of drugs and alcohol on fetal development are also very prominent in the etiology of severe mental retardation. These factors collectively account for 20–30% of cases (McQueen, Spence, Winsor, Garner, & Pereira, 1986). Prenatal causes are much more common causes of severe mental retardation than perinatal and postnatal factors combined.

Perinatal factors, such as hypoxia, infections, or prematurity account for approximately 11% of cases of severe mental retardation. Studies of postnatal causes, such as trauma or neglect, have yielded inconsistent results. The most commonly reported prevalence rate for trauma/neglect is 3% of severe cases; however, rates varied from 1 to 13%, according to McLaren and Bryson (1987).

Chromosomal abnormalities account for substantially less mild than severe mental retardation (7% vs. up to 40%, respectively). Prenatal etiologies in general are less frequent causes of mild mental retardation, and multifactorial causes account for 11–23% of cases. Hypoxia during the perinatal period is an important factor in 19% of mild cases, according to a study by Hagberg, Hagberg, Lewerth, and Lundberg (1981a). Fifteen percent of persons with mild mental retardation experienced postnatal trauma or neglect.

Arbitrary separation of the causes of mental retardation into distinct biological and psychosocial or environmental categories is being replaced by a broader, multivariate biopsychosocial perspective. Most researchers investigating the causes of mental retardation have reported only what they considered to be the most plausible single etiology. Multiple causes may be present in as many as 50% of the cases of mental retardation (Coulter, 1996).

PREVALENCE

The prevalence of mental retardation in American society varies according to the method employed to ascertain prevalence rates (agency case registries vs. population screening), age (higher during the school years), and gender (higher in males). Estimates derived from total population screening have identified 0.7% and 0.55% of individuals in the general population as having severe and mild mental retardation, respectively. Prevalence figures identified from the analysis of case registries and agency surveys are somewhat lower for both severe (0.35%) and mild (0.35%) mental retardation (McLaren & Bryson, 1987). Using the lower prevalence rates (0.7%) and assuming a current U.S. general population of 264,271,393 persons, 1.849 million individuals in the United States were mentally retarded in 1996. The higher prevalence rate, based on total population screening (1.25%), yields a larger figure of 3.303 million persons (U.S. Bureau of the Census, 1996). The number of persons with mental retardation in the United States can therefore be roughly estimated to be between 2 and 3 million persons, divided fairly equally between those with highly significant degrees of mental retardation and those with relatively mild limitations.

In general, the lower the intellectual level, the higher the probability of associated disabling conditions. The most common secondary physical disabilities include cerebral palsy or other motor impairment, which are present in 20–30% of persons with mental retardation, seizure disorders (15–30%), and visual or hearing impairments (10–20%) (McLaren & Bryson, 1987). Behavioral or psychiatric disorders, which impose particularly difficult challenges from the standpoint of community inclusion, are present in 15% to over 35% of all persons with mental retardation (Reiss, 1994). Recent progress in the assessment and treatment of persons with the dual diagnosis of mental retardation and behavioral/psychiatric disorder is discussed later in this chapter as an example of current innovations with this most vulnerable subgroup of persons with intellectual disabilities.

EARLY HISTORY OF SERVICES

The first epidemiological study of mental retardation was undertaken by the Commonwealth of Massachusetts in 1846 by Samuel Gridley Howe (1848). The study confirmed the presence of 514 individuals with mental retardation in Massachusetts and recommended the establishment of an experimental residential "training school" for 13 pupils. The residential school was modeled after similar efforts in France and Switzerland and opened in a wing of Boston's Perkins School for the Blind in 1848. The new school's program drew on the approach to individualized instruction developed by Jacob Periera (1715–1780) with hearing-impaired persons, by Jean-Marc-Gaspard Itard (1774–1838) with the Wild Boy of Aveyron (Itard, 1962), and, especially, from the pathbreaking synthesis of Edouard Seguin (1812–1880).

Seguin, Itard's student, pioneered the educational program at the Bicêtre Asylum's special school for children with mental retardation in Paris in the early 1840s. He demonstrated that people with "incurable" mental retardation could often be taught to speak, write, count, and develop disciplined work habits. Seguin's innovation was first to recognize society's obligation to educate every child. His "physiological method" combined physical, mental, and moral components and demonstrated that children with mental retardation could be educated (Seguin, 1856). This led to the initial development of institutions in the United States and Europe as state "schools" or "training" centers.

By 1880, the training schools envisioned by Howe and Seguin had evolved into custodial asylums with reduced emphasis on educating residents and returning them to community life (Wolfensberger, 1976). In 1900, there were 25 state mental retardation institutions operating in the United States with a nationwide census of 15,000 persons (Kuhlman, 1940). Many institutions had developed extensive lands for farming. Residents worked farms, laundries, and shops, not so much to develop skills for community out-placement, but rather to contribute to the self-sustaining economy of the institution.

The census of state mental retardation institutions swelled to 55,466 persons by 1926 (Lakin, 1979). Switsky et al. (1988) described institutions of this era as increasingly structured "like a hospital for the care of sick animals rather than as a place for the special education of human children and adults" (p. 28). The sterilization of institutional residents was commonplace during the first half of the twentieth century. Between 1907 and 1939, for example, more than 30,000 mentally disabled persons in 29 states were sterilized unknowingly or against their will (U.S. Holocaust Museum, undated; Wolfensberger, 1981).

Although the Great Depression and World War II inhibited progress and innovation in service delivery in the United States, there were several bright spots.

In Massachusetts, Fernald's (1919) Waverly studies had demonstrated that, with proper support from their families, individuals with mental retardation could function well in the community. Wallace (1929) also discredited the link between mental retardation and criminality. New York State introduced foster family care in the 1930s, authorizing the state to pay for the maintenance of persons with mental retardation in family homes (Vaux, 1935). Research subsequently confirmed the positive effects of placement in foster or adoptive homes (Skeels & Harms, 1948; Speer, 1940; Wells & Arthur, 1939) and the benefits of preschool intervention programs (Lazar & Darlington, 1982; Skeels, Updegraff, Wellman, & Wilhams, 1938).

Between 1920 and 1967, however, as Americans left the farms for the cities in great numbers, institutions quadrupled in size to almost 200,000 residents (Lakin, 1979). Every American state except Nevada opened one or more state-operated institutions. Some of the institutions were constructed new, but about a third of the facilities were converted tuberculosis hospitals or military bases (Braddock & Heller, 1985). The average facility population was 1,422 residents in 1962 (Survey and Research Corporation, 1965). Several facilities, such as Willowbrook in New York and Lincoln and Dixon in Illinois, housed 4,000–6,000 residents. In 1960, despite growing evidence to the contrary, American society still viewed persons with mental retardation as a group that needed to be controlled by segregation, sterilization, and isolation.

Innovation in the States

EXPANSION OF COMMUNITY LIVING

The election of John F. Kennedy to the presidency in 1960 ushered in the modern era of mental retardation services in the United States. On October 11, 1961, Kennedy issued an unprecedented presidential statement regarding the need for a national plan in the field of mental retardation. "We as a nation," he said, "have for too long postponed an intensive search for solutions to the problems of the mentally retarded. That failure should be corrected" (Kennedy, 1961, p. 196). Kennedy appointed the President's Panel on Mental Retardation, which in 1962 presented 95 broad and far-reaching recommendations. These extended from issues of civil rights to the need for scientific research on etiology and prevention. The panel called for a substantial downsizing of institutional facilities and an expansion of community services, and, most important, it clearly embraced the principle of normalization (Wolfensberger, 1972) as a guide to future innovation in service delivery.

Many of the 95 recommendations of the President's Panel (1962) were enacted into law by the 88th Congress as Public Laws 88-156 and 88-164. Public Law 88-156, the Maternal and Child Health and Mental Retardation Planning Amendments of 1963, doubled the spending ceiling for the existing Maternal and Child Health State Grant Program and established a new mental retardation planning grant program in the states. The planning effort was unique in the history of the field in that federal legislation required all 50 participating states to produce comprehensive plans for the development of improved residential, community, and preventive services.

In 1967 the nation's institutional census peaked at 194,650 individuals residing in 165 freestanding state-operated mental retardation institutional facilities (U.S. Department of Health Education and Welfare, 1972). Since 1968, however, the number of individuals with mental retardation served in state-operated facilities with 16 or more beds has declined between 3 and 5% each year for 29 consecutive years. The residential census in the nation's state institutions was 59,737 persons in 1996 (Braddock, Hemp, Parish, & Westrich, 1998).

States' efforts to "reform" institutions in the 1970s gave way to efforts to reallocate institutional resources to community services activities. States began closing institutions in significant numbers for the first time in the early 1980s (Braddock & Heller, 1985). On January 31, 1991, New Hampshire closed Laconia Developmental Center and became the first state in the country to provide all of its services to people with mental retardation in the community (Covert, MacIntosh, & Shumway, 1994). By 1995, 32 states had closed 95 state mental retardation institutions, and 18 more closures were scheduled to occur by the year 2000 (Braddock et al., 1998). Through 1998, all institutions have been closed in the states of Alaska, New Mexico, Rhode Island, Vermont, West Virginia and in the District of Columbia.

Institutional phase-downs and closures have been accompanied by a growing emphasis on supported community living for individuals with developmental disabilities. The expansion of community residential settings nationally is illustrated in Figure 8.1, which charts the growth of group homes, supervised apartments, and supported living settings nationwide over a 35-year period

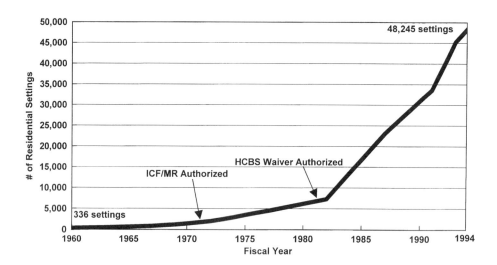

Figure 8.1   United States Community residential settings for persons with developmental disabilities, 1960–1994. Source: Braddock and Hemp, 1996.

from 1960 to 1994. The total number of out-of-home long-term care community settings in the United States, excluding foster homes, grew from 336 settings in 1960 to 48,245 settings in 1994. There were an additional 16,464 foster home settings in 1994, up from 5,332 settings in 1977 (Hauber, Bruininks, Hill, Lakin, & White, 1984); these figures are not included in Figure 8.1 due to the lack of comparable data for the earlier years. The total number of individuals served in community residential settings in the United States grew from fewer than 5,000 persons in 1960 to more than 181,000 in 1994 (Prouty & Lakin, 1995). Much of this tremendous expansion in community services was fueled by the federal-state partnership in the Medicaid Home- and Community-Based Services (HCBS) Waiver Program.

In addition to residential services, the states provide an array of day and work programs and other support services. This array of nonresidential supports is available to many residential clients and to large numbers of persons living at home. In 1996, a total of 305,460 persons participated in sheltered workshops and other facility-based day programs. There also were 86,540 workers with developmental disabilities in supported employment. Early intervention programs served 150,593 infants and toddlers with developmental disabilities and other children at risk of developmental delays. Family supports were provided to 268,000 children or adults with developmental disabilities living at home. These family supports included direct financial subsidies in 20 states for nearly 20,000 families. Respite care (114,000 families) and other family supports (138,000 families) were also provided. States provided case management and service coordination services to more than 650,000 children and adults with developmental disabilities in 1996 (Braddock et al., 1998).

THE HCBS WAIVER

The HCBS Waiver was authorized in 1981 as an amendment to Title XIX of the Medicaid Statute and permits federal reimbursement for a wide array of community services and supports. These include habilitation training, respite care and other family supports, case management, supported employment (for individuals formerly institutionalized), supported living, and many other types of assistance in homelike, community environments. Assistive technology, physical, occupational, and speech therapies, and behavior management are also reimbursed under the HCBS Waiver. Medicaid's Intermediate Care Facilities for the Mentally Retarded (ICF/MR) program, in contrast, reimburses primarily services in large institutional settings and provides more than 90% of all federal-state funding for such institutions nationwide. The HCBS Waiver Program supports individuals only in community settings, including apartments, small homes, and the family's home. Room and board costs are not reimbursable under the Waiver. However, HCBS Waiver clients are eligible to receive federal income maintenance payments under Supplemental Security Income/Aid to Dependent Children (SSI/ADC), and these funds are frequently used to pay for room and board. In 1996, federal-state HCBS Waiver spending nationally totaled $4.8 billion. Fifty states were participating (Braddock et al., 1998).

THE EXAMPLE OF MICHIGAN

In the 1980s, a number of states, including Michigan, New Hampshire, and Colorado, initiated substantial expansion of community living programs and dramatically reduced their reliance on state-operated residential institutions. The major innovations employed in these states included expanding family support programs, developing extensive networks of small group homes, introducing supported employment programs in lieu of sheltered workshops, introducing independent case management, and providing individualized placements in apartments and other home-like, family-scale settings, which were integrated into typical neighborhoods and communities throughout the state.

The State of Michigan is a particularly good example of a state government's innovative role in the transformation of the mental retardation service delivery system during the 1980s (Braddock & Hemp, in press). Michigan is also an interesting example because its institutionally oriented service system typified those of most other states as late as 1979, when approximately 80 cents of every dollar spent on mental retardation residential care in Michigan was allocated to state institutions. In addition, Michigan is an instructive example because it is the first heavily populated, industrialized state to be very close to having all of its mental retardation services provided in community and family settings. In 1996, only 362 residents remained in state institutions, down from a peak figure of 12,615 in 1965.

In addition to class action litigation focusing on the Plymouth Center (*Michigan ARC v. Smith*, 1978), four developments in Michigan facilitated the transformation of the state's system of mental retardation services. First, advocacy efforts and professional leadership led to the opening of the Macomb-Oakland Regional Center in 1973. The Center emphasized a family-support philosophy that stressed principles of family preservation and permanency planning (Taylor, 1991; Taylor, Lakin, & Hill, 1989). Second, the state subsequently enacted community mental health legislation that structured incentives for county boards of mental health and mental retardation to provide community services for county residents who were institutionalized. Michigan then closed nine state institutions between 1981 and 1996.

A third factor was Michigan's development of a strong cash subsidy program for families (Meyers & Marcenko, 1989). The subsidy provides about $250 per month for families earning up to $60,000 annually. The most frequent uses of subsidy payments are for clothing, education aids and toys, general household expenses, sitters, diapers, transportation, and medical expenses and health-related needs (Herman, 1991). The Michigan cash subsidy program, in combination with approximately $5,500 annually that individuals with mental retardation also receive in federal SSI/ADC payments, provided support for 4,400 individuals with mental retardation and their families in 1996 (Braddock & Hemp, in press). The cash subsidy and SSI payments combined were less than one-tenth of the annual cost of institutional services in Michigan, and were one-fifth of the cost of group home placements in the State. Other states, including Illinois and Wisconsin, have modeled their cash subsidy programs on Michigan's example.

Fourth, an additional 6,000 families in Michigan in 1996 received respite care and other family support such as counseling and additional in-home services. Michigan's family support philosophy and programs have had two direct impacts on the Michigan mental retardation service system. First, Michigan places proportionately fewer individuals with mental retardation in out-of-home placements than the average state. Second, Michigan's out-of-home placement rate in 1996 was 21% lower than the U.S. average.

The level of institutional spending in Michigan began to decline in 1980. In subsequent years, as institutions closed, institutional spending declined rapidly and funds "saved" were reallocated to finance community residential alternatives and family support. Initially, six-person group homes were established under the ICF/MR program. In recent years, Michigan rapidly expanded supported living through the use of the HCBS Waiver—from services for 616 persons in 1988 to 4,418 persons in 1996. Michigan began spending more for community services than for congregate (16+ beds) residential care in 1982, as shown in Figure 8.2. In 1996, Michigan allocated 96% of total mental retardation resources for family and community services, compared to a national figure of 65%. The FYs 1977–1996 resource allocation profile for Michigan, illustrated in Figure 8.2, shows the fiscal consequences of the State's transformation from an institution-dominated service system to one characterized almost exclusively by community and family support programs.

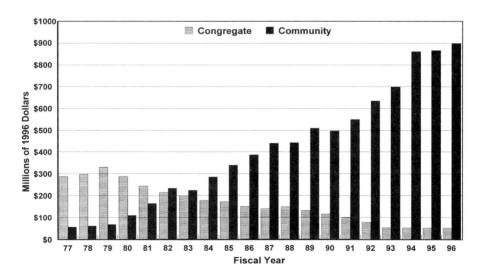

Figure 8.2 Michigan: Adjusted public spending, 1977–1996. Source: Braddock and Hemp, in press.

DIFFUSION OF INNOVATION ACROSS THE STATES

Innovation in mental retardation service delivery systems is clearly illustrated in the Michigan example. Michigan exemplifies the rapid growth of community services and family support programs set against an equally dramatic decline in reliance on large state or privately operated institutional facilities. The overall national trend is not so dramatic as Michigan's or those in other states, such as New Hampshire, Rhode Island, Vermont, Maine, Nebraska, North Dakota, Arizona, Minnesota, and Colorado, that have taken the lead in community-based care. However, virtually every American state is now participating in the transformation to community and family-based services to a significant extent. Figure 8.3 compares the structure of the nation's residential service system in 1977 and in 1996.

As shown in Figure 8.3, the institutional census declined from 149,892 persons in 1977 to 59,726 in 1996. During this period, the number of persons

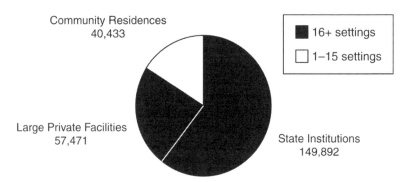

1977 Residential Services Total: 247,796

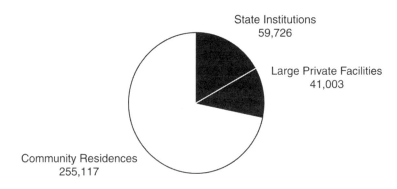

1996 Residential Services Total: 355,846

Figure 8.3 United States Persons with mental retardation in out-of-home settings. Source: Braddock, Hemp, Parish, and Westrich, 1998.

with mental retardation living in community residential settings with 15 or fewer persons increased fivefold from 40,433 to 255,117 individuals. In 1977, only 16% of all residents in formal out-of-home placements lived in community settings; in 1996, 72% of residents lived in such settings. Moreover, in 1996, 56% of the community residents reported in Figure 8.3 lived in settings with six or fewer residents. Figure 8.3 excludes mentally retarded residents in nursing homes, which declined from 42,424 residents with mental retardation in 1977 (National Center for Health Statistics, 1977) to 38,438 in 1996 (Braddock et al., 1998).

The transformation of services from an institution-dominated service system to a community living approach is clearly reflected in the financing of mental retardation services as well. During the 1977–1996 period, total federal, state, and local spending for mental retardation services in the nation grew from $3.5 billion to $22.8 billion. The total cost of operating state institutions, however, has remained fairly stable over the past 20 years. As the number of institutional residents declined by 67% (from 150,000 to 60,000), the costs per resident rose 150% in real economic terms. The average yearly expenditure for institutional residents in the United States in 1996 was $95,630 ($262/day).

The states have exhibited great variation in the extent to which they have allocated financial resources for mental retardation services over the past two decades. States that adopted community living objectives somewhat earlier than others—like Michigan, Nebraska, and most New England states—spent 60–75% of their total aggregate expenditures across the entire 20-year 1977–1996 period for community services, compared to 25–40% of funding for institutional facilities with 16 or more beds. Most states, however, spent far more in the aggregate for institutional operations than for community services when total expenditures for the entire 20-year period are taken into account. In 1996 the United States spent roughly twice the resources for community mental retardation services that it spent for congregate care services in public and private institutions ($15.5 billion vs. $7.4 billion).

The three main revenue sources for the $15.5 billion in 1996 funding for community services in the United States are federal, state, and local governments. Fifty-five percent of community funding derives from state own-source tax revenues, and 5% comes from local funds (county or municipal). The remaining 40% of revenues to finance community services comes from federal funds. One-third of the federal funding is associated with the HCBS Waiver Program; 30% is ICF/MR monies for facilities with 15 or fewer beds; 14% is noninstitutional Medicaid funds; 9% comes from the Social Services Block Grant Program or sundry small federal grant programs; and 14% is income maintenance payments for HCBS Waiver participants.

Emergence of Supported Community Living and Related Innovations

In the past two decades, many states and service providers have developed a rich variety of alternatives to institution-based services under the rubric of "supported community living." Services developed have included supports for people living at home through service vouchers, cash subsidies, respite care, in-home behavioral therapy, and other family support services. In the community, residential care models have been refined through the implementation of smaller and more personalized group living arrangements, supported apartment living, client-owned or -leased homes, and expanded foster care and adoption programs. Integrated recreational and leisure activities (Schleien & Ray, 1988), early intervention programs for infants and young children from birth to age 3 (Guralnick, 1996; Lazar & Darlington, 1982), specialized services for older adults with mental retardation (Heller, 1997; Sutton, Factor, Hawkins, Heller, & Seltzer, 1993), and programs for persons with mental retardation and emotional problems (Reiss, 1994; Reiss, Levitan, & McNally, 1982) have also been initiated on a larger scale.

BASIC PRINCIPLES

Supported community living, according to Lakin (1996), refers to "the development and provision of assistance to people with mental retardation, their family members and other sources of 'natural support' in ways that help them live their lives in settings and participate in activities that contribute to their personal goals, quality of life and community." The best contemporary supported living programs for persons with mental retardation are characterized by the following features:

- Separating the selection and the financing of the client's home, work, and recreational settings from the services and supports he or she needs to participate in those settings;
- Providing a home so that the person with mental retardation "controls his or her own front door" and lives with whom he or she chooses to live, according to his or her chosen lifestyle;
- Facilitating the opportunity to choose productive employment and volunteer work activities;
- Requiring service providers to be less intrusive and more respectful in how they bring services and supports into people's homes, job sites, and other settings;
- Ensuring that consumers exercise increased choice and control over the services and supports they receive and from whom they receive them;
- Learning new ways to adjust to market demands for individualized services, instead of utilizing comprehensive contracts to care for groups of individuals;
- Focusing on quality of life and desired personal outcomes as defined by individuals and families receiving services in all program evaluation activities;
- Providing specialized services for individuals with substantial behavioral, communication, and health needs in the settings in which the

individuals live rather than making the individual live where the services are located (Lakin, 1996, p. 3).

EMPIRICAL SUPPORT FOR COMMUNITY LIVING

The efficacy of supported community living is grounded in research. Positive changes in functional skill levels or adaptive behaviors have been documented in numerous community integration studies (Larson & Lakin, 1989). Studies of family attitudes have also indicated that the great majority of parents of formerly institutionalized persons with mental retardation are consistently satisfied with the benefits of their relative's community living experience (reviewed in Larson & Lakin, 1991).

Several studies have also focused on the comparability of costs between state-operated institutions and community living facilities (Bensberg & Smith, 1984; Knobbe, Carey, Rhodes, & Horner, 1995). The comprehensive averaged costs of community living programs across seven studies completed between 1979 and 1995 were 85% of the costs of institutional programs. The differences in institutional and community costs were primarily accounted for by lower wages and fringe benefits for private (community) workers compared to their public-sector counterparts. Given that employee turnover is inversely correlated with wage levels, it follows that most studies of turnover in mental retardation facilities have found appreciably higher rates of turnover in privately operated community facilities than in state institutions (Braddock & Mitchell, 1992).

Studies of waiting lists in the states show that, in 1991, an estimated 60,000 people with mental retardation were on waiting lists in those states for residential services, and 120,000 persons were waiting for related services such as day habilitation, vocational services, case management, family subsidy, and other services (Hayden & DePaepe, 1994). These figures seem conservative given the prevalence data discussed at the beginning of this chapter. In fact, only about 9% of all individuals with mental retardation in the United States are currently in supervised out-of-home placement settings. The remaining 91% of the 3.3 million persons with mental retardation in our society are living independently or with their families.

As families age, however, and as more attractive and more numerous community living opportunities evolve in the nation's communities, the demand for supported community living can be expected to increase. The Individuals with Disabilities Education Act (PL 94-142 as amended by PL 101-476), which requires a free and appropriate education for all children and youth with disabilities in the United States, has heightened parents' sense of entitlement to community living as their children reach adulthood. The Americans with Disabilities Act of 1990, which prohibits discrimination against disabled persons in employment, public accommodations, and public services (Wehman, 1993; West, 1991), can be expected to increase the demand for residential and vocational services in the coming years.

The limited supply of community residential services and their associated costs have put family support programs higher on the states' agendas. In 1992, family support programs were being offered in virtually every state (Braddock, Hemp, Bachelder, & Fujiura, 1995). These programs were not begun until the 1980s and today represent a relatively modest but growing component of the mix of services being offered in the states. In the years ahead, however, given efforts to curtail open-ended entitlement spending in Washington, there will be a great deal of pressure on the states to keep demand for the most costly services at a minimum. The most costly services are residential facilities and day habilitation programs operated with full-time staff.

Family support programs and related initiatives in permanency planning can be expected to grow rapidly in the next decade. Anticipated future shortages in direct support staff in institutional and community programs will bring a greater emphasis to less staff-intensive approaches. There are currently more than 350,000 direct support staff working in institutional and community settings. Rates of pay are low, often at or near the minimum wage for entry-level workers. The low birth rates of the 1960s and 1970s, coupled with greater competition among service providers to retain these workers, will pose formidable staffing challenges for community agencies and institutional programs.

COMMUNITY PARTICIPATION AND INCLUSION

The principle of normalization is the centerpiece of community participation. Normalization assumes that people's social roles are enhanced by age-appropriate activities in settings in which those activities usually occur, by having friends and other associates who are themselves valued socially in the community, and by participating in typical social, cultural, and economic roles in the community (Lakin, 1996). Research and advocacy efforts regarding the issue of "quality of life" for people with mental retardation is a more recent development evolving from the normalization principle. A key feature of "quality of life" is the right of the person with mental retardation to make choices about his or her life and to define what the quality of that life will be (Edgerton, 1990; Goode, 1994; Schalock, 1990).

The integration of people with mental retardation into community settings has been extremely challenging for the field. Relocating tens of thousands of individuals from institutions and nursing homes to community settings has necessarily been a complicated, expensive, and politically divisive process (Braddock & Heller, 1985) that has required enormous amounts of advocacy and community education (Seltzer, 1984; Sigelman, 1976). However, physical integration implies mere presence in the community and does not guarantee that desired social or interpersonal relationships will be established with typical community members (Bercovici, 1983; Bogdan & Taylor, 1987). What is sought for people with mental retardation is a socially valued role in the community (Wolfensberger, 1983).

"Person-centered planning" is a method used to facilitate social inclusion in valued roles. The method involves individuals in a person's support network coming together to create a vision of what the person with mental retardation wants. An action plan is then developed to describe what can be done to enhance the individual's social connectedness. Social inclusion facilitators are also often utilized to help individuals with mental retardation find a sense of belonging in the community (Abery & Fahnestock, 1994). Alternative or augmentative communication devices and other assistive technologies also help facilitate meaningful social relationships (Alm, 1993).

PERSONAL AUTONOMY AND SELF-DETERMINATION

Personal autonomy is a primary component of adult behavior in our society, and autonomy has emerged as an important goal for people with mental retardation. The development of personal autonomy skills is a formal part of the instructional approach of many special education and community living programs today. This is occurring through the teaching of choice making and assertiveness skills and by integrating them into the daily lives of individuals with mental retardation (Abery, Rudrud, Arndt, Schauben, & Eggebeen, 1995; Hoffman & Field, 1995). At the National Conference on Self-Determination (1989), persons with intellectual disabilities produced seven recommendations related to self-determination and residential living. The recommendations called for (1) enabling people to control their own futures; (2) supporting state and local self-advocacy organizations; (3) reshaping attitudes of professionals currently working with persons with disabilities to value autonomy and choice; (4) including self-determination as a top priority in preservice and inservice training of professionals and paraprofessionals; (5) providing courses in self-assertion for persons with disabilities; (6) reinforcing friendships between people with and without disabilities; and (7) facilitating the involvement of people with disabilities in their own program planning sessions (National Conference, 1989, in Lakin, 1996).

Organized self-advocacy is another important manifestation of the emergence of autonomy and self-determination (Dybwad & Bersani, 1996; Longhurst, 1994). Membership in local and statewide self-advocacy groups like People First is growing rapidly. Hayden and Senese (1996) identified more than 1,000 self-advocacy groups, some in every state. This represented almost a threefold expansion in the number of groups since 1990 (Longhurst, 1994). In 1995, self-advocacy groups established a national organization called Self Advocates Becoming Empowered (SABE). SABE has formed a board of directors that consists entirely of persons with intellectual disabilities, secured formal nonprofit status, and begun holding national meetings. SABE has also developed an advocacy agenda that calls for the phase-down and closure of all state-operated mental retardation institutions in the United States (Dybwad & Bersani, 1996). The self-advocacy movement is certain to grow in the years ahead, reinforcing the developing priority of personal autonomy and self-determination. Further reinforcement of this self-advocacy theme is likely to stem from the inclusion of autonomy and self-determination objectives in quality assurance requirements for supported community living programs throughout the country.

INTEGRATED EMPLOYMENT

Until recently, employment opportunities for persons with mental retardation were restricted to sheltered workshops and adult activity centers. The work was menial, and workers were paid token wages. Institutions practiced peonage with residents until this practice was outlawed by the Fair Labor Standards Act Amendments of 1967. Also, a priority requiring an expansion of supported employment for clients served in the state-federal vocational rehabilitation program was established by the 1986 Rehabilitation Act Amendments. Supported work has permitted tens of thousands of persons with mental retardation to obtain meaningful employment and to experience the inclusion, social participation, and self-esteem that come with real work (Rusch, Chadsey-Rusch, & Johnson, 1991). Wehman, Revell, and Kregel (1995) reported that 70% of supported employment clients served by more than 4,000 community agencies nationally were persons with mental retardation. Applied behavior analysis has been demonstrated to be an extremely effective instructional tool for teaching employment skills for persons with mental retardation (Snell, 1987).

The earnings of supported employment participants remain low, however; wages were $107 a week in 1993, and most workers were employed part time. Wehman, Revell, and Kregel (1995) noted in their National Survey of Supported Employment Implementation that relatively few persons with severe mental retardation were involved in supported work programs. Additional effort is needed to build on the important gains of the past decade in the supported employment field. Cost-benefit studies indicate that supported work generates savings for taxpayers in addition to improving social and psychological client outcomes (Lewis, Johnson, Bruininks, & Kallen, 1994).

INNOVATION WITH PERSONS WITH BEHAVIORAL DISORDERS

Persons with mental retardation often have high levels of exposure to extremely negative social conditions, including restricted opportunities for personal development and education, forced segregation and isolation from their families and friends, social stigma, discrimination in employment, exploitation, and abuse. Mentally retarded people are also usually acutely self-aware of the deprivations they endure, and this awareness evokes a heightened sense of frustration, loneliness, anxiety, anger, depression, an expectation of failure, poor self-concept, and an increased risk of developing mental health disorders.

The presence of a mental health disorder in a person with mental retardation imposes significant vulnerabilities such as barriers to community integration and social inclusion. These disorders, and the lack of appropriate treatments for them, are factors that can lead to institutionalization and reinstitutionalization and represent a common basis for failure in community residential and work placements (Bruininks, Hill, & Morreau, 1988). In the past two decades, however, extensive research and innovation has improved our understanding of the epidemiology and treatment of mental health disorders in people with mental retardation (Nezu, Nezu, & Gill-Weiss, 1992; Reiss, 1994).

Thirty-three epidemiological studies, conducted primarily in the past 15 years, have indicated that from 15% to more than 35% of persons with mental retardation have disorders significant enough to require specialized mental health services (Reiss, 1994). The great variations in prevalence rates in these studies were attributable to differences in sampling techniques, classification categories, and rating systems. Reiss has also suggested that lower prevalence rates were found in studies that relied on retrospective case files, whereas higher prevalence rates were associated with states that collected new data through professional interviewers. The lowest prevalence rates were found among individuals living in community settings, while higher rates were found among residents of state institutions.

This vulnerability of people with mental retardation to psychopathology was not fully recognized in the literature prior to the mid-1980s—after a phenomenon described as "diagnostic overshadowing" was elucidated by Steven Reiss and his colleagues at the University of Illinois at Chicago. Reiss, Levitan, and McNally (1982) conducted field experiments that clearly demonstrated the general tendency of clinicians to underdiagnose mental health disorders in persons with mental retardation. Clinicians often presumed that behavioral problems in people with mental retardation were a consequence of the mental retardation, rather than a separate mental illness. Diagnostic overshadowing, coupled with a severe shortage of trained mental health clinicians interested in working with people with mental retardation, thus led to serious inattention to the development and implementation of specialized treatments and services for a large segment of the population of persons with mental retardation. The situation began to improve in the 1980s with the development and application of new treatments and service models, including specialized outpatient services, specialized day services and inpatient units.

The outpatient model typically provides diagnostic services, individual and group psychotherapy, cognitive therapy, reinforcement therapy, and drug therapy. Consumer demand has been greatest for adolescents and young adults between the ages of 15 and 29. Two-thirds of the persons referred to the specialized outpatient mental health clinic at the University of Illinois at Chicago's Institute on Disability and Human Development were in this age range. The challenges associated with the transition to adulthood, coupled with the loss of the school as a support system as the young adult "ages out," seem to cause the high rate of referrals in this age group (Bouras, Brooks, & Drummond, 1993; Reiss & Trenn, 1984). There are a number of outpatient programs currently operating in the United States that are affiliated with major research universities such as Ohio State University (Nisonger Center), the University of Rochester (Davidson et al., 1993), and Harvard University (Institute for Community Inclusion). Some of the nation's large community residential services providers have begun to develop in-house treatment programs for their clients with emotional problems. Also, the University-Affiliated Cincinnati Center for Developmental Disorders (Woodward & Pederson, 1991) has developed a comprehensive curriculum guide for training community mental health professionals, including those working in the nation's extensive network of community mental health centers.

Outpatient mental health programs increasingly serve as community supports that help to keep people with mental retardation out of residential institutions or other restrictive congregate care facilities. Relatively few methodologically rigorous outcome data have been produced on the interventions employed in these settings, although descriptive statistics have been published on several of the more widely emulated models (summarized in Reiss, 1994). Behavioral skills training approaches (e.g., Benson, Rice, & Miranti, 1986; Matson & Andrasik, 1982) are generally more effective with persons with mental retardation than cognitive approaches, such as rational-emotive therapy (RET), modeling, and self-instruction. Prout and Cale (1994), however, provided case study evidence of the success of RET with persons with mental retardation, and Dowrick and Biggs (1983) report a successful interaction using a self-modeling approach with video feedback to address learned helplessness and other problem behaviors. Szymanski (1980a) reported positive outcomes in individual and group psychotherapy. Reiss and Aman (1998) have also recently published a manual in which they identify best practices in psychopharmacological approaches to therapy for persons with mental retardation. In addition, therapeutic techniques such as play, art, and music therapy may also be useful treatment modalities (Bowen & Rosal, 1989; Zagelbaum & Rubino, 1991).

Regardless of the model upon which psychotherapy is based, several special considerations apply to working with persons with intellectual disabilities (Reiss, 1994; Schiller & Schaaf, 1997). First, interview techniques need to be adapted to the person's cognitive level. The therapist must use concrete language, frequently assess the person's understanding, and also acknowledge his or her own feelings about mental retardation. Second, therapy should be directive. Sessions must be carefully structured and specific instructions provided to explain the purpose of the sessions and to clarify what is expected. When therapy does not progress as anticipated, alternative approaches or simpler ways of approaching therapy should be considered. Third, appropriate goals need to be established. It is crucial in this regard to recognize possible discrepancies between the goals of the referring agency and the person served. Fourth, the therapist should intervene in the person's total environment and be ever mindful that the therapy is part of a comprehensive support system (Nezu, Nezu, & Gill-Weiss, 1992).

Virtually all states have also created inpatient observation and stabilization units for clients in behavioral crises. The units in state mental retardation institutions typically serve people with severe intellectual disabilities, while those in state psychiatric hospitals work with people with mild degrees of intellectual impairment. Specialized inpatient units in state institutions are controversial. Notwithstanding the occasional need for a secure and controlled environment for a very small number of persons, it is preferable to effect behavioral change in the environment in which it arises (Carr & Durand, 1985; Reiss, 1994). As noted by Samuel Gridley Howe (1866) and Newman and Emerson (1991), congregating behaviorally disturbed people in a group setting with staff reinforces negative models of behavior and creates a chaotic environment that impedes consistency in the approach to treatment. Inpatient treatment units are inconsistent with a community integration and social inclusion philosophy. However, most states still find it necessary to maintain a small number of behavior units for their most challenging residents. Over the next decade it is likely that the utilization of these specialty units will continue to diminish, and community-based providers will play steadily increasing roles in the provision of both inpatient and crisis intervention services. For example, Menolascino and Stark (1984) developed a well-known university-based inpatient unit at the University of Nebraska's Psychiatric Institute. Staffing included a psychiatrist, a psychotherapist, four nurses, one-to-one staffing of paraprofessionals, a social worker, and a psychologist. The program serves no more than 15 persons at a time (Reiss, 1994).

The first nationally significant day services program for mentally retarded people with challenging behaviors was developed in 1973 at the Rock Creek Foundation in Silver Springs, Maryland (Smull, Fabian, & Chanteau, 1984). It served people with mental retardation who also had chronic mental illness. The program included psychotherapy, activity programming, and vocational services and was especially notable for promoting meaningful client input and control into the development of an individualized habilitation plan. Fletcher (1988) has also described a model day services program, known as Beacon House, in Ulster County, New York. The program provides a group method of treatment, with individual and drug therapy used adjunctively. Gains in socialization skills, impulse control, self-esteem, and problem-solving skills were observed in Fletcher's outcome study (cited in Reiss, 1994). The day program model for persons with mental retardation who also have a chronic mental illness is particularly useful in preventing institutionalization.

Until professionals in the generic mental health system can be induced to provide the mental health services required by a significant percentage of the population of persons with mental retardation, specialized support such as outpatient clinics, inpatient units, day programs, and crisis intervention will need to be provided through the mental retardation service system. Research continues to be needed to evaluate the outcomes of the numerous therapies that are being employed in specialized settings today, and greater emphasis should be placed on training clinicians to specialize in working with this challenging population. Federal leadership might include the establishment of a priority for a mental retardation research center in which investigations into the emotional problems of persons with mental retardation is the central theme. The National Institute of Mental Health has been relatively inactive in this area of "dual diagnosis" and should initiate more collaborative research and training activities with the Mental Retardation Branch of the National Institute on Child Health and Human Development. The National Institutes of Health (1989) consensus conference on the development and treatment of destructive behavior in persons with developmental disabilities focused on the most-difficult-to-treat subcomponent of the dually diagnosed population. This consensus conference is an example of collaborative, agencywide leadership from the NIH on this important topic.

Implications for Service Delivery, Policy, and Education

This chapter has provided a brief analysis of trends and innovations in the mental retardation field. People with mental retardation are emerging from a dark and neglected past in our society and becoming more accepted and valued members of the community. Our country, like other economically developed countries, has passed through cruel and oppressive periods in which people with mental retardation were segregated in institutions, sterilized, and treated exceedingly inhumanely. Even during long periods of this oppression, however, innovative services such as foster care and community placement were being developed and implemented on a small scale in selected state settings.

In retrospect, the important historical benchmarks in the provision of services to persons with mental retardation in the United States include the establishment of the first publicly financed residential school in Boston in 1848, authorization of the first public school special classes for mentally retarded children in major U.S. cities around the turn of this century, and, in the mid-twentieth century, the leadership of the federal government's legislative and then executive branches in promoting the adoption of federal financial assistance programs in mental retardation research, personnel training, service provision, and income maintenance.

In the 1970s, the entry of the federal judiciary into the civil rights arena was a critical event for individuals with mental retardation and their families. Federal courts recognized rights to a free, appropriate public education, to freedom from cruel and unusual punishment, to habilitation in the least restrictive environment, and, in 1990, through the Americans with Disabilities Act, to freedom from discrimination in employment, public accommodations, and public services. The federal government has played an immensely important role in the mental retardation field since the appointment of President Kennedy's Panel on Mental Retardation in 1961. It must not be forgotten that, as conditions deteriorated in residential institutions, states' rights arguments precluded significant federal leadership and innovation in the field of mental retardation for the 110-year period between 1850 and 1960.

In the 1990s, states, communities, families, and individuals with mental retardation themselves have been innovators in the provision of mental retardation services across the lifespan. The federal government has provided extensive financial resources to promote services and supports, but local communities and families, coupled with state government and professional leadership, have been the principal sources of the creative energy and resources to implement path-breaking innovations in areas like supported living, family support, supported employment, and specialized programs for mentally retarded persons with emotional disorders. Today, a dominant trend has clearly been established in the United States and internationally toward family support and community living and away from the segregated institutional model of the nineteenth century.

The United States today, however, still shows considerable variation among and within individual states in the degree of commitment to innovative family and community mental retardation services. States have chosen their residential living priorities—institutional or community services—by maximizing acquisition of ICF/MR reimbursements to sustain ever more expensive state institutions or, in recent years, by aggressively pursuing HCBS Medicaid Waiver funds, closing institutions, and significantly expanding supported community living. Although most states have tried to address both institutional and community living objectives simultaneously, few have done so with equal dedication to both objectives due to the high costs involved in operating dual systems. In many states, such as Illinois, parent groups associated with institutions, such as the Voice of the Retarded, and employee unions like the American Federation of State, County and Municipal Employees (AFSCME) have been formidable political adversaries for community living advocates seeking to phase down or close state facilities and to reallocate the resources thereby freed to community objectives.

Notwithstanding well-organized opposition, by the year 2000, fewer than 50,000 persons will probably reside in the nation's state-operated mental retardation institutions, and the census will continue to fall rapidly in future years as it has for every one of the past 30 years. The number of states operating institution-free service delivery systems is likely to double from four states today (New Hampshire, Maine, Rhode Island, and Vermont) to eight or more states before the year 2000. By the year 2000 or shortly thereafter, the first heavily populated state (Michigan) is likely to close its remaining institutions, supplying additional momentum in the nation's large states to close their remaining institutions while accelerating the development of supported community living and family support programs.

The decentralization and privatization of services in community settings will certainly continue with strong momentum. However, the environment in which services and supports are now financed is likely to change significantly as a result of four powerful trends: (1) federal spending reductions in the Medicaid program, which will reduce the rate of the growth of community resources in the mental retardation field (Braddock & Hemp, 1996); (2) the growth of managed care in the states, which may restrict access to disability services and reduce costs (Smith & Ashbaugh, 1995); (3) a general shift of program authority and resources in health and human services from Washington to the states; and (4) a growing emphasis on providing supports for people with mental retardation that are flexibly tailored to meet individual and not facility or group needs (Dufresne & Laux, 1994; Smull & Danehey, 1994). Researchers will be challenged over the next decade to investigate the impacts of these trends on mental retardation service innovations in the 50 states.

The innovations in service delivery that we have seen are being accompanied by a number of associated educational innovations. The current emphasis on natural supports and self-help in the mental retardation field parallels developments in mental health (Abell & Tracy, 1990; Katz, 1992; Naparstek, Biegel, & Spiro, 1982) and in independent living for persons with physical disabilities (DeJong, 1979). This emphasis on self-advocacy across the spectrum of physical and mental disability constituencies will grow in significance as it becomes more fully understood and accepted by professionals, parents, service providers, and university training programs. For example, interdisciplinary "disability studies" preservice training programs and research centers seem poised to emerge over the next decade in several major American universities. Such programs may be anchored in liberal arts colleges, schools of social work, education schools, health sciences colleges, university affiliated programs in developmental disabilities, or in some combination of these settings. Disability studies programs should be modeled in part after the interdisciplinary centers and training programs in women and gender studies, African American studies, and Latino studies. As with these "area studies" or "cultural studies" programs, disability studies will incorporate a variety of disciplinary perspectives to advance our understanding of the disabling experience in social, political, economic, and related contexts. In some universities, undergraduate and graduate degree programs in disability studies may also be offered.

Just as the Civil Rights Act of 1964 was an important catalyst in the United States for developing area studies programs in race and gender, the Americans with Disabilities Act of 1990 was a watershed civil rights statute that set the stage for people with disabilities to push higher education to become more academically responsive to their needs. There is progress to report. In January 1996, the board of trustees of the University of Illinois authorized the establishment on its Chicago campus of the first interdisciplinary Ph.D. program in disability studies in a public research university in the United States. The National Institute on Disability and Rehabilitation Research (NIDRR) has also commissioned two major disability studies textbooks, which are being edited by faculty at the Institute on Disability and Human Development at the University of Illinois at Chicago in association with faculty at other leading universities in the United States and abroad. Degree programs in disability studies have also been established at Syracuse University, the University of Delaware, Temple University, and the University of Maine. The University of California at Berkeley is presently considering the establishment of an undergraduate major in disability studies.

The development of disability studies curricular initiatives and interdisciplinary research centers represents an exciting new innovation in the evolution of the disability field. Disabled scholars have particularly crucial roles to play in ensuring the success of a disability studies movement in higher education. The NIDRR, the National Center for Medical Rehabilitation and Research in NIH, and the Office of Special Education and Rehabilitative Services in the U.S. Department of Education also have vital leadership roles to play in nurturing the emergence of disability studies initiatives in higher education. The agencies should continue to utilize their research and training grant resources to stimulate the creation of disability studies programs, centers, and institutes in the United States and worldwide.

REFERENCES

Abell, N., & Tracy, E. M. (1990). Special issue: Applications of social support and social network interventions in direct practice. *Journal of Applied Social Sciences, 15*(1).

Abery, B. H., & Fahnestock, M. (1994). Enhancing the social inclusion of persons with developmental disabilities. In M. F. Hayden & B. H. Abery (Eds.), *Challenges for a service system in transition: Ensuring quality community experiences for people with developmental disabilities* (pp. 83–119). Baltimore, MD: Paul H. Brookes.

Abery, B., Rudrud, L., Arndt, K., Schauben, L., & Eggebeen, A. (1995). Evaluating a multicomponent program for enhancing self-determination of youth with disabilities. *Intervention in School and Clinic, 30,* 170–179.

Alm, N. (1993). The development of augmentative and alternative communication systems to assist with social communication. *Technology and Disability, 2*(3), 1–18.

American Association on Mental Retardation. (1992). *Mental retardation: Definition, classification, and systems of supports.* Washington, DC: Author.

Bensberg, G. J., & Smith, J. J. (1984). *Comparative costs of public residential and community residential facilities for the mentally retarded.* Lubbock: Texas Tech University, Research and Training Center in Mental Retardation.

Benson, B. A., Rice, C. J., & Miranti, S. V. (1986). Effects of anger management training with mentally retarded adults in group treatment. *Journal of Consulting and Clinical Psychology, 54,* 728–729.

Bercovici, S. M. (1983). *Barriers to normalization: The restrictive management of retarded persons.* Baltimore, MD: University Park Press.

Bogdan, R., & Taylor, S. J. (1987). Conclusion: The next wave. In S. J. Taylor, D. Biklen, & J. Knoll (Eds.), *Community integration for people with severe disabilities* (pp. 209–213). New York: Teachers College Press.

Bouras, N., Brooks, D., & Drummond, K. (1993). Community psychiatric services for people with mental retardation. In N. Bouras (Ed.), *Mental health in mental retardation.* New York: Cambridge University Press.

Bowen, C. A., & Rosal, M. L. (1989). The use of art therapy to reduce the maladaptive behaviors of a mentally retarded adult. *Arts in Psychotherapy, 16,* 211–218.

Braddock, D., & Heller, T. (1985). The closure of mental retardation institutions I: Trends in the United States. *Mental Retardation, 23*(4), 168–176.

Braddock, D., & Hemp, R. (1996). Medicaid spending reductions and developmental disabilities. *Journal of Disability Policy Studies, 7*(1), 1–32.

Braddock, D., & Hemp, R. (in press). Toward family and community: A comparative analysis of mental retardation services in Massachusetts, New England, and the United States. *Mental Retardation.*

Braddock, D., Hemp, R., Bachelder, L., & Fujiura, G. (1995). *The state of the states in developmental disabilities* (4th ed.). Washington, DC: American Association on Mental Retardation.

Braddock, D., Hemp, R., Parish, S., & Westrich, J. (1998). *The state of the states in developmental disabilities* (5th ed.). Washington, DC: American Association on Mental Retardation.

Braddock, D., & Mitchell, D. (1992). *Residential services and developmental disabilities in the United States: A national survey of staff compensation, turnover, and related issues.* Washington, DC: American Association on Mental Retardation.

Bruininks, R. H., Hill, B. K., & Morreau, L. E. (1988). Prevalence and implications of maladaptive behaviors and dual diagnosis in residential and other service programs. In J. A. Stark, F. J. Menolascino, M. H. Abarelli, & V. C. Gray (Eds.), *Mental retardation and mental health: Classification, diagnosis, treatment, services* (pp. 3–29). New York: Springer-Verlag.

Carr, E. G., & Durand, V. M. (1985). Reducing behavior problems through functional communication training. *Journal of Applied Behavior Analysis, 18,* 111–126.

Coulter, D. L. (1996). Prevention as a form of support: Implications for the new definition. *Mental Retardation, 34*(2), 108–116.

Covert, S. B., MacIntosh, J. D., & Shumway, D. L. (1994). Closing the Laconia state school and training center: A case study in system change. In V. J. Bradley, J. W. Ashbaugh, & B. C. Blaney (Eds.), *Creating individual supports for people with developmental disabilities: A mandate for change at many levels* (pp. 197–211). Baltimore, MD: Paul H. Brookes.

Davidson, P. W., Cain, N. N., Sloane-Reeves, J. E., Giesow, V. E., Quijano, L. E., Van Heyningen, J., & Shoham, I. (1993). *Crisis intervention for community-based persons with developmental disabilities and concomitant behavioral and psychiatric disorders.* Unpublished manuscript, University of Rochester.

DeJong, G. (1979). Independent living: From social movement to analytic paradigm. *Archives of Physical Medicine and Rehabilitation, 60*(10), 435–446.

Dowrick, P. W., & Biggs, S. J. (Eds.). (1983). *Using video: Psychological and social applications.* Chichester, UK: Wiley.

Dufresne, D., & Laux, B. (1994). From facilities to supports: The changing organization. In V. J. Bradley, J. W. Ashbaugh, & B. C. Blaney (Eds.), *Creating individual supports for people with developmental disabilities: A mandate for change at many levels* (pp. 271–280). Baltimore, MD: Paul H. Brookes.

Dybwad, G., & Bersani, Jr., H. (Eds.). (1996). *New voices: Self-advocacy by people with disabilities.* Cambridge, MA: Brookline Books.

Edgerton, R. B. (1990). Quality of life from a longitudinal research perspective. In R. L. Schalock (Ed.), *Quality of life: Perspectives and issues* (pp. 149–160). Washington, DC: American Association on Mental Retardation.

Fernald, W. E. (1919). A state program for the care of the mentally defective. *Mental Hygiene, 3*, 566–574.

Fletcher, R. (1988). A country systems model: Comprehensive services for the dually diagnosed. In J. A. Stark, F. J. Menolascino, M. H. Albarelli, & V. C. Gray (Eds.), *Mental retardation and mental health: Classification, diagnosis, treatment, services* (pp. 254–264). New York: Springer-Verlag.

Goode, D. A. (Ed.). (1994). *Quality of life for persons with disabilities—international perspectives and issues.* Cambridge, MA: Brookline Books.

Guralnick, M. (1996). *The effectiveness of early intervention.* Baltimore, MD: Paul H. Brookes.

Hagberg, B., Hagberg, G., Lewerth, A., & Lindberg, U. (1981a). Mild mental retardation in Swedish school children. I. Prevalence. *Acta Paediatrica Scandinavica, 70*(4), 441–444.

Hagberg, B., Hagberg, G., Lewerth, A., & Lindberg, U. (1981b). Mild mental retardation in Swedish school children. II. Etiologic and pathogenic aspects. *Acta Paediatrica Scandinavica, 70*(4), 445–452.

Hauber, F. A., Bruininks, R. H., Hill, B. K., Lakin, K. C., & White, C. C. (1984, Sept.). *National census of residential facilities. Fiscal year 1982* (project report number 19). Minneapolis: University of Minnesota, Department of Educational Psychology.

Hayden, M. F., & DePaepe, P. (1994). Waiting for community services: The impact on persons with mental retardation and other developmental disabilities. In M. F. Hayden & B. H. Abery (Eds.), *Challenges for a service system in transition: Ensuring quality community experiences for people with developmental disabilities* (pp. 173–206). Baltimore, MD: Paul H. Brookes.

Hayden, M. F., & Senese, D. (1996). *Self-advocacy groups: 1996 Directory for North America.* Minneapolis: University of Minnesota, Research and Training Center on Community Living, Institute on Community Integration.

Heller, T. (1997). Older adults with mental retardation and their families. In N. Bray (Ed.),

International review of research in mental retardation. (Vol. 20, pp. 99–136). New York: Academic Press.

Herman, S. E. (1991). Use and impact of a cash subsidy program. *Mental Retardation, 29,* 253–258.

Hoffman, A., & Field, S. (1995). Promoting self-determination through effective curriculum development. *Intervention in School and Clinic, 30,* 147–156.

Howe, S. G. (1848). *Report made to the legislature of Massachusetts upon idiocy.* Boston, MA: Collidge & Wiley.

Howe, S. G. (1866). *In ceremonies on laying the cornerstone of the New York State Institution for the Blind at Batavia, Genesee, Co., New York.* Batavia, NY: Henry Todd.

Itard, J. M. G. (1962). *The wild boy of Aveyron.* New York: Meredith Publishing Company.

Katz, A. H. (Ed.). (1992). *Self-help: Concepts and applications.* Philadelphia: Charles Press.

Kennedy, J. F. (1961). Statement by the president regarding the need for a national plan in mental retardation. In the President's Panel on Mental Retardation, *National action to combat mental retardation* (pp. 196–201). Washington, DC: U. S. Government Printing Office.

Knobbe, C. A., Carey, S., Rhodes, L., & Horner, R. (1995). Benefit-cost analysis of community residential versus institutional services for adults with severe mental retardation and challenging behavior. *American Journal on Mental Retardation, 99*(5), 533–541.

Kuhlman, F. (1940). One hundred years of special care and training. *American Journal of Mental Deficiency, 45,* 18–24.

Lakin, C. (1996). *Research on community integration of persons with mental retardation and related conditions: Current knowledge, emerging challenges and recommended future directions.* Washington, DC: National Institute on Disability and Rehabilitation Research.

Lakin, K. C. (1979). *Demographic studies of residential facilities for mentally retarded people: A historical review of methodologies and findings.* Minneapolis: University of Minnesota, Center for Residential and Community Services.

Larson, S. A., & Lakin, K. C. (1989). Deinstitutionalization of persons with mental retardation. Behavioral outcomes. *Journal of the Association for Persons With Severe Handicaps, 14,* 324–332.

Larson, S. A., & Lakin, K. C. (1991). Parental attitudes about residential placement before and after deinstitutionalization: A research synthesis. *Journal of the Association for Persons With Severe Handicaps, 16,* 25–38.

Lazar, I., & Darlington, R. B. (1982). Lasting effects of early education. *Monographs of the Society for Research in Child Development, 47*(2–3, Serial No. 195).

Lewis, D. R., Johnson, D. R., Bruininks, R. H., & Kallsen, L. (1994). Accounting for costs of habilitation training, sheltered workshops, and supported employment. *Education and Training in Mental Retardation, 28*(1), 75–89.

Longhurst, N. A. (1994). *The self-advocacy movement: A demographic study and directory.* Washington, DC: American Association on Mental Retardation.

Matson, J. L., & Andrasik, F. (1982). Training leisure time social interaction skills to mildly mentally retarded adults. *American Journal of Mental Deficiency, 86,* 533–542.

McLaren, J., & Bryson, S. E. (1987). Review of recent epidemiological studies of mental retardation: Prevalence, associated disorders, and etiology. *American Journal on Mental Retardation, 92*(3), 243–254.

McQueen, P. C., Spence, M. W., Winsor, E. J., Garner, J. B., & Pereira, L. (1986). Causal origins of major mental handicap in the Canadian Maritime Provinces. *Developmental Medicine and Child Neurology, 28,* 697–707.

Menolascino, F. J., & Stark, J. A. (Eds.). (1984). *Handbook of mental illness in the mentally retarded.* New York: Plenum.

Mercer, J. R. (1973). *Labeling the mentally retarded: Clinical and social systems perspectives on mental retardation.* Berkeley: University of California Press.

Meyers, J. C., & Marcenko, M. O. (1989). Impact of a cash subsidy program for families of children with severe developmental disabilities. *Mental Retardation, 27,* 383–387.

Michigan ARC v. Smith, 475 F. Supp 990 (E.D. Mich. 1979) (filed Feb. 21, 1978).

Naparstek, A. J., Biegel, D. E., & Spiro, H. R. (1982). *Neighborhood networks for humane mental health care.* New York: Plenum.

National Center for Health Statistics. (1977). *National nursing home survey.* Washington, DC: Author.

National Conference on Self-Determination. (1989, January). *29+ Recommendations from the conference participants.* Minneapolis: University of Minnesota, Institute on Community Integration.

National Institutes of Health. (1989). *Final report of the consensus development panel on treatment of destructive behaviors in persons with developmental disabilities.* Bethesda, MD: Author.

Newman, I., & Emerson, E. (1991). Specialized treatment units for person with challenging behaviors. *Mental Handicap, 19,* 113–119.

Nezu, C. M., Nezu, A. M., & Gill-Weiss, M. J. (1992). *Psychopathology in persons with mental retardation: Clinical guidelines for assessment and treatment.* Champaign, IL: Research Press.

President's Panel on Mental Retardation. (1962). *A proposed program for national action to combat mental retardation.* Washington, DC: U.S. Superintendent of Documents.

Prout, H. T., & Cale, R. L. (1994). Individual counseling approaches. In D. C. Strohmer & H. T. Prout (Eds.), *Counseling and psychotherapy with persons with mental retardation and borderline intelligence* (pp. 103–142). Brandon, VT: Clinical Psychology Publishing.

Prouty, R., & Lakin, K. C. (Eds.). (1995, June). *Residential services for persons with developmental disabilities: Status and trends through 1994.* Minneapolis: University of Minnesota, Research and Training Center on Community Living, Institute on Community Integration.

Reiss, S. (1994). *Handbook of challenging behavior: Mental health aspects of mental retardation.* Worthington, OH: IDS Publishing Corp.

Reiss, S., & Aman, M. G. (Eds.). (1998). *Psychotropic medications and developmental disabilities: The international consensus handbook.* Washington, DC: American Association on Mental Retardation.

Reiss, S., Levitan, G., & McNally, R. (1982). Emotionally disturbed mentally retarded people: An underserved population. *American Psychologist, 37*(4), 361–367.

Reiss, S., & Trenn, E. (1984). Consumer demand for outpatient mental health services for mentally retarded people. *Mental Retardation, 22,* 112–115.

Rusch, F., Chadsey-Rusch, J., & Johnson, J. (1991). Supported employment: Emerging opportunities for employment integration. In L. Meyer, C. Peck, & L. Brown (Eds.), *Critical issues in the lives of people with severe disabilities* (pp. 145–169). Baltimore, MD: Paul H. Brookes.

Schalock, R. L. (1990). Where do we go from here? In R. L. Schalock (Ed.), *Quality of life: Perspectives and issues* (pp. 235–240). Washington, DC: American Association on Mental Retardation.

Schiller, W. J., & Schaaf, K. (1997). *Multimodal functional analysis and intervention: A training program for Illinois Department of Mental Health and Developmental Disabilities staff.* Chicago: Institute on Disability and Human Development, University of Illinois at Chicago.

Schleien, S. J., & Ray, M. T. (1988). *Community recreation and persons with disabilities: Strategies for integration.* Baltimore, MD: Paul H. Brookes.

Seguin, E. (1856). Origins of the treatment and training of idiots. *American Journal of Education, 2,* 145–152.

Seltzer, M. (1984). Correlates of community opposition to community residences for mentally retarded persons. *American Journal of Mental Deficiency, 89*(1), 1–8.

Sigelman, C. (1976). A Machiavelli for planners: Community attitudes and selection of a group home site. *Mental Retardation, 14*(1), 26–29.

Skeels, H. M., & Harms, I. (1948). Children with inferior social histories: Their mental development in adoptive homes. *Journal of Genetic Psychology, 72,* 283–294.

Skeels, H. M., Updegraff, R., Wellman, B. L., & Williams, H. M. (1938). A study of environmental stimulation, an orphanage preschool project. *University of Iowa Studies in Child Welfare, 15*(4).

Smith, G., & Ashbaugh, J. (1995). *Managed care and people with developmental disabilities: A guidebook.* Alexandria, VA: National Association of State Directors of Developmental Disabilities Services.

Smull, M. W., & Danehey, A. J. (1994). Increasing quality while reducing costs: The challenge of the 1990s. In V. J. Bradley, J. W. Ashbaugh, & B. C. Blaney (Eds.), *Creating individual supports for people with developmental disabilities: A mandate for change at many levels* (pp. 59–78). Baltimore, MD: Paul H. Brookes.

Smull, M. W., Fabian, E. S., & Chanteau, F. B. (1984). A special program for mentally retarded/mentally ill citizens: The Rock Creek Foundation. In F. J. Menolascino & J. A. Stark (Eds.), *Handbook of mental illness in the mentally retarded* (pp. 235–248). New York: Plenum.

Snell, M. E. (1987). *Systematic instruction of persons with severe handicaps* (3rd ed.). Columbus, OH: Charles E. Merrill.

Speer, G. S. (1940). The intelligence of foster children. *Journal of Genetic Psychology, 57,* 49–55.

Survey and Research Corporation. (1965, July). *Mental Retardation Program Statistics of U. S.–A report to the Department of Health, Education and Welfare pursuant to Contract PH-86-64-99.* Washington, DC: U.S. Department of Health, Education and Welfare.

Sutton, E., Factor, A., Hawkins, B. A., Heller, T., & Seltzer, G. B. (Eds.). (1993). *Older adults with developmental disabilities: Optimizing choice and change.* Baltimore, MD: Paul H. Brookes.

Switzky, H. N., Dudzinski, M., Van Acker, R., & Gambro, J. (1988). Historical foundations of out-of-home residential alternatives for mentally retarded persons. In L. W. Heal, J. I. Haney, & A. R. Novak Amado (Eds.), *Integration of developmentally disabled individuals into the community* (2nd ed., pp. 19–35). Baltimore, MD: Paul H. Brookes.

Szymanski, L. S. (1980a). Individual psychotherapy with retarded persons. In L. S. Szymanski & P. E. Tanguay (Eds.), *Emotional disorders of mentally retarded persons: Assessment, treatment, and consultation* (pp. 131–148). Baltimore, MD: University Park Press.

Szymanski, L. S. (1980b). Psychiatric diagnosis in retarded persons. In L. S. Szymanski & P. E. Tanguay (Eds.), *Emotional disorders of mentally retarded persons: Assessment, treatment, and consultation* (pp. 61–81). Baltimore, MD: University Park Press.

Taylor, S. J. (1991). Toward families for all children. In S. J. Taylor, R. Bogdan, & J. A. Racino (Eds.), *Life in the community: Case studies of organizations supporting people with disabilities* (pp. 19–34). Baltimore, MD: Paul H. Brookes.

Taylor, S. J., Lakin, K. C., & Hill, B. K. (1989). Permanency planning for all children and youth: Policy and philosophy to govern out-of-home placement decisions. *Exceptional Children, 55*(6), 541–549.

U. S. Bureau of the Census. (1996, Dec.). *Population Estimates Program, Population Division.* Washington, DC: Author.

U. S. Department of Health, Education, and Welfare. (1972, Sept.). *Mental retardation source book of the DHEW.* Washington, DC: Author, Office of the Secretary, Office of Mental Retardation Coordination.

U. S. Holocaust Memorial Museum. (Undated). *The mentally and physically handicapped victims of the Nazi era.* Washington, DC: The Museum.

Vaux, C. L. (1935). Family care of mental defectives. *Journal of Psycho-Asthenics, 40,* 168–189.

Wallace, G. L. (1929). Are the feebleminded criminals? *Mental Hygiene, 13*(1), 93–98.

Wehman, P. (1993). *The ADA mandate for social change.* Baltimore, MD: Paul H. Brookes.

Wehman, P., Revell, G., & Kregel, J. (1995). *Supported employment from 1986–1993: A national program that works.* Manuscript submitted for publication.

Wells, J., & Arthur, G. (1939). Effect of foster-home placement on the intelligence ratings of children of feebleminded parents. *Mental Hygiene, 23,* 277–285.

West, J. (1991). *The Americans with Disabilities Act: From policy to practice.* New York: Milbank Memorial Fund.

Wolfensberger, W. (1972). *The principle of normalization in human services.* Toronto: National Institute on Mental Retardation.

Wolfensberger, W. (1976). On the origin of our institutional models. In R. Kugel, & A. Shearer (Eds.), *Changing patterns in residential services for the mentally retarded* (rev. ed., pp. 35–82). Washington, DC: President's Committee on Mental Retardation.

Wolfensberger, W. (1981). The extermination of handicapped people in World War II Germany. *Mental Retardation, 19*(1), 1–7.

Wolfensberger, W. (1983). Social role valorization: A proposed new term for the principle of normalization. *Mental Retardation, 21*(6), 234–239.

Wolfensberger, W., & Menolascino, F. (1970). Reflections on recent retardation developments in Nebraska I: A new plan. *Mental Retardation, 8,* 20–24.

Woodward, H. L., & Pederson, E. L. (1991). *A model for developing mental retardation/mental illness intervention services in existing community mental health centers.* Cincinnati, OH: University-Affiliated Cincinnati Center for Developmental Disabilities.

Wyatt v. Stickney, 344 F.Supp. 373, 387 (M.D. Ala. 1972), affíd sub nom, Wyatt v. Aderholt, 503 F.2d. 1305 (5th Cir. 1974).

Zagelbaum, V. N., & Rubino, M. A. (1991). Combined dance/movement, art, and music therapies with a developmentally delayed, psychiatric client in a day treatment setting. *Arts in Psychotherapy, 18,* 139–148.

9

Innovations in Treating Alcohol Problems

ALLEN ZWEBEN

SUSAN ROSE

Redefining Alcohol Abusing Populations

Within the past 20 years, there has been a growing public acceptance of alcohol abuse as a sociomedical problem rather than a moral deficiency and an increasing awareness of the scope and pervasiveness of the problem. Professionals have recognized that alcohol abuse plays a prominent role in a substantial number of social problems, including domestic violence, unemployment, homelessness, and criminal behavior. Problems with alcohol use have been cited in employee absenteeism, unplanned pregnancy (Ewing, 1991), intentional suicides, homicides (CSAP, 1995), and child abuse and neglect (CWLA, 1992). It is estimated that 18 million persons in this country have experienced some problems with drinking (CSAP, 1995).

Within this vulnerable population, there is wide variation in patterns of consumption, degree of pathology, coping mechanisms, family resources, and community strengths available to ameliorate these problems. Individuals with alcohol use problems reflect a heterogeneous population and include those with mild to moderate difficulties stemming from alcohol use and those with severe difficulties. Those with moderate difficulties are afflicted with intrapersonal, interpersonal, or social problems without as yet experiencing the medical complications, physiological reactions (e.g., withdrawal symptoms), and psychiatric problems typically found in a chronic alcohol-abusing population. These individuals have had periodic absences from work, strained relationships with family members or employers, and more mild to moderate emotional difficulties such as guilt about the drinking episodes. Some have had extensive periods of abstinence from alcohol use. Others have been drinking moderately and only recently have increased their consumption levels. To differentiate them from so-called alcoholics or alcohol-dependent clients, individuals with mild to moderate alcohol difficulties have been termed "early-stage problem drinkers," "risky drinkers," "alcohol abusers" (DSM-IV category), or "nondependent alcohol clients."

Although the causal connection is not always clear, these nondependent clients have been linked with a variety of social ills such as domestic violence, trauma injuries, low productivity in the workplace, juvenile crime, suicides, homicides, and drinking and driving offenses (IOM, 1990). Estimates of the scope vary, but it has been widely reported that nondependent drinkers make up the vast majority of individuals with alcohol-related problems in this country (Sobell & Sobell, 1993). For example, the majority of individuals convicted of drinking and driving offenses can be categorized as nondependent drinkers (Single, 1996). While the social costs are difficult to calculate, the economic costs of the full range of alcohol problems in reduced productivity, premature death, and treatment has been estimated to be $98 billion in 1990 (USDHHS, 1993), and the costs of health care utilization for treating alcohol problems has been estimated to be $114 billion in 1993 (CSAP, 1995).

This chapter examines issues and practices related to the treatment needs of alcohol-abusing populations. Particular emphasis is placed on the brief intervention model, an approach deemed to be suitable for large numbers of individuals afflicted with alcohol problems. The rationale for the model, along with its task components, are delineated. How the brief intervention has been applied in health care settings is described. Evidence for the effectiveness of the model is critically reviewed. Discussion is focused on how health care practitioners might utilize brief intervention technology with individuals deemed to be at risk for alcohol problems. Recommendations are offered for enriching curricula in addictive behaviors for the purpose of improving the delivery of health services among diverse client groups.

SUBPOPULATIONS AT RISK

It is estimated that 15.3 million persons in this country met the DSM III-R criteria for alcohol abuse and dependence in 1988 (USDHHS, 1990). Rates of alcohol problems are greater for males than females and are highest in the younger age groups, decreasing with increasing age.

Subpopulations at greatest risk of harm from alcohol use problems include women of child-bearing age and adolescents, young white men, and African American men. As part of the Behavioral Risk Factor Surveillance System of the Centers for Disease Control, the prevalence of alcohol consumption among pregnant women was reported as 20% (Serdula, Williamson, Kendrick, Anda, & Byers, 1991); yet the identification of problem drinking among this group of women is limited. In a study of the negative consequences of alcohol use by women, Ewing (1991) reported that 97% of 135 women identified as having alcohol and other drug problems at delivery stated that their pregnancy was unplanned. Unintended pregnancy and potential fetal damage may indeed be one of the first results of risky drinking for women of child-bearing age.

Large numbers of high school–age girls are reported to drink occasionally in ways that lead to dangerous situations and negative consequences (Thompson & Wilsnack, 1984); yet relatively few schools or adolescent treatment programs identify this as a primary problem. Rates of heavy drinking peak among younger white males and female adolescents and decrease with age (USDHHS, 1993). While 7% of all drinkers experienced moderate levels of dependence symptoms and 10% experienced moderate levels of drinking-related consequences in 1989, alcohol dependence symptoms and drinking-related consequences were highest for male drinkers between the ages of 18 and 29.

National surveys have reported that African American persons abstain from drinking at higher rates and have lower rates of heavy drinking. However, African American males' rates of heavy drinking peak at a later age than those of white males. This later course of heavy drinking may account for the higher incidence of alcohol-related health problems reported by African American males.

A New Paradigm for the Treatment of Alcohol Problems

Definitions of alcohol-related behavior that rely heavily on medical and psychiatric conceptions were introduced in the third edition of the *Diagnostic and Statistical Manual of Mental Disorders* (APA, 1980) and remain in use in the current, most recent fourth edition (APA, 1994). These definitions assert a dichotomy between dependence and abuse, differentiating them by the presence of tolerance or withdrawal symptoms. Within this disease model, alcoholism is considered a progressive disorder and the course of the "illness" is expected to worsen unless abstinence is achieved and maintained. Thus, regardless of the level of severity of alcohol problems, abstinence-oriented treatment approaches are deemed to be the most viable approach for treating alcohol disorders.

This overreliance on medical models for diagnostic criteria (Kirk & Kutchins, 1992) often misses the drinker who is neither dependent nor abusive yet who drinks in a manner that could potentially cause medical and psychosocial problems. In recognition of the notion that individuals who drink excessively differ in the severity of their alcohol problems, the World Health Organization adopted the term "alcohol dependency syndrome" (Skinner & Allen, 1982). This broader definition of alcohol use problem behaviors encompasses the reality that individuals can be placed on a continuum ranging from those with severe difficulties (e.g., medical complications) to those with mild or moderate difficulties (e.g., interpersonal stress) that stem from the drinking. The new paradigm emphasizes that alcohol use problem behaviors are not necessarily degenerative, and therefore it is believed that some individuals afflicted with alcohol problems can return to moderate drinking without eventually succumbing to a pattern of dependent drinking.

In response to this new paradigm, health care policy has shifted its focus beyond those who are dependent drinkers to include those who are nondependent as well (IOM, 1990). These outreach efforts have resulted in an increase in the amount of resources devoted to more vulnerable at-risk groups (Weisner & Room, 1984). For example, in most states, health maintenance organizations and insurance carriers are required by law to include substance abuse treatment services in the mental health care packages offered to their customers. At the same time, corporations have included assessment and intervention for substance use problems as part of the benefits package offered to their employees.

Courts have mandated that drinking and driving offenders undergo assessment and treatment as an alternative to incarceration. The purpose of these changes is to detect and intervene in these problems before they become more severe.

This increasing attention to individuals with varying levels of alcohol problem behaviors parallels the attention given to health promotion and early intervention strategies in the health care system in general. To attend to the diversity of clients seen for alcohol problems, greater emphasis has been placed on providing a *continuum of treatments* that reflects the continuum of behaviors, motivations, capacities, and needs of this diverse and vulnerable client group. Such treatments are aimed at a continuum of outcomes that include improving consumption patterns (e.g., controlled drinking), reducing the harmful consequences of the abuse, and encouraging abstinence for those experiencing more severe consequences of drinking.

Treatment Needs of Persons with Alcohol Use Problems

What increases the vulnerability of persons with alcohol use problems is their low level of awareness about their alcohol misuse and the related consequences stemming from these negative behaviors. For example, one study indicated that only 9% of individuals in social service settings were able to acknowledge drinking as a primary problem (Demone et al., as cited in Corrigan & Anderson, 1985). When seen in nonspecialized settings, these individuals are, for the most part, focused on the issues that initially brought them into the setting, such as marital conflict, domestic violence, and employment problems and have not as yet made a connection between their alcohol use and these psychosocial issues (Cooney, Zweben, & Fleming, 1995; Zweben & Barrett, 1997). Even among the more dependent population, frequent heavy drinkers with higher incomes and educational levels are less likely to report both dependence symptoms and alcohol-use-related consequences than those with lower incomes and less education (USDHHS, 1993).

Due to the low severity of their alcohol use problems, many of the nondependent drinkers have not as yet experienced pressures from family, friends, or employers to address these problems. Family members may not have experienced sufficient hardship to feel it necessary to coerce the drinker to seek help for his or her problems. Thus, it is not surprising that nondependent clients do not feel the need to seek help for their alcohol use difficulties and have been termed *nonhelp-seeking* by community health clinics (Heather, 1989).

Practitioners in health care settings who are interested in engaging these clients in formal treatment have encountered enormous obstacles that in turn have contributed to low compliance rates. Studies routinely report that the majority of alcohol-abusing clients fail to enter or remain in treatment programs. For example, failure rates for referrals to alcohol treatment programs range from 70% to 90% in North America (Babor, Ritson, & Hodgson, 1986; Soderstrom & Cowley, 1987). Similarly, immediate dropout rates (i.e., clients who do not stay past the first session) are about 44% in programs studied in the United Kingdom (Rees, Beech, & Hore, 1984; Thom et al., 1992).

This lack of compliance can be partially attributed to both practitioners' restrictive perspectives on alcohol problems (i.e., "alcoholic" or not) and their lack of the intervention skills necessary for addressing the treatment needs, diverse capacities, and resources of these at-risk clients (Cook et al., 1983). Practitioners have failed to keep pace with the changing definitional paradigms for treating alcohol problems, and, consequently, their perceptions of nondependent drinkers are often incompatible with these clients' own perceptions of their problems. Unlike chronic alcohol clients, nondependent clients do not see themselves as having a "disease" that renders them "powerless" (i.e., lacking control) to regulate their negative behaviors, as many have already demonstrated an ability to cut down or control their consumption levels. Consequently, they are more interested in reducing their consumption levels than in abstaining (Sanchez-Craig et al., 1984). In short, messages delivered by practitioners about alcohol use and its related problems represent a radical departure from these clients' own thinking about their problems.

The use of conventional techniques such as "breaking down denial" and "labeling" (e.g., being designated as alcoholic) have often proven to be counterproductive and ineffective in engaging persons with alcohol problems in treatment (Miller, 1983). Since there are few alternatives to traditional, intensive programs in the United States, clients with identified alcohol use problems are typically referred to conventional treatment facilities. Such programs usually require a commitment to abstinence, regular attendance at Alcoholics Anonymous meetings, and participation in a treatment regimen that includes alcohol and drug education and group therapy. Given the circumstances of nondependent clients and their perceptions of their problems, many are not ready to accept the rigorous demands or expectations laid out for participants in traditional treatment programs. In short, the focus of traditional treatment programs is not applicable to the range of issues encountered by nondependent alcohol clients and might even become a major barrier to their acceptance of treatment.

Brief Intervention as an Alternative Model for Treating Alcohol Problems

On the basis of research involving nicotine abusers (Ockene et al., 1991; Richmond & Heather, 1990) and studies conducted primarily in Europe (cf. Bien et al., 1993 for a comprehensive review of the literature), brief intervention has been considered a suitable alternative to more intensive traditional interventions, particularly for individuals with low to moderate alcohol use problems. Studies conducted primarily in hospital settings have affirmed the utility of brief interventions for effecting changes in drinking and drinking-related problems. Bien and his colleagues (1993) reviewed 32 clinical trials involving brief intervention modalities. They concluded: "There is sufficient evidence to warrant the implementation of brief motivational interventions in a variety of settings. . . . Substantial proportions of people presented with or referred for alcohol problems may be responsive to this approach, allowing more extensive treatments to be focused on those who benefit differentially from it" (p. 322).

Brief interventions convey the expectation that the potential for change is possible through the efforts of the individual, rather than by the directions of the practitioner. The interventions are aimed at enhancing self-directed efforts for change. Rather than reinforcing notions of illness, dependency, and the need for long-term treatment, brief interventions convey the optimistic message that, with the support of others, the individual has the inherent coping resources to modify the negative behaviors, immediately for some, eventually for others.

The brief treatment approach is grounded in the principles of motivational psychology and natural recovery (Miller & Rollnick, 1991; Prochaska & DiClemente, 1984). The underlying assumption of the model is that individuals have the inherent coping resources to initiate and maintain change with minimal involvement of the practitioners. Such change is initiated through interventions that involve decision-making processes. The decision to change is activated when the benefits derived from the substance use behavior are outweighed by the costs of continuing them. The benefits might involve the belief or expectation that substance use can improve social performance, reduce stress and anxiety, and enhance pleasurable events. The costs may be direct or immediate, such as financial problems, legal difficulties, and medical consequences, or indirect and not immediate, such as the problems that result when abusive behaviors begin to threaten supportive relationships, personal values, ideals, and beliefs. Individuals who are subject to external pressures such as loss of employment, marital separation and incarceration resulting from alcohol use are more amenable to change than those lacking such pressures.

Brief treatment is seen as a mechanism to initiate or facilitate this self-changing process. This treatment provides an opportunity for the individual to rationally assess whether the benefits derived from the abusive behaviors are worth the actual and potential costs incurred because of them. Also, the individual is asked to consider whether there are feasible and acceptable alternatives that can serve the same functions as the abusive behaviors. These alternatives might include spending time with family rather than "drinking buddies" in order to satisfy interpersonal needs for companionship or attending self-help meetings instead of visiting regularly the neighborhood saloon.

The likelihood of changing the alcohol use behaviors is associated with the individuals' level of self-efficacy about the problem behaviors (Miller & Rollnick, 1991). Self-efficacy is defined as the individuals' belief about whether or not she or he can execute a positive response to the negative behaviors (Bandura, 1977). Individuals possessing a high degree of self-efficacy are able to recognize and accept the risks associated with drinking and at the same time are ready to undertake the necessary action steps to change the behavior. Individuals who are cognizant of the risks stemming from alcohol use experience a sense of dissonance about the problem behaviors and are ready to adopt alternative behaviors in order to reduce the dissonance or restore emotional equilibrium ("peace of mind"). In contrast, individuals with low self-efficacy tend to deny the risks associated with drinking and consequently avoid taking the necessary action steps to address the problems.

A critical component of the brief intervention model is the emphasis placed upon client choice, particularly in the selection of drinking goals and the creation of a plan to change the behavior. This is a key component of the model and differentiates it from traditional disease-oriented approaches such as 12-step treatment programs. Unlike traditional approaches, it expects clients to have input to all aspects of treatment planning such as formulating drinking goals and devising strategies to achieve these goals (Rollnick, Heather, & Bell, 1992). These decision-making activities involve clarifying and negotiating differences between practitioner and client concerning such matters as the severity of alcohol problems and related issues (e.g., whether to involve the marital partner in the sessions). Successful negotiation of the treatment contract positively affects the outcome of treatment (Sobell & Sobell, 1987, 1993).

TASK COMPONENTS OF THE BRIEF INTERVENTION MODEL

A summary description of the task components of the brief intervention model is provided here. For a complete description of the techniques associated with these activities, see Miller, Zweben, DiClemente, and Rychtarik (1992).

Self-esteem Building

One of the major tasks is to improve the client's self-esteem and self-image. Extensive efforts are made to affirm and reinforce attitudes and beliefs about change. The individual is presented with a rationale for his or her involvement in treatment and complimented for being involved. Any efforts to change problem behaviors currently and in the past are explored and affirmed. At the same time, ambivalence about change is normalized, and labeling (e.g., alcoholic) is strictly avoided. Confrontational strategies commonly used in traditional programs are replaced with collaborative approaches to facilitate the client's commitment to change.

Increasing Awareness

Another task component is to have the individual present his or her own argument for change. The method used to achieve this goal is consciousness-raising (i.e., increasing the individual's awareness of the costs and consequences of the alcohol-abusing behavior). Feedback is presented on standardized tests on drinking practices, along with discussion of events or conditions (e.g., family, work, and legal issues) that might affect the cessation or continuation of the problem behavior. Such information helps to clarify and resolve discrepancies between practitioner and client about the severity of substance use and related problems.

Standardized instruments found to be useful in this phase include the Alcohol Use Disorders Test (AUDIT) (Babor & Grant, 1992) and the Drug Use Questionnaire (DAST-20) (Skinner, 1994). The University of Rhode Island Change Assessment (URICA) (Prochaska & DiClemente, 1992) and the Readiness to Change Scale (Heather et al., 1993) are useful in assessing clients' awareness level of alcohol problems and their willingness to change their behavior. Specific diagnostic tools include the Addiction Severity Index (ASI) (McClellan et al., 1992) and biological markers such as gamma glutamy transference (GGT). The latter two instruments have been commonly used by practitioners in the feedback session to enhance clients' motivational levels.

Enhancing Commitment to Change

The purpose of treatment is to obtain and enhance the individual's commitment in order to enable him or her to undertake the requisite action steps for resolving the problem. This model employs a step approach in order to obtain a commitment to change. Individuals are requested to identify specific action steps that will lead to changing the alcohol abusing behavior. This may entail sustaining a period of abstinence prior to attempting to cut down on their drinking or allowing the spouse to pick up the client's weekly salary check to avoid spending the money at the neighborhood bar. Techniques such as *optimizing* (e.g., "What do you think will work for you?") and *prioritizing* (e.g., "Of all the things you mentioned, which is the most important step to take at the present time?") are used to facilitate a commitment to change. Individuals are encouraged to explore the pros and cons of specific actions to affirm these decision-making activities. Individuals who remain uncertain or ambivalent about addressing these problems are offered a number of options such as (1) continuing what they are currently doing, (2) doing nothing at all, or (3) thinking further about the problem. Providing a menu of options is consistent with the goal of enabling the client to take ownership of the problem.

Carrying out Directives

Once an agreement is reached about proposed action steps, the individual is requested to carry out specific directives. A time frame is established for completing specific action steps. A monitoring form is given to clients to review their progress. This recording form is viewed as a mechanism to reinforce the client's commitment to change. A tentative plan may entail the following: (1) informing family members, friends, and employers about the treatment plan; (2) becoming involved in activities or events that are incompatible with drinking behavior, such as attending church services regularly, going to AA fellowship meetings, or maintaining active involvement with family rituals (e.g., dining regularly with family members, celebrating birthdays and holidays, sharing household tasks, or visiting relatives and friends).

Forestalling Relapse

The task is to sustain the benefits derived from the intervention and to prevent future relapse. The present model recognizes that the individual may occasionally have a drinking episode even if committed to an abstinence goal. Such episodes are viewed as normative or expected during the course of the recovery period. The individual is viewed as having the coping and social resources to handle the "slip" or "setback" without requiring additional treatment.

Discussion is centered on relapse prevention methods. The practitioner identifies potential "high-risk" situations that may cause the individual to resume drinking. A client is advised to examine methods in the past that were found to be effective in handling high-risk situations. Strategies are devised to handle drinking episodes. This may entail returning to abstinence and tracing situations and events that may have led to the setback.

Application of Brief Intervention Approaches in the Health Care Field

Brief interventions have been employed differentially in different settings with various kinds of alcohol clients. The task components of brief intervention can be covered in a single session of advice, as in the Orford and Edwards study (1977) (discussed later) or in a four-session treatment regime that utilizes a repertoire of motivational counseling strategies (e.g., Project MATCH) (Project MATCH Research Group, 1997). In primary care settings such as physicians' offices and emergency rooms, brief intervention components have been employed opportunistically to address the alcohol problems of nondependent clients. Such interventions are incorporated into a health promotion approach employed by health care providers for the secondary prevention of alcohol problems (Fleming et al., 1997). Depending upon the nature of the setting (e.g., emergency room, staff model HMO, EAP setting, or private physician's office), the task components are covered in a single, 15- to 30-minute session or in two 30- to 60-minute interviews (e.g., feedback and booster sessions).

The task components are carried out in four separate steps: (1) feedback, (2) goal formation, (3) advice, and (4) referral. Feedback is aimed at increasing clients' awareness of the negative consequences of the drinking behavior (Fleming et al., 1997). This helps to change clients' misperceptions or misunderstandings about the severity of the alcohol problems. This is followed by the formulation of goals about the drinking pattern (e.g., establishing criteria or cutting points for daily or weekly consumption level). Treatment goals are often aimed at reducing harm (e.g., cutting down on the drinking), rather than at achieving abstinence. Advice is focused on identifying action steps that might be taken to change the drinking pattern and making plans for achieving them. A referral for further counseling is provided if warranted and desired. Booster sessions or a referral for additional counseling is sometimes offered (Elvy et al., 1988; Fleming et al., 1997). Together these strategies help to mobilize clients' coping resources, thereby resulting in behavioral change (Heather, 1994).

In specialized settings, such as "carve-out," first-line alcoholism treatment programs, brief interventions have been employed as stand-alone treatments for individuals help seeking with higher levels of alcohol problem severity than those seen in primary care settings (Chick et al., 1988; Drummond et al., 1990; Edwards & Taylor, 1994; Heather, 1995, 1996; Zweben et al., 1988). Unlike health care providers, the individuals who conduct the interventions are considered to be specialists in treating addictive disorders (cf. Edwards et al., 1977; Project MATCH Research Group, 1997; Zweben et al., 1988). As in primary care settings, there is some variability in terms of the level of intensity associated with different components of the intervention. However, the basic steps and components (i.e., feedback, advice, goal formation, and referral) are similar to those found in primary care settings. Because of the higher level of severity of alcohol problems, the assessment interview is usually more comprehensive (3 hours in some cases) than the interview conducted in primary care settings (Orford et al., 1977; Zweben et al., 1988). Due to the length of the assessment battery, the assessment interview is ordinarily conducted prior to the feedback and advice session. Data are obtained on a variety of issues that may impact on the drinking (e.g., marital relationships), as well as on consumption patterns and related symptoms. The feedback/advice session (90 minutes) is more detailed and exhaustive than that conducted in primary care settings. In addition, in accordance with the circumstances and conditions of the clients, specialists are typically more interactive and exploratory in the interviews than are health care providers.

More recently, to enhance the potency of the intervention, an array of motivational counseling techniques has been incorporated into the brief intervention approach (Donovan et al., 1994). Such techniques are aimed at resolving clients' underlying ambivalence, uncertainty, or resistance toward changing the drinking behavior and have been found to have demonstrated efficacy in terms of treatment compliance and enhancing commitment to change (Bien et al., 1993). They include such strategies as delaying commitment to change, eliciting self-motivational statements, and deploying discrepancy (Miller, Zweben, DiClemente, & Rychtarik, 1992). For example, with regard to deploying discrepancy, the practitioner externalizes the clients' ambivalence by pointing out the disparity between "where they are and where they want to be" in terms of addressing the alcohol problems (Miller, Zweben, DiClemente, & Rychtarik, 1992; Project MATCH Motivational Enhancement Therapy [MET] Manual, p. 8). (See Project MATCH MET Manual for a complete description of these techniques.) Another ingredient in the mix of strategies employed to increase the potency of the intervention is involvement of significant others (Zweben, 1991). Unlike brief interventions employed in primary care settings, this augmented approach is typically conducted in from 4 to 6 60-minute sessions. This allows the practitioner maximum opportunity to address motivational issues.

While brief interventions vary in terms of intensity, goals, targeted groups, and intervention components, the principles remain the same (Bien et al., 1993; Heather, 1995, 1996). They all place great emphasis on personal responsibility for change, client choice, increased self-efficacy, and the promotion of optimism for change (Donovan et. al., 1994).

A Case Example

To further understand the components of this methodology, we here provide a case example of how brief intervention is applied in a community-based mental health setting.

The Drinking Check-up is a brief intervention program aimed at clients with low to moderate alcohol problems. The program is situated in a regional community health center. This mental health center offers a variety of treatment services, including family therapy, grief and loss counseling, sexual adjustment therapy, special-needs therapy for adolescents and persons with AIDS, and employee assistance for area employees and their families. Unlike earlier brief intervention programs (Miller & Sovereign, 1989), the significant other (SO) (i.e., spouse, family member, friend, or employer) is considered an essential part of the Drinking Check-up and is asked to participate in all aspects of the treatment, including information gathering, goal setting, treatment planning, and relapse prevention. It is expected that the SO will play an important role in enhancing the motivation and resolve of the drinking partner to overcome the alcohol problems.

This is a 4-session treatment program over a 9- to 10-week period. The sessions entail the following: (1) preparatory interview, (2) feedback session, (3) 1 or 2 booster sessions and emergency sessions (only if necessary). Individuals are referred to the Drinking Check-up program internally by workers who conduct intake assessments and externally by assessment workers in DWI (Drinking While Intoxicated) programs and employee assistance programs. Eligibility is determined by the use of screening devices such as the Michigan Alcoholism Screening Test (MAST) (Selzer, 1971) and the Alcohol Use Disorders Test (AUDIT) (Babor & Grant, 1992). Criterion scores have been established for inclusion in the program.

Once eligibility is determined, clients are requested to complete a comprehensive battery of tests dealing with matters related to alcohol use. Information is gathered on medical history, family concerns, situations associated with drinking episodes, coping abilities, and other issues. These data are used for goal setting, problem solving and decision making with regard to the cessation or continuation of problem drinking.

Immediately after the assessment interview, the individual and the SO meet with the practitioner to prepare them for the feedback session. In this session, reasons for entering treatment are discussed, costs and benefits of drinking are reviewed, and any ambivalence about change is explored. Also, the rationale for having the SO present is reviewed. Techniques such as role induction, the deployment of discrepancy and the eliciting of self-motivational statements (Miller et al., 1992; Zweben et al., 1988) are frequently employed.

This preparation interview is followed by the feedback session. Here the practitioner reviews relevant material from the assessment battery, such as pattern of alcohol use, high-risk situations, and coping capacities with regard to these risk situations. Efforts are made to forge a consensus with the individual and the SO concerning (1) the severity of alcohol problems, and (2) relevant issues pertaining to the drinking episodes (e.g., communication concerns, employment problems, leisure time, negative emotions, and interpersonal matters). A considerable amount of time is devoted to the negotiation of drinking goals. At issue is whether moderate drinking is a reasonable goal at this time. Individuals who do not demonstrate an ability to maintain control over drinking behavior, have major medical problems, and lack support for achieving moderate drinking are usually advised to abstain for period of time. Techniques such as delaying commitment are employed in cases where overt ambivalence is expressed about proposed drinking goals (Zweben et al., 1988).

Once a consensus is reached about the drinking, a plan is developed for reaching this objective. If moderate drinking is the goal, the practitioner negotiates frequency of drinking and amounts. Also, on the basis of information supplied in the assessment battery, circumstances for drinking are reviewed. This way, safeguards are developed to forestall relapse. For example, a client might negotiate a plan to drink only on weekends (e.g., two drinks a day) when he is relaxed and not under considerable stress from the job. Constructive input from the SO is particularly important in formulating a treatment plan to ascertain whether specific objectives are feasible or achievable, considering the client's circumstances.

Plans are made to address risk situations found to be associated with alcohol misuse. Various options are explored, such as avoiding certain people and places, choosing leisure-time activities that are incompatible with drinking, and obtaining support from natural helping relationships (e.g., family, friends, clergy) to help sustain the benefits of treatment and to reinforce the commitment to change. This session concludes with a discussion of relapse prevention. Prevention techniques are identified on the basis of past episodes where the client effectively dealt with a "slip." Tactics such as immunization and normalization are employed to improve the coping capacities of clients (Zweben & Barrett, 1993). This involves identifying negative reactions that resulted from the "slip," such as feelings of guilt or self-blame, and "normalizing" these responses. The client is requested to develop an action plan to refrain from further drinking, such as participating in activities that are incompatible with drinking (e.g., attending AA meetings). In this way, the client is "immunized" against relapse.

Booster sessions are provided to monitor progress and to address lingering problems such as ongoing ambivalence or fear about change. Efforts are made to reinforce client's coping resources and to review future barriers to change. Client performance in the interim period is an indication of whether previous goals need to be modified (e.g., returning to abstinence goal if there are too many slips).

Efficacy Studies of Brief Intervention

Initially, brief interventions were employed as minimal or control treatment conditions in studies that examined the efficacy of more intensive traditional approaches. However, by virtue of their effectiveness, brief interventions have become a viable alternative to more intensive interventions or no interventions, particularly for individuals with low to moderate alcohol problems.

Beginning with the work of Orford and Edward (1977), evidence has suggested that a brief treatment regime, often consisting of only one session, was as effective across a number of outcome measures dealing with drinking and related problems as more traditional approaches. Their original study was followed by Chick, Lloyd, and Crombie (1985) who found that a single counseling session produced significantly better outcomes at 12-month follow-up than routine medical care. The sample consisted of men admitted to a medical unit who were subsequently identified as problem drinkers. The authors concluded that brief interventions for problem drinkers is a promising approach, especially for individuals with some degree of social support.

Zweben, Pearlman, and Li (1988) compared outcomes after 8 sessions of outpatient treatment and after a single session of "advice." The study included individuals who had low to moderate levels of alcohol problems and whose partners were willing to be involved in the treatments. Approximately 60% of the subjects in both treatment groups were rated as "much improved" at eighteen months after the initial interview. However, there were no between-group treatment outcome differences.

Elvy, Wells, and Baird (1988) conducted a referral compliance study with problem drinkers seen on a medical ward of a New Zealand hospital. Eligible individuals were randomly assigned to either a referral compliance or a control group condition. Individuals in the former group received feedback on their drinking practices and a discussion about their need for formal intervention, while the latter received only routine assessment. Details of the assessment interview were sent back to the individual's general practitioner. Significant differences were found between the referral and the control groups on acceptance rates for alcoholism treatment; 67% of the referral group, compared to 37% of the controls, were subsequently enrolled in an alcoholism counseling program. However, there were few differences between the experimental and the control groups at the 18-month follow-up with respect to drinking and related measures. This study provides support for utilizing brief intervention as a mechanism to motivate the individual to seek treatment for alcohol problems, rather than as vehicle for resolving the problems.

A seminal study was conducted by the World Health Organization (WHO) (Babor & Grant, 1992). This study was conducted in health care centers in 10 countries involving a total of 1,655 subjects. The design required that subjects be assigned to one of three groups. One received 5 minutes of advice (experimental group A); one received 5 minutes of advice plus 15 minutes of counseling and a self-help pamphlet (experimental group B); and one received a 20-minute health interview (control group C). Findings showed an advantage to the two experimental groups (groups A and B) over the control group (group C). However, subjects in the advice group (A) fared as well in terms of decreased levels of consumption and related negative consequences as their counterparts in the counseling group (B).

Both Wallace et al. (1988) and Anderson and Scott (1992) conducted randomized control trials of brief intervention with nonhelp-seeking clients seen in primary care settings. Clients were seen in physician offices in Great Britain. These studies reported that the intervention group did significantly better than the control group in reducing alcohol consumption. However, in the Anderson and Scott study, this difference was found only in men. Nonetheless, both studies suggest that a brief intervention is a useful approach in reducing alcohol consumption in these nonhelp-seeking populations.

Project MATCH (Project MATCH Research Group, 1997) contrasted a brief treatment (4 sessions), termed motivational enhancement therapy (MET), with two more intensive treatment modalities (12 sessions), cognitive behavioral therapy (CBT) and a 12-step facilitation approach (TSF). Unlike subjects in some of the other studies, clients in the MATCH study constituted a broad range of problem drinkers with differing levels of severity of alcohol problems. Overall, each of the three treatments performed equally well in terms of drinking and related measures. Unlike prior matching research, severity of clients' alcohol problems was not associated with intensity of treatment; individuals with severe alcohol problems did as well in MET as in the other two treatment modalities (CBT and TSF).

As is customary in reviewing outcome research, it is important to note some limitations in these studies. It is often unclear whether observed differences between outcomes for brief treatment and those for more intensive modalities could be attributed to the characteristics of the therapists (e.g., empathy) who conducted the intervention rather than to the particular treatment modality. Another issue pertains to the integrity of the brief intervention approach. Further assurance may need to be provided that amount of exposure to treatment is significantly lower for brief intervention clients than for those assigned to more intensive treatment. Such an issue was raised about the Orford and Edwards study (1977). In this study, questions were raised about whether the amount of treatment differed significantly for clients assigned to the brief advice condition and for those assigned to the "average package of care" (Mattick & Jarvis, 1994). Nonetheless, there is no firm basis to refute the conclusions drawn by Bien et al. (1993) in their meta-analysis of brief intervention studies. The authors concluded that there no evidence indicating that the extensive alcohol treatments such as those offered in traditional treatment settings are more effective than brief interventions across a broad range of individuals seen for alcohol problems.

Questions for Future Research

The evidence suggests that brief intervention can be used in lieu of more intensive interventions, particularly for individuals with low to moderate severity of alcohol problems. These findings provide some directions for future studies on this topic.

Studies of brief intervention have differed in the number of sessions and kinds of brief intervention components (e.g., feedback, advice, referral, and motivational counseling techniques) used with clients. Due to their special circumstances, some clients, such as those seen in emergency rooms, have received fewer components of the treatment package (i.e., feedback and advice only) and, consequently, have been offered fewer sessions (usually one session) than those in other settings. At present, it is unknown whether there are incremental benefits to including the full repertoire of strategies of the brief intervention model.

Another area of concern centers on the extent to which findings on brief intervention can be generalized to client groups seen in nonhospital-based community settings such as educational, vocational, and social service settings. Thus far, most of the research has been conducted in hospital-based programs. The apparent effectiveness of brief intervention may be related to the setting in which it is being conducted. Conceivably, the medical aspects of the setting can be an important active ingredient of the brief approach. It may be easier to link alcohol problems to health-related issues (e.g., injuries resulting from accidents) than to social matters (e.g., marital conflict). In short, individuals may be more inclined to accept the model when it is delivered in health care settings than when it is delivered in social service facilities.

Other concerns deal with the importance of having the significant other (SO) play an active role in brief intervention (cf. Sobell & Sobell, 1993; Zweben, 1991). It is unclear what the relative contribution of involving the SO is to the apparent success of brief intervention (Zweben & Barrett, 1993). SO-involved brief intervention studies discussed earlier (see Chick et al., 1985; Orford & Edwards, 1977; Zweben et al., 1988) were not designed to test this unique feature. Consequently, further studies will be needed to compare brief treatments with and without SO involvement.

Future studies will need to examine the long-term impact of brief intervention in areas related to health costs and utilization. Only one study (Kristenson et al., 1983) has been conducted on extended outcomes of brief intervention, and these researchers found the long-term outcomes to be positive.

With reduced financing for substance abuse treatment services, a premium has been placed on the development and implementation of brief intervention treatment program for the secondary prevention of alcohol problems. Targeted for these programs are managed care organizations, settings where a sizeable proportion of these at-risk clients can be found. The National Institute on Alcoholism and Alcohol Abuse (NIAAA) has been a strong advocate of the development and implementation of brief intervention technology. An NIAAA manual on screening and brief intervention for alcohol problems has been developed for physicians and has received wide distribution in health care settings (NIAAA, 1995).

Implications for Practice, Service Delivery, Policy, and Interdisciplinary Education

Multiple forces have driven the development of brief interventions in the field of alcoholism. First, in light of the increasing magnitude and scope of alcohol problems, there is compelling empirical evidence for the efficacy of brief interventions for treating the range of these problems. Second, the potential for use of this innovation by clinical practitioners is a positive influence. Clinicians from many disciplines practice in a wide variety of settings with persons experiencing a range of severity of physical, social, and psychological problems related to alcohol use. In specialized hospitals and clinics that provide alcohol treatment, for example, social workers represent the bulk of the professional staff (Googins, 1984) and are therefore prime candidates for conducting brief intervention. Third, the motivational counseling techniques and values that underlie these innovations are consistent with the principles and practices of those professions committed to work with society's more vulnerable populations. Thus, incorporating brief interventions into standard practice protocols for treating persons with the full range of alcohol problems has significant implications for human service professionals engaging in direct practice. The acceptance of brief interventions can bring about significant change in service delivery systems, practice patterns, and education of practitioners.

In order to implement brief interventions in practice, clinicians need skills in screening, assessment, and motivational counseling techniques. They need to become more skillful in screening for nondependent problem drinkers, especially in the use of specific instruments for enhancing motivation for treatment. Such instruments can be of enormous practical use in the implementation of brief intervention in both primary and secondary settings.

SERVICE DELIVERY

Broad changes in the service delivery system are pushing the development of more efficient, comprehensive, cost-effective methods of treatment for persons with alcohol-related problems. Clinicians practicing in both public and private settings have become sensitized to the need to develop more cost-conscious methods of treating vulnerable populations as public systems of care increasingly migrate toward the use of managed-care methods. More and more individual practitioners and clinicians in agency settings are influenced by managed-care organizations, and they are called upon to use treatment methods that are effective and consistent with the principle of "parsimony," the principle that the least treatment is the best treatment. Providing the same intensity of treatment to all persons with alcohol-related problems is inconsistent with a system that attempts to match the intensity and frequency of treatment to the level of dysfunction.

The greater use of brief intervention will increase the gatekeeping function of clinicians in both primary and secondary settings. In primary clinical settings, such as free-standing outpatient clinics and voluntary social service agencies, brief intervention serves to identify and provide appropriate treatment for nondependent problem drinkers at an earlier point, thereby reducing the likelihood of comorbidity. For clients with a more chronic course, brief intervention can act as a type of triage and motivational enhancement for successful referral to more specialized alcohol treatment programs.

In secondary clinical settings such as hospitals, employee assistance programs (EAPs), schools, and child welfare systems, brief intervention serves as a case-finding technique, reducing barriers to care by identifying and treating alcohol-use problems that complicate the primary focus of care. For example, while parental alcohol abuse has been cited as a primary cause of increases in reports of child abuse and neglect, child deaths, and increased placement rates in the past five years, the child welfare service system is not designed to address parental alcohol problems (Tracy, 1994). Treatment resources are scarce for alcohol-dependent women (Abbott, 1994), and there is a lack of risk assessment models for rational decision making on the risk of harm to children with alcohol-abusing parents. Yet, child welfare workers must continue to provide services to families with alcohol-abuse problems while protecting children from risk of further harm. The use of brief intervention can assist in protecting children from harm by identifying the level of alcohol abuse and enhancing the motivation of parents and caretakers to reduce problem drinking or seek more intensive treatments.

PRACTICE

Practice patterns of clinicians are developed in response to a multiplicity of influences, including but not limited to a responsiveness to new information about effectiveness of particular models or interventions, societal and professional values, and structural issues, such as cost and payment provisions. Brief intervention is an enormously useful component of a standard protocol package in the treatment of persons with alcohol problems when paired with empirically validated screening instruments and pertinent medical necessity criteria. The development of standard intake protocols for early identification and brief intervention that can be used in a variety of settings with diverse populations is a critical first step in changing the practice patterns of clinicians in outpatient and inpatient settings. Without such protocols, clinicians will continue to rely on skills in diagnosis and intervention that are targeted to chronic or dependent drinkers and the social, physical, psychological, vocational, and interactional problems they experience.

Screening and identifying at intake alcohol problems other than severe alcohol dependence has not been a usual part of agency practice. Googins (1984) reports that only 40% of social service agencies indicated that questions about an individual's drinking history (or that of family members) were included in their intake procedures. Corrigan and Anderson (1985) reported that social workers often lack familiarity with methods of assessing alcohol problems and, consequently, are reluctant to identify such problems in their clients. Tracy (1994) notes that child welfare workers often doubt even their right to ask parents about drinking and drug use because they lack the necessary interviewing skills for assessing alcohol problems.

Most clinicians in outpatient primary settings are also deficient in early diagnosis and intervention with alcohol clients (Van Wormer, 1989). This lack of skill will continue to present problems for these practitioners as the recognition of the increasing scope of alcohol use problems inevitably leads to increased numbers of persons requiring intervention. Incorporating brief intervention into basic practice knowledge requires all clinicians to develop rudimentary skills in assessment, diagnosis, and treatment of persons with nondependent drinking problems. These skills must be integrated into the practice regimes of both individual and family practitioners, not just used as a case-finding technique for referral to more specialized settings.

EDUCATION

Changing practice patterns to include a wider range of diagnostic and intervention skills will require a change in the education and training of graduate students and practicing clinicians. All clinical practitioners should be educated in assessment and treatment of alcohol problems, since it is inevitable that they will encounter such persons in the course of their practice. For example, Fleming and Barry (1992) report that clinicians in ambulatory care settings can expect that 15 to 20% of their adult patients will have a history of alcohol disorder and 8 to 10% will currently have such a disorder.

In educational institutions, knowledge and skill development in relation to the use of brief intervention should be incorporated into both baccalaureate and graduate-level practice programs across disciplines. Knowledge about addictive behaviors should be included in core curriculum courses, and the number of specialized courses in addictive behaviors in undergraduate and graduate curricula should be increased (CSAP, 1995). Course content should include information about epidemiology and pharmacological effects of alcohol, theories of alcohol and other drug use, problems in definitions and descriptions of alcoholism, findings of outcome studies comparing different treatments, approaches, and differential application, exploration of attitudes about alcohol use and alcoholism, administration of alcoholism treatment programs, including the effects of legislation, the roles of social control agencies, and policies related to advertising, prevention, legal issues, pricing, and availability of alcohol (Corrigan & Anderson, 1985; CSAP, 1995).

Dissemination of studies that address the effectiveness of brief intervention should be actively pursued through a variety of professional media as a means of educating professional clinicians in the rationale for the use of brief interventions. Empirical evidence that supports the probability of a more positive prognosis using brief intervention should be included, not just in professional journals specific to the field of alcoholism treatment, but also in professional journals with a more generalized social work or clinical focus, such as child welfare, mental health, women's issues, gerontology, and health.

Such material might also be included through in-service training workshops for persons in both primary and secondary settings. Clinicians practicing in primary settings might benefit from training in how to integrate assessment for alcohol-related problems in a more generalized psychosocial assessment. In secondary settings, clinicians might be trained in the use of standardized screening instruments and brief intervention as a method of case finding and referral to more specialized treatment settings. In training practitioners in secondary settings, specific connections must be made to the primary purpose of the setting and to the ways that undiagnosed and untreated alcohol-related problems act as a barrier to the treatment of presenting problems (e.g., marital dissatisfaction, domestic violence, and job performance) in these settings. The focus of such education and training should be on a public health approach, with an emphasis on primary prevention and the early intervention aspects of secondary prevention.

Summary and Conclusions

The treatment environment in which clinicians have practiced in the past was characterized by a focus on persons with chronic alcohol use problems, persons with severe symptomatology and disability related to their alcohol use, and persons who were defined as help seeking. Key concepts were the notion of alcoholism as a disease with a chronic and ever downward-spiraling course that required acceptance of loss of control and complete abstinence on the part of the client. Because of the definitional rigidity, clients often sought help at the apex of their most severe drinking episodes and had to convince the clinician of their desire to change. It was common to find that clients were not accepted for treatment unless they were willing to commit to lifelong abstinence. This practice environment supported the growth of a class of clinicians who possessed a restricted set of skills geared to chronic or dependent client populations. These skills included dramatic techniques to "break down denial" to deal with the chronic underlying "resistance" that was understood to be a part of the "disease."

The current practice environment is characterized by a broadened definition of alcohol problems that includes a wider range of patterns of consumption and greater range in the extent of problems related to drinking. Persons who experience problems related to their drinking do not always seek help for their drinking but sometimes seek it for a variety of other life problems; they are therefore defined as nonhelp-seeking for alcohol problems. Due to this greater definitional flexibility, persons with alcohol problems are finding help at earlier stages and from a greater variety of sources, such as court-mandated diversion programs, primary care physicians, voluntary family support agencies, employee assistance programs, and health maintenance organizations. The use of inpatient stays is lessening as a result of the influence of managed-care organizations that demand reduced intensity of care and are reluctant to approve expensive alternatives. While the motivation to change is still valued by clinicians, more attention is being given to developing strategies for treating the involuntary client (Ivanoff, Blythe, & Tripodi, 1994), or what has been termed the prevoluntary client (Hepworth & Larson, 1993).

These changes in the client population demand changes in the skills of clinicians. A restricted repertoire of skills or treatment approaches may be a barrier to effective alcohol treatment. Clinicians must be innovative in treating the range of severity presented by persons with alcohol problems. They must be trained in a variety of approaches, employ these methods in a wide variety of settings, and learn how to integrate them into their standard practice package.

Resistance to incorporating brief intervention in standard practice knowledge can be seen in this continuing push for specialization of method embraced by the profession. The emerging professional guild that has developed to treat alcoholism and other substance abuse problems, certified alcoholism counselors (CAC) and those with other specific qualifiers and designations, is a part of the larger alcohol treatment industry. This professional protectionism supports disease models of alcoholism and the belief that anyone who treats a person for alcohol misuse must possess a specific set of unique skills and have the technology to deliver those skills. To change this paradigm is to face the challenge of changing a set of beliefs and ideological assumptions about the nature of alcoholism and its treatment. Such change is difficult in and of itself, but it also suggests an economic consequence. Those who are currently providing this level of treatment might become less employable unless they are able to change both their belief systems and the set of techniques that they strongly believe has been helpful to them and will be helpful to others. This belief system is strong, runs counter to empirical evidence, and denies the movement of the field toward briefer methods encouraged by managed-care organizations. It is a potent barrier to change that must be addressed.

The use of these more effective brief interventions, however, is compatible with managed behavioral health care settings and may provide the best opportunity to intervene and treat persons with alcohol use disorders. Since more than 70% of Americans visit a doctor's office at least once every two years, brief intervention can facilitate this interface with managed-care methods in both commercial markets and public systems. It utilizes a shorter-term treatment method and reduces costs by providing more targeted treatment. Brief intervention has been shown to be effective for those with less severe alcohol use problems, and there is increasing evidence that it may even have benefit for those experiencing more severe problems.

Finally, the use of more effective brief interventions can provide greater incentives for the integration of alcohol treatments into general health care services, where the treatment of many mental health disorders is moving. The current view of alcohol treatment services as a "carve-out" both in public and private service delivery systems separates it from the mainstream of managed behavioral and physical health care systems. Brief intervention might provide a stronger impetus to provide alcohol-related treatment services as a "carve-in" and help to bridge this gap. As long as this separation continues, the disparity in private insurance coverage and expenditure of public funds for alcohol treatment and other areas of health care will likely persist, and those most vulnerable to the ravages of alcohol misuse problems will continue to be underserved.

REFERENCES

Abbott, A. A. (1994). A feminist approach to substance abuse treatment and service delivery. *Social Work in Health Care, 19*(3/4), 67–83.

American Psychiatric Association. (1994). *Diagnostic and statistical manual of mental disorders* (4th ed.). Washington, DC: Author.

Anderson, P., & Scott, E. (1992). The effect of general practitioners' advice to heavy drinking men. *British Medical Journal, 87,* 891–900.

Babor, T. F., & Grant, M. (Eds.). (1992). *Project on identification and management of alcohol-related problems, report on phase II: A randomized clinical trial of brief interventions in primary health care.* Geneva, Switzerland: World Health Care Organization.

Babor, T. F., Ritson, E. B., & Hodgson, R. J. (1986). Alcohol-related problems in the primary health care setting: A review of early intervention strategies. *British Journal of Addiction, 81,* 23–46.

Bandura, A. (1977). Self-efficacy: Toward a unifying theory of behavioral change. *Psychological Review, 84,* 191–215.

Bien, T. H., Miller, W. R., & Tonigan, J. S. (1993). Brief interventions for alcohol problems: A review. *Addiction, 88,* 315–336.

Center for Substance Abuse Prevention. (1995). *Curriculum modules on alcohol and other drug problems for schools of social work.* Washington, DC: Author.

Chick, J., Lloyd, G., & Crombie, E. (1985). Counseling problem drinkers in medical wards: A controlled study. *British Medical Journal, 290,* 965–967.

Chick, J., Ritson, B., Connaughton, J., Steward, A., & Chick, J. (1988). Advice versus extended treatment for alcoholism: A controlled study. *British Journal of Addiction, 83,* 159–170.

Child Welfare League of America. (1992). *Children at the front: A different view of the war on alcohol and drugs.* Washington, DC: Author.

Cook, D., Fewell, C., & Riolo, J. (1983). Introduction. In D. Cook, C. Fewell, & J. Riolo (Eds.), *Social work treatment of alcohol problems* (pp. xiii–xix). New Brunswick, NJ: Journal of Studies on Alcohol.

Cooney, N. L., Zweben, A., & Fleming, M. F. (1995). Screening for alcohol problems and at-risk drinking in healthcare settings. In R. K. Hester & W. R. Miller (Eds.), *Handbook of alcoholism treatment approaches* (2nd ed., pp. 45–60). Boston: Allyn & Bacon.

Corrigan, E., & Anderson, S. (1985). Graduate social work education in alcoholism. In E. Freeman (Ed.), *Social work practice with clients who have alcohol problems* (pp. 335–350). Springfield, IL: Charles C. Thomas.

Donovan, D. M., Kadden, R. M., DiClemente, C. C., Carroll, K. M., Longabaugh, R. H., Zweben, A., & Rychtarik, R. (1994). Issues in selection and development of therapies in alcoholism treatment matching research. *Journal of Studies on Alcohol* (Supplement 12), 101–111.

Drummond, D. C., Thom, B., Brown, C., Edwards, G., & Mullan, J. (1990). Specialist versus general practitioner treatment of problem drinkers. *Lancet, 336,* 915–918.

Edwards, G., Orford, J., Egert, S., Guthrie, S., Hawker, A., Hensmen, C., Mitcheson, M., Oppenheimer, E., & Taylor, C. (1977). Alcoholism: A controlled trail of "treatment" and "advice." *Journal of Studies on Alcohol, 38,* 1004–1031.

Edwards, G., & Taylor, C. (1994). A test of the matching hypothesis: Alcohol dependence, intensity of treatment, and 12-month outcome. *Addiction, 89,* 553–561.

Elvy, G. A., Wells, J. E., & Baird, K. A. (1988). Attempted referral as intervention for problem drinking in the general hospital. *British Journal of Addiction, 83,* 83–89.

Ewing, H. (1991, April 19). *Management of the pregnant alcoholic/addict.* Paper presented at the American Society of Addictions Medicine Scientific Conference, Boston, MA.

Fleming, M. F., & Barry, K. L. (1992). *Addictive disorders: A practical guide to treatment.* Chicago: Mosby/Yearbook Medical Publishers.

Fleming, M. F., Barry, K. L., Manwell, L. B., Johnson, C., & London, R. L. (1997). Brief physician advice for problem drinkers: A randomized controlled trial in community based primary care practices. *Journal of the American Medical Association, 277*(13), 1039–1045.

Googins, B. (1984). Avoidance of the alcoholic client. *Social Work, 29*(2), 161–166.

Heather, N. (1989). Psychology and brief intervention. *British Journal of Addictions, 84,* 357–370.

Heather, N. (1994). Brief intervention strategies. In R. H. Hester & W. R. Miller (Eds.), *Handbook of alcoholism treatment approaches: Effective alternatives* (pp. 105–122). Needham Heights, MA: Allyn & Bacon.

Heather, N. (1995). Interpreting the evidence on brief intervention: The need for caution. *Alcohol & Alcoholism, 30,* 287–296.

Heather, N. (1996). The public health and brief interventions for excessive alcohol consumption: The British experience. *Addictive Behaviors, 6,* 857–868.

Heather, N., Rollnick, S., & Bell, A. (1993). Predictive validity of the Readiness to Change Questionnaire. *Addiction, 88,* 1667–1677.

Hepworth, D. H., & Larson, J. A. (1993). *Direct social work practice: Theory and skills* (3rd ed.). Belmont, CA: Wadsworth.

Institute of Medicine (IOM). (1990). *Broadening the base of treatment for alcohol problems.* Washington, DC: National Academy Press.

Ivanoff, A., Blythe, B. J., & Tripodi, T. (1994). *Involuntary clients in social work practice: A research-based approach.* New York: Aldine De Gruyter.

Kirk, S. A., & Kutchins, H. (1992). *The selling of DSM: The rhetoric of science in psychiatry.* New York: Aldine DeGruyter.

Kristenson, H., Ohlin, H., Hultin-Nosslin, M., Trell, E., & Hood, B. (1983). Identification and intervention of heavy drinking in middle-aged men: Results and follow-up of 24–60 months of long-term study with randomized controls. *Alcoholism: Clinical & Experimental Research, 20,* 203–209.

Mattick, R. P., & Jarvis, T. (1994) Brief or minimal intervention for 'alcoholics'? The evidence suggests otherwise. *Drug and Alcohol Review, 13,* 137–144

McLellan, A. T., Kushner, H., Metzger, D., Peters, R., Smith, I., Grissom, G., Pettinati, H., & Argeriou, M. (1992). The fifth edition of the Addiction Severity Index. *Journal of Substance Abuse Treatment, 9,* 199–213.

Miller, W. R. (1983). Motivational interviewing with problem drinkers. *Behavioral Therapy, 11,* 147–172.

Miller, W. R., & Rollnick, S. (1991). *Motivational interviewing: Preparing people to change addictive behavior.* New York: Guilford Press.

Miller, W. R., & Sovereign, R. (1989). The drinking check-up: A model for early intervention in addictive behaviors. In T. Loberg, W. R. Miller, P. Nathan, & G. A. Marlatt, (Eds.), *Addictive behaviors: Prevention and early intervention* (pp. 219–231). Amsterdam: Swets & Zeitlinger.

Miller, W. R., Zweben, A., DiClemente, C. C., & Rychtarik, R. G. (1992). *Motivational enhancement therapy (MET): A clinical research guide for therapists treating individuals with alcohol abuse and dependence* (DHHS Publication No. ADM 92-1894). Washington, DC: U.S. Government Printing Office.

National Institute on Alcohol Abuse and Alcoholism. (1995). *The physician's guide to helping patients with alcohol problems* (NIH publication No. 95-3769). Washington, DC: U.S. Department of Health and Human Services, National Institutes of Health.

Ockene, J. K., Kristeller, J., Goldberg, R., Amick, T. L., Pekow, L., Hosmer, P. S., Quirk, M., & Kalan, K. (1991). Increasing the efficacy of physician-delivered smoking interventions: A randomized clinical trial. *Journal of General Internal Medicine, 6*, 1–8.

Orford, J., & Edwards, G. (1977). Alcoholism: A comparison of treatment and advice, with a study of the influence of marriage. *Institute of Psychiatry Mandsley Monographs, 26.* New York: Oxford University Press.

Prochaska, J. O., & DiClemente, C. C. (1984). *The transtheoretical approach: Crossing traditional boundaries of therapy.* Homewood, IL: Dow Jones-Irwin.

Prochaska, J. O., & DiClemente, C. C. (1992). Stages of change in the modification of problem behavior. In M. Hersen, R. Eisler, & P. M. Miller (Eds.), *Progress in behavior modification* (Vol. 28, pp. 183–218). Sycamore, IL: Sycamore Publishing.

Project MATCH Research Group. (1997). Matching alcoholism treatments to client heterogeneity: Project MATCH posttreatment drinking outcomes. *Journal of Studies on Alcohol, 58*(1), 7–29.

Rees, E. W., Beech, H. R., & Hore, B. D. (1984). Some factors associated with compliance in treatment of alcoholism. *Alcohol and Alcoholism, 19*, 303–307.

Richmond, R., & Heather, N. (1990). General practitioners intervention for smoking cessation: Past results and future prospects. *Behavioral Change, 7*(3), 110–119.

Rollnick, S., Heather, N., & Bell, A. (1992). Negotiating behavior change in medical settings: The development of brief motivational interviewing. *Journal of Mental Health, 1*, 25–37.

Sanchez-Craig, M., Annis, H. M., Bornet, A. R., & MacDonald, K. R. (1984). Random assignment to abstinence and controlled drinking: Evaluation of a cognitive-behavioral program for problem drinkers. *Journal of Consulting and Clinical Psychology, 52*, 395–404.

Selzer, M. (1971). The Michigan Alcoholism Screening Test: The quest for a new diagnostic instrument. *American Journal of Psychiatry, 127*, 1653–1658.

Serdula, M., Williamson, D. F., Kendrick, J. S., Anda, R. F., & Byers, T. (1991). Trends in alcohol consumption by pregnant women: 1985 through 1988. *Journal of American Medical Association, 265*(7): 876–879.

Single, E. (1996). Defining harm reduction. *Drug and Alcohol Review, 14*, 287–290.

Skinner, H. A. (1994). *Computerized Lifestyle Assessment.* Toronto: Multi-Health Systems.

Skinner, H. A., & Allen, B. A. (1982). Alcohol dependence syndrome: Measurement and validation. *Journal of Abnormal Psychology, 91*, 199–209.

Sobell, M. B., & Sobell, L. C. (1987). Conceptual issues regarding goals in the treatment of alcohol problems. *Drugs and Society, 1*(2/3), 1–38.

Sobell, M. B., & Sobell, L. C. (1993). Treatment for problem drinkers: A public health priority. In J. S. Baer, G. A. Marlatt, & R. J. McMahon (Eds.), *Addictive behaviors across the lifespan: Prevention, treatment, and policy issues* (pp. 138–157). Beverly Hills, CA: Sage Publications.

Soderstrom, C. B., & Cowley, R. A. (1987). A national alcohol and trauma center survey. *Archives of Surgery, 122*, 1067–1071.

Thom, B., Brown, C., Drummond, C., Edwards, G., Mullan, M., & Taylor, C. (1992). Engaging patients with alcohol problems in treatment: The first consultation. *British Journal of Addiction, 87*, 601–611.

Thompson, K., & Wilsnack, R. (1984). Drinking problems among female adolescents:

Patterns and influences. In S. Wilsnack & L. Beckman (Eds.), *Alcohol problems in women* (pp. 37–65). New York: Guilford Press.

Tracy, E. M. (1994). Maternal substance abuse: Protecting the child, preserving the family. *Social Work, 39*(5), 534–540.

U.S. Department of Health and Human Services. (1990). *Seventh special report to the U.S. Congress on alcohol and health* (DHSS Publication No. ADM 90-1656). Washington DC: Superintendent of Documents, U.S. Government Printing Office.

U.S. Department of Health and Human Services. (1993). *Eighth special report to the U.S. Congress on alcohol and health.* (ADM 291-91-003, NIH Publication No. 94-3699). Washington, DC: U.S. Government Printing Office.

Van Wormer, K. (1989). Co-dependency: Implications for women and therapy. *Women & Therapy, 8*(4), 51–63.

Wallace, P., Cutler, S., & Haines, A. (1988). Randomized controlled trial of general practitioner intervention in clients with excessive alcohol consumption. *British Medical Journal, 297,* 663–668.

Weisner, C., & Room, R. (1984). Financing and ideology in alcohol treatment. *Social Problems, 32*(2), 167–184.

Zweben, A. (1991). Motivational counseling with alcoholic couples. In W. R. Miller & S. Rollnick (Eds.), *Motivational interviewing, preparing people to change addictive behavior* (pp. 225–235). New York: Guilford Press.

Zweben, A., & Barrett, D. (1993). Brief couples treatment for alcohol problems. In T. V. O'Farrell (Ed.), *Treating alcohol problems: Marital and family interventions* (pp. 353–380). New York: Guilford Press.

Zweben, A., & Barrett, D. (1997). Facilitating compliance in alcoholism treatment. In B. Blackwell (Ed.), *Treatment compliance and the therapeutic alliance* (pp. 277–293). New York: Gordon & Breach.

Zweben, A., Pearlman, S., & Li, S. (1988). A comparison of brief advice and conjoint therapy in the treatment of alcohol abuse: The results of the marital system study. *British Journal of Addiction, 83,* 899–916.

10

Innovation in Practice with Homeless Populations

Partnership in the Struggle for Empowerment

JUDITH A. B. LEE

Homelessness is an American tragedy. Ideally, this chapter should be about the eradication of homelessness through the creation of affordable housing opportunities, with services available for all low-income Americans, especially those who are most vulnerable by virtue of poverty, race, gender, age, mental and/or physical or disabilities, or other stigmatized and marginalized statuses. But that chapter in American history is yet to be written.

I began my work with homeless people in New York City's municipal women's shelters in 1982. Then, I was struck that 18-year-olds just discharged from foster care and frail elderly women slept side by side with addicts, alcoholics, and women with profound mental illness who often raged through the night (Lee, 1989, 1994a, 1994b). As one young woman, Carla, noted, "My bed is bounded on one side by a murderer just released from jail and on the other side by a strung-out prostitute. I have all I can do to keep my sanity and my sense of who I am." She added, "My biggest job is to keep clean. To use the bathroom I have to line up for toilet paper, and I am scared to use the open showers. Getting ready for a job interview is a major challenge, but I try because I want to resume care of my little girl. Now I have to grow up fast. I think I'm in shock."

In 1982, New York's shelters exemplified my grandmother's worst fears of the poorhouse (NASW News, 1983). I intervened with top human resources (HRA) administrators, as well as with shelter directors and the women directly, individually and in groups (Lee, 1989, 1990, 1994b). Years later, the HRA would implement, on a small scale, my suggestions for homogeneous shelters that address the needs of distinct vulnerable groups, first with substance-abusing men, then with mentally ill women. But horrendous conditions still exist. The "lucky" who get in from the cold still sleep on the floors of sanctuaries and on cots in armories. Human beings still live under bridges, in the subterranean bowels of the subway system, and in cars, shanties, or cardboard boxes. For example, "Bushville," a shanty town on Manhattan's Lower East Side, stood for six years, until 1993, when it was leveled by bulldozers in an illegal sweep. The photographer and art professor Margaret Morton documented the care and attention the residents took with their structures before they were destroyed. Residents of Bushville stated that they found shelters unsafe, unsanitary, and dehumanizing (Safety Net, 1994).

The current political scene presses government to take even less responsibility for the provision of housing and services than it did in 1982 (Edwards, Cooke, & Ried, 1996; Ewalt, 1996; Jansson & Smith, 1996). Election-year federal and state "welfare reform" raises the probability of massive poverty and homelessness of children, parents, and other adults who can't "toe the mark" and work (AJO, 1996; Freeman, 1996). Some analysts say that homelessness, having increased dramatically during the past three decades of affluence for the well off, approaches the proportions it reached during the Great Depression of the 1930s (Blau, 1992; Rossi, 1989). Deregulation, fixed-rate tax cuts that benefit only the rich, the deindustrialization of the economy, and the business community's competitive "lean and mean" response, including the assault on labor unions and the resulting unemployment and underemployment, has left working-class and poor Americans with less money (Blau, 1992). In a 1982 shelter group meeting, Carla concluded that "homelessness is the fruit of oppression." The broken fibers of American society must be rewoven to include basic rights to housing for all people.

Who Are the Homeless Now?

Efforts to count and categorize "the homeless" have taken much energy to produce some fairly accurate generalizations. The homeless represent a heterogeneous variety of impoverished people who are without permanent housing due to the low-income housing crisis and to their own biopsychosocial vulnerabilities, which make competing for scarce resources problematic. The deinstitutionalization of the mentally ill is a major factor in homelessness for about a third of the homeless population (Blau, 1992). The affordable-housing crisis started during the Reagan years when the federal housing budget was slashed by more than 80%. More than a million families remain on waiting lists for public housing, and in many cities lists for subsidized housing are closed (Johnson & Lee, 1994). The Clinton administration has recently funded the rebuilding of selected dilapidated low-income projects in 73 large cities. While this is well received by project residents, it does little for the unhoused as the number of units will not be increased.

Federal spending in all programs that benefit poor children and families declined dramatically during the 1980s, while military spending increased 40% (Nunez, 1994, p. 19). The introduction of McKinney Programs, funded through the U.S. Department of Housing and Urban Development through the Stuart B. McKinney Homeless Assistance Act of 1987, have provided some relief to homeless people, but these programs are limited in scope. Shelter Plus Care, for example, provides rental assistance for permanent housing for homeless adults with mental illness, substance abuse disabilities, or AIDS. Yet this is time-limited funding that can easily be revoked. Section 8 Housing Certificates, sporadically available to a range of homeless people, are also highly effective but politically vulnerable forms of relief for homelessness (Rog, Holupka, & McCombs-Thornton, 1995). Private-sector and nonprofit corporation efforts to create affordable low-income housing units have developed demonstration projects. Although the Corporation for Supportive Housing has created about 30,000 such units (CSH, 1996) they do not even begin to diminish the lowest estimate of the number of homeless people.

Estimates of the prevalence of homelessness vary greatly, depending on the methodology and definitions, the time of year the studies were undertaken, and the purpose for which the data were collected (Bachrach, 1992; Bassuk, 1995; Baxter & Hopper, 1981; Straw, 1995; Whitbeck & Simons, 1993). Government has consistently yielded the lowest counts (228,372 in the 1991 U.S. census), while advocates for the homeless have estimated the number of homeless at about 1.5 to 3 million (Blau, 1992). In 1989 a 7-day study of shelter users in 178 large cities reported an estimate of 500,000 to 600,000 homeless. By the early 1990s the federal government had accepted this estimate, along with figures that indicated as many as 7 million persons were homeless at some time during the late 1980s (Executive Order No. 12848, 1993). A nontraditional study by Link et al. (1995) based on telephone inquiries to 1,507 households found that a shocking 14% (26 million) of Americans were homeless (including those who doubled up with other people) during the 5-year period 1985–1990. Developing stringent definitions of literal homelessness and doubling up (virtual homelessness), their 1995 follow-up study confirmed that the magnitude of homelessness is much larger than had been previously reported (Bassuk, 1995). The categories of homelessness and the counts themselves have us hamstrung in efforts to deal with the problem (Hopper, 1995).

African Americans are overrepresented among the homeless, and young single mothers with small children make up the largest and fastest-growing category of the homeless population (Johnson & Lee, 1994; Nunez, 1994; Thrasher & Mowbray, 1995). While adult men still make up more than half of the homeless population (Blau, 1992), at least a third of the homeless are families headed by a woman. Extreme poverty, pregnancy and single parenthood, youth, the lack of labor market skills, and other biopsychosocial vulnerabilities, including domestic violence, substance abuse, mental illness, family disruptions, trauma (earlier sexual and/or physical abuse), and minority status are the highest risk factors among women (Lee & Nisivoccia, 1997). Research on homelessness has demonstrated the presence of mental health problems, alcohol and substance abuse and psychological distress among homeless people (Thrasher & Mowbray, 1995). Substance abusers may be mothers with children as well as single adults (Homan et al., 1993). Homeless women unaccompanied by their children tend to have higher rates of substance abuse, and they also admit more readily to the problem. But homeless families have higher rates of substance abuse, domestic abuse, and child abuse, more mental health problems, and weaker social support networks than their housed counterparts (Robertson, 1991; Shinn, Knickman, & Weitzman, 1991). Prevalence rates of single and coexisting mental and substance abuse disorders vary by population subgroup and range from high estimates of 60% to 85% (Baum & Burnes, 1993) to more than 40% for alcohol abusers, 25% to 30% for drug abusers, and one-third for mental illness (Argeriou & McCarty, 1990; Blau, 1992; CSH, 1996; Lee & Nisivoccia, 1997). Studies also show that psychological trauma and mental and substance abuse disorders can be secondary to the horrific experience of homelessness (Goodman, Saxe, & Harvey, 1991). Some authors stress the importance of pathology in determining homelessness (Baum & Burnes, 1993), while others stress macro/structural forces (Blau, 1992; Leibow, 1993). It is clear that micro and macro factors must be combined to explain "causality" and to create adequate policies and programs (Bassuk & Saloman, 1993; Lee & Nisivoccia, 1997). The Corporation for Supportive Housing states that, while housing is imperative, for 70% of the homeless, housing is not enough. Services must be made available with permanent housing to stop the revolving door of homelessness (CSH, 1996).

In this chapter, I focus on innovative programs and practice approaches in working with homeless people. Since the population is so diverse, I discuss a particular program and highlight three nonexclusive categories of homeless women as particularly vulnerable subgroups within the homeless population: women with children, women with substance abuse problems, and women with chronic mental illness.

Issues in Practice and Service Delivery

Religious and humanitarian organizations were the first to respond to the crisis of homelessness in the late 1970s. In both municipal and private-sector shelters, professionally trained social workers were later arrivals on the scene. In many places, shelters are still operated by those who see charity and service as an outgrowth of religious commitment. However, the need for differential assessment and intervention and the requirements of funding sources eventually prompted the hiring of social workers and other clinicians. While professional social workers and other staff had much to teach each other, tensions could run high. Hence, social workers needed to learn how to enact the mediation role in a new host setting (Schwartz, 1994).

Although social workers and other providers were often zealous in their advocacy for their clients, few had vision that went beyond notions of "advocating for" and "caring for the less fortunate." Some programs were extremely hard on the more vulnerable clients, expecting them to "reform" and to "pick themselves up," while others practiced acceptance and did not "judge" (or assess) in any way, creating little opportunity for change or for the management of debilitating personal conditions and problems in living. As the complex needs of heterogeneous shelter residents became more apparent, it became clear that many different approaches to sheltering and rehousing residents were needed. Over time, several major changes took place in practice, service delivery and programs.

Innovations in Service Delivery and Programs: Housing Plus Services

As it was recognized that homelessness was a combined macro/structural and micro/individual problem, programs and services took on a "Housing Plus" focus. Even the most ideal programs must bend to the pragmatic reality of offering service not only when it is appropriate but when there is no place else for the client to go. Yet it is worthwhile to describe ideal thinking and practice. The multitier concept of sheltering seeks to meet needs along a continuum of service. On the one end is the emergency shelter, with enriched services; in the middle is the transitional living facility; and on the far end is permanent housing with supportive services. The actual living structures and programs that operationalize these concepts in sheltering may take a variety of forms. Each is distinguished from basic-level sheltering (just a bed for an overnight or extremely short stay) by the addition of services intended to help people move beyond homelessness to relative self-sufficiency. In general, innovative sheltering approaches have moved from charity to empowerment, from "catch-all" to population specific programs; from a temporary or crisis mentality to the provision of sheltering and permanent housing with ongoing services. In some programs, empowerment-based interventions, both personal and political, take place. The idea is that, with resources and knowledge, people can empower themselves, their families, and their communities to move from victim to victor status. They can develop awareness and take actions that go beyond attaining housing to a level of personal and political transformation (Beyond Shelter, 1995; Lee, 1991, 1994a).

THE CONTINUUM

Enriched Service Emergency Shelters

Basic shelters open primarily at night and offer minimal services and emergency intervention and referral only. Enriched service shelters are open 24 hours and offer an array of services ranging from individual assessment and referral to on-site individual and group counseling to housing groups, clinics, and life skills programs that deal with job preparation, educational options (e.g., tutoring, G.E.D. programs), AIDS and other health-oriented issues, and parenting skills. Lengths of stay are often longer (several months or more), accommodating the need for individualized plans. At the emergency shelter stage, assessment skills are critical in helping individuals find suitable temporary or permanent housing. Some areas utilize drop-in centers for mentally ill and substance-abusing persons to offer another level of connection and outreach. Some of these programs utilize an empowerment philosophy; examples include the Holy Innocents Outreach Program in Portland, Maine (Cohen & Johnson, 1996), Deborah's Place in Chicago, Sistering in Toronto (Breton, 1989), and The Open Door in New York City (Pathways Press, 1996).

Most service-enriched shelters have responded to the differential problems of substance abusers and persons with mental illness. Some are known as "dry" shelters that emphasize sobriety, recovery, and substance-abuse treatment (Argeriou & McCarty, 1990). Others assess substance abuse and mental health problems and refer clients to appropriate treatment services. Shelters may also utilize rules about sobriety and curfews to encourage recovery. Some offer 12-step programs on the premises, and others encourage attendance in outside 12-step programs. Some shelters are set up exclusively for the needs of people with chronic mental illness, while others specialize in families, mothers, and children. Services are geared to the population served. Many now provide group services that include socialization, education, treatment, life skills, parenting, tutoring and recreation for children, and empowerment on the personal and political level. Enriched shelters become centers for referral or treatment as well as for education and skill development, not just places to sleep. As people get back on their feet economically and biopsychosocially, they may move to subsidized housing if it is available, to low-income projects, to market-rate housing, or to transitional or permanent housing programs with services.

In some states "transitional shelters" house individuals for up to a year as enriched services are provided to help them get ready for independent housing. The St. Louis "Families with a Future" research demonstration project, aimed at substance-abusing mothers and their children, is an example of a transitional shelter for families. Extensive case management and comprehensive family and child development support services produced effective services that enabled families to attain and sustain housing (Homan et al., 1993). Conceptually, the transitional shelter falls between the enriched service shelter and the transitional living facility.

Transitional Living Facilities

In observing the revolving-door phenomenon among clients, it was recognized that some individuals were not ready to move into their own apartments. They needed a period of time in which they could have their own space (ranging from cubicles to single rooms to full apartments) but still be part of a program that would more fully prepare them to live independently. Transitional living facilities were developed to meet this need. Residents can stay in TLFs for 2 years while completing educational and vocational programs and developing job skills, parenting skills, and daily living skills. Parents may be reunited with children who were in foster care. A range of services are given to replenish healthy family life. In some TLFs, residents are encouraged to attend outside treatment or recovery programs. Some facilities have such programming incorporated into their structures. Residents also participate in the TLF's supportive community milieu and utilize on-site individual and group counseling. Since the average age of the homeless population is 31 and most homeless people lack educational and job preparation, TLFs meet a need for a period of preparation that is often denied them (Johnson & Lee, 1994). TLFs also provide a form of sheltered living for those in recovery from substance abuse or domestic abuse and violence. There are TLFs for single adults and for mothers and families with children. The plight of homeless children is well documented (Bassuk &

Gallagher, 1990; Boxhill, 1990; Hall & Maza, 1990; Rivlin, 1990; Wright, 1990). TLF programming may include a focus on children and include recreational space and a day-care and after-school center so that mothers may enter the workforce or attend school. Counseling and activity groups for children may also be part of the program. A holistic and empowering approach is utilized in most TLFs. While nationwide studies have not been done, most TLFs demonstrate a very low rate of residents returning to homelessness. For example, of the 40 families who "graduated" from My Sisters' Place II, a 2-year TLF in Hartford, Connecticut, over a 3-year period, only two were known to utilize shelters again. Other studies bear this out (Shlay, 1994). Some TLFs provide follow-up services in the early stages of independent living to help ensure success. On occasion, residents are able to move on to home ownership through affirmative action and first-home buyers programs.

Permanent Housing with Services

Service-enriched permanent housing, also known as supportive housing, is primarily for homeless individuals and families who can live independently but who have severe disabling conditions to manage, such as chronic mental and physical illness (including AIDS) or chemical dependence. A variety of models of supportive housing have been effective in helping even "hard-core" homeless individuals to maintain housing, maintain recovery from chemical dependence, maintain compliance with psychotropic medications and reduce hospitaliza-tions, maintain some level of employment, and generally find a higher quality of life (CSH, 1996). Cluster House and The Travelers Hotel, under the auspices of the Urban Pathways Programs in New York City and the executive direction of Joan E. Ohlson, are longstanding examples of model programs of supportive housing with services (Pathways Press, 1996). Supportive housing programs show retention rates of nearly 85% for even the hardest-to-house people. They are relatively cost-effective compared to revolving-door use of shelters, emergency room care and hospitalizations, incarcerations, and often dilapidated market-rate housing. Supportive housing is designed to break the cycle of homelessness by providing opportunities for stability and self-sufficiency in attractive, safe, relatively low-cost, not-for-profit housing (CSH, 1996; Fine, 1994). (In the CSH model, a nonprofit housing development corporation is in partnership with a nonprofit social service provider that encourages, motivates, and makes a full array of services available.)

McKinney funds have made possible several demonstration projects that clearly show that homeless people with serious mental illness can be reached, are willing to accept services, and can remain in community based housing with services. The projects represent several styles of providing housing with on-site services. For example, the Boston Project compared two distinct housing pro-grams. The independent living (IL) program offered scattered-site apartments and single-room-occupancy housing with minimal communal aspects; the other program was a "consumer-run group home" (an Evolving Consumer Household or ECH) that initially had 24-hour live-in staff but later became consumer-run as residents were able to assume control. The latter was conceptualized as community living with consumer empowerment. The preliminary findings indicate that the ECHs had somewhat better results in some areas of living than the independent living set-up. But all 115 participants in the study were remarkably successful at staying housed over a 2.5-year study and follow-up period. Intensive clinical case management seemed to be a positive factor in these and other successful models of supportive housing. Clustered site-housing with intensive clinical case management services and emphasis on coming together communally for consumer empowerment is another model successfully utilized at My Sisters' Place III, a program for formerly homeless chronically mentally ill women (and families) in Hartford, Connecticut (Lee, 1994). The fourth tier of My Sisters' Place opened in 1998, has 30 one-bedroom apartments, 40% of which are for the chronic mentally ill, 10% are for persons with HIV/AIDS, 20% are for homeless without special needs, and the rest are for low-income individuals from the general population. Outreach to shelters and to homeless individuals living on the streets is an important component of this and most supportive-housing programs. This supportive-housing endeavor will have an array of services available. It will encourage and motivate but not mandate their usage. This is another model of enriched-services housing that has been found to be effective in reducing homelessness and integrating the formerly homeless into the community (CSH, 1996).

Another concept of permanent housing with services is the provision of Section 8 housing subsidies with case management services designed for seriously troubled families. The Homeless Families Project (HFP) was designed as a 2-year initiative (later extended to 5 years) with funding provided to a lead agency in nine sites to coordinate case management and other needed services such as substance abuse treatment. Six hundred and one families were studied in nine states over an 18-month time period. While the sites represented different models and intensities of service programs, early findings suggest that 86% of clients were still in Section 8 housing at the end of the study. Residential stability was found to be high and suggested that some families can be moved directly to permanent housing with Section 8 certificates if services are provided (Rog, Holupka, & McCombs-Thornton, 1995).

In summation, programs that successfully rehouse the homeless represent a continuum of services in order to meet a variety of needs. Differential assessment and intervention are basic to meeting these needs. Beyond rehousing, programs that help people empower themselves personally and politically go the next step in restoring self-esteem and relative self-sufficiency.

Empowering the Homeless: Innovations in Practice

Empowerment is an idea whose time has come. The aim for the homeless is not simply to house them but to have them gain the internal, economic, and political power to redefine themselves as proactive and political participants in society. Many scholars are researching and conceptualizing empowerment practice (Gutiérrez, 1990; Lee, 1991, 1994a; Mancoske & Hunzeker, 1989; Parsons, 1991). Some have related empowerment concepts and principles specifically to working with people who are homeless (Banyard & Graham-Bermann, 1995; Breton, 1989; Lee, 1990, 1991, 1994a, 1994b; Thrasher & Mowbray, 1995; Toro, Trickett, Wall, & Salem, 1991). My own work with homeless populations was highly influential in the development of the empowerment approach to social work practice (Lee, 1991, 1994a). While considering the effects of biopsychosocial vulnerability and pathology, empowerment work with homeless people emphasizes their inherent strengths, self determination, and coping abilities in the face of the major life crisis of homelessness. It encourages the development of critical consciousness and the ability to reflect and act on the personal and political levels of making change happen. Empowerment is neither a psychological concept nor a political concept. For people who experience oppression, as the homeless do, empowerment is a blending of the personal/clinical and the political. Empowering homeless people moves beyond individual problem solving to end personal homelessness to a level of awareness that catalyzes collective and community action. The empowerment of homeless people can be seen on a continuum of overcoming external and internalized obstacles and gaining knowledge, resources, and skill that culminates in attaining and maintaining personal resources, especially housing and collective action toward structural change. Some may attain only the first step while others move on to a level of collective responsibility, community building, and political action.

THE EMPOWERMENT APPROACH

The empowerment approach makes connections between social and economic injustice and individual pain and suffering (Lee, 1994a). Utilizing empowerment theory as a unifying framework, it presents an integrative, holistic approach to meeting the needs of members of oppressed groups, including the homeless population. This approach adapts an ecological perspective, as advanced by Carel Germain (1979, 1990) and Toro, Trickett, Wall, and Salem (1991), among others. The ecological perspective helps us to see the interdependence and connection of all living and nonliving systems and the transactional nature of all relationships. It focuses on the potentialities of people and the nutritive and noxious qualities of environments (Germain, 1979, 1990; Germain & Gitterman, 1995; Lee, 1989). Potentialities are the power bases that exist in all of us when there is a "goodness of fit" between people and environments. By definition, poor people and oppressed groups like the homeless seldom have this "fit" as injustice stifles human potential. To change this unfavorable equation, people must examine the forces of oppression, name them, face them, and join together to challenge them as they have been internalized and encountered in external power structures. The greatest potentiality to tap is the power of collectivity, people joining together to act, reflect, and act again in the process of praxis fueled by mutual caring and support and standing on common ground (Lee, 1994a).

Fifocal Vision: Multiple Perspectives

Five perspectives are used to develop an empowerment practice framework. These multifocal or "fifocal lenses" also determine the view of the client. They are: (1) the historical perspective, learning a group's history of oppression, including a critical-historical analysis of related social policy; (2) an ecological perspective, including a stress-coping paradigm and other concepts related to coping, a transactional view of ego functioning that takes oppression into account, and cognitive behavioral concepts such as problem solving and cognitive restructuring of the false beliefs engendered by internalized oppression, and a strengths perspective; (3) ethclass and (4) feminist perspectives that appreciate the ceilings imposed by class and race and gender and the concept that power may be developed by all; and (5) a critical perspective that analyzes the status quo. In addition to this fifocal perspective, the empowerment approach is based on values, principles, processes, and skills that are integrated into an overall conceptual framework. Helping processes include assessing and supporting strengths and ego functioning; challenging false beliefs; negotiating and challenging external obstacles and unjust systems; developing pride in peoplehood; problem solving and problem posing; consciousness raising and dialogue; and building collectivity. In this model, "clients" and workers teach and empower each other. These processes may be used one to one, in small groups, and in the wider community, including for political activity. The group, in particular the "empowerment group," is the heart of empowerment practice. The uniqueness of this approach is the synthesis of the personal/clinical and the political in a direct practice approach relevant to homeless populations (Lee, 1994a).

Critical consciousness and knowledge of oppression is power. Power also comes from healthy personality development and growth in the face of oppression, which fuels the ability to influence others and includes self-esteem/identity, self-direction, competence, and relatedness. Clinical and political interventions that challenge the external and internal obstacles to the development of these attributes are essential. Workers and consumers of services are partners in these interventions. Transformation occurs as people are empowered in relationships with a worker and others "in the same boat" who use consciousness raising to see, act, and reach for alternatives. Transformation is a process and an outcome of throwing off oppression in one's own life and that of the community. It is achieved through talking about problems in the context of structural inequity and using "codes," visual, dramatic, artistic, musical, and other means to help people think about and plan to act on oppressive realities. It requires anger at injustice and the dehumanization of poverty, negative valuations, and the culture of personal greed (Mancoske & Hunzeker, 1989). The strengths perspective of Saleebey (1992) can also be utilized in the empowerment of people who are homeless (Thrasher & Mowbray, 1995).

Empowerment Further Defined

Empowerment "deals with a particular kind of block to problem-solving: that imposed by the external society by virtue of a stigmatized collective identity" (Solomon, 1976, p. 21). Webster's Eighth Edition defines the word empower thus: "to give power or authority to; to give ability to, enable, permit." This implies that power can be given to another. This is very rarely the case (Parsons,

1991). The empowerment process resides in the person, not the helper. It can be motivated but not bestowed (Simon, 1990, 1994).

There are three interlocking dimensions of empowerment: (1) the development of a more positive and potent sense of self; (2) the construction of knowledge and capacity for more critical comprehension of the web of social and political realities of one's environment; and (3) the cultivation of resources and strategies, or greater functional competence, for attainment of personal and collective social goals, or liberation. Mancoske and Hunzeker further define empowerment as using interventions that enable those with whom we interact to be "more in control of the interactions in exchanges . . . and the capacity to influence the forces which affect one's life space for one's own benefit" (1989, pp. 14, 15).

Empowerment practice also addresses resource problems, problems of asymmetrical exchange relationships, problems of powerlessness and of inhibiting, constraining, or hindering power structures, and problems related to arbitrary social criteria or values. Powerlessness is basically low social attractiveness resulting from poor resources (personal strengths and skills, material resources, and knowledge) (Staub-Bernasconi, 1992). To help empower, we must first learn to speak openly about power with clients; then engage in examination and promotion of power bases stemming from personal resources—biopsychosocial strength (which may include compliance with medication for persons with mental illness, working a recovery program for people who are substance abusers, and education and job training for homeless mothers and fathers); socioeconomic power; and access to political and collective power structures. Economic empowerment is a critical element in empowerment practice. For example, "Baked in the Hood" is a New York City (East Harlem)-based economic enterprise that provides jobs and job training in the bakery business for homeless heads of families.

Empowerment in Action

To illustrate the empowerment approach in action with homeless populations, I present excerpts of empowerment group work, political activities and individual and family oriented empowerment practice at My Sisters' Place (MSP), a four-tier program for homeless and formerly homeless women and children and men in Hartford, Connecticut.[1] MSP shelter, the "first tier," was founded in 1983 by a small group of nuns and feminist women who initially ran it on a volunteer basis. There are now four tiers.

MSP is a 24-hour, 18-bed service-enriched shelter for women and children located in a predominantly low-income African American community. The

---

[1]Special credit for helping develop the empowerment approach and contributors of practice for this chapter goes to the women and staff of My Sisters' Place, especially Judith Beaumont, executive director and activist for peace and justice; Gail Bourdon, program director of MSP III and supervisor of clinical staff in the shelter and Mary Seymour Place; and Evelyn Thorpe, residential director of MSP.

shelter is a comfortable and homey older house (a former convent located on church property but not affiliated with the church). There are seven bedrooms, a large kitchen for communal meals, a "coffee" room, a dining-living room that doubles as the group meeting room and children's play space, and a small outdoor play and picnic space. Some bedrooms are private rooms for one family, and some are shared. The shelter can accommodate 18 people. The clinical social worker has a private office, while the shelter manager and staff share an office off the "coffee room."

MSP II is a 2-year-stay transitional living facility for women and children located a few blocks from MSP in a large, beautifully renovated brick factory building. It consists of offices for the executive director, program director and clinical social worker; 20 apartments of various sizes; a multipurpose room for large meetings and activities, including children's groups and women's group meetings; a library with several computer terminals for child and adult use; a separate study area; a fully equipped day-care program for children from birth to age 3; and a large outdoor play and picnic space.

MSP III is a scattered-site residential support program for formerly home-less, chronically mentally ill women (with and without children) who hold the leases on their own apartments, which are mostly clustered in a safe residential part of the city on a bus line and near relevant services. MSP III serves 19 consumers, using a team approach with a high ratio of professional (MSW and BSW) staff to clients (1:4 ratio).

The fourth tier, *Mary Seymour Place* (named after one of Hartford's promi-nent African American women of the early twentieth century), is a supportive permanent-housing program. This new and attractive brick building houses 30 single adults in one-bedroom apartments, offers community meeting and recreation spaces, and has an array of services available. Practice illustrations will be drawn from the first three programs, which have been in operation for 14 years, 6 years, and 9 years, respectively.

EMPOWERMENT IN THE SHELTER: TAKING SUBSTANCE ABUSE SERIOUSLY

The population of the shelter is mainly younger women of color (ages 18–35, African American and Puerto Rican women), usually accompanied by their children. Women with chronic mental illness are accepted as long as they are not a danger to themselves or others, and women who abuse substances are accepted as long as they are not actively using during their stay. The shelter connects women who abuse substances with appropriate treatment and resi-dential services and also strongly encourages recovery. There is an AA group that meets on the premises one night a week. Twelve-step groups and other drug and alcohol programs in the community are also utilized. Many of the women in residence are dealing with addictions to cocaine, heroin, and/or alcohol. Polysubstance abuse is frequent in the younger cohort. Alcohol abuse is particularly life threatening, since it progresses quickly and there is a high rate of death among African American female alcoholics (Gary & Gary, 1985; NCADD, 1990).

Alcohol and other substance abuse adds to the family's vulnerabilities and becomes an important contributing risk factor for homeless mothers. There are multiple health risks for infants and children whose homeless mothers use alcohol and other substances including cigarettes. More than one-third of homeless mothers smoke during pregnancy (Weinreb, Browne, & Benson, 1995). Substance-abusing mothers are less likely to obtain prenatal care and other health services, which leads to detrimental affects on fetal and infant development. Homeless mothers have a higher rate of child abuse and/or neglect or involvement with child protective services agencies, compared to other poor families. Homeless women with children more often report patterns of domestic violence toward themselves and their children than do poor housed mothers, and they often have histories of substance abusing partners that contributed to the homelessness (Lee & Nisivoccia, 1997).

The Shelter Empowerment Group

The shelter empowerment group blends a variety of personal issues related to homelessness, including substance abuse and recovery, with critical consciousness regarding oppression and the slavery of addiction. The focus of the group is on the dynamic connection of the personal and the political. With some groups this work may also take place in a serial fashion, attending first to the personal and later to the political level of concern. The worker is an empathic listener and problem poser, asking critical questions to stimulate discussion and reflection. Members are asked to share experiences, thoughts, and feelings and then to analyze problems on the personal, institutional/systems, and cultural/political levels. The development of a code (picture, chart, song, or poem) is sometimes used by the group to further stimulate consciousness raising. The group members then reflect on their thoughts, feelings, and actions in an ongoing process of praxis, which is action-reflection-action. Empowerment groups also build on strengths and promote ethnic and gender pride and knowledge, which bolsters self-esteem (Lee, 1994a). Two brief examples of shelter empowerment groups at work are presented in this chapter.

Addiction as Part of the Contract with the Shelter Empowerment Group

Present in the first example are two social workers for the group, an African American woman who is learning the empowerment approach and a white (Franco-American) woman experienced in this approach. (She is the "I" in the extract). Eight women are present: five African Americans, two Puerto Ricans, and one white (Italian American), ages 19 to 36. (All are mothers; six have children in tow). This is an ongoing, open-ended weekly group; therefore the worker must explain the group's purpose when new members join.

I began by welcoming the three women who are new to the group today and asked them to tell a little about themselves and why they're here. As each one shared, the others echoed their stories. I said, everyone here has had a difficult time before coming here. This group is an opportunity to talk about the things they have experienced and the problems they face that make finding housing difficult. Sometimes they face discrimination and prejudice. Some of the problems are personal, like the ones with relationships you have already described, or trouble with drug and alcohol abuse for yourself or someone close to you. Daria said, that's me! And Maritza said, me too. I just got out of a drug program and have nowhere to go. I said, it was courageous to share that. It is a hard struggle, and one we will work on together here. My co-worker said, drugs are oppressive. Daria said, they made me a slave. Maritza said, and they made me a fool! (She told her story). . . . (Lee, 1994a)

In another, similar meeting, the members work on their addictions:

In response to a critical question about the forces that created their homelessness, Michaela discussed her cocaine addiction. After she told her story, Ramona shared her alcohol addiction but noted that the rules of the Shelter and the Twelve Step meetings have helped her stay sober. Michaela agreed and told how she had gone to NA and AA meetings to help her with her "temptations." I said, this is what the group is about . . . talking about and helping each other with those things that brought them down . . . to the point that they became homeless. The group members indicated sadly that they have had to "go it alone." I said, it can be very difficult alone and suggested that while they are here they might be able to help one another and possibly continue to help one another after they leave here.

Dora said, finding an apartment is the easy part. The difficult part is keeping it. I said, that is right and we have begun to hear from some group members that it was drugs or alcohol that brought them down. Dora said she does pot (marijuana) but she has never done alcohol or other drugs like the other members. My co-worker said that pot is much more potent now than it was a few years back. I replied that whether it is pot, harder drugs like cocaine and crack, or alcohol, they are all drugs. Ramona and Michaela said that they all get you high, and the group members agreed. Ramona described how addicts often exchange food for drugs and how they will use food money for drugs and then say they do not have any money. I nodded and asked if drugs were a problem for those who had been quiet up until now or if they had other things that brought them to the shelter. . . . (Lee, 1994a)

For further examples of empowerment group work in a variety of shelters, see Lee (1994a).

Empowerment group work in shelters can motivate recovery and prepares individuals for more meaningful participation in 12-step groups. At MSP and other family shelters, parenting groups also make connections to the effects of drug and alcohol abuse on children and parenting. Empowerment work also takes place in individual counseling with the clinical social worker. The milieu itself encourages empowerment, recovery, and self-sufficiency, but affordable housing remains a problem. MSP documented that 44% of the women who left the shelter between September 1995 and September 1996 obtained permanent housing. (In this time period, Section 8 subsidies were frozen.)

MSP has also held "alumnae groups" for shelter "graduates." One such group, the Successful Women's Group, is discussed fully in Lee, 1994a. The story of Shandra Loyal, a founding member of this group is told in Lee, 1994a, and updated and expanded here.

An Intergenerational Case Study Involving MSP's Three Operating Programs

Shandra Loyal and Selina, Her Mother

Shandra is a pretty, dark skinned, intelligent, somewhat overweight 26-year-old who began her empowerment work at MSP 6 years ago when she entered the shelter during her seventh month of pregnancy. Although she had worked full time since her vocational high school graduation, she was sleeping on the floor at her grandmother's home. Her mother was struggling with depression and her own recovery from drugs. Shandra wisely chose not to live with the baby's father and his family as he was drug dealing and physically abusive to her, although she did not disclose this at the time. By the time her daughter was a month old, she moved into subsidized housing, established her household, and returned to work.

Several months later she became a founding member of the Successful Women's Shelter Alumnae group. She developed a close bond with another group member and with the group's coworkers (myself and Judy Beaumont, the executive director). While Shandra tended to be a quiet yet thoughtful participant, she did work on speaking up more in all aspects of her life. An ongoing area of growth for her was in balancing the culturally appropriate but sometimes excessive demands of an African American daughter, sister, grandchild, and mother with her own needs. It is remarkable that Shandra has always remained drug- and alcohol-free and thereby also had to assume a highly responsible role in her family. Her life as a working mother and caretaker was all-consuming. Her strengths were many, but so were her burdens.

About a year later, she contacted me from the inpatient unit of the local psychiatric facility, where she had been admitted for uncontrollable crying on the job and suicidal ideation. It was then that she shared the history of Thomas's violent abuse. This first, and very frightening, psychiatric hospitalization was on the eve of Thomas's release from prison. There were several other stressors as well.

It was extremely important to lower the stress levels dramatically, ensure proper medical follow-up, work with her on the safety factors related to Thomas's return, and teach problem-solving skills. Since this was accomplished with Gail Bourdon from MSP III, consciousness-raising activities were included. The manifestations of oppression in Shandra's life were obvious: battering by the man she cared for and depended on, racial and gender prejudice on the job, economic cutbacks and hardship, and second-rate service offered by the health system. Oppression as well as depression were defined as the problem foci and part of the agreed-upon contract. As social workers, we had to tolerate, however, that once safety plans were in place, the relationship with Thomas would have to proceed according to Shandra's sense of urgency and on her timetable, not ours. It took an additional year and much reflection for Shandra to completely let go of Thomas. Eventually Shandra was able to end the relationship with Thomas, move to a suburban town, complete a cosmetology course, work out of her home, and enter college. With the help of MSP's social work students, she obtained state-of-the art medical care for migraines and connected with support systems in her new town, including a group for women of color, where she continued empowerment work. Although she also mourned the death of her beloved grandmother during this time, she did not have a reoccurrence of major depression. Shandra briefly entered another abusive relationship but was able to get out of it before it got physically violent. She has been able to complete nine college credits and is currently carrying a full course load and working a half-time job. Tomika is a happy, bright, outgoing first grader who loves school. When her mother, Selina, was evicted from her housing, Shandra referred her to MSP.

Selina: From Consumer to Shelter Worker

Selina, 46, divorced from a drug-addicted husband and newly evicted, was also struggling with dysthymia (lifelong serious low-grade depression) and recovery from cocaine abuse. Like her daughter, she had one previous psychiatric hospitalization for depression. She also had inpatient and outpatient drug treatment. She had recently lost her job as a secretary. She grieved the loss of her mother. Her young adult sons who lived with her abused drugs and alcohol and took the rent money for drugs. Selina was overwhelmed and was withdrawing into depression. She turned to Shandra, who referred her mother to MSP Shelter. Selina entered with much sadness and feelings of shame and relief. She responded immediately to the support available. A very intelligent woman, she was able to use the shelter stay to reflect on her situation and to begin to act. She connected to a local mental health agency and began to work a 12-step recovery program. In a few months, she started a 12-step program in her church.

Selina felt the need for continued support in her recovery and restoration of mental health and requested admission to MSP II (The TLF). She was an excellent candidate for this program and eagerly participated in the empowerment group and vocational preparation program upgrading her computer skills. She worked on her unresolved grief and parenting issues with the clinical social worker. She continued her recovery work and leadership in her 12-step group. She participated in the political activities of MSP. She also volunteered in the shelter. A year later, she was hired as a part-time shift supervisor. She has special skill in motivating substance abusers toward recovery. In a recent empowerment group meeting, Selina quoted a 1970s feminist slogan (from a Helen Reddy song), "I am woman, hear me roar." She told her story of despair, loss, and struggle and concluded, laughing, that she never thought "that white woman's song" would describe her—but it does. She said she feels empowered and wants to help others. Moreover, she added, "I *am* doing it—and I know I *can* continue to do it."

The examples thus far have focused on personal and interpersonal empowerment. Yet, a primary tenet of empowerment practice is that the personal is political. The political level of empowerment is achieved when consciousness is raised to include knowledge of structural inequities and when individuals act to challenge or change conditions of oppression. Selina's awareness of her oppression as a woman and her new sense of power illustrate her political level of consciousness. In the following group meetings, we see MSP program residents joining together to challenge Connecticut's "welfare reform" package and to develop consciousness and knowledge to utilize their rights to vote and influence public policy.

Two Examples of Personal/Political Empowerment

MSP II and Welfare Reform

The residential director records:

The women at MSP II invited a top administrator of the local AFDC program to a life skills meeting to discuss what Connecticut's welfare reform would mean to them. The man discussed the new policy realities that women on AFDC would need to get a job within a 21-month time period. One woman in disbelief asked how her children would eat if she didn't get a permanent job? She worked for a temp agency. Another said that she was trying to work, too, but her skills (crocheting, sewing) were not marketable here. The administrator told the women about an entrepreneurial program for low-income women at a local college. The resident was interested but wisely asked how you started a business with no capital even if you went to classes on it? Other women shared their histories of being the last hired and the first fired from low-paying jobs. Another said that she was hoping to take advantage of the rental subsidies now available for TLF graduates but worried that she'd lose her job and have no income "out there on her own" with three children. The administrator eventually said that he could see the problems that the new policies caused for mothers and children. He gave them names of influential people to contact. The women decided to devote the next meeting to strategizing letter writing and lobbying on their own behalf.

MSP III: Political Awareness and Voter Registration

The program director records:

Recent empowerment meetings at MSP III have been devoted to preparations for the coming presidential and local elections. This is a seven-week process, as this work proceeds slowly and sequentially for persons with mental illness. The first meeting was on registering to vote. The process of voter registration and reasons for it were discussed. Some women accompanied others to register to vote. One woman took her test for citizenship so that she could vote in this election.

Then two meetings were devoted to reviewing the issues in the coming elections. The women brought in newspaper articles and watched TV ads about the local and presidential candidates' views. They were asked to raise issues related to themselves as women, parents, and SSDI and mental health consumers. The issues of health care reform and managed care were discussed from all angles. The women shared their experiences with managed care. They developed positions on their views on two or three issues, then identified candidates who supported their views.

For the next meeting, they listened to a tape of the presidential debate and discussed the issues and viewpoints that affected them. The next meeting consisted of practicing voting with a dummy voting machine. Following that, they discussed a local newspaper article on the African American struggle for the right to vote and the struggle for women's suffrage. Many felt they had to use their rights to vote. They also identified how they continue to struggle as African American and Latina women.

In another meeting, they went together to the City Hall where there was an actual voting machine they could practice on. Several were fearful of the curtain and confused about the levers. Several went together to the polls. Watching women who have lived on the streets and spent years in mental hospitals empower themselves in this way was truly exciting.

A by-product of this "talking and doing" preparation was the leadership roles that emerged in the group at this point in time. S., who has been very ill, was able to take on the role of welcoming and guiding the newer group members as they attempted new tasks. B. continued in her role as scribe and narrator. Others researched the newspapers on the issues and so forth. Self-esteem soared.

BRENDA: THE PERSONAL/POLITICAL EMPOWERMENT
OF A WOMAN WITH MENTAL ILLNESS.

The following example illustrates how one member of the MSP III group, Brenda, develops her political skills, which in turn raises her sense of efficacy as well as self-esteem:

Brenda Gary, a 40-year-old African American woman with multiple physical problems and chronic paranoid schizophrenia, experienced periods of intermittent homelessness for 5 years. Leaving her children with relatives, she moved cyclically from the streets to the hospital to several shelters. Then she entered the shelter's residential support program, which set her up in her own apartment and offered daily support and empowerment services. Recently Brenda volunteered to testify at public hearings on proposed state cutbacks of mental health programs. This is an excerpt from her testimony.

> We need our programs to keep us aware of life's possibilities. No matter what you want to be, it's possible. These programs kept me on track and looking forward to life. If the state cuts these programs, the state also cuts the good that they do. . . . We have a women's group every week. We talk about what goes on in our lives—the problems we experience and solutions to them by getting feedback from each other. . . .

To get Brenda and her peers to this point, the worker, Gail Bourdon, prepared the empowerment group to understand the issues and the process of testifying before asking for their participation.

> Early the next evening we went to testify. Brenda patiently waited two hours in line and the additional 2 1/2-hours before testifying. Brenda and I presented our testimony in the Hall of the House of Representatives. It was a striking image to see Brenda, in her woolen hat, speaking so well from the seat of the minority leader. One senator thanked Brenda for her testimony and shared how moved she was by Brenda's effort. Brenda was clearly the group leader that night.

The group then reflected on their actions in the next meeting. The worker invited praxis, the members' reflections on the process of testifying and going to the legislative hearing.

> I asked the group members who went how it was for them and each replied affirmatively. Vicky added, I feel like I could do that sometime . . . I feel the strength. The entire group agreed, noting that they had a voice and were heard. Ida said that those who simply sat there also brought support and power in numbers, so they had a presence as well as a voice. . . . Brenda added, it's good to know that I can accomplish things even with a mental illness. Sometimes people think you can't do things because you have a mental illness. I live with the illness, but this does not mean I am not able to take care of business. The other members thoughtfully agreed. (Lee, 1994a)

The careful preparation of the group members paid off in their confident action. In all of these examples, one can see that personal and political empowerment are part of the same process and outcome.

It is important to note that housing stability and the intense services provided by MSP III have a significant role in helping program residents maintain housing, utilize mental health services, and reduce hospitalizations. Brenda, for example, has experienced some periodic decompensation over the eight years she has been in the program, but she has never been rehospitalized. She, like almost all of the other program residents, has retained her housing. Documentation shows that the MSP III program is clearly effective. There is concern at this point that managed-care guidelines are attempting to redefine programs like MSP III as temporary instead of permanent. Such programs now have to show that a certain percentage of clients are discharged to other programs or to their own supervision. It is hoped that providers and consumers may be empowered together to resist arbitrary criteria for discharge when the service needs of the chronically mentally ill are ongoing.

IMPLICATIONS FOR FUTURE POLICY, PRACTICE, AND RESEARCH AGENDAS

This chapter has highlighted many program and practice innovations in working with homeless populations, particularly with homeless women with and without children, some of whom suffer from substance abuse disorders and others of whom have chronic mental illness. Innovative programs often represent a continuum of services according to the differential needs of this heterogeneous population. One program, My Sisters' Place in Hartford, was presented in detail to illustrate innovative programs and empowering social work practice. Yet minimal programs for the homeless, and worse, no programs at all, exist alongside such full-service innovative programs.

POLICY IMPLICATIONS

Needed policy initiatives to better meet the needs of homeless persons include the following:

1. A nationwide timetable for the eradication of homelessness.
2. Adequate development of affordable housing.
3. Adequate provision of Section 8 subsidies and rental assistance programs.
4. Provision of ethnic- and gender-sensitive transitional and permanent rehabilitative housing programs for homeless-individuals with special needs, especially chronic mental illness and substance dependency and dual disorders.
5. Provision of health and mental health services for homeless individuals.
6. Educational and vocational training opportunities, with job placements for young homeless mothers and fathers as well as for single employable individuals.

7. Health, mental health, and educational services for homeless children.
8. Availability of a continuum of services to the homeless that utilizes differential assessment and intervention.
9. Provision of specialized housing and levels of service for different populations.
10. Recognition of the need for shelter and economic stability throughout the rehabilitation process, especially for those with long term disabilities.

PRACTICE IMPLICATIONS

Social workers and other helping professionals who work with homeless individuals, particularly women with children, need preparation that includes the following:

1. A thorough knowledge of the principles of empowerment practice that appreciates ethnic and class differences; an ecological view; ego-supportive and cognitive-behavioral intervention abilities; and a critical view of oppression.
2. The ability to connect the substance abuse issues of women to gender, class, and racial oppression.
3. In-depth training in the assessment of, intervention with, and treatment of women with substance abuse problems, including an appreciation of the value of 12-step programs and the skilled use of the group modality.
4. In-depth training in the provision of services and referral sources for persons with mental illness, and the ability to detect illnesses that may not yet be formally diagnosed by a mental health provider.
5. Skills in promoting consciousness raising and cultural pride, guiding praxis, and facilitating action to change not only maladaptive behaviors but the society that contributes structurally to homelessness. Skills in implementing the empowerment group approach and individual empowerment work.
6. Knowledge and skill in family-oriented work and in developing culturally sensitive parenting skills.
7. A strengths perspective that does not minimize pathology of any sort.
8. A family and community perspective that looks beyond the individual woman to her connection and contribution to her family and her community.
9. Social work school curricula that are responsive to the needs of homeless individuals and that teach practice approaches, such as the empowerment approach and the strengths perspective, that have relevance to multilevel work with homeless populations.

RESEARCH

There is a plethora of studies about who the homeless are, how to engage them in services, and what kinds of housing and supportive services are effective in work with them. In this writer's opinion, it is not more research that is needed in these areas, but a focus on utilizing existing research findings to further develop relevant policy, program, and practice. Nonetheless, further research to guide practice and service delivery is suggested as follows:

1. Longitudinal studies that demonstrate the journey of homeless individuals through the currently uneven gamut of housing and service provision systems may be a helpful step in designing and obtaining resources for the continuum of services described in this chapter.
2. Studies that show the strengths and coping activities of homeless people may further illustrate how to enact an empowerment and strengths perspective with populations faced with many internal and external obstacles.
3. Empowerment is a multilevel concept that cannot be measured in simplistic ways. Qualitative studies documenting the self-perceived journey toward empowerment in the lives of homeless individuals exposed to empowerment practice could be useful in further grounding this practice concept as it is applied to homeless populations.

Conclusion

Service providers must be trained in differential assessment and intervention and in empowerment-oriented social work practice to enact the goal of going beyond housing people to helping people to act for themselves. It is hoped that resources to make all programs responsive to the needs of heterogeneous populations will be available through public and private funding sources. McKinney funding must be increased to go beyond demonstration projects. Federal Section 8 subsidies are clearly effective for all types of homeless individuals and need to be available on a consistent basis, along with funding for services. Public- and private-sector partnerships are especially useful. Most important, it is hoped that empowered citizens (including consumers of services) will work toward eradicating the American tragedy of homelessness with appropriate affordable housing and services. As noted, there is a full range of literature and ample research on what works. The next step is to make it happen.

REFERENCES

American Journal of Orthopsychiatry. (1996). Special Issue on Welfare Reform and the Real Lives of Poor Women, *66*(4).

Argeriou, M., & McCarty, D. (Eds.). (1990). *Treating alcoholism and drug abuse among homeless men and women: Nine community demonstration grants.* New York: Haworth Press.

Bachrach, L. (1992). What we know about homelessness among mentally ill persons: An analytical review and commentary. In H. R. Lamb, L. Bachrach, & F. Kass (Eds.), *Treating the homeless mentally ill* (pp. 13–40). Washington, DC: American Psychiatric Association.

Baker, S. R. (1994). Gender, ethnicity, and homelessness. *American Behavioral Scientist, 37*(4), 461–475.

Banyard, V., & Graham-Berman, S. A. (1995). Building an empowerment policy paradigm: Self-reported strengths of homeless mothers. *American Journal of Orthopsychiatry 65*, 479–491.

Bassuk, E. (1993). Social and economic hardships of homeless and other poor women. *American Journal of Orthopsychiatry, 63*, 340–347.

Bassuk, E. (1995). Dilemmas in counting the homeless: Introduction. *American Journal of Orthopsychiatry. 65*, 318–319.

Bassuk, E., & Gallagher, E. M. (1990). The impact of homelessness on children. In N. A. Boxhill (Ed.), *Homeless children: The watchers and the waiters* (pp. 79–93). New York: Haworth Press.

Bassuk, E., & Salomon, A. (1993, Dec.). The heart of the social contract. *Readings: A Journal of Reviews and Commentary in Mental Health, 8*(4), 8–12.

Bassuk, E., & Weinreb, L. (1993). Homeless pregnant women: Two generations at risk. *American Journal of Orthopsychiatry, 63*, 348–357.

Baum, A., & Burnes, D. (1993). *A nation in denial: The truth about homelessness.* Boulder, CO: Westview Press.

Baxter, E., & Hopper, K. (1981). *Private lives/public spaces.* New York: Community Service Society.

Berman-Rossi, T. (1994). *Social work practice: The collected writings of William Schwartz.* Itasca, IL: F. E. Peacock Publishers.

Beyond Shelter. (1995). Connecticut Coalition to End Homelessness Newsletter: 5.

Blau, J. (1992). *The visible poor.* New York: Oxford University Press.

Bourdon, G. (1996). *From homelessness to domiciled living: The journey of persons with severe mental illness.* Unpublished dissertation proposal. Boston: Simmons College School of Social Work.

Boxhill, N. A. (Ed.). (1990). *Homeless children: The watchers and the waiters.* New York: Haworth Press.

Breton, M. (1989). The need for mutual aid groups in a drop-in for homeless women: The sistering case. In J. A. B. Lee (Ed.), *Group work with the poor and oppressed* (pp. 47–59). New York: Haworth Press.

Breton, M. (1991). Toward a model of social groupwork practice with marginalized populations. *Groupwork 4*(1), 31–47.

Buckner, J., Bassuk, E., & Zima, B. (1993). Mental health issues affecting homeless women: Implications for intervention. *American Journal of Orthopsychiatry, 63*, 385–399.

Burt, M. (1995). Critical factors in counting the homeless: An invited commentary. *American Journal of Orthopsychiatry, 65*, 334–339.

Cohen, M. B., & Johnson, J. M. (1996, Feb.). *Voicing the homeless experience: A student project in self-directed group work.* Paper presented at 42nd APM, Council on Social Work Education, Washington, DC.

Corporation for Supportive Housing (CSH). (1996). *An introduction to supportive housing.* Unpublished literature accompanying "In Our Backyard," an educational video about supportive housing. New York: Author.

Dattalo, P. (1991). Moving beyond emergency shelters: Who should fund low-income housing? *Social Work, 36*(4), 297–301.

Edwards, R., Cooke, P., & Ried, P. N. (1996). Social work management in an era of diminishing federal responsibility. *Social Work 41*(5), 468–480.

Ewalt, P. (1996). Social work in an era of diminishing federal responsibility: Setting the practice, policy and research agenda. *Social Work 41*(5), 439–440.

Executive Order No. 12848, U.S. Department of Housing and Urban Development. (1993). *Priority Home! The federal plan to break the cycle of homelessness* (HUD-1454-CPD).

Fine, A. (1994, April). To end homelessness permanently. *Community Jobs: The National Employment Newspaper for the Non-profit Sector,* p. 5.

Freeman, E. M. (1996). Welfare reforms and services for children and families: Setting a new practice, research, and policy agenda. *Social Work 41*(5), 521–532.

Gary, L., & Gary, R. (1985). Treatment needs of black alcoholic women. In F. Brisbane & M. Womble (Eds.), *Treatment of black alcoholics* (pp. 97–114). New York: Haworth Press.

Germain, C. B. (1979). *Social work practice: People and environments.* New York: Columbia University Press.

Germain, C. B. (1990). Life forces and the anatomy of practice. *Smith College Studies in Social Work 60,* 138–152.

Germain, C. B., & Gitterman, A. (1995). *Life model approach of social work practice: Advances in theory and practice* (2nd ed.). New York: Columbia University Press.

Goodman, L. (1991). The prevalence of abuse in the lives of homeless and housed poor mothers: A comparison study. *American Journal of Orthopsychiatry, 61,* 489–500.

Goodman, L., Saxe, L., & Harvey, M. (1991). Homelessness as psychological trauma. *American Psychologist, 46*(11), 1219–1225.

Gutiérrez, L. (1990). Working with women of color: An empowerment perspective. *Social Work, 35*(2), 149–155.

Hall, J. A., & Maza, P. L. (1990). No fixed address: The effects of homelessness on families and children. In N. A. Boxhill (Ed.), *Homeless children: The watchers and the waiters* (pp. 35–48). New York: Haworth Press.

Homan, S., Flick, L., Meaton, T. M., & Mayer, J. (1993). Reaching beyond crisis management: Design and implementation of extended shelter-based services for chemically dependent homeless women and their children. *Alcoholism Treatment Quarterly, 10*(3–4), 101–112.

Hopper, K. (1995). Definitional quandaries and other hazards in counting the homeless: An invited commentary. *American Journal of Orthopsychiatry, 65,* 340–347.

Hudson, H. (1985). How and why Alcoholics Anonymous works for blacks. In F. Brisbane & M. Womble (Eds.), *Treatment of black alcoholics* (pp. 11–30). New York: Haworth Press.

Jansson, B., & Smith, S. (1996). Articulating a new nationalism in American social policy. *Social Work, 41*(5), 441–451.

Johnson, A., & Lee, J. (1994). Empowerment work with homeless women. In M. Pravder (Ed.), *Women in context: Toward a feminist reconstruction of psychotherapy* (pp. 408–432). New York: Guilford Press.

Lee, J. A. B. (1989). An ecological view of aging: Luisa's plight. *Journal of Gerontological Social Work, 14*(1–2), 175–190.

Lee, J. A. B. (1990). When I was well, I was a sister: Social work with homeless women. *Jewish Social Work Forum 26,* 22–30.

Lee, J. A. B. (1991). Empowerment through mutual aid groups: A practice grounded conceptual framework. *Groupwork 4*(1), 5–21.

Lee, J. A. B. (1994a). *The empowerment approach to social work practice.* New York: Columbia University Press.

Lee, J. A. B. (1994b). No place to go: Homeless women. In A. Gitterman & L. Shulman (Eds.), *Mutual aid, vulnerable groups, and the life cycle* (pp. 268–293). New York: Columbia University Press.

Lee, J. A. B., & Nisivoccia, D. (1997). Substance abuse and homeless mothers: Multiple oppression. In E. P. Congress (Ed.), *Multicultural perspectives in working with families* (pp. 288–310). New York: Springer.

Leibow, E. (1993). *Tell them who I am: The lives of homeless women.* New York: Free Press.

Link, B., Phelan, J., Bresnahan, M., Steuve, A., Moore, R., & Susser, E. (1995). Lifetime and five-year prevalence of homelessness in the United States: New evidence on an old debate. *American Journal of Orthopsychiatry, 65*, 347–354.

Mancoske, R. J., & Hunzeker, J. M. (1989). *Empowerment-based generalist practice: Direct services with individuals.* New York: Cummings and Hathaway.

McCarty, D., Argeriou, M., Heubner, R., & Lubran, B. (1991). Alcoholism, drug abuse, and the homeless. *American Psychologist, 4*(11), 1139–1148.

NASW News. (1983, Sept.). Who's looking out for the homeless? Interview with Judith A. B. Lee. *NASW News 28*(8), 4–5.

National Council on Alcoholism and Drug Dependence. (1990). *Fact sheet.* New York: Author.

National Institute on Alcohol Abuse and Alcoholism. (1985). *Alcohol use among U.S. ethnic minorities.* Research Monograph No. 18. Rockville, MD: U.S. Department of Health and Human Services.

National Institute on Drug Abuse. (1994, June). Women and drug abuse. Rockville, MD: Press Office of the National Institute of Drug Abuse.

Nunez, R. D. (1994). *Hopes, dreams and promises: The future of homeless children in America.* New York: Institute for Children and Family, Homes for the Homeless.

Parsons, R. (1991). Empowerment purpose and practice principles in social work. *Social Work with Groups. 14*(2), 7–21.

Pathways Press. (1996). Newsletter of Urban Pathways, 575 Eighth Avenue, New York, New York.

Rivlin, L. G. (1990). Home and homelessness in the lives of children. In N. A. Boxhill (Ed.), *Homeless children: The watchers and the waiters* (pp. 49–63). New York: Haworth Press.

Rog, D. J., Holupka, S., & McCombs-Thornton, K. L. (1995). Implementation of the homeless families program: Service models and preliminary outcomes. *American Journal of Orthopsychiatry, 65*, 502–513.

Rossi, P. H. (1989). *Without shelter.* New York: Priority Press.

Safety Net. (1994, March 4–6). Sweeps: Moving people and the problem out of sight. *Safety Net: The Newsletter of the Coalition for the Homeless.* New York: Author.

Saleebey, D. (Ed.). (1992). *The strengths perspective in social work practice.* New York: Longman.

Schwartz, W. (1994). The social worker in the group. In T. Berman-Rossi (Ed.), *The collected writings of William Schwartz* (pp. 167–198). Originally published in 1968. Itasca, IL: Peacock Press.

Shlay, A. B. (1994). Running on empty: Monitoring the lives and circumstances of formerly homeless families and children. *Journal of Social Distress and the Homeless, 3*(2), 135–162.

Shinn, M., Knickman, J. R., & Weitzman, B. C. (1991). Social relationships and vulnerability to becoming homeless among poor families. *American Psychologist, 46*, 1180–1187.

Simon, B. L. (1990). Rethinking empowerment. *Journal of Progressive Human Services, 1*(1), 27–39.

Simon, B. L. (1994). *The empowerment tradition in social work practice.* New York: Columbia University Press.

Solomon, B. (1976). *Black empowerment: Social work in oppressed communities.* New York: Columbia University Press.

Staub-Bernasconi, S. (1992). Social action, empowerment, and social work: An integrating theoretical framework. *Social Work with Groups, 14*(3/4), 35–52.

Straw, R. (1995). Looking behind the numbers in counting the homeless: An invited commentary. *American Journal of Orthopsychiatry, 65*, 330–333.

Thrasher, S. P., & Mowbray, C. T. (1995). A strengths perspective: An ethiographic study of homeless women with children. *Social Work, 2*, 93–101.

Toro, P., Trikett, E., Wall, D., & Salem, D. (1991). Homelessness in the United States: An ecological perspective. *Psychologist, 46*, 1208–1218.

U.S. Department of Health and Human Services, Center for Mental Health Services. (1994). *Making a difference—Interim status report of the McKinney demonstration program for homeless adults with serious mental illness* (DHHS Publication No. SMA 94-3014). Washington, DC: Author.

Weinreb, L., Browne, A., & Benson, J. D. (1995). Services for homeless pregnant women: Lessons from the field. *American Journal of Orthopsychiatry, 65*, 492–501.

Weinreb, L., & Buchner, J. C. (1993). Homeless families: Program responses and public policies. *American Journal of Orthopsychiatry, 63*, 400–409.

Whitbeck, L., & Simons, R. (1993). A comparison of adaptive strategies and patterns of victimization among homeless adolescents and adults. *Violence and Victims, 8*, 135–152.

Wright, J. D. (1990). Homelessness is not healthy for children and other living things. In N. A. Boxhill (Ed.), *Homeless children: The watchers and the waiters* (pp. 64–78). New York: Haworth Press.

Part IV

Innovations in Practice and Service Delivery with the Elderly

11

Innovations in Institutional Care from a Patient-Responsive Perspective

EVA KAHANA

BOAZ KAHANA

HEIDI T. CHIRAYATH

The need for long-term care for the aged is affecting increasing numbers of older adults and their families in our aging society. The key component of long-term care in the United States continues to be palliative residential care offered in nursing homes. In 1990, 1.6 million elderly resided in nursing homes, constituting 5.1% of the population over age 65 (U.S. Bureau of the Census, 1993). Within the most rapidly growing age group in the United States, those over 85, 24.5% are nursing home residents. Life in nursing homes poses challenges for both staff and elderly residents of such facilities. Approaches to enhancing care continue to be a source of public debate and controversy for politicians, policymakers, and practitioners who serve the elderly (Estes & Swan, 1993). Thus, it is indeed ironic that the topic of nursing home care has attracted scant attention from scientific researchers in the past two decades, with only a very small portion of research dollars funding inquiry in this area. In a paper written by the first author (Kahana, 1973), humane treatment of the elderly in nursing homes was discussed. This chapter presents a welcome opportunity to revisit this issue almost 25 years later. We do so with the added objective of considering innovative programs in nursing home care that use a patient-responsive perspective to guide our analysis.

Public concern about the quality of life in nursing homes has resulted in legislation to ensure that basic rights of elderly patients are safeguarded (OBRA, 1987). There have been major initiatives to eliminate restraints and to consider end-of-life wishes of elderly patients (Brown, 1989). Ombudsmen programs are now mandated by most states (Kahana, 1994), and utilization reviews ensure that level of care (skilled or basic) is appropriately matched to resident needs.

Paralleling the absence of research interest in nursing home care, there has also been relatively little published evidence of systematic program innovation to develop overall policies or environmental changes to better serve nursing home residents. It is noteworthy in this context that many clinical efforts toward program enhancement remain unknown to the scientific community because they are not documented in the published literature. At the same time, there are numerous examples of targeted program initiatives or interventions to address specific goals such as restraint reduction or better management of incontinence. The aim of this chapter is to challenge both researchers and practitioners in the field of aging to remove the cobwebs of disinterest and to direct the searchlights of inquiry and innovation to this challenging area. To facilitate such efforts, a three-pronged approach is taken.

In the first part of the discussion, we provide an overview of the broad array of goals, approaches, and types of interventions that characterize special programs in nursing home settings. This framework sets the stage for a review of recent program initiatives and practices implemented in nursing home settings and published in the scientific literature. In the second part of our discussion, we attempt to organize and review recent programs and practice innovations and focus particularly on initiatives that are aimed at improving overall quality of resident life.

In the third and final part of the chapter, we move beyond reports of existing programs and develop a conceptual framework for patient-responsive care in nursing homes that can guide future initiatives and identify neglected areas that require intervention.

Goals and Approaches of Intervention in Nursing Homes

Nursing homes provide residential settings for housing and caring for the frailest, oldest, and socially most isolated group of older adults. With an average age of 85, the typical nursing home resident is a cognitively impaired widowed older woman who has difficulty performing even basic activities of daily living (Jette, Branch, Sleeper, Feldman, & Sullivan, 1992).

It is a well-accepted axiom that most older adults enter nursing homes involuntarily and with minimal choice in selecting a particular facility (George & Maddox, 1989). Frail elderly as well as members of other age groups prefer home care to nursing home care (Steel, 1992). As long-term care becomes increasingly available in the community, those requiring institutional care represent a highly select group of the most vulnerable (Hing, 1987). Consequently, any therapeutic efforts to enhance the functioning of this group represent a regimen of limited objectives. Nevertheless, nursing home settings can serve important therapeutic and rehabilitative functions and can enhance the quality of life of frail elders by ensuring comfort and some measure of autonomy (Agich, 1993). In a welcome contrast with prior work, which generally emphasized the deficiencies of nursing homes, recent research has begun to identify criteria for high quality of care and even excellence in nursing home settings (Andersen, 1987; Brittis, 1996).

In the gerontological literature, it has been customary to refer to older adults living in nursing homes as residents, a designation based on the tradition of residential care once provided to relatively intact older adults in homes for the aged (Tobin & Lieberman, 1976). However, the frail older person who lives in a skilled nursing home is, for all practical purposes, a patient being cared for in the context of a medical model of care. Hence, we concur with the position advocated by anthropological researchers in nursing homes (Henderson & Vesperi, 1995) that the terms "patient" and "resident" may be interchangeably used to depict the reality of nursing home life. We thus employ both expressions in our discussion of nursing home life.

Because of the limited personal, social, and financial resources of the elderly in nursing homes, residents are known to be characterized by extreme environmental docility (Lawton, 1980). These elderly individuals are highly susceptible to environmental influences, displaying great responsiveness to the stimuli of institutional life. Because of this environmental docility, frail older residents are at high risk when the nursing home environment presents negative social or physical characteristics. At the same time, resident docility also holds promise for magnifying positive effects of programs and interventions that are oriented to enhancing quality of life.

Like other parts of the health care system, nursing homes face pressures to deliver economical care. Nursing home services are generally paid for by third-party payers, and hence consumers exercise little control over services (Estes & Swan, 1993). Economic influences dictate that direct care of elderly persons living in nursing homes be generally provided by paraprofessional staff working for low wages and possessing minimal training and skills. Professional staff have limited direct patient contact in such settings, and physicians' orders are often delivered by phone (Fortinsky & Raff, 1995–96). Registered nurses' duties are largely limited to supervising other staff and dispensing medication. Social work staff, where available, typically focus on intake and residential transfer services and play some formal roles in maintaining contact with families and resolving conflicts involving staff and family members of residents (Vladeck, 1980). Reimbursement is generally unavailable for psychotherapy and psychiatric care, which generally involves diagnosis and administration of psychotropic drugs.

Programmatic innovation in nursing homes is a particularly exciting and much needed arena for intervention, because it confronts barriers posed by funding constraints, organizational climate, and client characteristics. Limited staff resources of nursing homes must be juxtaposed against a high level of patient need. Staff must care for physically frail and often cognitively impaired older persons who may exhibit psychological distress and behavioral disturbances. These behavioral disturbances are compounded by the propensity of the frail aged to have difficulty in walking, to experience falls, to develop incontinence, and to endure sleep disturbances. Existing programs of intervention in nursing homes are generally aimed at reducing disruptive and problem behaviors of residents and at improving function. Interventions are usually sought that do not require costly professional treatments and are also likely to yield readily discernible benefits. Since impairments due to chronic illness are not readily treatable, some interventions center on enhancing resident comfort by removing iatrogenic influences of the nursing home environment. Although programs to enhance resident autonomy have been widely advocated (Kane, 1991), few actual interventions have been implemented to achieve such goals.

Program Innovation in Nursing Homes

ORGANIZING FRAMEWORK

In presenting a review of existing interventions, we conducted a systematic search of the literature, using databases in psychology, sociology, social work, medicine, nursing, and nutrition. We decided to use a broad time-frame in considering program innovation. Restricting our review to a limited time-frame would have omitted a great deal of important program innovation developed during prior decades that represent promising areas of program development and are yet to be fully realized or widely implemented. We thus include innovations on the basis of either creativeness of approach or novelty or recency of implementation.

In conducting our review of the literature, we also discovered a notable absence of organizing frameworks for classifying innovation and program implementation in this area. To make a contribution to filling this void, we present a framework for organizing existing program innovations and at the same time identify gaps in programming along important areas of resident need. We conclude our illustrative summary of program innovations by presenting a new framework of Patient-Responsive Care (PRC), which can guide future program development in nursing home care.

Programs or interventions in nursing homes may be better understood when classified based on intended resident or organizational outcomes as well as the locus of interventions, or the major target of interventions. Table 11.1 depicts a means/ends typology we propose for classifying nursing home interventions along these salient dimensions. The table outlines interventions that seek to achieve goals for residents, staff, and families. These goals may be achieved alternatively by targeting the resident, the physical and social environment of the nursing home, or staff, family, and community in the design of interventions. The actual methods or content of interventions may then be placed in the cells of the table. Elements of the table include existing approaches to intervention as well as the potential patient-responsive interventions that we advocate in the concluding section of our chapter.

As shown in Table 11.1, goals of interventions in nursing homes generally have a resident-related focus. The majority of programs described in the literature aim to enhance residents' functioning or their quality of life. These goals are achieved either through medically oriented efforts to reduce impairments and disability or through psychosocial programs to improve residents' psychosocial well-being. However, to appreciate the full range of program initiatives, readers should note that some programs have goals that are organization or family centered. That is, they aim to enhance organizational efficiency, increase staff satisfaction, or enhance the well-being of family members. It is useful to note

TABLE 11.1
Means/Ends Typology of Nursing Home Interventions

Goals	Target/Locus of Intervention							
		Patient		Physical Environment	Social Environment	Staff Organization	Family	Community
	Management-Oriented Process	Therapeutic Process	Patient-Responsive Process	Prosthetic Process	Prosthetic Process			
A. Achieve Resident-Focused Goals								
1. Improve health and physical function								
a. Reduce impairment and disability		upper body exercise	self-medication	hip protectors				
b. Reduce nutritional problems		exercise		diet supplements				
c. Reduce incontinence	diapering scheduled toileting	pelvic exercise		computerized monitoring system				
d. Reduce mobility problems/falls		lower body exercise medication reduction		alarms restraint reduction				
e. Reduce behavioral problems	limit behavioral choices	reinforce behavioral competence			ecological PE fit approach			
2. Improve resident psychosocial well-being		group therapy life review relaxation therapy	support patient autonomy			hugging week staff education	hugging week	pet therapy inter-generational programs
B. Achieve Staff-Related Goals					build staff-resident relations	empowerment support groups		
C. Enhance Family Well-Being		educational programs support programs			family council		group therapy	

these distinctions as we turn to the horizontal axis of our model and consider the locus of interventions. Here it is evident that diverse goals may be achieved by interventions directed at effecting changes in patients, the physical or social environment, staff, family, or the community. Certain goals are more likely to be achieved through interventions that target patients, while others may call for targeting the environment. Nevertheless, goals are, at least theoretically, independent of the locus of interventions. The usefulness of this distinction may be illustrated when we consider that some family-oriented programs may be aimed at increasing resident well-being by involving families more closely in caring for residents, while others may be directed at reducing family burden through group therapy and may, in fact, serve to reduce family involvement with residents. In both of these examples, the family is the locus of intervention, but in the former case resident-oriented goals are served, whereas in the latter case the well-being of family members is the goal.

Embedded in the structural framework just outlined are the cells, which represent the specific content and method of interventions. Implicit in the framework but not modeled, there are also complex and important considerations of social processes. To appreciate the divergent processes that characterize program development and implementation, it is useful to note that programs typically reflect the philosophies and traditions of the disciplines from which they originate. Medicine, nursing, the allied health professions, psychology, and social work each has a distinct set of traditions that influence the types of programs created. It is beyond the scope of this chapter to review these alternative traditions, but readers may appreciate program differences, keeping in mind that they may arise from alternative disciplinary orientations. Examples of differences may include focus on therapeutic interventions (psychology), programs that enhance patient function (nursing or medicine), and interventions that empower patients (social work).

In Table 11.1 we have further subdivided interventions that target patients or the physical and social environment on the basis of processes that reflect management-oriented, therapeutic, patient-responsive, or prosthetic approaches to intervention. Looking at the cells of Table 11.1, it is readily seen that interventions aimed at reducing patient impairment or disability generally target the patient as the locus of intervention. In contrast, approaches to improving patient psychosocial well-being tend to target staff, family, or the community. In terms of process, management-oriented, therapeutic, and prosthetic approaches appear to be most common. Very few patient-responsive interventions were discerned in our literature review.

The organizational climate of managed care may serve to foster management-oriented interventions. The prevailing ethos of consumer advocacy (Burger, Fraser, Hunt, & Frank, 1996), as well as practice guidelines within the field of social work, espouse an empowerment-oriented approach (Cox & Parsons, 1994). Improvements in physical and social functioning of residents are sought by programs that are generally based on a therapeutic orientation. Numerous nursing interventions aimed at enhancing ambulation or continence also reflect this approach.

While therapeutic programs may often involve efforts to reduce patient impairments through exercise or the development of better coping skills, prosthetic approaches involve interventions that may reduce environmental demands or create a more supportive atmosphere. Such interventions generally aim to improve the physical or social environment or to enhance responsiveness of staff to achieve their objectives.

In evaluating social processes that define patient-oriented interventions, major distinctions exist in the relationship between staff, who design and implement programs, and residents, who are the presumed beneficiaries of these interventions. Management-oriented approaches often treat patients as objects of intervention who must be manipulated to achieve desired objectives. Thus, for example, in programs to deal with incontinence, staff may diaper all residents who need assistance in toileting at regular intervals. Residents may be awakened at night for such care, regardless of whether they are wet. In contrast, therapeutic programs seek to enhance capabilities of residents by using accepted professional means such as pelvic exercise. Accessible toilets near patient's beds represent prosthetic interventions to deal with incontinence. Enhancing staff responsiveness to resident requests for toileting reflects patient-responsive prosthetic approaches to intervention.

Therapeutic, prosthetic, and management-oriented approaches do not imply responsiveness to resident preferences. Instead, each typically applies an expert's definition about goals to be addressed and approaches to be used to achieve objectives. Autonomy- or empowerment-oriented approaches have been advocated in the social work literature as an alternative to management-based or therapeutic interventions (Kane, 1991). In fact, empowerment of elderly and disabled persons was the theme of the 1997 professional meetings of Systems Science in Health Social Services for the Elderly and Disabled (SYSTED) (Heuman, 1997). These approaches are predicated on respect for resident autonomy and suggest active involvement of residents in designing interventions to assist them (Cox & Parsons, 1994). Such approaches also consider resident involvement in determining level of participation in interventions.

Since residents living in nursing homes are typically too frail and powerless to demand or even practice active consumer involvement in programs designed to aid them, few programs have been reported in the literature that actually utilize these empowerment-based approaches. In the concluding part of our chapter, we propose an alternative to designing and implementing interventions that we term Patient-Responsive Care. This approach calls for a systematic and empathetic discernment by staff of resident perspectives and preferences. The approach we advocate is broadly related to earlier work of the first author on person-environment fit as a determinant of resident well-being in nursing homes (Kahana, 1973; Kahana, Liang, & Felton, 1980). Such ecological orientations go beyond commonly used prosthetic approaches and call for a comprehensive thrust to meet the articulated needs and preferences of residents. Environments may be matched to resident needs by altering the physical or social environment and by enhancing staff responsiveness in an effort to improve residents' quality of life (Kahana, Kahana, & Riley, 1989).

In the following review and discussion of existing programs, we classify interventions in some cases on the basis of the treatment goals and in others on the basis of the locus of intervention. This mixed use of intervention axes reflects the themes that emerged from our review of the literature. The framework we presented will be referred to throughout our review to clarify commonalties and differences relevant to goals, value orientations, processes, and locus of interventions.

REVIEW OF PROGRAMS REPORTED IN THE LITERATURE

In this section of the chapter, we provide a broad, illustrative review of nursing home-based interventions reported in the literature. Our review is not intended to be comprehensive but instead provides a backdrop of prior programming in major areas of intervention and illustrates how innovative approaches can provide direction for future research and program development. In our presentation of specific programs we organize our review to proceed from a description of programs that reflect a medical orientation to those that reflect a social orientation. We begin with medical/nutritional programs, review programs aimed at reducing incontinence and falls, and then turn to programs aimed at enhancing psychological well-being, reducing behavioral problems, and enhancing quality of life through family and staff-based interventions.

Interventions to Improve Health and Physical Function

Reducing impairment and disability.   Gerontological researchers have documented the typical progression of the frail elderly from illness to physical impairment and then to disability and reduced quality of life (Kahana & Kahana, 1996; Kahana, Kahana, Namazi, Kercher, & Stange, 1997). This cascade of disability has been shown to have serious repercussions for the quality of life of the elderly. Medical programs in the nursing home may intervene at various stages along this cascade. Yet researchers aptly point out that interventions aimed at slowing the disablement process are ineffective when targeted to the extremely frail elderly. These individuals will still need nursing home care, despite even highly successful innovation (Schnelle, MacRae, Ouslander, Simmons, & Nitta, 1995).

Our review of innovative programming to reduce disablement highlights those interventions that consider both physical and psychosocial functioning of nursing home residents and take resident satisfaction into account as a measure of program success. Most interventions aimed at improving resident physical functioning are either therapeutic or prosthetic, with prosthetic approaches sometimes serving preventive functions. Such programs include the use of hip protectors to reduce fractures (Lauritzen, Petersen, & Lund, 1993) and efforts to improve knee flexion and range of motion in order to prevent further regress in ambulation. One therapeutic program (Mollinger & Steffen, 1993) stopped an iatrogenic practice by determining that splinting a knee to produce a prolonged stretch was no more effective than manual stretching.

Two interventions stand out in this area as moving beyond promoting physical health and physical function to improving overall resident quality of life.

The first, a Danish study (Wagner, Wahlberg, & Worning, 1994), sought to both decrease drug consumption among residents and improve their autonomy and locus of control. The program permitted competent residents to administer their own medications and succeeded in reducing drug consumption for a number of years following the intervention. The second program (Plautz & Timen, 1992) aimed at improving both physical function and self-image by helping residents sit more erectly in wheelchairs. In terms of physical health, this intervention aimed to improve pulmonary, cardiovascular, and gastrointestinal functioning. The intervention moved beyond the medical model by recognizing that an elderly person's appearance in a wheelchair affects other people's perceptions of them. Beyond improvement in functioning, the intervention served to raise residents' self-esteem and communication, due to their improved appearance. This program illustrates the point that innovation can address simultaneously physical and psychosocial aspects of resident well-being with positive synergistic effects.

Programs to reduce nutritional problems.   Eating is hindered by diverse ailments that commonly afflict the elderly, such as dental problems, cognitive impairment, mobility problems, and dysphasia (swallowing disorder). One study reports nutritional deficits in up to 85% of nursing home patients (Mion, McDowell, & Heaney, 1994). In addition, institutional food, especially when it is constrained by dietary restrictions, can be unappetizing to residents. Meals in nursing homes are seldom matched to the cultural or personal customs and preferences of residents. Poor nutrition, in turn, is widely recognized as contributing to susceptibility to illness and disability.

Published reports of nutritional interventions in nursing homes were found by the authors to be sparse, as has been documented by other researchers (Abbasi, Basu, Parsa, Alverno, & Rudman, 1993). A common goal of nutritional efforts is to increase functioning and nutrition through dietary supplements. One program in the Netherlands improved the weight of residents through the use of vitamin-fortified fruit juices (van der Wielen, van Heereveld, deGroot, & van Staveren, 1995).

Nutritional programs have also been instituted in order to counteract weight loss and poor appetite or to bring about improvements in medical conditions or physical functioning (Johnson, Dooley, & Gleick, 1993). One innovative program utilized nutrition to help decrease falls and improve mobility of nursing home residents (Fiatarone, O'Neill, Doyle, Clements, Roberts, Kehayias, Lipsitz, & Evans, 1993). This intervention combined the use of multinutrient supplements and lower body exercise to reduce muscle weakness. Another initiative explored the link between dietary protein and pressure ulcers (Breslow, Hallfrisch, Guy, Crawley, & Goldberg, 1993). The program introduced high-protein nutritional formulas to malnourished patients with skin ulcers and found decreases in the surface areas of their ulcers in response to the nutritional intervention.

These programs illustrate the application of nutritional interventions to address a wide variety of medical issues. Typically they involve dietary changes using a medical model; few programs have been published that are concerned with social or psychological aspects of eating or that use meals to enhance the psychological well-being of residents. Considering the highly social nature of eating, it may be useful to incorporate food into various efforts at enhancing social life and experiences of older adults. Such initiatives informally take place in recreational programs that serve refreshments. There is little evidence, however, from the published literature that formal initiatives or evaluations have taken place in this area. Nutritional programs would also represent a most promising arena for enhancing personal control through more extensive choices and enhancing cultural continuity through provision of culturally familiar and preferred foods (Kahana, Kahana, Sterin, Fedirko, & Taylor, 1993; Langer & Rodin, 1976).

Programs to reduce incontinence.   Urinary incontinence has been recognized as a highly prevalent problem among nursing home residents (Qualey, 1995). It is a condition that demands major expenditures of time and effort on the part of staff and one that undermines the quality of life of residents. While OBRA (1987) has placed specific requirements on nursing homes for assessing and managing incontinence (HCFA, 1989), most incontinent residents in nursing homes are cared for by diapering or, in some instances, by scheduled toileting (Schnelle, Newman, & Fogerty, 1991).

Most interventions that address urinary problems are management oriented, rather than therapeutic (Ouslander & Schnelle, 1993). They generally involve some form of time-bound intervention to encourage frequent and regular emptying of the bladder. Most programs involve little verbal interaction and often result in residents being treated as objects (Ouslander & Schnelle, 1993). Although ideally such programs should be individualized, staffing constraints and institutional schedules are generally cited as reasons for the unresponsiveness of staff to individual toileting needs and the reliance on programs in which patients are toileted according to a fixed timetable.

Interventions to reduce incidence of incontinence range from behavioral techniques that provide reinforcement for maintenance of bladder control (Pinkston, Howe, & Blackman, 1986–87) to high-tech approaches that use computer-based monitoring in incontinence management systems (Schnelle, McNees, Crooks, & Ouslander, 1995). An underlying assumption of most treatment programs is that a behavioral dysfunction is being remedied by special staff interventions and through the use of skilled nursing techniques. Yet a closer evaluation of successful programs suggests that at least part of the solution involves removal of environmental barriers to maintenance of continence.

There is little information, at present, linking reduced wetness rates to improved quality of life for residents. In fact, there is some evidence that eliminating toileting schedules, which disrupt resident sleep, may represent one useful area of intervention (Morton, 1995). Here, the positive impact comes from removing the iatrogenic effects of toileting programs that may actually undermine quality of resident life.

Staff responsiveness to patient needs and preferences is particularly important in dealing with the common problems of incontinence in nursing homes. For many frail residents, a vestige of personhood and dignity relates to the ability to maintain continence. Finding ways to respond to toileting requests by residents and individualizing toileting programs thus represents an important area for future intervention in nursing homes. Programs where patients are prompted to request toileting assistance may hold particular promise in this area (Ouslander & Schnelle, 1993).

Programs to enhance mobility and prevent falls (restraint reduction).   Due to their physical impairments, nursing home residents are often limited in mobility and are at high risk for experiencing debilitating and potentially life-threatening falls. Annual incidence of falls in nursing homes are reported as 0.4 to 3.6 falls per bed, with a mean of 1.4 falls (Rubenstein & Wieland, 1993). Diverse factors contribute to the risk of falls, ranging from confusion to visual impairments, unstable gait, and dizziness (Lipsitz, Jonsson, & Kelley, 1991). The unfamiliar nature of the nursing home terrain and other environmental risk factors are also likely to raise the risk of falls among residents. Side effects of drugs may contribute to risk factors for falling. Multiple risk factors are often present, which may operate synergistically.

Residents prone to falling have in the past often been secured through physical restraints. Such restraint use may have played a role in increasing resident vulnerability to falls by further deconditioning residents. In a major study (Tinetti, Liu, & Ginter, 1992), fall-related injuries were ten times higher for residents who had been restrained during the previous year than for those who had not. On an organizational level, restraint reduction efforts have been a major thrust of nursing home–based program innovations and development.

Preventive interventions for falls generally include identification of risk, particularly after falls have occurred. High-risk persons have been referred to exercise programs and provided with alarm systems or other protective devices (Jagella, Tideiksaar, Mulvihill, & Neufeld, 1992). Educational programs have also been used to improve the prescription and management of medications. Involvement of a consulting pharmacist has been an innovative approach in attempting to reduce the negative effects of polypharmacy among nursing home residents who are at high risk for falls (Gurwitz, Soumerai, & Avorni, 1990).

A literature review of exercise-based interventions provides conclusive evidence for the effectiveness of diverse exercise programs in reducing falls (Province et al., 1995). As muscle strength and tone are increased, the likelihood of falls is reduced. The success of these approaches is illustrated in an exercise program in which major increases in muscle strength were observed among nonagenarians who participated in weight training programs (Fiatarone, Marks, Ryan, Meredith, Lipsitz, & Evans, 1990).

A more prosthetic or ameliorative orientation to reducing falls without improving function is the use of alarm systems that are activated when patients move too far forward in their chair or wheelchair or try to get out of their wheelchair unassisted (Widder, 1985). Although at times these devices may go off too late to prevent falls, they may still serve a useful function, since they summon assistance promptly after the fall. Ideally, preventive, therapeutic, and prosthetic approaches could be combined to reduce the likelihood of falls.

Programs to reduce behavioral problems.   Interventions to limit or manage behavioral problems of nursing home residents include efforts aimed at improving behavioral competence as well as at curbing manifestations of behavioral dysfunction. Therapeutic interventions seek to address and ameliorate causes of dysfunction, while management-oriented ones simply reduce the incidence of behaviors that are deemed undesirable by staff. A review of published program innovation in this area reveals a focus primarily on management-based efforts.

Most programs aim to limit disruptive behaviors, primarily among demented patients. Programs in this area range from pharmacological approaches to restraint use and, often, use behavioral techniques, reinforcing desired behaviors, using time-outs when undesirable behaviors are shown, and employing differential reinforcement when proper actions are exhibited by the resident (Cooper, 1994).

One innovative approach reported for dealing with behavioral problems involves an ecological model for management of aggressive behaviors in the nursing home (Cox, 1993). The ecological model considers the behavioral problems of residents to be a function of interactions between resident attributes and the physical and social environment of the nursing home. Interventions based on this model thus include careful evaluation of both person and environment and involves efforts to implement both behavioral approaches and environmental change.

An interesting issue raised in this area of behavioral problems relates to cognitively intact residents who engage in undesirable behaviors such as refusal to eat or drink. Here the limits of resident autonomy are being tested, and the appropriateness of interventions must be explored. A Swedish study (Mattiasson & Andersson, 1994) examined staff attitudes about this issue and found that 50% of staff personally endorsed the right of patients to die if they refuse to eat. However, only 20% indicated that their unit would permit patients to refuse nourishment. Some patient-responsive approaches such as validation therapy (Feil, 1982) have also been advocated as holding promise for reducing disruptive behaviors.

Programs to Enhance Resident Psychosocial Well-being

Programs aimed at enhancing psychological well-being of nursing home residents come closest, at least in theory, to being responsive to patients' needs and preferences. Some of these programs are also aimed at improving social functioning of residents. As such, they may reflect an overlap between therapeutic and palliative modalities on the continuum of interventions that we have proposed.

Diverse interventions to address psychosocial goals have been described in the literature. Established therapeutic modalities that have reported success in nursing home settings include life review techniques (Butler, 1980–81) and approaches to personal construct therapy in which older adults derive healing experiences through supported story telling (Viney, 1993). The second group of interventions introduces some form of affective stimulation to reduce depression and to enhance positive affective states. Interventions of this type range from touching and hugging programs to use of visits by pets. One innovative and successful example of efforts to provide a positive affective climate in nursing home settings was a hugging week throughout one nursing home that recognized and addressed the deprivation from affective touching experienced by many residents (Weisberg & Haberman, 1989). This program was found to have broad organizational impact and benefited staff and families, as well as residents. Programs that introduce visits by pets have also been found to increase social behaviors and to enhance psychological well-being (Hendy, 1987; Perelle & Granville, 1993).

In terms of more traditional therapeutic interventions, reminiscence-based therapies have been among the most widely employed. Findings evaluating the effectiveness of these programs reveal mixed results, with resident characteristics as well as therapist training influencing outcomes. A number of unique and targeted intervention programs have been aimed at enhancing coping resources (such as self-esteem), and internal locus of control among residents. These range from group therapy to progressive relaxation therapy (Bensink, Godbey, Marshall, & Yarandi, 1992). Some limited successes have been achieved by these interventions. Nevertheless, a careful analysis of results reveals that the therapeutic hour provides only limited respite from the generally depersonalizing experiences of resident life in nursing homes.

Family- and Community-oriented Programs

The importance of contacts between representatives of the community and institutionalized elders has been underscored in the seminal work of Goffman (1961). Such contacts help break down barriers between the real world and the world of those in institutions. Yet programs which build on this widely acclaimed notion have been slow to emerge.

Programs involving families may be broadly classified in two categories. The first group reflects an interest in treating family members to address their presumed feelings of guilt and to reduce the burdens and distress of family members. Supportive or educational group approaches have been used to address these objectives. (Drysdale, Nelson, & Wineman, 1993; Hamel, 1995). It is noteworthy that family therapy programs of this type often define families as the problem and may take a patronizing approach toward them.

A second genre of family-centered interventions acknowledges that involving families in the care of residents may have benefits both to the family members and to nursing home residents. Programs of this type can help break down barriers between families and nursing home staff and may reduce alienation by families, who typically feel unwelcomed by nursing home administration and staff. Support-group formats as well as family council programs have reported success in bringing family and staff closer together (Campbell & Linc, 1996). The full potential of such programs is yet to be realized, for there is a tremendous helping potential in family members, who are major stakeholders in quality of care.

There are very few accounts of programs that involve community volunteers in the published literature. The literature may provide an underestimate of actual programming involving community volunteers, since clinical accounts attest to the high prevalence of such programs. Perhaps intergenerational programs (Camp, this volume) represent the most innovative trend in this field.

Staff-centered Programming

Three main objectives emerge as drivers of staff-centered programming. The first focuses on supporting and empowering staff. Nursing assistants in nursing homes report high levels of stress and burnout, as well as lack of input into patient care (Diamond, 1992; Tellis-Nayak & Tellis-Nayak, 1994). Interventions in this area include the development of support groups for nursing assistants (Wilner, 1994). Such groups may serve as a forum to share problems and ideas and may decrease stress and boost staff self-confidence. In addition, programs often involve a component of team-building among staff.

A second goal of staff-centered intervention is to provide staff training about aging or about the experiences of life as a resident. Often staff report not being able to assist residents because they are unfamiliar with the problems they face (Bonnel, 1995). The aim of such programs is not only to facilitate better understanding of residents by staff but also to improve care through such understanding. Programs aimed at staff development often involve educational sessions in which staff are familiarized with various topics in aging (Chandler, Rachal, & Kazelskis, 1986), including relevant issues such as sexuality among the aged (White & Cantania, 1982) and definitions of elder abuse (Hudson, 1992). Other programs involve experiential learning about the problems that the frail elderly residents face every day. One educational program combined learning about the psychosocial components of aging with an experiential focus on the physical limitations of the elderly (Norburn, Nettles-Carlson, Soltys, Read, & Pickard, 1995). "They [staff members] were fed pureed food, tried to listen and understand with the radio blaring and cotton in their ears, read the newspaper and tried to find the bathroom while wearing 'cataract glasses' and 'glaucoma glasses' "(Norburn et al., p. 41). After their exposure to resident life, staff reported feeling more supportive of residents' needs and empowered to play a more active role in care planning.

A third goal of staff-centered programs is to facilitate the relationship between residents and staff. Interventions may aim to personalize residents to the staff through interviews or discussion sessions between residents and staff (Abood, 1992). Alternatively, intervention may be conducted in the context of providing staff with success in implementing some component of patient care. One such program encouraged staff to foster residents' self-care behaviors, such as bathing and dressing (Blair, 1995). This goal was achieved by facilitating communication between the staff and residents. The staff helped the residents set up goals to achieve, encouraged their progress, and cheered their achievements. Follow-up measures indicated that, compared to a control group, residents who worked with staff on self-care goals showed significant and lasting improvements over time. This innovative plan achieved multiple objectives through teamwork between residents and staff. It helped residents meet their own physical needs while building independence and self-esteem.

Another patient-responsive intervention aimed to build more personal, trusting relationships between staff and residents (Taival & Raatikainen, 1993). Assessment of residents' well-being was based on their own assessment, not on staff opinions. This intervention improved patients' physical and psychological well-being, as well as their relationships with staff.

Staff-centered programs encompass diverse goals and many different types of program initiatives. They do not necessarily create patient-responsive care but are often involved in implementation of patient responsive programs.

Working Toward a Model of Patient-Responsive Care and Intervention

The foregoing review of existing interventions presented a broad array of useful and targeted approaches to improving patient function and quality of life in nursing homes. The specific innovative programs we reviewed were illustrative, rather than exhaustive. Some of the most promising innovations were those that recognized that intervention is most effective when physical and social needs are considered simultaneously (e.g., Plautz & Timen, 1992). Multidimensional interventions are particularly useful because frailty and functional limitations of nursing home residents are typically extensive and multidimensional. Physical, social, and psychological limitations of residents must also be considered in the context of the restricted life space of the nursing home and the environmental docility of residents. It is useful to recognize, in planning interventions, that personal and environmental factors interact to place the elderly at risk. These influences can also converge in maximizing benefits through program innovation. Interventions may thus be best designed and implemented by multidisciplinary teams adept at employing prosthetic as well as therapeutic orientations.

A major limitation of the majority of interventions reviewed is their orientation to improving care from the staff's perspective and their narrow focus, leaving them unable to alter the most problematic features of life in a total institution (Goffman, 1961; Henry, 1963). Placing diverse programs in the framework of the means/ends typology we presented in Table 11.1, it becomes apparent that patient-responsive processes are relatively infrequent in implementing nursing home–based intervention.

In the remainder of this chapter, we attempt to capture this important and potentially valuable area for developing future interventions. To do so, we must set the stage for a paradigm shift in considering the needs of nursing home residents. Discussion in the literature about alternative philosophies of care is relatively scarce. Traditional medical models of acute care (Wolinsky, 1982), social work models of empowerment (Cox & Parsons, 1994), interdisciplinary models of rehabilitation (Hahn, 1991), or the populist models of consumerism (Heumann, 1997) do not readily fit the needs or constraints of frail and old-old nursing home residents. The acute care medical model is predicated on curability of illness, which does not fit patterns of chronic illness in the old-old. The empowerment model of social work makes questionable assumptions about the interest and willingness of staff to share power. It also assumes extensive involvement of professional staff in the care of patients in nursing home settings. In an era of managed care, such involvement is increasingly rare. The rehabilitation model is based on goals of enhanced function, leading to reintegration of clients into the community. Such options are seldom open to institutionalized elders. Consumerism, which is an emerging movement for self-care and self-empowerment, presupposes the availability of control and choices that are in reality available only to those who directly purchase services. Frail elders, who are generally sustained in nursing homes through third-party payments, have little chance to exercise such control.

Patient responsive care as advocated here is guided by a communitarian philosophy advocated by sociologists (Etzioni, 1993). This approach is predicated on a value system that is consistent with the ethical principles articulated in service literature on rehabilitation and in biomedical ethics (Beauchamp & Childress, 1989). Principles of beneficence and nonmalficence underlie the delivery of all health care services. These well-established principles call for "doing good" and avoiding doing harm to patients (Erlanger & Roth, 1985). Principles of autonomy figure importantly in empowerment-oriented approaches to care and in consumerist orientations. Principles of justice and fidelity reflect a desire to promote fair treatment and to honor commitments made to clients. In addition to these principles, patient-responsive care is predicated on a principle of empathy, that is, a propensity to perceive and respond to the wishes of persons receiving care (Spiro, 1993).

The major requisite of patient-responsive care is an understanding and an appreciation of nursing home life from the patient's perspective. To achieve this, it is useful to consider some of the unstated paradoxes of institutional life for the elderly. Ten of the paradoxes noted by the first author during participant observation in nursing homes are noted here. Several of the areas of incongruity have also been alluded to in prior studies of nursing home residents (Gubrium, 1975; Laird, 1979; O'Brien, 1989).

1. Nursing home residents are deprived of their customary home environments just as they are most vulnerable to change.
2. Residents are expected to accommodate routines set by others when they are most in need of personalized attention.
3. Residents are expected to be compliant when the stakes are high for being assertive.
4. Residents are given minimal information about their condition and treatment when knowledge could be a source of power.
5. Residents cannot initiate communication with their doctors when they are most in need of medical attention.

6. Residents have limited access to individual staff time when staff are their major source of social interaction.
7. Residents must be vigilant about their surroundings amid the loss of normal cues and capabilities.
8. Residents are treated as objects when given personal care even as they try to hold on to remnants of their human dignity.
9. Residents are exposed to interminable waits when their needs are most pressing.
10. Residents are often seen as management problems by staff but view themselves as people with pasts and uncertain futures.

Attention by staff to these and other often overlooked paradoxes of institutional life can motivate staff to take a more empathetic stance in working with residents in nursing homes.

ELEMENTS OF PATIENT-RESPONSIVE CARE

Patient-centered or patient-focused care has been advocated in the medical literature (Stewart, Brown, Weston, McWhinney, McWilliam, & Freeman, 1995). Yet, even as the focus is on the patient, decisions about the patient's needs are typically made by staff. Most attempts at formal needs assessment also involve expert judgments about resident needs. Sometimes it is the health care professional's appraisal of what he or she would want that gets reported as the patient's perspective. Yet, we recognize that it would not be therapeutic or even feasible to have nursing home care become totally driven by patient preferences. Hence, the approach proposed here is "Patient-Responsive Care." Only through a conscious and systematic effort to understand the domains of residents' perspectives can we arrive at formulating Patient-Responsive Care.

Development of practices and programs that are responsive to patients and that help diminish the paradoxes of institutional life requires an appreciation of resident needs and preferences. Systematically considering the residents' perspectives on daily life in a nursing home can help in making programs salient to the daily experience of the individual resident. Maslow's (1970) hierarchy of needs provides a useful context for classifying the full array of resident needs and organizing them in a hierarchical fashion. Thus, for example, programs that target residents' social function may hold little interest for older adults whose most basic physical needs have not been met. Residents may thus express disinterest in attending a carefully planned community birthday party or a group therapy session, simply because they fear that there will be no one there to take them to the toilet when needed. Consequently, priority must be placed on meeting more immediate needs first; only then can staff move toward creating programs that address higher order needs.

HIERARCHY OF NEEDS OF THE NURSING HOME PATIENT

The hierarchy of patient needs we propose is seen as invariant across diverse conditions as well as across diverse nursing home environments. Four major areas of need are to be met by staff: reducing physical distress, meeting basic physiological needs, meeting emotional needs, and meeting social needs.

The needs outlined here are broadly related to Maslow's hierarchy of needs and are adapted from a framework we are developing to consider patient responsive care for elderly in acute care hospital settings (Kahana, Kahana, & Taylor, 1997). We recognize that cognitively impaired and frail elders may be limited in their ability to articulate and communicate their needs, and thus a major challenge of Patient-Responsive Care is to elicit expression of needs and preferences. However, we consider traditional approaches to need assessments that are based on objective test data to be of limited value in assessing patients' perspectives. We advocate, instead, empathetic listening to the patient's lived experience as a basis for developing Patient-Responsive Care. Such listening involves the creation of a staff environment in which residents do not fear sanctions if they express needs or place demands on staff. It also involves active efforts on the part of staff to solicit expressions of resident need. The specific areas of unmet needs should be articulated by residents. The framework offered here will organize staff inquiry about areas of need.

Alleviating Discomfort

Discomforts such as pain, dizziness, or nausea are experienced by many nursing home residents due to physical frailty and multiple chronic illnesses. Contributing to physical discomfort may also be medical regimens or the nursing home environment itself. Pain may be due to poor circulation or arthritis. Discomforts may be caused by dressings or by a catheter. The resident may also suffer from backache or soreness due to a lumpy or soft mattress provided by the nursing home. Diminishing physical discomforts represents the first challenge to be met in providing Patient-Responsive Care. This is an area where communication with physicians and skilled nurses becomes important. Side effects of medications need to be dealt with and attention needs to be directed to proper nutrition and exercise. Only when physical discomfort is minimized can interventions to meet higher-order needs become effective.

Meeting Physical Needs

The second major area of needs involves the basic physiological needs of hunger, thirst, toileting, sleep, temperature regulation, and breathing. These are needs that healthy people living in the community routinely meet without difficulty. However, for the frail nursing home resident, each of these needs can pose major challenges. Nursing home residents are likely to have difficulty in meeting their basic physiological needs, in part due to illness and physical limitations and in part due to environmental barriers posed by the nursing home. To the extent that environments and care are not individualized, some residents will find problems in meeting their physical needs even in situations where the majority are comfortable.

In describing issues related to physiological needs of residents, we provide some examples where environmental barriers may present problems. In terms of hunger, problems arise when residents are given diets to which they are not accustomed or when trays are placed out of reach of a bedridden resident. In regard to temperature regulation, many nursing homes do not offer temperature controls that can be regulated for individual residents. Since the majority of residents prefer extreme warmth during the winter, the temperature may be set too high for meeting the needs of those elderly who are uncomfortable in excessive heat.

Restful sleep is very important for the maintenance of physical and psychological well-being, yet sleep is often disrupted in nursing home settings in an effort to implement toileting programs or to turn residents in order to avoid bedsores. Older adults often seek fresh air by opening windows. However, in most nursing homes windows are not designed to open. Toileting needs are particularly acute for frail residents in wheelchairs. In many nursing homes, even cognitively intact residents find it difficult to obtain assistance in being taken to the toilet when needed. Other, more cognitively impaired residents find it difficult to operate the devices designed to call for a nurse and hence cannot communicate their needs. The average wait for a response by an aide to requests for assistance may be staggeringly long. As these examples illustrate, lack of Patient-Responsive Care in meeting these most basic of human needs, may result in psychological problems and unmet psychological needs, to which we next turn.

Meeting Emotional Needs of Residents

Emotional needs of residents include a broad array of normal human needs. However, aging, frailty, and institutionalization also result in special areas of need. Four areas of emotional need may be identified as particularly salient to elderly nursing home residents. These include: harm avoidance, personhood, dependency, and autonomy. We illustrate approaches of Patient-Responsive Care by focusing on harm avoidance and personhood. Extensive discussions of issues of autonomy and dependency have been presented in the literature (Agich, 1993)

Residents need to feel secure and unharmed in the face of frailty. The extreme vulnerability experienced by old-old persons with physical, sensory, and cognitive limitations calls for constant reassurance that those caring for them will not hurt or neglect them. Patient-Responsive Care in this area demands that there be reassuring touching and verbal communication whenever personal care is provided. Patients must be actively queried about their concerns and specific reassurance provided in areas of fear. Typical concerns may involve fears of falling out of bed or having a medical emergency that goes unnoticed. Patients are typically also fearful of being lifted on a hoyer lift or bathed in tubs where they are suspended while bathing

A second area of unique emotional concerns for nursing home residents involves the need to maintain a sense of personhood and respect in the face of losses and institutionalization. Examples of concerns in this area include fears that requests, wishes, and opinions of the resident may be disregarded. This emotional need is exacerbated in nursing home settings where there is little individualization of care. Patient-Responsive Care must seize opportunities to acknowledge resident opinions. The challenge is to do so in ways that are meaningful to residents. Patient-Responsive Care is not about choices in pictures to color but about acknowledgment that the resident truly matters. One example may be a staff member who spontaneously discusses a sports event or asks advice from a resident. Spiritual needs of residents and their concerns about having a "good death" also need to be acknowledged through empathetic listening and sensitively responsive comments.

Meeting Social Needs

The primary social needs and concerns of residents are for maintaining meaningful social ties with family and maintaining some sense of attachment with those in their immediate social environment, including both staff and other residents. A major social need concerns the fear of abandonment by family and the outside world (Oliver & Tureman, 1988). Residents may make frantic and apparently unnecessary demands that staff contact members of their family. Such actions are likely to mask emotional needs for close human contact and attachments. Patient-Responsive Care calls for active listening by staff for these signals. Instead of vacuous reminders that "your children were here just a few days ago" residents' concerns should be heard and empathetically acknowledged. Active efforts by staff to create meaningful bonds with residents reflect examples of patient-responsive care.

Designing Patient-Responsive Intervention and Care

A patient-responsive orientation to care suggests guidelines for intervention that build on Gestalt approaches to care such as "milieu therapies." Such interventions were anchored in ecological approaches and enjoyed an era of popularity in the 1960s. In addition, orientations that break down the barriers between the institution and the outside world by bringing representatives of the familiar outside community into the institution or taking residents back into the community would diminish the "totalistic features of institutions" (Goffman, 1961). Some of these ideas have been articulated in a treatise on humane treatment of the elderly in nursing homes (Kahana, 1973).

Exemplifying such approaches, aides who care for elderly patients on a regular basis may be trained to redefine their jobs from providing custodial care to providing therapeutic measures. Thus, for example, it is typical for frail elders on a nursing home rehabilitation unit to receive occupational and physical therapy to enhance their ability to perform activities of daily living such as dressing or eating independently. At the same time, little is done to reinforce or encourage such independence outside the therapy program. Daily meals provide tremendous opportunities for socialization, as well as a motivating context to improve self-care, nutrition, and morale. Programmatic attention to residents during meals could go a long way toward achieving improvements in their physical function as well as their psychosocial well-being. Personnel delivering meals could easily be trained to engage in conversation with residents during meals, explaining what the resident is eating and contributing to the enjoyment of the meal. Meaningful choices can also be provided in the framework of meals, at a minimum allowing residents choices in desserts and beverages.

In terms of diminishing barriers with the outside world, church and community or neighborhood groups may be used as a framework for arranging for resident visits into the community. Encouraging families to take residents out for meals or to special events by assisting with transportation also holds great promise for Patient-Responsive Care by providing residents with a window to their past. Sharing information about treatment regimens and medications can enhance a sense of involvement and allay anxieties, even among patients with limited cognitive abilities.

Organizationally, an important requisite for implementing such Gestalt approaches is breaking down communication barriers and establishing lines of communication between families and staff and among different levels of staff. What is being urged echoes Hillary Clinton's (1995) adage about children: "It takes a village."

In a recent study on markers of excellence in nursing home care, Brittis (1996) has found that the major unifying thread among nursing homes that were judged by both residents and staff to be excellent was not a programmatic, policy, or resource-based distinction but a fundamental connection between residents and staff. Brittis terms this unique positive ingredient "sharing destinies."

Most U.S. nursing homes are characterized by an absence of this emotional connection wherein individual staff regularly express affection, affirmation, and communication in dealing with individual residents (Savishinsky, 1991; Vladeck, 1980). Volunteers and family members are major natural sources of connectedness for residents, and encouraging their active involvement in residents' lives can facilitate Patient-Responsive Care (Bumagin & Hirn, 1989; Oliver & Tureman, 1988).

The discussion thus far has taken us from considering alternative objectives and value orientations of nursing home-based programs to a review of examples of programs in diverse areas of need and to consideration of the relevance and impact of selected interventions from an actual resident's perspective. Our review of program innovations published in recent years reveals a preponderance of highly targeted and specific therapeutic interventions generally aimed at enhancing specific functions or targeting specific concerns. A major limitation of such targeted approaches is their lack of salience to the broad aspects of the day-to-day lives of elderly patients. A concerted and successful attempt to focus on special areas of need such as restraint reduction or the disruptive behaviors of Alzheimer's patients appears to have diverted attention from more general milieu-based interventions.

Our thoughts on the relative irrelevance of many existing programs to the daily life of a resident should not be taken to imply a cynical view that such programs are useless or unnecessary. Existing programs simply reflect our belief in the need to approach daily life and care in the nursing home and any special interventions as related parts of the whole of residents' daily lives. Special programs are just one small component of the overall care experienced by residents. Interventions that have the promise of high impact and salience must reflect a desire to enhance overall care rather than reflect a brief departure from routinized ongoing care practices. Most important, they must be responsive to patient or resident needs.

Intervention generally requires at least some additional expenditure of funds by the nursing home. Such funding may be increasingly difficult to obtain in an era of cost containment. The challenge in this era of managed care is how to undertake positive program initiatives without increasing costs. Patient-Responsive Care is care with a soul and care with common sense. Such care need not be very costly. Patient-Responsive Care may be enhanced even using the vantage point and terminology of good business practice. We may view the resident as a customer; pleasing the customer and paying heed to his or her wishes can readily result in Patient-Responsive Care.

In evaluating existing interventions, we located relatively few examples of patient-responsive intervention. However, many other helpful and high-impact programs are initiated and implemented by nursing home staff and by clinicians sensitive to the service needs and perspectives of residents and never find their way into the literature. It is important to acknowledge that there are fundamental divisions among clinical, practice, and research domains that serve as barriers to the dissemination of clinical programs to the scientific community. The very professionals most prominently committed to developing practice innovation that are high impact and relevant to the daily needs of older residents may lack the training, the temperament, and the time and resources necessary to design program evaluations and write them up for publications in scientific journals. Conversely, the scientists best equipped to design, implement, and get funding for scientifically sound innovative programs tend to work in academic settings. Often they design intervention programs for nursing homes while lacking familiarity with the day-to-day living situations or perspective of residents or staff.

Innovative programs have been noted, guided by diverse disciplinary orientations. It is also noteworthy that some of the most remarkable integrative programs have been developed outside the United States, particularly in the Scandinavian countries, where program development in caring for the aged has been a national policy priority (Williamson, Evans, Powell, & Hesse-Biber, 1982).

Patient-Responsive Care involves humanizing the nursing home environment and working toward creating a therapeutic community. The authors have long advocated such approaches (Kahana, 1973), following up on the seminal work of social scientists such as Goffman (1961) and Henry (1963). The challenge still stands, as growing numbers of older adults will live the final days of their lives within the confines of nursing homes. It is our hope that the attempt of this chapter to juxtapose "what is" with a framework of "what can be" may contribute to development of more Patient-Responsive Care in nursing homes.

REFERENCES

Abbasi, A. A., Basu, S. N., Parsa, A., Alverno, L., & Rudman, D. (1993). Nutritional problems in the nursing home population; opportunities for clinical interventions. In L. Z. Rubenstein, & D. Wieland (Eds.), *Improving care in the nursing home* (pp. 195–215). Newbury Park, CA: Sage Publications.

Abood, L. M. (1992). *An examination of congruence in resident and staff perceptions of the nursing home experience.* Unpublished doctoral dissertation, State University of New York at Binghamton.

Agich, G. J. (1993). *Autonomy and long-term care.* New York: Oxford University Press.

Andersen, B. R. (1987). What makes excellent nursing homes different from ordinary nursing homes? *Danish Medical Bulletin, Special Supplement Series No. 5,* 7–11.

Beauchamp, T. L., & Childress, J. F. (1989). *Principles of biomedical ethics* (3rd ed.). New York: Oxford University Press.

Bensink, G. W., Godbey, K. L., Marshall, M. J., & Yarandi, H. N. (1992). Institutionalized elderly: Relaxation, locus of control, self-esteem. *Journal of Gerontological Nursing, 18*(4), 30–36.

Blair, C. E. (1995). Combining behavior management and mutual goal setting to reduce physical dependency in nursing home residents. *Nursing Research, 44*(3), 160–165.

Bonnel, W. B. (1995). Managing mealtime in the dependent group dining room: An educational program for nurse's aides. *Geriatric Nursing, 16*(1), 28–32.

Breslow, R. A., Hallfrisch, J., Guy, D. G., Crawley, B., & Goldberg, A. P. (1993). The importance of dietary protein in healing pressure ulcers. *Jounal of the American Geriatric Society, 41*(4), 357–362.

Brittis, S. (1996). *Sharing destinies: Staff and residents' perspectives on excellence in high quality nursing homes in London, England, and New York City, U.S.A.* Unpublished doctoral dissertation, Sociology Department, Case Western Reserve University, Cleveland, OH.

Brown, R. (1989). *The rights of older persons* (2nd ed.). Carbondale: Southern Illinois University Press.

Bumagin, V. E., & Hirn, K. F. (1989). *Helping the aging family: A guide for professionals.* New York: Springer.

Burger, S. G., Fraser, V., Hunt, S., & Frank, B. (1996). *Nursing homes: Getting good care there.* San Louis Obispo, CA: Impact Publishers.

Butler, R. N. (1980–1981). Life review: An unrecognized bonanza. *International Journal of Aging and Human Development, 12*(1), 35–38.

Campbell, J., & Linc, L. (1996). Support groups for visitors of residents in nursing homes. *Journal of Gerontological Nursing, 22*(2), 30–35.

Chandler, J. T., Rachal, J. R., & Kazelskis, R. (1986). Attitudes of long-term care nursing personnel toward the elderly. *Gerontologist, 26*(5), 551–555.

Clinton, H. R. (1995). *It takes a village: And other lessons children teach us.* New York: Simon & Schuster.

Cooper, J. W. (1994). Managing disruptive behavioral symptoms: Today's do's and don't's. *Nursing Homes, 43*(1), 54–56.

Cox, C. (1993). Dealing with the aggressive nursing home resident. *Journal of Gerontological Social Work, 19*(3–4), 179–192.

Cox, E. O., & Parsons, R. J. (1994). *Empowerment-oriented social work practice with the elderly.* Pacific Grove, CA: Brooks/Cole.

Diamond, T. (1992). *Making grey gold: Narratives of nursing home care.* Chicago: University of Chicago Press.

Drysdale, A. E., Nelson, C. F., & Wineman, N. M. (1993). Families need help too: Group treatment for families of nursing home residents. *Clinical Nurse Specialist, 7*(3), 130–134.

Erlanger, H. S., & Roth, W. (1985). Disability policy: The parts and the whole. *American Behavioral Scientist, 28*(3), 319–346.

Estes, C. L., & Swan, Y. (1993). *The long-term-care crisis: Elders trapped in the no-care zone.* Newbury Park, CA: Sage Publications.

Etzioni, A. (1993). *The spirit of community.* New York: Touchstone.

Feil, N. (1982). *V/F validation, the Feil method: How to help disoriented old-old.* Cleveland, OH: Edward Feil Productions.

Fiatarone, M. A., Marks, E. C., Ryan, N. D., Meredith, C. N., Lipsitz, L. A., & Evans, W. J. (1990). High-intensity strength training in nonagenarians. *Journal of the American Medical Association, 263,* 3029–3034.

Fiatarone, M. A., O'Neill, E. F., Doyle, N., Clements, K. M., Roberts, S. B., Kehayias, J. J., Lipsitz, L. A., & Evans, W. J. (1993). The Boston FISCIT study: The effects of resistance training and nutritional supplementation on physical frailty in the oldest old. *Journal of the American Geriatric Society, 41*(3), P333–P337.

Fortinsky, R. H., & Raff, L. (1995–1996). Changing role of physicians in nursing homes. *Generations, 19*(4), 30–35.

George, L., & Maddox, G. (1989). Social and behavioral aspects of institutional care. In M. Ory, & K. Bond (Eds.), *Aging and health care: Social science and policy perspectives* (pp. 116–141). London: Routledge.

Goffman, E. (1961). *Asylums: Essays on the social situation of mental patients and other inmates.* Garden City, NY: Doubleday.

Gubrium, J. (1975). *Living and dying at Murray Manor.* New York: St. Martin's Press.

Gurwitz, J. H., Soumerai, S. B., & Avorni, J. (1990). Improving medication prescribing and utilization in the nursing home. *Journal of the American Geriatrics Society, 38,* 542–552.

Hahn, H. (1991). Alternative views of empowerment: Social services and civil rights. *Journal of Rehabilitation, 57*(3), 17–19.

Hamel, G. (1995). Guilt: A hidden problem in caregiving. *Provider, 21*(11), 59–60.

Health Care Financing Administration (HCFA). (1989). Medicare and Medicaid requirements for long-term-care facilities. *Federal Register, 54*(21).

Henderson, J. N., & Vesperi, M. D. (1995). *The culture of long-term care: Nursing home ethnography.* Westport, CT: Bergin & Garvey.

Hendy, H. M. (1987). Effects of pet and/or people visits on nursing home residents. *International Journal of Aging and Human Development, 25*(4), 279–291.

Henry, J. (1963). *Culture against man.* New York: Vintage.

Heumann, L. (Ed.). (1997). *Proceedings of the Sixth International Conference on Systems Sciences in Health-Social Services for the Elderly and Disabled (SYSTED).* Chicago: SYSTED.

Hing, E. (1987). Use of nursing homes by the elderly: Preliminary data from the 1985 National Nursing Home Survey. *NCHS Advancedata, 135,* 1–11.

Hudson, B. (1992). Ensuring an abuse-free environment: A learning program for nursing home staff. *Journal of Elder Abuse and Neglect, 4*(4), 25–36.

Jagella, E., Tideiksaar, R., Mulvihill, M., & Neufeld, R. (1992). Alarm devices instead of restraints? *Journal of the American Geriatric Society, 40*(2), 191.

Jette, A., Branch, L., Sleeper, L., Feldman, H., & Sullivan, L. (1992). High-risk profiles for nursing home admission. *Gerontologist, 32*(5), 634–640.

Johnson, L. E., Dooley, P. A., & Gleick, J. B. (1993). Oral nutritional supplement use in elderly nursing home patients. *Journal of the American Geriatric Society, 41*(9), 947–952.

Kahana, B., Kahana, E., Namazi, K., Kercher, K., & Stange, K. (1997). The role of pain in the cascade from chronic illness to social disability and psychological distress in late life. In J. Lomrantz & D. Mostofsky (Eds.), *Pain in the elderly* (pp. 185–206). New York: Plenum.

Kahana, E. (1973). The humane treatment of old people in institutions. *Gerontologist, 13,* 282–289.

Kahana, E., & Kahana, B. (1996). Conceptual and empirical advances in understanding aging well through proactive adaptation. In V. Bengston (Ed.), *Adulthood and aging: Research on continuities and discontinuities* (pp. 18–41). New York: Springer.

Kahana, E., Kahana, B., & Riley, K. (1989). Person-environment transactions relevant to control and helplessness in institutional settings. In P. S. Fry (Ed.), *Psychological perspectives of helplessness* (pp. 121–154). Alberta, Canada: Elsevier Science Publishers.

Kahana, E., Kahana, B., Sterin, G., Fedirko, T., & Taylor, R. (1993). Adaptation to institutional life among Polish, Jewish, and Western European elderly. In C. Barresi & D. Still (Eds.), *Ethnicity and long-term care* (pp. 144–158). New York: Springer.

Kahana, E., Kahana, B., & Taylor, H. (1997, August). *Institutional care from a patient-centered perspective.* Proceedings of the annual meeting of the American Sociological Association.

Kahana, E., & Kiyak, A. (1984). Attitudes and behavior of staff in facilities for the aged. *Research on Aging, 6,* 395–416.

Kahana, E., Liang, J., & Felton, B. (1980). Alternative models of person-environment fit: Prediction of morale in three homes for the aged. *Journal of Gerontology, 35,* 584–595.

Kahana, J. (1994). Reevaluating the nursing home ombudsman's role with a view toward expanding the concept of dispute resolution. *Journal of Dispute Resolution, 94,* 217–233.

Kane, R. (1991). Personal autonomy for residents in long-term care. In Y. Birren, J. Rowe, J. Lubben, & D. Deuthman (Eds.), *Quality of life in the frail elderly* (pp. 315–334). San Diego: Academic Press.

Laird, C. (1979). *Limbo: A memoir about life in a nursing home by a survivor.* Novato, CA: Chandler & Sharp.

Langer, E. J., & Rodin, J. (1976). The effects of choice-enhanced personal responsibility for the aged: A field experiment in an institutional setting. *Journal of Personality and Social Psychology, 34,* 191–198.

Lauritzen, J. B., Petersen, M. M., & Lund, B. (1993). Effect of external hip protectors on hip fractures. *Lancet, 341*(8836), 11–13.

Lawton, M. P. (1980). *Environment and aging.* Monterey, CA: Brooks/Cole.

Lipsitz, L. A., Jonsson, P. V., & Kelley, M. M. (1991). Causes and correlates of recurrent falls in ambulatory frail elderly. *Journal of Gerontology, 46,* 114–122.

Lundervold, D. A., Young, L., & Jackson, T. H. (1993). Factors influencing nurses' acceptability of treatments for problem behaviors of nursing home residents: Initial results. *Clinical Gerontologist, 12*(3), 31–40.

Maslow, A. H. (1970). *Motivation and personality.* New York: Harper & Row.

Mattiasson, A. C., & Andersson, L. (1994). Staff attitude and experience in dealing with rational nursing home patients who refuse to eat and drink. *Journal of Advanced Nursing, 20*(5), 822–827.

Mion, L. C., McDowell, J. A., & Heaney, L. K. (1994). Nutritional assessment of the elderly in the ambulatory care setting. *Nurse Practitioner Forum, 5*(1), 46–51.

Mollinger, L. A., & Steffen, T. M. (1993). Knee flexion in institutionalized elderly: Prevalence, severity, stability, and related variables. *Physical Therapy, 73*(7), 437–446.

Morton, A. (1995). Nighttime incontinence. *Contemporary Long-Term Care, 18*(10), 62–64.

Norburn, J. E. K., Nettles-Carlson, B., Soltys, F. G., Read, C. D., & Pickard, C. G. (1995). Long-term care: Organizational challenges and strategies. *Journal of Gerontological Nursing, 21*(8), 37–44, 54–55.

O'Brien, M. (1989). *Anatomy of a nursing home: A new view of residential life.* Owings Mills, MD: National Health Publishing.

Oliver, D. B., & Tureman, S. (1988). *The human factor in nursing home care.* New York: Haworth Press.

Omnibus Reconciliation Act of 1987(OBRA). (1987). Public Law 100–203, *Congressional Record, 133*(205), Part 3.

Ouslander, J. G., & Schnelle, J. F. (1993). Assessment, treatment, and management of urinary incontinence in the nursing home. In L. Z. Rubenstein & D. Wieland (Eds.), *Improving care in the nursing home: Comprehensive reviews of clinical research* (pp. 131–159). Newbury Park, CA: Sage Publications.

Perelle, I. B., & Granville, D. A. (1993). Assessment of the effectiveness of a pet-facilitated therapy program in a nursing home setting. *Society and Animals, 1*(1), 91–100.

Pinkston, E. M., Howe, M. W., & Blackman, D. K. (1986–1987). Medical social work management of urinary incontinence in the elderly: A behavioral approach. *Journal of Social Service Research, 10*(2/3/4), 179–194.

Plautz, R., & Timen, B. (1992). Positioning can make the difference. *Nursing Homes, 41*(1), 30–33.

Province, M. A., Hadley, E. C., Hornbrook, M. C., Lipsitz, L. A., Miller, J. P., Mulrow, C. D., Ory, M. G., Sattin-Tinetti, M. E., & Wolf, S. L. (1995). The effects of exercise on falls in elderly patients, a preplanned meta-analysis of the FICSIT trials. *Journal of the American Medical Association, 273*(17), 1341–1347.

Qualey, T. L. J. (1995). An approach to elderly incontinence. *Nursing Management, 26*(4), 48S–T.

Rubenstein, L. Z., & Wieland, D. (1993). *Improving care in the nursing home: Comprehensive reviews of clinical research.* Newbury Park, CA: Sage Publications.

Savishinsky, J. S. (1991). *The ends of time: Life and work in a nursing home.* New York: Bergin & Garvey.

Schnelle, J. F., MacRae, P. G., Ouslander, J. G., Simmons, S. F., & Nitta, M. (1995). Functional incidental training, mobility performance, and incontinence care with nursing home residents. *Journal of the American Geriatric Society, 43*(12), 1356–1362.

Schnelle, J. F., McNees, P., Crooks, V., & Ouslander, J. G. (1995). Use of a computer-based model to implement an incontinence management program. *Gerontologist, 35*(5), 656–665.

Schnelle, J. F., Newman, D. R., & Fogerty, T. E. (1991). Assessment and quality control of incontinence care in long-term nursing facilities. *Journal of the American Geriatric Society, 39*, 165–171.

Spiro, H. (1993). *Empathy and the practice of medicine.* New Haven: Yale University Press.

Steel, K. (1992). Homeward bound. *Caring, 11*(10), 9–12.

Stewart, M., Brown, J. B., Weston, W. W., McWhinney, I. R., McWilliam, C. L., & Freeman, T. R. (1995). *Patient-centered medicine: Transforming the clinical method.* Thousand Oaks, CA: Sage Publications.

Taival, A., & Raatikainen, R. (1993). Finnish nursing homes: Client well-being and staff development. *Journal of Gerontological Nursing, 19*(2), 19–24.

Tellis-Nayak, V., & Tellis-Nayak, M. (1994). Quality of care and the burden of two cultures: When the world of the nurse's aide enters the world of the nursing home. *Generations, 18*, 39–40.

Tinetti, M. E., Liu, W. L., & Ginter, S. F. (1992). Mechanical restraint use and fall-related injuries among residents of skilled nursing facilities. *Annals of Internal Medicine, 116,* 369–374.

Tobin, S. S., & Lieberman, M. A. (1976). *Last home for the aged.* San Fransico: Jossey-Bass.

U.S. Bureau of the Census. (1993). *Nursing home population: 1990* (C. Taeuber, CPH-L137 ed.). Washington, DC: U.S. Government Printing Office.

van der Welen, R. P., van Heereveld, H. A., deGroot, C. P., & van Staveren, W. A. (1995). Nutritional status of elderly female nursing home residents; the effect of supplementation with a physiological dose of water-soluble vitamins. *European Journal of Clinical Nutrition, 49*(9), 665–674.

Viney, L. L. (1993). *Life stories: Personal construct therapy with the elderly.* Chichester, Australia: John Wiley & Sons.

Vladeck, B. C. (1980). *Unloving care.* New York: Basic Books.

Wagner, L., Wahlberg, V., & Worning, A. M. (1994). Drug consumption among elderly—a four-year study. *Scandinavian Journal of Caring Sciences, 8*(2), 113–117.

Weisberg, J., & Haberman, M. R. (1989). A therapeutic hugging week in a geriatric facility. *Journal of Gerontological Social Work, 13*(3–4), 181–186.

White, C. B., & Cantania, J. A. (1982). Psychoeducational intervention for sexuality with the aged, family members of the aged, and people who work with the aged. *International Journal of Aging and Human Development, 15*(2), 121–138.

Widder, B. (1985). A new device to decrease falls. *Geriatric Nursing, 6*(5), 287–288.

Williamson, J. B., Evans, L., Powell, L. A., & Hesse-Biber, S. (1982). *Politics of aging: Power and policy.* Springfield, IL: Charles C. Thomas.

Wilner, M. A. (1994). Working it out: Support groups for nursing assistants. *Generations, 18,* 39–40.

Wolinsky, F. D. (1982). Assessing the effects of the physical, psychological, and social dimensions of health on the use of health services. *Sociological Quarterly, 23*(2), 191–206.

12

Innovations in Managing Alzheimer's Disease

CAMERON J. CAMP

JEANNE M. MATTERN

In this chapter, we review a number of interventions for managing Alzheimer's disease (AD) that are innovative because of their recent development as interventions for this population, their perspectives/orientation, and their origins. Rather than assuming that maintenance of existing abilities should be the goal of intervention for AD, as is often the case today, these interventions assume that improved levels of functioning are quite possible. For these interventions, reductions in problems associated with AD are a by-product of successful intervention, rather than a primary focus.

In addition, these interventions have been imported from research programs initially developed outside the area of AD, such as, neuropsychological rehabilitation and developmental psychology. Thus, these interventions represent some fresh perspectives in the area of cognitive intervention for dementia. They have a rehabilitation orientation and are firmly grounded in theoretical bases. It is our assumption, as scientist-practitioners, that theory-driven interventions are those most likely to be successful when applied to AD populations. We offers these examples as cases in point and as a glimpse of future directions in designing interventions for managing AD.

Finally, we have selected examples of interventions that were designed for an individual with AD, small groups of persons with dementia, and dyads of persons with AD and preschool children. We hope that by presenting examples of innovations targeted at such a diversity of implementation levels, we will be able to demonstrate the breadth and versatility that interventions based on rehabilitation principles can achieve.

Preparation of this manuscript was supported in part by grants from the Sihler Mental Health Foundation and the Alzheimer's Association to the first author.

Alzheimer's Disease: A Form of Dementia

Dementia refers to a gradual and progressive deterioration of cognitive functioning. Memory impairment is a hallmark of dementia, especially loss of memory for newly acquired information. Dementia is also accompanied by other deficits such as language disturbances, impairments in carrying out motor functions, failure to recognize or identify objects, and disturbances in the ability to plan, organize, or reason abstractly. Like a fever, dementia is symptomatic and can be caused by a variety of underlying conditions, some of which are treatable and reversible.

The most common cause of dementia is Alzheimer's disease (AD). It is estimated that more than 4 million persons in the United State have AD, representing about half of all cases involving dementia. AD is a neurological disorder characterized by the presence of abnormal deposits called neuritic plaques between nerve cells in the brain, tangled masses called neurofibrillary tangles inside nerve cells, reduced levels of neurotransmitters, and extensive cell death. The onset of the disease is gradual, but, as the disease progresses, symptoms become more acute. Eventually, persons with AD lose all ability to function independently and must receive extensive care. This form of dementia is progressive and irreversible, ultimately ending in death (generally 7 to 9 years after initial diagnosis).

STAGES OF AD

AD has been described as progressing in stages. There are several staging systems, the most general of which refers to early, middle, and late stages of progression, with late stages referring to highly advanced dementia and subsequent severe levels of disability. The most widely used staging system was developed by Reisberg and his colleagues (Reisberg et al., 1982). In this classification scheme, called the Global Deterioration Scale (GDS), typical behavioral patterns are used to delineate specific stages.

The GDS has seven stages. Stages 1–4 are considered to be "predementia," indicating that a clinically significant level of impairment has not yet developed, but signs of impairment that might progress to dementia at a later time are evident. Stage 1 describes behavior and cognitive abilities typical of normal adulthood, with no subjective complaints or memory deficits. A person in Stage 2, Forgetfulness, resembles a normal aging adult. Subjective complaints are made of mild forgetfulness regarding misplacing familiar objects, well-known names, and so on, but no clinical evidence of cognitive deficit is seen. At Stage 3, labeled Early Confusional, there are manifestations of deficits in some areas, such as difficulty in retention of new information, inability to travel to unfamiliar locations, tendencies to lose or misplace something of value, and word- or name-finding deficits. Coworkers begin to see poor performance. Decreased performance is seen in demanding social or employment situations. Anxiety and denial are present, but objective measures of memory deficits are seen only in intensive interviews and assessments. Stage 4, labeled Late Confusional, indicates moderate cognitive decline, detected through clinical interviews. Problem areas include decreased knowledge of current events and recent personal history, concentration deficits, and difficulty with traveling and finances. However, there are generally no deficits in orientation to time and place or in recognition of familiar persons, faces, and locations. Denial and withdrawal from challenging situations are used as defense mechanisms. Flattening of affect may also be seen. A person who has advanced to Stage 4 in this system will be observed closely, for they are potentially transitional between predementia and dementia. Any further decline may be indicative of progressive dementia.

Moderately severe decline becomes evident in Stage 5, labeled Early Dementia. Patients now require some assistance recalling major and relevant aspects of their lives (e.g., their address and phone number, names of grandchildren). Disorientation occurs frequently regarding time, date, season, and place. Individuals at this stage still retain knowledge of important facts (e.g., own name, name of spouse, children). No assistance is required at this stage for most activities of daily living (ADLs). However, some persons may require assistance in choosing appropriate clothing. Middle Dementia is Stage 6. In this stage a person exhibits severe cognitive decline, occasionally forgetting even the names of children or spouse. Patients are unaware of recent events, date, season, or year. Some knowledge of the past is retained, but this too becomes very sketchy. Some assistance is required with ADLs (e.g., toileting, ambulation), and diurnal rhythm is frequently disturbed. However, patients are almost always able to recognize their own name and to distinguish between the familiar and the unfamiliar in the immediate environment. Emotional and personality changes such as agitation, delusional and obsessive behaviors, and loss of willpower occur at this stage. Speech becomes very limited (e.g., patients use short sentences and answer questions with either yes or no). Stage 7, labeled Late Dementia, is marked by the loss of psychomotor skills (e.g., ambulation, ability to sit up, smile, hold head up). Neurological signs and symptoms of decline are present (e.g., seizures). Frequently the person may refrain from speaking at all. Increased assistance is required with ADLs such as toileting and feeding. Death results, usually due to coronary or respiratory failure.

RISK FACTORS FOR AD

A crucial problem facing those who attempt to formulate strategies for managing AD is the finding that "it is very likely that Alzheimer disease is not a single disease and that it results from sets of complex interactions among biological variables overlaid on a genetic predisposition and influenced by environmental, cultural, and educational experiences and exposures" (Radebaugh, Buckholz, & Khachaturian, 1996, p. 3). These factors can be contributors in and of themselves, or they may exacerbate biological influences in AD. At the very least, a number of variables have been shown to correlate with the occurrence of AD, and these have been labeled risk factors.

Mayeaux (1996) reviewed several risk factors identified with AD. These include both genetic and environmental factors. Though space does not allow an extensive elaboration of genetic research in AD, at least four different chromosomes and corresponding genes on these chromosomes have been implicated in increased risk for developing AD. Many of these genes involve early-onset (before age 50) cases, which are quite rare. The APOE gene's variants, or alleles, have been associated with late-onset AD. But, even in this case, expression of this genetic predisposition varies across ethnic groups. As a result, genetic counseling for AD risk may be premature until more is learned about factors that influence the expression of genes related to AD development.

Other risk factors include depression, occupational exposure to glues, fertilizers, and pesticides, head injury, and (among women) thyroiditis. Factors that have been tentatively linked to decreased risk include use of estrogen supplements (among women), some anti-inflammatory drugs, smoking (though this carries other risks, of course), and high levels of education (Mayeaux, 1996).

The case of education is an example of the limits of our knowledge of AD and of the problems facing development of management strategies for AD based on such knowledge. Mayeaux (1996) notes that there are at least five different explanations for a correlation between education level and AD. Low education could lead to poor performance on diagnostic tests (detection bias); high education could alter brain function or structure (cognitive reserve); low education could be related to another risk factor, such as exposure to toxins at work (confounder); attaining a low educational level might be an initial, early symptom of AD (direct effect); or low education might cause AD (causal link).

The major risk factor for developing AD is age. Approximately 3–4% of persons ages 65–74 have AD, but estimates of persons over age 85 with AD range from 20% to almost 50%. Since persons over the age of 85 represent the fastest-growing group of our population, AD represents a significant and growing public health concern. It is the third most costly disease after cancer and heart disease (Ernst & Hay, 1994). The cost of caring for a person with AD in the United States is $47,000 per year, whether the care is delivered in a nursing home or in a home setting. When lost earnings and productivity are included, each case of AD costs substantially more (Thal, 1996). The cost for society in general is about $80–$90 billion per year, and it is estimated that the actual number of persons with AD could begin to double every twenty years.

Rehabilitation as an Innovative Approach to Managing AD

Most services for persons with AD have focused on the presumption that, because they have a progressive disorder, maintaining adults with AD at their current levels of functioning and providing a nonchallenging, comfortable environment is the best approach. In long-term care, for example, this has led to the establishment of Special Care Units (SCUs) in nursing homes. These usually focus on persons in the early stage of dementia, where ADLs and self-care are not problematic. The idea is to create the atmosphere of a group or boarding home as much as possible, that is, to create a warm and familiar environment. Persons with AD have difficulty adjusting to changes in their environment, so provision of familiar settings and social support is important for them when entering a new facility to reduce confusion, anxiety, agitation, and depression (e.g., Mayeaux, 1996).

A related model, driven by market potential, is behind the rapid expansion of assisted living facilities for older adults. Under the best of circumstances, a medical model of care is replaced by a psychosocial support system. However, in advanced stages of dementia, increased physical care needs often override psychosocial philosophy. Staff are often overwhelmed in facilities serving persons with advanced dementia because caring for their physical needs is very time-intensive. As a result, the need to continually provide personal and medical care precludes other forms of care. These models of care reflect a philosophy that emphasizes attempts to maintain individuals at current levels of functioning or at least to slow down the progressive decline of dementia. We next discuss a different, recently evolving approach to caring for persons with AD and related dementias.

ORIGINS OF REHABILITATIVE INNOVATION FOR AD

An innovative approach to managing problems associated with AD is based on the philosophy of rehabilitation. Such an approach emphasizes recapturing lost or abandoned abilities, reducing disabilities, or restructuring activities so that they can be successfully accomplished in spite of deficits attributable to AD. Interventions that could accommodate or compensate for losses in cognitive abilities should have a substantial impact on the ability of older adults to maintain their independence.

Researchers in cognition and aging report that older adults' most preserved abilities, on which interventions should be based, involve the use of environmental supports and cues found in familiar surroundings and the use of aspects of cognition that are relatively spared by aging, such as automatic skills and implicit memory (Hess & Pullen, 1996; Howard, 1996; Smith & Earles, 1996). While these researchers have worked primarily with normal older adults, the same principles apply to interventions for persons with AD.

In Great Britain, researchers in cognitive rehabilitation have a history of applying their techniques to populations with dementia. Wilson (1989) and Moffat (1989) describe how the disciplines of behavioral psychology, neuropsychology, and cognitive psychology have provided a framework for understanding and designing memory-therapy programs and rehabilitation techniques for the memory-impaired and confused elderly. These strategies were derived through various methods including standardized assessment, clinical interviews, and direct observation of memory-impaired/brain-damaged individuals.

Improving memory performance has been accomplished through a variety of techniques. For example, interventions involving care providers in at-home settings have included the use of external aids (electronic cueing devices, diaries, computers), environmental adaptations (labeling objects), internal strategies (first-letter cueing), rehearsal and repetitive practice, reminiscence therapy (reviewing old photos and objects), memory games and exercises, and reality orientation (using signposts). The need for both individual and group interventions is also stressed (Moffat, 1989; Wilson, 1989). We next describe an intervention from this research area that has been applied to both normal older adults as well as persons with AD through Stage 6 of the GDS and that was designed to be implemented at the level of the individual.

Spaced-Retrieval (SR): An Intervention for Individuals with AD

BACKGROUND OF SR

As an example of an intervention for older adults with dementia, Moffat (1989) described a case study involving a woman in her late fifties with AD who was living alone and having difficulty remembering the names of objects. An intervention was attempted using a technique originally developed in a lab setting with younger adults (Landauer & Bjork, 1978) initially called expanding rehearsal and later called spaced-retrieval (SR) when used in the context of re-mediating memory disorders (Schacter, Rich, & Stampp, 1985). The intervention was carried out in the client's home by a patient aide (an untrained helper attached to the community psychiatric nurse).

Before training, the client could not retain the name of an object for longer than a few minutes. Twenty target items were selected for training. In this intervention, the name of an object was practiced, and then retention of the name was checked after 2 min. If the client remembered the name, the next retention interval was doubled (if not, she was given the correct name, allowed to repeat it, and the time interval was halved). After three training sessions, the majority of the 20 words could be named (Moffat, 1989). This case study by Moffat is an example of how a rehabilitative intervention can be used to improve the status of a person with dementia.

THEORETICAL BASIS OF SR

SR utilizes two technologies. One is the shaping procedure from behavior modification techniques. This involves shaping—the reinforcement of successive approximations to a desired behavior. Successful recall is intrinsically reinforcing for older adults, especially those who have been confronted by a failing memory system. Learning theory, therefore, serves as one theoretical base for this intervention. In this particular case, the principles of shaping are applied to memory, and the desired behavior is long-term retention of information.

In addition, SR takes advantage of a neuropsychological rehabilitation principle called "errorless learning" (Baddeley, 1992; Wilson, Baddeley, Evans, & Shiel, 1994). The idea behind errorless learning is that there are two types of learning/memory systems. The first, called declarative memory (Squire, 1992, 1994), involves conscious learning and retrieval. It is what most persons refer to when they use the term "memory," and this system is impaired from the earliest stages of AD; attempts to utilize declarative memory, especially for learning and retaining new information, generally meet with failure. For example, the ability to learn and remember information from personal or autobiographic memory, such as what you were doing 10 minutes ago or what you ate for breakfast, is part of this system.

The other memory system in Squire's model is referred to as procedural or nondeclarative memory. It involves the use of well-learned processes and the unconscious acquisition and retrieval of new information. It is believed that much if not most new learning found in persons with memory disorders takes advantage of unconscious learning. But in order to learn and retain information, persons with memory disorders generally must practice or work with the new information. Since they cannot recall personal episodes, they cannot use the past as a basis for correcting any errors they might make while learning new information. Only if they are not allowed to make errors will they learn new information accurately. Otherwise, incomplete or inaccurate learning will take place. This is why it is so important for persons with AD to have success when recalling information in the SR procedure, and why each trial must end with a correct recall.

DESCRIPTION OF THE SR INTERVENTION

Camp and his associates (Camp & McKitrick, 1992; Camp et al., 1993; Camp & Stevens, 1990; Camp, Foss, O'Hanlon, & Stevens, 1996; Camp, Foss, Stevens, & O'Hanlon, 1996) have extended the original application of SR in a number of areas. First, they modified the procedure so that recalling target information is based on a variety of expanding time intervals. Initially, information is immediately recalled. Then, intervals are expanded (e.g., 5 sec, 10 sec, 20 sec, 40 sec, 60 sec). When a person has successfully retained information for 60 sec, intervals expand by 30 sec each trial (60 sec, 90 sec, 120 sec, and so on). Of course, other expansion schedules may also be used (e.g., 60 sec, 120 sec, 240 sec, and so on). If a person with AD fails at recall, he or she is given the correct answer, asked to repeat it, and then tested next at the interval where the person was last successful before expanding the intervals again.

IMPLEMENTATION OF SR

As mentioned earlier, most work with SR in persons with AD has taken place with persons in the early or middle stage of dementia. Though a relatively new intervention, the number of applications of SR is impressive. It has been used to train persons with AD to learn the names of family members, caregivers, and everyday objects, the locations of important items, and even strategies.

For example, Camp, Foss, Stevens, and O'Hanlon, (1996) describe a study in which persons with AD were trained, using SR, to learn and use a strategy involving calendars. Single-day calendars were placed in the homes of persons with AD, on which were listed daily tasks to be accomplished, appointments, and other information of use to the person with AD. These individuals were trained to remember and execute the strategy of looking at the calendar when they wanted to remember what was important for that day. Persons in this study, under normal circumstances, could not remember new information after a period of a few minutes (or sometimes a period of a few seconds). However, after SR training, 87% of these persons could recall the strategy after a one-week interval, with the majority learning the strategy within three training sessions.

After learning the strategy, participants also demonstrated the ability to use the strategy effectively (Camp et al., 1996).

In one case, a man who initially was so impaired that he could not repeat the strategy verbally was able to effectively use this intervention. On one occasion, he read a task involving watering outdoor plants, went outside, then returned and told his wife that it had rained. He then inquired if there was anything he should do instead of watering the plants (Stevens, O'Hanlon, & Camp, 1993). This illustrates that the strategy learned was not just a string of words that could be verbalized when cued but instead was a true process that could be integrated into everyday contexts.

Much more work has to be done in developing this innovation. As a technology, SR is still in its infancy. Optimal recall scheduling, whether or not to overtrain newly acquired information, the amount of information which can be learned using this procedure, and other aspects must be determined. Likewise, the length of time information learned using SR that can be retained and the circumstances which maximize its recall and use by persons with AD must be explored. But SR appears to be an extremely potent intervention, and time invested in developing this innovation should prove worthwhile.

Next we present an intervention—Question-Asking Reading (QAR)—that is designed to engage groups of persons with AD and related dementias, rather than with single individuals, as was the case with SR. The QAR innovation was designed specifically for persons in Stage 5 of the GDS, though persons with good social and listening skills at Stage 6 can take part as well.

Question-Asking Reading: A Group Intervention

BACKGROUND OF QAR

The next innovation we discuss, QAR, was designed to fit within the context of a long-established procedure, Reality Orientation. Care providers in adult day care centers and long-term care facilities have long used the technique called Reality Orientation (RO) when working with confused older adults, many of whom have AD. Though we are not describing RO as an innovation, it is necessary to understand this procedure as a means of showing the context into which QAR was implemented. RO is a procedure that attempts to create or recreate awareness of current time, place, and person. In use for more than 30 years, it was designed to be a 24-hour-a-day process in which staff and family members remind the older adult of the current time, place, who the person is, and who staff or family members are. Environmental cues are an adjunct part of this intervention, as are RO classes (Holden & Woods, 1982, 1995; Wilson, 1989; Woods, 1996).

RO classes are group activities, usually held for 30 minutes to an hour on a regular basis, in some facilities every day. They generally consist of practicing items of verbal orientation (e.g., time, date, month, location, names of participants and staff). Part of this group activity usually involves a reading of current events by a staff member to the group. Though RO is designed to be an all-day, total-environment intervention, in actuality RO classes are often the primary or only means of delivering this intervention (Holden & Woods, 1995; Woods, 1996).

The effectiveness of RO has been hotly debated. Proponents note that verbal orientation improves for persons in RO compared to no-treatment controls and claim that other learning may also improve (Woods, 1996). Critics state that RO simply trains verbal responses, has little or no impact on behavior, and serves to frustrate as much as help (e.g., why orient people to the fact that they've been put into a nursing home?) and that time spent in RO could be put to better use through behavior modification or other interventions (Stokes, 1996; Zarit, Orr, & Zarit, 1985). An extended discussion of this topic is beyond the scope of this chapter. There are, however, three important points regarding RO that should be noted: (1) it has already been implemented, in the form of RO classes, in thousands of facilities nationally; (2) having the longest history and most widespread acceptance of psychosocial interventions for confused older adults, it will remain in place for some time; and (3) it is implemented by line staff such as nursing assistants in long-term care facilities or aides in adult day care. We view RO as an established, rather than an innovative, intervention for managing AD.

It was within this context that the next innovation we discuss was developed. In this case, the administrator of an adult day care center in the New Orleans, Louisiana area, made a request to the first author. She reported that when staff members read current events to clients during RO classes, few clients paid attention (some slept), and there was little interaction among participants. Further, she noticed a high refusal rate to attend classes. The administrator asked if the reading activity could be modified so that it would become more effective. The innovation we now describe for managing AD, Question-Asking Reading (QAR), was designed to fit within the structure of existing RO programs.

THEORETICAL BASIS OF QAR

QAR is based on Vygotsky's (1978) concept of the zone of proximal development—a context in which an ability can be demonstrated with support, even though the same ability could not be demonstrated by the individual acting alone—and originates in the sociohistorical school of Luria, Vygotsky, and Leont'ev of the former Soviet Union (Cole & Griffin, 1983; Stevens, King, & Camp, 1993). The sociohistorical school of psychology emphasizes the role of others as mediators in an individual's learning and development. Significant others, such as parents and teachers, as well as the general social system, are seen as playing a pivotal role in development. Features of the external world gradually become internalized in an individual's mind and ways of knowing.

Vygotsky (1978) saw the role of the teacher and society as one of creating zones of proximal development for the child, who is constantly led forward by meeting challenges that initially can be accomplished only with assistance. With practice, the child masters each task to the point that it can be done without assistance. As tasks are mastered, the zone of proximal development moves forward, and more and more sophisticated tasks can be accomplished without assistance. This approach to developmental psychology has several attractive features that lend themselves to cognitive rehabilitation, and Vygotsky's student, Luria, became a founding father of neuropsychological rehabilitation (Christensen & Caetano, 1996; Luria, 1979). The use of zones of proximal development has been suggested as a way of organizing cognitive support for dementia patients (Cavanaugh et al., 1989).

Thus, both RO and Vygotsky's approach, represented here by the QAR intervention, emphasize the use of external aids and social supports. However, RO's goal is to reorient persons with AD to time and place. In QAR, orientation is not relevant. Instead, the focus of the QAR intervention is to raise the amount and quality of social interactions and cognitive function—that is, to use QAR to create a zone of proximal development. Successfully taking part in a reading activity and engaging in a group discussion on the topic covered is the goal of QAR for person with AD. Knowing whether the day is Monday or Tuesday is simply not germane within this context.

DESCRIPTION OF QAR

Stevens, King, and Camp (1993) developed QAR as an intervention for clients with dementia at an adult day care center. Their intervention distributes the task of reading across group members. QAR requires the reading group to follow a scripted procedure when reading a short text.

Text scripts were taken from materials used in adult literacy training and involved topics such as the history of beer and the behaviors of whales. As part of the script, clients were given questions to ask about the text they read. Use of a scripted procedure and an interesting text served to facilitate clients' interactions with the text and with one another. The role of the staff member was to redirect discussion to the text and questions and to facilitate group interaction. Group members could help each other answer scripted questions about the text (e.g., "What is the main point of the story?," "Ask about a specific detail in the story.") and were free to elaborate on one another's comments. Use of a group setting, scripted procedures, and an interesting text helped create a zone of proximal development.

IMPLEMENTATION OF QAR

In an initial study involving adult day care clients with dementia (primarily Stage 5, a few at Stage 6), clients in QAR groups demonstrated higher levels of verbal interactions, more extended discussions, and greater sustained attention than were seen in usual group reading activities of RO classes at the same adult day care center. The QAR intervention increased retention of stories' contents, as well as the amount of verbal interaction among group members. A staff member who was trained to implement the intervention was able to maintain the levels of improvement originally achieved by the experimenter over the course of a 3-week follow-up period (Stevens, King, & Camp, 1993).

In a later study with adult day care clients (using a sample with a larger proportion of persons at Stage 6), Stevens et al. (in press) trained two staff members at each of two adult day care centers to implement the QAR procedures.

In each center, one staffer initially implemented the QAR procedure, while a second used the same reading materials but presented them in the fashion normally used within a RO class. Later the second staffer implemented QAR. In all cases, QAR procedures again significantly increased verbal interaction within reading groups. Memory of the content of stories was not improved by QAR, possibly because samples in this second study were substantially more impaired on mental status measures than were the subjects in the initial Stevens et al. (1993) study. Again, it was clearly demonstrated that lay persons (staff in this case, often with only a high school education) could implement this cognitive intervention.

QAR has been successfully implemented within long-term care facilities with residents in middle-stage dementia (Stephens, personal communication, Oct., 1996). In this form of the intervention, residents are given an object or picture descriptive of the theme of the day's story on leaving QAR. Nursing home staff then use the object as a topic of conversation with the resident. Thus, QAR is being used to facilitate communication between caregiving staff and residents outside the context of the story-reading activity itself.

To the staff in these QAR studies, the most dramatic outcomes had nothing to do with researchers' outcome measures. They were most impressed by the fact that QAR participants at the centers actually wanted to attend class and, once the sessions started, remained where they were and took part in the group activities during the entire 30 to 45 minutes of each session. These behaviors were in great contrast to the former refusals to participate in classes and/or the lack of attention displayed by many of these same individuals when QAR was not used. We hypothesize that taking part in QAR became associated with positive affect resulting from successful task performance and socialization experiences. In other words, it seems reasonable that clients with dementia who took part in QAR learned to associate going to the activity with pleasant emotions. This would fit within Squire's model of nondeclarative memory; classical condition seems to be part of the nondeclarative memory system, a learning and memory system relatively spared in dementia until its final stage (Squire, 1992, 1994).

Future work in this area will involve developing generic training materials so that staff in a variety of settings (especially if they already have RO classes in place) can implement QAR groups. Initial research has been conducted to determine effects of QAR participation outside the reading activity. Informally, we have observed that QAR participants begin to form social groups in day care settings, but this needs to be better documented. Stevens et al. (1996) found that, when QAR was implemented within a long-term care facility, residents were more verbally expressive during and after the QAR activity than were residents who participated in usual nursing home activities. In addition, we are interested in determining if QAR can be used to better orient clients to ongoing activities in a facility; for example, a story could involve events that will take place later in the day or week. Finally, we wish to explore other ways of creating zones of proximal development for persons with AD and related dementias.

This research is being conducted at Menorah Park Center for the Aging, a multiprogram campus that includes long-term care, assisted living as well as independent living apartments for older adults, a child care center for employees' children, and an adult day care center that serves the general Cleveland community. It is in the adult day care center that we have been conducting our research with the QAR intervention. We next describe an intervention that is designed for persons at the same GDS stages as those taking part in QAR. In fact, at Menorah Park's adult day care center, clients alternate taking part in QAR and the next intervention we describe on different days. This next intervention, however, is designed for dyads of persons with AD/preschool children rather than for groups of persons with AD per se. The idea that developmental psychology and neuropsychological rehabilitation can share common concepts and create cross-fertilization of ideas is personified in a pilot intergenerational intervention for persons in early and middle stages of dementia that we have recently begun (Camp et al., 1997).

An Intergenerational Montessori-Based Program

BACKGROUND OF THE INTERGENERATIONAL PROGRAM

Intergenerational activities between older persons (60 years and older) and children (ages 3 to 5 years) are viewed as beneficial to both generations (Fruit et al., 1990; Short-DeGraff & Diamond, 1996) and are increasing in number nationally. A major difficulty in designing intergenerational programs is the selection of appropriate activities. Difficulties may be further compounded when the older person suffers from AD or a related dementia. Short-DeGraff and Diamond (1996) conclude that one-to-one activities between young children and older adults with dementia should be limited to very simple activities (e.g., listening to music). Cognitive disabilities of the older persons challenge effective intergenerational programming. To meet this challenge, a pilot program was started at the Menorah Park Center for the Aging to enable older adults with dementia to effectively engage preschool children one to one.

THEORETICAL BASIS OF THE INTERGENERATIONAL PROGRAM

Researchers have claimed that, during the late stages of dementia, cognitive abilities may be lost in reverse developmental order (first in, last out). This may be a useful guide in creating a intervention or innovation for persons with AD (Camp et al., 1993; Vance et al., 1996). The question then becomes one of selecting an approach on which to base a broad array of interventions that will be effective across a variety of individuals and levels of dementia.

The work of Vygotsky provided general principles for designing interventions but lacked an extensive set of specific exercises, materials, and technologies for implementing his theoretical ideas. Piagetian theory and research have generated a host of diagnostic exercises and materials, but the emphasis has been on accurately describing development rather than finding means to shape it or influence its course. As a result, we turned to the work of a person admired by Vygotsky for her ability to effectively teach cognitive skills to children—Maria Montessori.

The Montessori method of instruction has many dimensions that translate readily to the creation of activities for persons with dementia. Training is encapsulated within activities, called "lessons." Each lesson in Montessori is presented at its simplest level, with subsequent lessons increasing in complexity. Montessori also provides the structure that persons with dementia as well as preschool children need for optimal performance of activities (Vance et al., 1996). These activities involve environmental cueing, immediate feedback, high probability of success, and repetition.

Perhaps most important, the philosophy underlying the Montessori method is to create persons who are independent and able to make choices and who are treated with respect and dignity by being given meaningful work in environments designed to accommodate their needs. This is true for the education of children. It is also seen in the mission statements of adult day care centers and long-term care facilities.

DESCRIPTION OF THE INTERGENERATIONAL PROGRAM

At Menorah Park, a variety of both individual and group Montessori-based activities have been developed for dyads composed of persons with dementia and preschool children who attend an on-site child care center (Camp, Maish, & Daniels, 1996; Camp et al., 1997; Vance et al., 1996). Examples of Montessori-based activities include tool usage, seriation, finding hidden objects, personal care, sorting, matching, phonics, counting, and practicing motor skills. In the intergenerational program, staff first work individually with each older person and preschooler. All participants become familiar with the activities and the routine before actual intergenerational programming begins. Children and older persons are matched on cognitive ability level so that the older person will be somewhat more advanced and can serve as mentor to the preschooler. Older adults practice giving lessons to research assistants in the room that will be used for the program, while children are brought to the room to practice activities with research assistants. Once older adults and children have become used to the environment and to the general nature of Montessori activities, they are brought together for the intergenerational program.

IMPLEMENTATION OF THE INTERGENERATIONAL PROGRAM

Behavioral observations of eight older adults on the AD Special Care Unit of Menorah Park's long-term care facility were taken in the early, mid-, and late mornings (e.g., 9:00 A.M. to 10:00 A.M., 10:00 A.M. to 11:00 A.M., 11:00 A.M. to 12:00 P.M.). This was done both on days they worked with children (in the mid-morning time-frame) and on days they were not doing intergenerational programming. The first concern was whether residents would display inappropriate behaviors or anxiety while working with children. In more than 80 observation sessions, these were never seen. The next question of interest was whether residents would display disengagement (e.g., sleeping, staring into space). Again, disengagement was not seen while residents worked with children, though it was seen in early and late mornings. Finally, it was important to determine if the amount of disengagement was influenced outside the intergenerational interaction. For all residents, disengagement was substantially lower in late mornings after working with children compared to the amount seen in late mornings when residents did not work with children.

In this intervention, residents of long-term care and clients in adult day care who had dementia demonstrated a higher level of functioning than they did under normal circumstances. A zone of proximal development was created in which the context of teaching children created a purposeful goal, environmental supports for achieving the goal, and allowed these older adults to fulfill a useful social role. In the process of fulfilling this role, they performed at a more nearly normal level of functioning than was usually seen. In addition, children found the activities interesting and challenging, often choosing this program over recess. Persons with dementia in the adult day care center and in the Special Care Unit readily came when invited to teach, and they later told family members that they were working with the children.

The next endeavors in this area will involve expanding this pilot program to determine the extent and the size of the effects it can produce, as well as the best roles for persons at different stages of dementia to have in such programming. The development of training materials will follow so that this type of intergenerational programming can be created in other settings within existing frameworks of intergenerational programming. Finally, pilot work has started in order to explore the use of Montessori-based materials and lessons that might be used directly with persons in late stage dementia (Stage 7) by line staff (e.g., activities personnel or nursing assistants in long-term care settings).

Summary and Conclusions

IMPLICATIONS FOR RESEARCH AND PRACTICE

Michelle Bourgeois (1991) commented that attempts to effectively treat adults with dementia are encouraging; however, several issues need resolution before interventions can proceed most effectively. These issues include the selection of treatment targets, the modification and planning of interventions as AD progresses, and "long-term maintenance of therapeutic gains with dementing individuals" (Bourgeois, 1991). The innovations described in this chapter represent attempts to address these issues.

Selection of treatment targets (deciding what intervention to deliver and who will benefit from the intervention) is made more effective when interventions are firmly grounded in theory. The innovations described in this chapter represent theory-driven approaches to management of AD, designed to fit within existing program structures, such as reading activities or intergenerational visits; yet they take a radical departure from existing program content. Participants engage in more meaningful activities, and perform at higher levels of competence and for longer periods of time, than would normally be the case. This is reflective of a change in philosophy, from maintenance to rehabilitation. This is exactly what is meant by Vygotsky's zone of proximal development. These interventions are designed to create such zones. Furthermore, when engaged in these activities, persons with AD do not wander or sleep, become combative or aggressive, or demand attention. Such behaviors are incompatible with active participation. That is why such innovations are important in the management of AD. Persons allowed to behave more normally often behave less abnormally.

Bourgeois also noted the need to modify and plan interventions as AD progresses. These steps are also enhanced when interventions are grounded in a theory that maps on to the progress of dementia. The application of developmental psychology to dementia progress, on which much of our work is based, enables modification and planning to be successful. For example, as mentioned earlier, Montessori-based activities for persons in more advanced (Stage 6) levels of dementia are being developed. These involve both individual and group activities (Camp, Maish, & Daniels, 1996). As dementia progresses, activities are modified to accommodate greater degrees of impairment. Knowing the pattern in which cognitive abilities develop in children and the corresponding Montessori-based activities they can perform at each ability level gives us a reverse blueprint of what abilities can be expected to be lost and in what order in older adults as dementia progresses. Activities can then be adapted to current ability levels so that older adults with dementia are still challenged yet successful when engaged in activities.

An important issue to address at this point is the implications of creating such interventions for AD with regard to policy and practice. This addresses Bourgeois's last point on the need to act to maintain gains made through interventions. It is unfortunate that regulation and reimbursement systems usually lag behind innovative discoveries. New but successful interventions that cannot be classified within existing treatment and payment structures may not be implemented because service providers cannot receive third-party payments for providing them. In the case of AD, interventions aimed at improving memory functioning are simply not reimbursable. Such treatments must be incorporated within existing treatment goals that are already acceptable within current payment structures if they are to be implemented and maintained.

In the case of QAR, the intervention was designed to fit within the structure of existing RO classes so that currently employed staff could implement the intervention with little or no disruption in daily routine (other than greater participation by older adults). Likewise, the Intergenerational Program represents an attempt to modify the nature of current intergenerational programming within the facility (and others now taking part in pilot programs) so that older adults with AD and related dementias can become more active participants in such programming. Again, the goal is to create training materials so that regular staff can implement such programming within existing activity periods.

In the case of SR, a pilot project has been developed to examine how the SR intervention can be delivered within speech therapy sessions (Brush & Camp, 1998). Anomia (word-finding difficulty) is seen as a language disorder that can be treated by speech therapists and that is often associated with AD. For a referral to the therapist to be made, there generally must be a discernable and relatively abrupt decline in communication skills. If this could be documented, the speech therapist could use SR to train persons with AD in the acquisition of strategies (e.g., first-letter cueing) and/or the use of external memory aids (e.g., pocket notebooks) in order to cope with anomia. Speech therapists have now utilized SR to meet therapeutic goals for clients with AD and related dementias within billable therapy sessions. Long-term maintenance of these goals has also been documented.

Perhaps the best thing about the use of SR within a therapeutic session is that, as recall intervals for remembering a strategy increase, the time between recall intervals can be filled with other speech therapy activities. Thus, SR can be integrated into therapy sessions as an adjunct procedure, one that is a powerful intervention in its own right but that is superimposed upon a session that is fulfilling additional therapy goals. Again, our approach is to create innovative interventions that can be applied by professionals within the routine course of their daily activities.

IMPLICATIONS FOR POLICY

To date, existing service delivery systems are predicated on the belief that persons with AD and related dementias are poor candidates for rehabilitation, especially with regard to cognitive interventions. This is not the case, and many interventions for AD and related dementias based on this approach are now being described in the research literature (e.g., Camp & Foss, 1997). Successful cognitive interventions can reduce the need for more costly ones. For example, it is less costly to manage a problem associated with AD via a cognitive intervention (e.g., teaching a person to use a calendar to know what important appointment occurs today) than to sedate people in order to reduce the number of times they inquire about today's appointments. This is especially true over an extended time-frame, as is generally going to be the case with a chronic, progressive disorder such as AD. A change in policies to acknowledge the rehabilitative potential of persons with AD may be necessary before extensive benefits to persons with AD can be achieved. Since memory disorders underlie many of the problems affecting the management of AD, attempts to deal directly with the underlying cause of problems should become reimbursable. This will, however, require a departure from a system that still focuses on a medical model to determine how best to manage AD.

IMPLICATIONS FOR INTERDISCIPLINARY EDUCATION

Management of AD often involves interdisciplinary teams. We have, in this chapter, discussed working with staff in adult day care, long-term care, and speech therapy in the course of implementing interventions. In addition, we routinely become involved with social workers, nurses, physicians, and family caregivers. For example, McKitrick and Camp (1993) trained a number of caregivers to use SR as an intervention for persons with AD in their care. We are also interested in developing training regimens so that RNs in long-term-care units can teach SR intervention methods to nursing assistants. Thus, our work demands contact with professionals across a variety of disciplines. In order to be effective, we need to be sensitive to their job demands and to their disciplinary paradigms.

Models for creating interdisciplinary teams in long-term care to help implement interventions for dementia have been described in the literature (e.g., Lichtenberg, 1994; Sakauye & Camp, 1992). In order for innovative management of AD to exhibit long-term gains, similar models must be in place and be viable wherever persons with AD come into contact with professionals who deliver care. This implies that professionals in disciplines that will attempt to manage AD must be trained to work as part of an interdisciplinary team. Whether specific course work outside one's discipline, a minor or certification in interdisciplinary gerontology, or knowledge acquisition on the job, interdisciplinary education will become a necessity in the successful management of AD.

REFERENCES

Baddeley, A. (1992). Working memory. *Science, 253*, 556–559.
Bourgeois, M. S. (1991). Communication treatment for adults with dementia. *Journal of Speech and Hearing Research, 34*, 831–844.
Brush, J. A., & Camp, C. J. (1998). Using spaced retrieval as an intervention during speech-language therapy. *Clinical Gerontologist, 19*, 51–64.
Camp, C. J., & Foss, J. W. (1997). Designing ecologically valid memory interventions for persons with dementia. In D. G. Payne & F. G. Conrad (Eds.), *Intersections in applied and basic research* (pp. 311–325). Mahwah, NJ: Lawrence Erlbaum.
Camp, C. J., Foss, J. W., O'Hanlon, A. M., & Stevens, A. B. (1996). Memory interventions for persons with dementia. *Applied Cognitive Psychology, 10*, 193–210.
Camp, C. J., Foss, J. W., Stevens, A. B., & O'Hanlon, A. M. (1996). Improving prospective memory task performance in Alzheimer's disease. In M. A. Brandimonte, G. O. Einstein, & M. A. McDaniel (Eds.), *Prospective memory: Theory and applications* (pp. 351–367). Mahwah, NJ: Lawrence Erlbaum.
Camp, C. J., Foss, J. W., Stevens, A. B., Reichard, C. C., McKitrick, L. A., & O'Hanlon, A. M. (1993). Memory training in normal and demented elderly populations: The E-I-E-I-O model. *Experimental Aging Research, 19*, 277–290.
Camp, C. J., Judge, K. S., Bye, C. A., Fox, K. M., Bowden, J., Bell, M., Valencic, K., & Mattern, J. M. (1997). An intergenerational program for persons with dementia using Montessori methods. *Gerontologist, 37*, 688–692.
Camp, C. J., Maish, M. J., & Daniels, G. C. (1996, June). *Montessori-based activities for adults with dementia*. Workshop presented at the annual meeting of the Ohio Association of Adult Day Care, Columbus, OH.
Camp, C. J., & McKitrick, L. A. (1992). Memory interventions in Alzheimer's-type dementia populations: Methodological and theoretical issues. In R. L. West & J. D. Sinnott (Eds.), *Everyday memory and aging: Current research and methodology* (pp. 155–172). New York: Springer-Verlag.
Camp, C. J., & Stevens, A. B. (1990). Spaced-retrieval: A memory intervention for dementia of the Alzheimer's type (DAT). *Clinical Gerontologist, 10*, 658–661.
Cavanaugh, J. C., Dunn, N. J., Mowery, D., Feller, C., Niederehe, G., Fruge, E., & Volpendesta, D. (1989). Problem-solving strategies in dementia patient-caregiver dyads. *Gerontologist, 29*, 156–158.

Christensen, A., & Caetano, C. (1996). Alexandr Romanovich Luria (1902–1977): Contributions to neuropsychological rehabilitation. *Neuropsychological Rehabilitation, 6,* 279–303.

Cole, M., & Griffin, P. (1983). A socio-historical approach to remediation. *The Quarterly Newsletter of the Laboratory of Comparative Human Cognition, 5* (4).

Ernst, R. L., & Hay, J. W. (1994). The U.S. economic and social cost of Alzheimer's disease revisited. *American Journal of Public Health, 84,* 1261–1264.

Fruit, D., Lambert, D., Dellman-Jenkins, M., & Griff, M. (1990, Nov.). Intergenerational day care. Paper presented at the annual meeting of the Gerontological Society, Boston, MA.

Hess, T. M., & Pullen, S. M. (1996). Memory in context. In F. Blanchard-Fields & T. M. Hess (Eds.), *Perspectives on cognitive change in adulthood and aging* (pp. 387–427). New York: McGraw-Hill.

Holden, U. P., & Woods, R. T. (1982). *Reality orientation: Psychological approaches to the confused elderly.* London: Churchill Livingstone.

Holden, U. P., & Woods, R. T. (1995). *Positive approaches to dementia care* (3rd ed.). Edinburgh: Churchill Livingstone.

Howard, D. V. (1996). The aging of implicit and explicit memory. In F. Blanchard-Fields & T. M. Hess (Eds.), *Perspectives on cognitive change in adulthood and aging* (pp. 221–254). New York: McGraw-Hill.

Landauer, T. K., & Bjork, R. A. (1978). Optimal rehearsal patterns and name learning. In M. M. Gruneberg, P. Morris, & R. Sykes (Eds.), *Practical aspects of memory* (pp. 625–632). London: Academic Press.

Lichtenberg, P. A. (1994). *Psychological practice in geriatric long-term care.* New York: Haworth Press.

Luria, A. R. (1979). The making of mind. In M. Cole & S. Cole (Eds.), *The making of mind: A personal account of Soviet psychology* (pp. 17–188). Cambridge, MA: Harvard University Press.

Mayeaux, R. (1996). Development of a national prospective study of Alzheimer disease. *Alzheimer Disease and Associated Disorders, 10,* 38–44.

McKitrick, L. A., & Camp, C. J. (1993). Relearning the names of things: The spaced-retrieval intervention implemented by a caregiver. *Clinical Gerontologist, 14,* 60–62.

Moffat, N. J. (1989). Home-based cognitive rehabilitation with the elderly. In L. W. Poon, D. C. Rubin, & B. A. Wilson (Eds.), *Everyday cognition in adulthood and late life* (pp. 659–680). New York: Press Syndicate of the University of Cambridge.

Radebaugh, T. S., Buckholz, N. S., & Khachaturian, Z. S. (1996). Fisher symposium: Strategies for prevention of Alzheimer disease—overview of research planning meeting III. *Alzheimer Disease and Related Disorders, 10,* 1–5.

Reisberg, B., Ferris, S. H., Leon, M. J., & Crook, T. (1982). The global deterioration scale for assessment of primary degenerative dementia. *American Journal of Psychiatry, 139,* 1136–1139.

Sakauye, K. S., & Camp, C. J. (1992). Introducing psychiatric care into nursing homes. *Gerontologist, 32,* 849–852.

Schacter, D. L., Rich, S. A., & Stampp, M. S. (1985). Remediation of memory disorders: Experimental evaluation of the spaced-retrieval technique. *Journal of Clinical and Experimental Neuropsychology, 7,* 79–96.

Short-DeGraff, M. A., & Diamond, K. (1996). Intergenerational program effects on social responses of elderly adult day care members. *Educational Gerontology, 22,* 467–482.

Smith, A. D., & Earles, J. L. K. (1996). Memory changes in normal aging. In F. Blanchard-

Fields & T. M. Hess (Eds.), *Perspectives on cognitive changes in adulthood and aging* (pp. 192–220). New York: McGraw-Hill.

Squire, L. R. (1992). Memory and the hippocampus: A synthesis from findings with rats, monkeys, and humans. *Psychological Review, 99,* 195–231.

Squire, L. R. (1994). Declarative and nondeclarative memory: Multiple brain system supporting learning and memory. In D. L. Schacter & E. Tulving (Eds.), *Memory systems 1994* (pp. 203–232). Cambridge, MA: MIT Press.

Stephens, S. A., & Christianson, J. B. (1986). *Informal care of the elderly.* Lexington, MA: D.C. Heath & Company.

Stevens, A. B., Camp, C. J., King, K. A., & Bailey, E. H. (in press). Effects of a staff implemented therapeutic group activity for adult day care clients. *Aging and Mental Health.*

Stevens, A. B., King, C. A., & Camp, C. J. (1993). Improving prose memory and social interaction using question asking reading with adult day care clients. *Educational Gerontology, 19,* 651–662.

Stevens, A. B., Marshall, N. B., Wessel-Blaski, T., Baldwin, J., & Burgio, L. D. (1996, Nov.). *Influence of group structue on verbal interactions in nursing home activity programs.* Paper presented at the annual meeting of the Gerontological Society of America, Washington, DC.

Stevens, A. B., O'Hanlon, A. H., & Camp, C. J. (1993). Strategy training in Alzheimer's disease: A case study. *Clinical Gerontologist, 13,* 106–109.

Stokes, G. (1996). Challenging behaviour in dementia: A psychological approach. In R. T. Woods (Ed.), *Handbook of the clinical psychology of ageing* (pp. 601–628). Chichester, Great Britain: John Wiley & Sons.

Thal, L. J. (1996). Potential prevention strategies for Alzheimer disease. *Alzheimer Disease and Associated Disorders, 10,* 6–8.

Vance, D., Camp, C., Kabacoff, M., & Greenwalt, L. (1996). Montessori methods: Innovative interventions for adults with Alzheimer's Disease. *Montessori Life, 8,* 10–11.

Vygotsky, L. S. (1978). *Mind in society.* Cambridge, MA: Harvard University Press.

Wilson, B. A. (1989) . Designing memory-therapy programs. In L. W. Poon, D. C. Rubin, & B. A. Wilson (Eds.), *Everyday cognition in adulthood and late life* (pp. 615–638). New York: Press Syndicate of the University of Cambridge.

Wilson, B. A., Baddeley, A., Evans, J., & Sheil, A. (1994). Errorless learning in the rehabilitation of memory impaired people. *Neuropsychological Rehabilitation, 4,* 307–326.

Woods, R. T. (1996). Psychological "therapies" in dementia. In R. T. Woods (Ed.), *Handbook of the clinical psychology of ageing* (pp. 575–600). Chichester, Great Britain: John Wiley & Sons.

Zarit, S. H., Orr, N. K., & Zarit, J. M. (1985). *The hidden victims of Alzheimer's disease: Families under stress.* New York: New York University Press.

13

Innovative Intervention Approaches for Alzheimer's Disease Caregivers

DAVID W. COON
RICHARD SCHULZ
MARCIA G. ORY
AND THE REACH STUDY GROUP

Millions of Americans currently suffer from Alzheimer's disease and related dementing disorders (ADRD), and, unless advances in prevention and treatment are established quickly, the number of people with ADRD is expected to grow exponentially as the U.S. population ages (Schulz & O'Brien, 1994). The primary costs associated with providing care for persons with ADRD rest on the shoulders of their family members, most of whom care for their loved ones at home. Family caregivers often "add on" this caregiving responsibility to many already existing roles, such as grandparent, parent, worker, spouse, friend, and community member (Kramer & Kipnis, 1995; Pearlin, Mullan, Semple, & Skaff, 1990; Scharlach, 1994). The tasks and burdens associated with family caregiving are typically numerous and varied and often change across the course of the dementing illness. Caregiving responsibilities can include running simple errands, providing emotional support, managing behavioral disturbances, attending to physical needs, and remaining ever vigilant (Gold, Cohen, Shulman, Zucchero et al., 1995; Vitaliano, Russo, Young, Teri, & Maiuro, 1991; Wright, Clipp, & George, 1993). Given these often overwhelming responsibilities, caregiving for family members with dementia is associated with increased levels of depression, anxiety, and anger, as well as higher use of psychotropic medications, poorer self-reported physical health, and compromised immune function (Schulz, O'Brien, Bookwala, & Fleissner, 1995; Schulz, Visintainer, & Williamson, 1990). As a result, family caregivers are often described as "hidden patients" in need of outside

This work was supported by the National Institute on Aging and the National Institute for Nursing Research, AG/NR13255, AG/NR13265, NR/AG04261, AG/NR13289, AG/NR13297, AG/NR13305, AG/NR13313.

assistance and support to maintain their own health and functioning (Gallagher-Thompson, Coon, Rivera, Powers, & Zeiss, in press).

In response to the needs of family caregivers and their risk for negative health outcomes, researchers and services providers have developed or expanded a variety of psychosocial, technological, and environmental interventions designed to help people adjust to their caregiving roles and situations. Several informative research reviews published in the past several years examine the relative effectiveness of these interventions for family caregivers (Bourgeois, Schulz, & Burgio, 1996; Gallagher-Thompson, 1994; Knight, Lutzky, & Macofsky-Urban, 1993; Zarit & Teri, 1992). While the evidence is inconclusive regarding the superiority of any particular type of intervention, the research literature does identify several promising approaches: (1) strategies to increase caregivers' knowledge of dementia or understanding of their caregiving situation, (2) strategies to provide the caregiver with emotional and other forms of social support, (3) approaches directed at managing care recipient behavioral problems that often lead to caregiver mental and physical health deterioration, (4) the provision of community and home-based resources to support the caregiver, (5) strategies that modify the environment's effect on the care recipient and help support the caregiver, and (6) technological approaches (such as home-centered computer networks) to reduce distress and isolation and increase problem-focused coping strategies.

The existing literature reviews also raise important issues regarding the limitations of current caregiver intervention research. Most notably, the majority of interventions described in caregiver research are not explicitly theory-based or theory-driven. This practice frequently leads to intervention methods, designs, and measurement strategies that are all unrelated to one another and often generates study results that are in conflict with each other (Bourgeois et al., 1996; Knight et al., 1993). Treatment fidelity practices in particular are typically ignored in the caregiving literature, diminishing the replicability, generalizability, and interpretation of these intervention efforts. In addition, the majority of these studies report only the short-term effects of interventions, leaving the fundamental question of what happens to caregivers over time essentially unanswered. Often, the key outcomes of caregiver interventions are also not defined, measured, and monitored adequately. Moreover, the plethora of measures used to characterize intervention outcomes in the literature has also made the comparison of results across studies difficult. Another fundamental criticism is that the specific population of caregivers and care recipients targeted by many intervention studies, as well as their corresponding subject recruitment and retention strategies, are not sufficiently described. Finally, the vast majority of caregiving intervention studies have focused primarily on white family caregivers, neglecting racial and ethnic minority caregivers and ignoring the heterogeneous experience of caregiving within identified minority groups (Gallagher-Thompson, 1994; Gallagher-Thompson et al., in press).

The chief purpose of this chapter is to describe the innovative interventions of a new multisite family caregiver intervention research program entitled Resources for Enhancing Alzheimer's Caregiver Health (REACH) that addresses many of the criticisms raised in these recent reviews of the caregiving literature. The chapter also includes a concise presentation of the goals of the REACH Program and a brief description of how the REACH organizational components cooperate to help accomplish these key goals. The body of the chapter focuses on the descriptions of the various site-specific REACH interventions and then introduces the measurement strategy developed by REACH to capture outcomes of these interventions and to assess their proper implementation. The chapter concludes with a discussion of REACH efforts to tailor many of its interventions to meet the needs of a diverse population of family caregivers and proposes potential next steps and future studies in caregiver intervention research and service delivery.

Resources for Enhancing Alzheimer's Caregiver Health

Resources for Enhancing Alzheimer's Caregiver Health (REACH) is a unique, 5-year program sponsored by the National Institute on Aging (NIA) and the National Institute for Nursing Research (NINR) at the National Institutes of Health (NIH). REACH grew out of an NIH initiative that acknowledged the well-documented burdens associated with family caregiving, as well as the emergence of promising family caregiver interventions in the literature. These two areas of research provided the foundation for a systematic test of well-specified and theory-based intervention approaches. In 1995, NIH funded a set of six sites and a coordinating center to focus on interventions for family caregivers to ADRD persons at the mild or moderate level of impairment. This national research program includes an examination of different types of inter-ventions, all of which are based on theory-driven models of care: (1) Individual Information and Support strategies, (2) Group Support and Family Systems efforts, (3) Psychoeducational and Skill-Based Training approaches, (4) Home-Based Environmental interventions, and (5) Enhanced Technology Systems. In some cases, combinations of these general types are being explored. Because the caregiving experience in ethnic minority families is particularly neglected in the field, several of the REACH sites target specific groups of ethnic minority caregivers, and others are recruiting caregivers from several ethnic minority communities.

The six REACH intervention sites funded by NIH yield a multisite collabo-rative effort utilizing multidisciplinary staff to deliver a variety of interventions culturally tailored to meet the needs of a range of ethnic majority and minority populations. The study goals shared by all the REACH sites include (1) the design of theory-driven caregiving interventions to test hypotheses about intervention processes and their effect on family caregivers, (2) the specification of inter-vention components to understand the pathways through which interventions actually produce desired outcomes and to examine the effectiveness of a variety of psychosocial, behavioral, and technological interventions to strengthen family members' capacities to care for individuals with ADRD, (3) the development of standardized outcome measures to assess the impact of comparable strategies on caregivers and their care recipients, and (4) the creation of a common database to help compare the effectiveness of these different interventions across the range of identified populations. Finally, given the lack of well-described and well-controlled studies of this nature, REACH is designed to examine the feasibility and outcomes of different intervention approaches and their intensities, rather than to provide definitive information on the one best intervention strategy for enhancing caregiving.

Organizational Structure of REACH

The overall organizational structure of the REACH Program spans six intervention sites, a Coordinating Center, NIH program administrators from the NIA and NINR, a Steering Committee, cross-site workgroups, and an external advisory committee.

The chief responsibility for the REACH study rests with the Steering Committee which serves as the central decision-making body for all shared aspects of the REACH Program and is composed of the principal investigators from each of the intervention sites and the Coordinating Center, as well as the program administrators from NIA and NINR. However, six national intervention sites are ultimately responsible for the recruitment and retention of the number of subjects necessary to address site-proposed hypotheses regarding the effectiveness of their interventions relative to their site-specific usual care or minimal treatment conditions. When proposed sample sizes are combined across all the sites, the total number of caregivers to be recruited into the REACH study will be well over 1500. In addition, ethnic minority caregivers will be actively recruited at all six sites, with at least three sites planning to attain 50% minority recruitment for a possible total across sites of almost 600 minority caregivers. The vast majority of these minority caregivers are expected to self-identify as African American or Hispanic.

The Coordinating Center interacts regularly with the intervention sites and all other organizational components, serving as an information and communication center for the cooperative agreement. In addition, it contributes substantive methodological, analytical, and managerial expertise in the design, implementation, and evaluation of the national study to help meet the program's goals and objectives. The Coordinating Center is also responsible for assuring standardization of the collection, management, and quality control of the common data set in order to maximize the potential for cross-site comparability and analyses.

The REACH workgroups also help develop and coordinate many of the shared aspects of the REACH Program. Staffed by representatives from the intervention sites, the Coordinating Center, and the NIH, these workgroups and subcommittees utilize teleconferences and other forms of telecommunication to address both substantive and procedural program issues. All REACH workgroups work closely with one another to ensure that policies and procedures are consistent with features of the proposed study and forward key study design recommendations to the Steering Committee for discussion and final approval. For example, the Intervention Workgroup reviewed, critiqued, and sought consensus regarding the application of site-proposed interventions during the first year of the agreement, while the sites refined, pilot-tested, and modified their interventions in order to maximize both site-specific and cross-site intervention goals. This communication between sites and the Intervention Workgroup was designed to foster standardization of the application and general procedures of these unique interventions and thereby maximize the REACH Program's ability to combine and compare data across the six Intervention Sites. While certain issues were able to be uniform across all sites or among subsets of sites, many other issues will continue to vary across all sites given the uniqueness of the site-specific interventions and target populations.

Thus, the REACH Program's organizational components actively work together to meet the primary goals of the study—the development, implementation, and evaluation of the effectiveness of intervention programs provided to various groups of ethnic majority and minority caregivers. Two examples of the cooperative nature of these components in support of study goals and objectives include the following:

- *Sampling and recruitment efforts.* REACH developed a standardized screening tool to be used across sites to provide an appropriately diverse, yet well-defined target population. In the course of designing this screen, the Sampling, Recruitment, and Retention Workgroup created definitions for the care recipient and caregiver and in discussion with the Steering Committee developed both common and site-specific inclusion and exclusion criteria. As a result, the REACH study participant is clearly defined as an adult caregiver at least 21 years old who lives with and provides four or more hours of daily care to a family member suffering from at least two instrumental activities of daily living (IADL) or one activity of daily living (ADL) impairment (Katz, Ford, Moskowitz, Jackson, & Jaffe, 1963; Lawton, & Brody, 1969). This care recipient must have either a physician's diagnosis of ADRD or a recent Mini-Mental State Examination (MMSE) score less than or equal to 23 out of 30 (Folstein, Folstein, & McHugh, 1975). In addition, the caregiver must have been in the caregiving role at least 6 months, must be reachable by telephone, and must plan to stay in the area for the duration of the study. These definitions, when combined with the six sites' target populations, generate the potential for sizable proportions of ethnic minority caregivers and caregiving men, groups that are often neglected in caregiving research.
- *Cross-site standardization.* The Intervention Workgroup organized the development of cross-site and site-specific treatment fidelity assessments and the creation of intervention procedural manuals for each intervention to maximize replicability, generalizability, and interpretation of study results. It also encouraged standardization of intervention protocol components across subgroups of sites when standard practice across all sites was not feasible. For example, a subgroup of REACH sites will distribute similar ADRD educational material to participants at predetermined intervals and will create similar minimal support treatment

groups. Moreover, each site generated a site-specific Manual of Operations and Procedures that detailed sampling and design issues, subject recruitment and retention strategies, and intervention and data management activities, with a complementary set of treatment implementation and quality control procedures. These manuals will ultimately assist in intervention replication and outcome interpretation.

The REACH Program's Interventions for Family Caregivers

The REACH Program spans a diverse array of interventions that are well grounded in theoretical frameworks related to the caregiving stress process and its relevant mechanisms of change. The rich variety of these interventions, combined with the multidisciplinary background of their developers, produces a broad spectrum of theoretical frameworks. Therefore, two schematics were created to help organize the presentation of all REACH interventions. The first schematic, as seen in Figure 13.1, expands upon several models of caregiving stress (e.g., Lawton, Moss, Kleban, Glicksman, & Rovine, 1991; Pearlin et al., 1990; Russo, Vitaliano, Brewer, Katon, & Becker, 1995) and describes the caregiving context in which the REACH Program's interventions attempt to impact the psychosocial and health functioning of caregivers and, in some cases, assess these outcomes in their care recipients as well.

In part, the variety of interventions both within REACH and in the caregiving literature as a whole is a response not only to the large number of correlates related to caregiver burden and distress but also to the broad range of sociocultural contexts within which these interventions occur. As illustrated in Figure 13.1, family members provide care within a larger sociocultural context where four key components interact to influence outcomes of the caregiving experience. First, adults come to the caregiving context with their own set of strengths and vulnerabilities that can affect their experience of the caregiving process. These characteristics range from their own distinct psychosocial and physical health histories, coping strategies, and prior caregiving history to the multiple roles they hold (e.g., employee, grandmother, friend) and their potential to experience positive aspects of caregiving. Various demographic characteristics (e.g., age, ethnicity, gender, and sexual orientation) may also serve as strengths or risk factors for high stress in the caregiving role. Second, care recipient characteristics, including the levels of cognitive, functional, and behavioral deficits and their associated disturbances and dependencies can also substantially influence caregiving outcomes. Third, caregivers bring with them a variety of family and social support configurations that may or may not help buffer the impact of caregiver stress through physical assistance, information resources, and emotional support. And fourth, caregivers live and work in physical environments and situations that can either assist or impede their caregiving efforts. For example, employed caregivers may work for organizations with flextime policies and eldercare opportunities that ease rather than exacerbate family caregiving responsibilities.

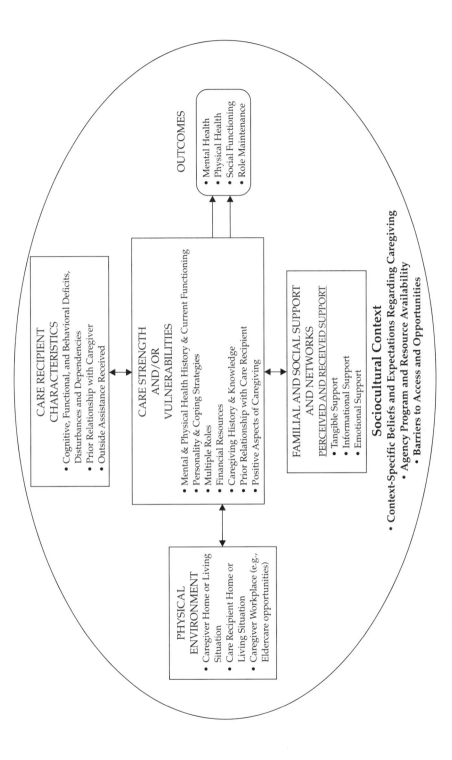

Figure 13.1 Context of Caregiving

Overall, these four components interact within a sociocultural context that holds specific beliefs and expectations regarding caregiving, and this context too can shape caregiver experiences. The sociocultural context also dictates the availability and accessibility of appropriate agencies and services that are able to meet the needs of caregivers and care recipients (e.g., culturally sensitive programs staffed with linguistically and culturally diverse staff). Finally, many of the factors in Figure 13.1 are not static but shift with changes in people's caregiving careers and their caregiving contexts. Pearlin and his colleagues developed the concept of caregiving as a career to help reflect the lengthy duration of the caregiving role, the time and energy extended in the organization of caregiving responsibilities over time, and the personal and professional transitions frequently influenced by caregiving tasks and activities (Pearlin, 1992; Skaff, Pearlin, & Mullan, 1996). Thus, multiple factors and influences can affect not only a caregiver's decision to enter into a chosen intervention program but also the overall impact and the effectiveness of that particular intervention.

The REACH Program's distinct interventions enter this context of caregiving at a number of points, ranging from the physical home environment and the family support system to the care recipients and the caregivers themselves. The second schematic organizes all the REACH interventions under five general categories. Due to the uniqueness of the REACH sites and their efforts to tailor their treatment strategies to specific caregiver populations, these interventions do not necessarily fit neatly into one category but tend to overlap categories. These five general types and their related REACH interventions appear in Figure 13.2 and are discussed in more detail in the following sections: (1) Individual Information and Support strategies that increase caregivers' understanding of dementia and their particular caregiving situation, (2) Group Support and Family Systems efforts that provide caregivers with multiple forms of social support, (3) Psychoeducational and Skill-Based Training approaches that teach caregivers coping and behavioral management strategies, (4) Home-Based Environmental interventions that modify the home environment's effect on the care recipient and support the caregiver, and (5) Enhanced Technology Systems such as home-centered computer/telephone networks that are designed to reduce caregiver distress and isolation.

INDIVIDUAL INFORMATION AND SUPPORT

These intervention strategies are designed to increase not only the family caregiver's understanding of dementia but also certain aspects of his or her particular caregiving situation. This is accomplished through one-to-one encounters between the caregiver and an interventionist and through the distribution of standardized educational material that covers relevant caregiving topics. Two of these REACH intervention strategies, the Minimal Support Condition and the Information and Referral Condition, are similar to many caregiver intervention approaches found in the community and hence do serve as REACH control or usual care approaches for four different sites. However, these REACH approaches go beyond typical usual care conditions by standardizing the frequency and duration of contact, as well as the specific educational material provided.

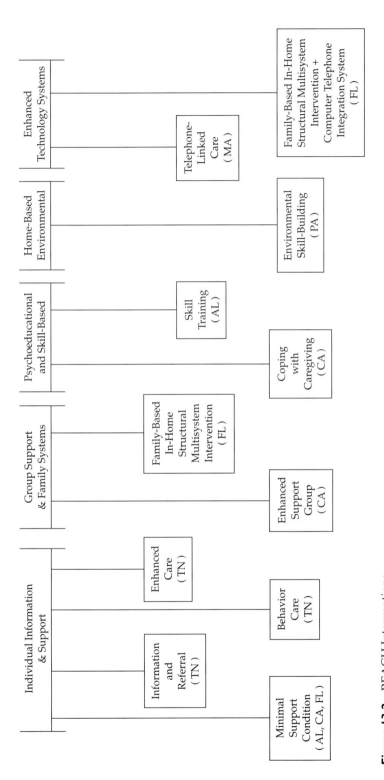

Figure 13.2 REACH Interventions

Minimal Support Condition (MSC) (Alabama, California, and Florida)

Three sites collaborated to develop this telephone-based one-to-one support-ive intervention, which consists of active listening and appropriately expressed empathy provided to REACH caregivers. The schedule of these telephone con-tacts mirrors the frequency of contacts for the other interventions at each of the sites involved. For example, caregivers at the California site will be telephoned once a week for ten consecutive weeks and then once a month for the next eight months to match the number and frequency of contacts with caregivers randomized to either one of its other two interventions. In addition to these tele-phone contacts, MSC interventionists also mail educational materials discussing dementia and caregiving issues to participants at pre-established time periods. Several important research and service rationales influenced the development of this common comparison group, rather than site reliance on a usual care or typical control condition. First, this choice is supported by empirical studies that suggest this type of telephone contact can be effective in the amelioration of distress with certain populations (Evans, Smith, Werkhoven, Fox, & Pritzl, 1986; Guy, 1995). This contact also supplies subjects with information and support in an effort to minimize differential drop-out between this and the other treatment conditions. Moreover, this type of brief telephone contact is supported by the presence of similar telephone-based programs in local community agencies. Finally, the inclusion of the MSC will help determine if participants who receive this one-to-one brief, supportive contact report results on outcome variables of caregiver distress that are similar to those described by caregivers in the more intensive individual and group interventions offered by these REACH sites. If the MSC intervention is comparable to more resource-intensive interventions on at least some key outcome measures, the MSC might then hold strong economic implications that could influence the design and administration of future intervention programs.

Information and Referral (Tennessee)

All three interventions investigated at the Tennessee site explore the feasi-bility of caregiver support provision within primary care settings. However, In-formation and Referral (I&R) is specifically designed to simulate the community standard of care for caregivers of individuals with Alzheimer's disease. At the conclusion of a primary care office visit, I&R interventionists give AD caregivers commercially available pamphlets on general topics about dementia and the telephone numbers of the local Alzheimer's Association and other national Alzheimer's resources. Caregivers in the I&R intervention will receive additional educational material on dementia-related health topics, such as nutrition and safety, at regularly scheduled office visits (typically four to six times a year, in accordance with usual Alzheimer's care). However, these materials will not address any behavioral interventions or stress management strategies found in Tennessee's other interventions. The provision of educational/informational material is well supported by a patient survey by Shank and associates (1991) that found that patients, particularly older adults, wanted to receive health education information at every office visit. Yet, these researchers also discovered that physicians needed to give the material directly to patients, since they would not ask for it themselves.

All three of Tennessee's interventions are based on the stress and coping model of Lazarus and his colleagues in which it is believed that educational interventions can help caregivers learn to better assess their ability to cope with the demands of their care recipients, as well as with their own reactions to these and other demands in their environment (Folkman et al., 1979; Lazarus & Launeir, 1978). The development of these interventions is also grounded in Becker's model (1992) in which treatment adherence is maximized by (1) simplifying information whenever possible and repeating it frequently, both orally and in writing, (2) facilitating the provider-patient relationship through the active involvement of the caregiver in the treatment process, and (3) enlisting the family/social support system in the change process whenever possible. Although all of Tennessee's interventions are discussed in the present general category because they each use interventionists to share information and educational material with the caregiver on a one-to-one basis, Tennessee's other two interventions embody noticeable features of the interventions categorized under Psychoeducational and Skill-Based Interventions, such as teaching the caregiver either specific skills to help manage care recipient problem behavior or self-management skills designed to increase his or her ability to cope with caregiver stressors.

Behavior Care (Tennessee)

Behavior Care builds on the usual care activities just described in Information and Referral but adds written material and individual counseling sessions focused on care recipient behavior management. These targeted counseling and education sessions identify specific problem behaviors the care recipients exhibit, such as wandering and aggressive behavior, and assess key losses in their activities of daily living. Initially, Behavior Care interventionists meet with caregivers at scheduled office visits to teach them how to better manage these problems and, by extension, how to help themselves cope better when they arise. These sessions are extended through supplemental phone calls between office visits that also discuss intervention material. Supplemental phone calls occur every 2 weeks for the first 3 months and then monthly thereafter whenever the caregiver is not seen in the primary care office. In agreement with usual Alzheimer's care, these visits will occur approximately four to six times a year. Finally, caregivers receive behavior-specific handouts identified through the in-person counseling sessions, and these handouts are used to reinforce material covered during both the in-person and telephone contact sessions.

Enhanced Care (Tennessee)

This treatment teaches specific stress and behavior management strategies to the caregiver through face-to-face meetings with the interventionist and written material provided at regularly scheduled visits to the primary care physician.

This material is given in addition to the general information in Information and Referral and the problem behavior management material in Behavior Care. Enhanced care counseling educates caregivers on successful cognitive and behavioral strategies that can help change negative thinking patterns. These changes may in turn help to reduce caregiver distress in caregiving contexts where the course of events cannot be altered. More specifically, these strategies will include topics such as relaxation training and the delineation of steps to use in order to cope with counterproductive thoughts and feelings. As in Behavior Care, supplemental phone calls will extend face-to-face counseling sessions between office visits. These phone calls are made every 2 weeks for the first 3 months and then monthly thereafter whenever the caregiver is not seen in the primary care office.

GROUP SUPPORT AND FAMILY SYSTEMS

These group and family intervention efforts are developed to help ease caregiver stress by encouraging caregivers to mobilize and utilize their informal and formal social support networks in order to increase their chances of receiving informational, emotional, and tangible forms of support when needed.

Enhanced Support Group (ESG) (California)

The ESG intervention is patterned after many support groups available to caregivers in the community and is targeted specifically to Anglo and Hispanic women. While there is a great deal of clinically based literature on the helpfulness of support groups for caregivers, very few well-controlled empirical studies have been conducted to date. This may be partially due to the fact that support groups vary considerably in such features as meeting frequency, type and amount of disclosure encouraged, and the length of time caregivers regularly attend. The rationale for support group interventions is firmly established in studies that have shown that the quality of one's support network can have a strong effect in moderating or buffering the impact of stress for both older and younger adults (e.g., Cobb, 1976; Dean & Lin, 1977; Finch, Okun, Barrera, Zautra, & Reich, 1989). However, in a study that directly examined the impact of support groups, these groups proved more helpful in their informational and peer support activities but were less successful in addressing members' own intrapsychic conflicts (Gonyea, 1989).

Since ESG mirrors the fundamental components of community-based support groups, the ESG also focuses primarily on developing peer support, rather than resolving intrapsychic conflicts or specifically teaching participants how to take care of their own needs. Still, it is possible that the development of peer support within the group may extend outside its boundaries and encourage caregivers to establish additional support systems that could buffer a variety of caregiving stressors. Since the family has traditionally been the major source of support among many Hispanic women, the role of social support (and, by extension, the role of support groups) may behave differentially in lives of Hispanic and Anglo caregivers. For example, Hispanic family members, when compared to their Anglo counterparts, appear to rely to a much greater extent on informal networks for various forms of help (Lockery, 1991; Weeks & Cuellar, 1981). Therefore, separate support groups will be offered for the two ethnic groups. However, differences in social support behavior may vary among Hispanic participants according to their level of acculturation, since the role of the family is changing in society and increased acculturation can often shift people's adherence to traditional values (Villa et al., 1993). Finally, the ESG is enhanced because initially it meets weekly rather than monthly (as is typically found in the community), and caregivers are given specific educational material about caregiving at predetermined intervals. These ESGs are held in local community agencies for the convenience and comfort of caregivers and are co-led by two professional REACH staff. The groups for Hispanic participants are co-led by bilingual and bicultural staff and are offered in both Spanish and English.

Family-Based Structural Multisystem In-Home Intervention (FSMII) (Florida)

Drawn from the work of Szapocznik and colleagues (1989) and targeted to both Anglo and Cuban American families in Florida, the FSMII is a therapy-based intervention that utilizes a family systems approach to enhance communication between caregivers and other family members. The overarching goal of the intervention is to identify existing problems in communication and to produce changes in interaction patterns that allow the caregiver to harness available family and community resources. Thus, the focus of change is not just the individual or the environment, but rather the transaction between the two. This transaction is then viewed as embedded within larger social and cultural systems. This approach was successfully implemented with depressed Cuban-born elders, and the current project seeks to extend this proven methodology to caregivers of individuals with dementia. FSMII proceeds through three general phases of treatment: (1) *joining*—the process of establishing the therapeutic relationship with the caregiver and other family members, (2) *diagnosis*—the identification of interactional patterns within the family or between systems that are linked to the caregiver's experience of burden and lack of support, and (3) *restructuring*—the process of creating new patterns of interaction. The goals of FSMII as applied to caregivers include not only the reduction of distress created by living with and managing a demented family member but also the enhancement of family functioning by identifying specific caregiver problems, assessing the efficacy of family problem-solving strategies, generating a range of accessible family resources, and building collaboration between caregivers and their families in their caregiving efforts. Family members participate in in-home family therapy sessions conducted by bilingual therapists. These sessions occur weekly for the first 4 months, biweekly for the next 2 months, and then monthly for the 6 months thereafter.

PSYCHOEDUCATIONAL AND SKILL-BASED TRAINING

REACH Psychoeducational and Skill-based Training approaches incorporate a group instructional component that addresses caregiver stress and distress through training the caregiver in practical, care recipient behavioral management strategies or teaching the caregiver effective coping strategies.

Coping with Caregiving (CWC) (California)

This psychoeducational class is firmly established in theories that articulate the role of cognitions and behaviors in negative affective states (Beck, Rush, Shaw, & Emery, 1979; Lewinsohn et al., 1982; Lewinsohn, Muñoz, Youngren, & Zeiss, 1986). CWC classes are designed to teach a limited number of mood management skills in order to help ameliorate the stress of caregiving and alleviate caregiver distress. Two key approaches are actively integrated into the intervention to achieve these objectives: (1) an emphasis on reducing negative affect by learning how to relax in the stressful situation, appraising the care receiver's behavior more realistically, and communicating assertively, and (2) an emphasis on increasing positive mood through acquisition of such skills as seeing the contingency between mood and activities, developing strategies to do more small, everyday pleasant activities, and learning to set self-change goals and reward oneself for accomplishments along the way. Theoretically, a good deal of these classes is built on the extensive writings of Bandura (1977, 1982, 1989), which document the powerful mediating effect of self-efficacy on various outcomes. Briefly stated, this theory predicts that individuals high in self-efficacy perceptions will engage in more adaptive behaviors, and it is people's change in their efficacy perceptions that actually enables interventions to work. Furthermore, these self-efficacy perceptions change even more when individuals can actually learn from modeling and performance-based feedback.

Thus, CWCs were designed to be small, interactive classes that foster the development of specific skills and encourage participants to practice these skills both in and out of class to reinforce learning and receive valuable feedback. Many of the same cultural issues discussed under the Enhanced Support Group intervention are applicable to CWC classes as well; consequently, separate classes are offered to Hispanic and Anglo caregivers. Moreover, CWC classes for Hispanic caregivers are offered in either English or Spanish by bilingual/bicultural professional staff. All CWC classes meet weekly for 10 weeks and then once a month thereafter for a total of eight booster sessions. These classes are composed of caregivers in the community and are held in local community agencies that many of the participants know and frequent. Since half of California's projected participant pool is composed of Hispanic caregivers, special emphasis has been placed on identification of agencies, organizations, and churches with strong ties to the Hispanic community.

Skill Training (Alabama)

Skill Training draws its rationale from the caregiver stress model of Haley and colleagues (1987), which emphasizes the relative influences of various components of the caregiving stress process on caregiver well-being. These components include caregiver stressors (e.g., care recipient behavioral deficits and excesses), caregiver appraisals of stress, and caregiver social support and coping responses (social activities and health behaviors). More recently, Haley and his colleagues have begun to explore similarities and differences among African American and white caregivers with regard to the caregiving stress process (Haley, Roth, Coleton et al., 1996; Haley, West, Wadley et al., 1995) and have utilized these findings to help guide the development of this particular intervention. Skill Training is also substantially based on the work of Burgio and his associates (e.g., Bourgeois, Burgio, Schulz et al., 1997; Burgio, 1997; Burgio & Bourgeois, 1992; Burgio, Jones, Butler, & Engel, 1988; Burgio, Scilley, Hoar et al., 1993), which investigates behavioral disturbances displayed by individuals with dementia, the negative impact these behaviors have on care recipients and caregivers, and the development of promising behavioral interventions to help treat these behavioral problems. As a result, this intervention combines care recipient-focused behavior management skill training and caregiver-focused problem solving training to help African American and white caregivers manage the stress and distress of their caregiving situations. The care recipient–focused skill training component teaches caregivers how to better address their family member's behavioral excesses (e.g., disruptive vocalization) and remediable deficits (e.g., excess dependence in self-care), which can contribute substantially to caregiver stress. In contrast, caregiver problem-solving skills training will address certain caregiver behaviors in order to increase the caregivers' ability to cope with caregiving stress. These targeted behaviors include such strategies as increasing pleasant events and social activities and encouraging positive health behaviors. The Skill Training intervention begins with a 3-hour group workshop offered in the community (e.g., at local churches or community centers) that encompasses didactic training, modeling techniques, role plays, and performance feedback. Participants will also be given a training manual and videotapes that review and reinforce these critical skills. Regular home visits to caregivers after the workshop help fine-tune these behavior management and self-management skills by collecting behavioral logs from the caregivers and establishing individualized caregiver and care recipient programs. Six home visits take place in the first 8 weeks following the workshop, and then another five bimonthly visits are made over the rest of the year. These last five visits alternate with five bimonthly therapeutic telephone calls, so that the caregiver receives monthly contact either in person or by telephone from Skill Training staff. The workshops of the Skill Training intervention are co-led by African American and white program staff, and home visits are made by culturally sensitive interventionists.

HOME-BASED ENVIRONMENTAL

In general, Home-Based Environmental interventions are designed to assist and support caregivers through educating them about the impact of the home environment on their care recipients' dementia behaviors. Caregivers are taught to identify problems, problem-solve solutions, and subsequently introduce effective modifications into the home. These strategies in turn help reduce the home environment's deleterious effect on care recipients by maximizing their awareness, orientation, safety, and functional ability.

Environmental Skill-Building Program (ESP) (Pennsylvania)

The purpose of ESP is to provide caregivers with the skills and technical support necessary to alter their home environments enough to help reduce the severity of behavioral problems that affect the performance of activities of daily living in their ADRD family members. This client-driven, home-based service is a standardized, 20-week reproducible program that seeks to educate caregivers about the impact of the environment on care recipients with dementia. ESP is grounded in an competence-environmental press framework (Lawton & Nahemow, 1973), and an extension of this framework that describes four hierarchical layers that can be manipulated to obtain just the right fit between a person's capabilities and environmental demands. These four hierarchical layers include a physical dimension (objects), a task dimension (daily routines), a social dimension (household composition and social resources), and a cultural dimension (shared values and beliefs) (Barris, Kielhofner, Levine, & Neville, 1985; Corcoran & Gitlin, 1991; Gitlin & Corcoran, 1996). As a care recipient's competence declines, the demands of unchanging objects and tasks can result in maladaptive behavior, including increased resistance to activities of daily living. Through intervention strategies directed at the four dimensions, ESP teaches caregivers the tools necessary to reduce particular behavioral stressors in the environment and to enable care recipients to function at higher levels of their abilities. In this intervention program, caregivers first learn to identify and prioritize problem areas encountered in the environment; then they begin to brainstorm, generate, and introduce individualized environmental strategies such as employing assistive devices, making home alterations, simplifying tasks, changing daily routines, and enlisting other family support and formal support services. These strategies can range from no-cost solutions such as establishing consistent routines for the care recipient, rearranging furniture, and removing household objects to various cost solutions such as installing grab bars, handrails, or stairglides. The rationale for this approach suggests that the use of these strategies will help reduce problematic environmental factors that lead to caregiver burden and strain. ESP begins with a 5-month, active phase that incorporates five home visits and one telephone call during which the occupational therapist educates the caregiver about the impact of the environment and implements individualized environmental strategies. The program continues with a maintenance phase over the next 6 months, during which these strategies are reinforced through an additional home visit and three telephone contacts.

ENHANCED TECHNOLOGY SYSTEMS

REACH encompasses two high-technology communication-based interventions that investigate the acceptability and utilization of technology-based services by ADRD caregivers to help reduce their isolation, enhance support, and provide support as well as respite functions.

Telephone-Linked Care (TLC) (Massachusetts)

Telephone-Linked Care reaches out to both white and ethnic minority caregivers (particularly African American and Hispanic caregivers) through a year-long telephone-based intervention designed to reduce caregiver stress. The design and development of the TLC system was heavily influenced by Pearlin's conceptual model of Alzheimer's caregivers' stress (Pearlin et al., 1990). The model suggests that the background and the context of caregiver stress, such as the caregiver's socioeconomic characteristics and caregiving history, as well as the caregiver's primary stressors, such as the care recipient's level of cognitive impairment and behavioral disturbances, can be mediated by the caregiver's personal and social resources to alter the main outcomes of stress (e.g., mental health symptoms, physical health limitations, and yielding of caregiver activities). This automated telecommunication system is available 24 hours a day and uses a computer-controlled human voice system to speak with caregivers at home. Caregivers press designated keys on the touch-tone keypad of their home phone to communicate with the system, allowing them access to a number of options tailored to meet caregivers' needs and preferences over time. The system houses a voice-mail caregiver support network designed to reduce social isolation, where caregivers can post messages on a voice-mail bulletin board or send them to one another for information and advice. Once a week, caregivers can report in to TLC about behavior problems exhibited by their care recipient and receive information on strategies to reduce them. The TLC system also monitors the caregiver's stress during this weekly conversation and makes recommendations and referrals when appropriate. Caregivers can also call in and access a geriatric nurse specialist's voice-mail and ask for special assistance regarding their caregiving situations. Through yet another option, TLC supports an activity/distraction conversation designed to conduct a 12-minute individualized conversation with the care recipient in order to distract him/her from problem behavior and give the caregiver a short break. Finally, the TLC system is able to manage large-scale use over long periods of time, and the Massachusetts site is especially interested in exploring the cost effectiveness of such a system.

Family-Based Structural Multisystem In-Home Intervention plus Computer Telephone Integration System (FSMII + CTIS) (Florida)

This intervention expands the FSMII described earlier with a computer telephone integration system that examines the effectiveness of using screen phones as a tool to augment the family-based therapeutic intervention. Screen phones are telephones with text that display screens and enhanced functions that expand basic telephone use through the addition of various computer inputs and outputs and, as a result, allow both voice and text to be sent and received during an interaction session. The rationale for this augmented intervention suggests that computer and communication technologies can be used effectively to facilitate communication linkages established in therapy and provide the caregiver with enhanced access to the therapist, family members (especially those at a distance), and other caregivers. CTIS can also provide access to formal support programs, such as information databases or services. Computer links and various forms of telecommunication similar to CTIS have already been found to be helpful with some populations (Czaja, Guerrier, Nair, & Landauer, 1993; Leirer, Morrow, Tanke, & Pariante, 1991). The CTIS system relies primarily on voice communication, accepts both Spanish and English text and voice messages, and is relatively simple and easy to use, since it makes use of the telephone, a highly familiar technology. It allows individuals to place regular phone calls, develop voice messaging systems (e.g., therapists will be able to leave messages to caregivers on an individual or family or group basis), and participate in conference calls of up to eight individuals at once. CTIS is also designed to incorporate several other functions including caregiver respite functions in which family members develop vignettes with activities and material to help interest and occupy the care recipient; orientation functions where the system provides orientation material and memos for the care recipient; and information functions with access to medication and nutrition information, and linkages to formal resources. In summary, FSMII + CTIS combines psychosocial and engineering solutions to enhance support and alleviate burden for family caregivers by facilitating family communication through the provision of messaging, conferencing, and respite functions.

Developing a Measurement Strategy

One of the most formidable challenges of multisite studies is the development of a common measurement battery. Meeting this challenge requires that a multidisciplinary team of investigators with widely varying perspectives reach consensus on what should be measured and how it should be done. This task is made all the more difficult if the measurement goals include psychosocial domains for which there may be limited consensus regarding standardized measurement approaches. Identifying measures suitable for culturally diverse populations adds yet another layer of complexity to the deliberation process. All of these challenges had to be addressed by the REACH investigators. In addition, the measurement strategy developed had to be suitable for a wide variety of interventions to be implemented at the six different sites.

In order to achieve these goals, a Measurement Workgroup, with representatives from each site and from the NIH, was convened to identify measures to be used in the study. This workgroup was asked to identify core areas of measurement, evaluate measurement options for the identified core areas, and achieve consensus in the selection of specific measures to be implemented. Before taking on the task of identifying measurement domains and specific measures, the Measurement Workgroup articulated several goals aimed at facilitating this process. First, it was agreed that the measures generated would serve multiple goals including (1) characterizing the samples, (2) enabling cross-sectional and predictive analyses, and (3) assessing intervention effects. It was felt that the core battery must minimally include a common outcome measure assessing caregiver health or functioning. Second, it was agreed that existing measures were to be evaluated on the following dimensions: internal reliability, convergent and discriminant validity, sensitivity to change, and absence of ethnicity or gender biases. Once these general operating rules were adopted, the group proceeded to identify specific measures, using a two-stage procedure involving, first, the selection of domains of measurement and, second, the prioritization of measures within domains.

In terms of prioritizing the domains of measurement, the most important domains identified included measures of intervention outcomes and measures that characterize the sample for purposes of generalization. Measures that assess the integrity and intensity of the interventions used were also given high priority. Other contextual and individual difference variables that might moderate or confound treatment effects were also included, although they were given somewhat lower priority than measures that characterize the samples and primary outcomes.

Once broad categories of measures were identified, specific measures within domains were prioritized by applying traditional psychometric criteria to the selection of measures. All appropriate psychometric criteria (reliability, validity, sensitivity) were applied to each measure, and the one considered to have the best psychometric properties on the basis of reports in the literature was selected. Special consideration was given to issues of internal reliability with diverse population groups in making final selections.

The final stage in the selection process involved the consideration of time-vs.-quality trade-offs. The goal was to construct a core measurement battery that required approximately one hour to administer. Because of this time constraint, trade-offs had to be made in terms of both measurement domains and in choosing specific measures within domains. All other things being equal, shorter measures were selected over longer ones. All measures selected, particularly the few, newly developed measures and those adapted from existing instruments, were extensively pretested before final decisions were made.

The Measurement Workgroup, with the final approval of the REACH Steering Committee, developed a core assessment battery to be administered across sites at baseline prior to randomization and subsequently at 6 months, 12 months, and 18 months after baseline assessment. In doing so, REACH sites gather data on caregivers past the most intensive phase of site interventions, addressing concerns raised in the literature about the duration of participant follow-up. The results of the workgroup's effort are summarized in Table 13.1. In order to characterize the care recipient, REACH assesses multiple domains, including sociodemographic characteristics, functional status as measured by ADL, IADL, and Mini-Mental State Examination, problem behaviors, and medication and service use. The remaining measures focus on the caregiver and included sociodemographic characteristics, medication and service use of the caregiver, health status and health behaviors, and affective status of the caregiver, including depressive symptomatology and state anxiety. To characterize the caregiving experience, the core battery assesses the amount of care provided, the vigilance demands of caregiving, and the positive aspects of caregiving. Finally, a number of contextual and individual difference variables are measured, including social support, social integration, negative interactions, and the religiosity or spirituality of the caregiver. The specific measure used within each of these categories is also identified in the table.

In addition to the core battery, Intervention Sites selected other measures

TABLE 13.1
REACH Core Measurement Battery

Measurement Domain	Name of Measure/Form	Citation/Source
CR demographics	CG sociodemographic information	Various sources
CR physical health	CR health	SF-36 and other health measures
CR physical impairment	ADL/IADL	Katz et al., 1963; Lawton & Brody, 1969
CR behavior	Revised Memory and Problem Behavior Checklist (RMBPC)	Teri et al., 1992
CR cognition	MMSE	Folstein et al., 1975
CR medications	CR medications	Transcription from containers
CG demographics	CG sociodemographic information	Various sources
CG burden	Revised Memory and Problem Behavior Checklist (RMBPC)	Teri et al., 1992
	Positive aspects of caregiving	Schulz et al., 1997 CHES
	ADL/IADL helping	FIM (Granger, Hamilton, Sherwin, 1986)
	Vigilance	New (Mahoney)
CG physical health	CG health & health behaviors	Archbold et al., 1986; AHEAD, HRS, DYNH
CG medications	CG medications	Transcription from containers
CG mental health/ well-being	CES-D Anxiety	Radloff, 1977 Spielberger et al., 1983
CG social support	Received support	Krause, 1995; Barrera et al., 1981
	Lubben Social Network Index (SNI)	Lubben, 1988; Berkman & Syme, 1979
	Negative Interaction Subscale	Krause, 1995
	Satisfaction with support	Krause, 1995
CG Religiosity	Religiosity	New from various sources
CG Social activities	Social activities	New (Haley)
Service utilization	Formal care and services	New from various sources including site-specific proposals
Cost	ADL/IADL Formal care and services	Additional questions added to ADL/IADL and formal care

intended to address their own individualized research objectives. All in all, these measures will help capture additional characteristics of site samples (e.g., range of acculturation) and identify other predictor, mediator, and moderator variables deemed appropriate to their populations. Sites with similar research interests and shared site-specific measures afford the additional opportunity for smaller sets of cross-site or subcore data analyses. Examples of such measures include Self-Efficacy for Caregiving (Zeiss, Gallagher-Thompson, & Bandura, 1992; revised Thompson, 1996), Screen for Caregiver Burden (Vitaliano et al., 1991), and the Cognitive Status and Caregiver Mastery Scales (Pearlin et al., 1990).

An important innovation of the REACH program is the development and application of measures aimed at assessing the extent to which treatments were implemented at each of the sites. Thus, besides simply defining each intervention and its relationship to outcomes, REACH has adopted several treatment fidelity concepts derived from a recent treatment implementation model put forth in the literature. Although treatments vary by site and many of these measures are of necessity specific to that site, they all fall into three general categories reflecting components of proper treatment implementation: treatment delivery, treatment receipt, and treatment enactment (Lichstein, Riedel, & Grieve, 1994).

The first concept, treatment delivery, refers to actions taken to ensure the accuracy of treatment presentation and to help delineate the differences between treatments to be compared. Treatment delivery can be affected by many issues, including therapist drift (e.g., additions or subtractions to treatment), therapist personality characteristics, and inadequate training of the interventionist. To help monitor and assess treatment delivery, every REACH site developed detailed intervention manuals and created separate manuals to help differentiate between interventions within their particular site. Several sites train interventionists with pilot subjects, provide ongoing supervision of intervention activities, audiotape intervention activities to evaluate protocol adherence, and give regular feedback to interventionists.

The second concept, treatment receipt, is designed to assess the amount of participant exposure to the intervention. Treatment receipt is weakened through numerous factors, including interventionist or participant shortcomings (e.g., poor communication and poor motivation), participant inattentiveness or comprehension deficits, and personality factors that either foster or erode the therapeutic relationship. Treatment receipt evaluations in the REACH Program range from attendance records, role-play exercises, and amount of hi-tech system utilization to pre-post knowledge tests and ratings of participant behavior on audiotaped intervention sessions.

The third concept, treatment enactment, describes the amount of practice or use of the intervention strategies by the participant both in and out of the intervention context. Participants are the primary change agents outside the intervention, and therefore they have the key responsibilities for treatment adherence, treatment extension, and change. While the level of responsibilities may vary across intervention types, at least some responsibilities exist in all interventions. Examples of treatment enactment evaluation activities include monitoring of homework assignments, use of suggestions received from automated telephone systems, review of activity log books for compliance with therapist recommendations, and analyses of structured performance measures.

A further goal of the REACH Measurement Workgroup is to develop a common set of metrics that can be used to assess treatment delivery, receipt, and enactment across the six sites. Examples of common metrics might include whether an intervention was delivered one-on-one or in a group setting, the amount of contact between interventionist and caregiver, and indicators that show the extent to which components of an intervention were comprehended, used, and resulted in new behaviors.

In summary, problems with intervention implementation in any one of the three implementation areas may erode both internal and external validity. Moreover, implementation difficulties will go unnoticed unless critical components of treatment delivery, receipt, and enactment are specified and assessed regularly (Bourgeois et al., 1996). As Lichstein and his associates assert (1994), one really cannot determine if a study is a fair test of a particular intervention when serious attention is not given to all three of these issues.

Tailoring of Interventions

The effort to tailor interventions to meet the needs of caregivers is an evident theme across the REACH sites. For example, Alabama, California, and Florida each tailored various components of their interventions to meet specific groups or subgroups of caregivers. Alabama developed intervention videotapes and print material sensitive to the range of needs expressed by both African American and white caregiver-care recipient dyads. Both California and Florida not only utilize bilingual and bicultural staff in their interventions with Hispanic caregivers but also developed conceptual translations of their interventions that incorporate culturally relevant content and process material that maintains the integrity of the interventions' theoretical frameworks. Similarly, California discovered in its previous intervention programs that women and men respond differently in caregiving classes and have tailored their current interventions solely toward female caregivers, with the hope of extending programs to male caregivers in the future (Ory & Schulz, 1996). REACH sites have also often tailored their interventions to meet the concerns of individuals with distinct caregiving situations that reflect their own particular caregiving contexts. Massachusetts's TLC program, Tennessee's Behavior Care and Enhanced Care Programs, and Pennsylvania's Environmental Skill-Building Program all afford caregivers the opportunity to receive individualized programs (within specific protocols) targeted to meet their informational, behavioral management, and stress management needs. Ultimately, the theme of tailoring may help uncover which interventions are more appropriate for different population groups, for different types of caregivers, and for different stages of dementia.

Recently, a debate has arisen in the literature over the best approaches to testing caregiver interventions (Mittelman & Gallagher-Thompson, 1996; Montgomery, 1996). Montgomery criticizes caregiver studies for defining their target populations within narrow clinical contexts and focusing their research questions too restrictively. As a consequence, the field is saddled with the difficulty of extending interventions developed in resource-intense clinical settings out into a gamut of sociocultural contexts, where they appear to be neither applicable nor financially feasible. However, Mittelman and Gallagher-Thompson (1996) suggest that researchers need to clearly identify effective interventions *first* and then tailor them appropriately to meet the needs of more diverse caregiving populations. If these interventions continue to be successful, researchers and practitioners could then modify them further to make them less resource intensive.

Two opposing intervention strategies are now emerging in the field. This debate contrasts the utility of focused intervention approaches developed to manage very specific caregiver problems against more comprehensive intervention efforts that combine several focused approaches, such as a program of individual counseling, peer support, and family therapy designed to address a broader range of caregiver issues. While highly focused caregiver interventions may be too limited in their scope, they typically encompass mechanisms of change that are relatively easy to isolate and test. In contrast, multimodal intervention approaches are by their definition more comprehensive but are not so easily tested, due to their many component parts and associated mechanisms of change. In response to some of these issues, the REACH Program has recognized that, while many of its interventions are indeed tailored to meet the needs of a diverse group of caregivers, this tailoring process needs to be balanced with the delineation of specific algorithms so that this research can go beyond clinical judgment and remain generalizable to the populations described.

Future Directions in Caregiver Intervention Research and Service Delivery

The REACH Program concentrates on characterizing and testing a variety of promising home- and community-based interventions for enhancing family caregiving and expands the study of the caregiving experience among several groups of racial and ethnic minority caregivers and caregiving men. The program's commitment to specify the components of these theory-based interventions and to critically examine their effectiveness through a set of standard outcome measures will help sort through the complex relationships among type of intervention, caregiver and care recipient variables, and intervention outcomes. Both the specification of these components and a thorough understanding of the theoretical underpinnings of these strategies is critical to the successful implementation of similar interventions in other populations and settings.

LINKING RESEARCH TO SERVICE DELIVERY

Any implications for practice, service delivery, and policy development that may grow out of the findings of the REACH Program will be strongly influenced by the desired outcomes targeted by the particular interventions involved. These relevant outcomes are intrinsically tied to the explanatory theories selected by the intervention sites that identified the needs of their caregiver populations and then shaped their specific intervention designs, accordingly. Once successful REACH interventions or specific components of these interventions are validated with their targeted populations, they must not only translate successfully into programs and services within a broader variety of practice environments but also adequately meet the needs of other caregiver populations in order to attract policymakers and secure stable funding sources.

It is very likely that the various REACH interventions will differentially affect distinct outcome variables, given the diversity of their explanatory theories and substantial differences in the ethnic and racial composition of the sites' target populations. However, the REACH study group must be prepared to address questions about the plausible chain of events between interventions and the wide range of outcomes examined in the caregiving literature. For instance, the psychoeducational Coping with Caregiving class may have a great impact on increasing cognitive and behavioral coping strategies that in turn should reduce caregiver anger and frustration. But the REACH group does not necessarily expect this intervention to affect other, broader outcomes such as the pace of social service utilization or the reduction of health care costs.

Still, it will be important for the REACH study to begin to explore the interrelationship between intervention success and some key components of the caregiving context, such as stage in the disease process or length of time in the caregiving career. Differences in intervention success across either disease stage or caregiving career might point to the need for community organizations and social service programs to provide multimodal caregiving intervention programs and services themselves or to establish stronger linkages with programs that provide services outside their purview. Similarly, the REACH study may find that the labor intensive small group or family interventions are highly effective in reducing caregiver psychological distress when compared to the study's technologically based interventions; in contrast, REACH's high-tech telecommunication approaches may prove more cost-effective and reach more people than their labor-intensive counterparts. Therefore, potential findings in the REACH Program might support programs that encompass telephone and on-line support services, referral information and educational material in the early stages of the disease, and more intensive family support interventions and skill-building classes to maximize caregiver coping capacities as the disease progresses. Such results suggest researchers and practitioners need to be flexible and comfortable with caregivers who are using multiple professional sources to help manage their caregiving situations.

The REACH Program may also shape future services and policies regarding who should be the primary focus of caregiver interventions to achieve specified outcomes (e.g., the primary caregiver, the caregiver-care recipient dyad, or the larger family unit) and how family caregivers will be identified and subsequently recruited. Successful interventions need an appropriate service delivery system to help recruit older individuals and families into intervention studies and programs, but, just as important, these systems are critical in order to maintain successful intervention components after the research funding ends. In response to this issue, some REACH sites have agreed to train interested agency staff in their interventions as the program progresses so that successful interventions can continue after the study ends. Moreover, results of the program may influence service and policy rationales regarding the structure and presentation of caregiver interventions including: (1) the duration and intensity necessary for interventions to achieve and maintain success on relevant caregiver outcomes, (2) the utility of a variety of intervention settings, including caregiver homes, local churches and community agencies, and primary care offices, (3) the selection of intervention mediums such as individualized or class-based skill instruction, technological interactions, and family therapy, as they relate to different caregiving contexts, and (4) the use of multidisciplinary staff in effective intervention delivery. The REACH teams both within and across sites consist of staff members that reflect the multidisciplinary nature of caregiver research and intervention approaches and suggest the importance of interdisciplinary gerontological training designed to meet the needs of our aging population. The breadth of REACH interventions suggest that such training might include a foundation of basic research principles and their relationship to practice, an understanding of biological and psychosocial theories and processes of adult development and aging, substantial exposure to theories of behavior change and their application to direct practice, a grasp of the importance of technological advances in the lives of the elderly and impediments to its perceived acceptability and utility, and the continuing development of one's cross-cultural awareness and competence.

FUTURE RESEARCH EMPHASES

The next generation of caregiver research studies might focus on identifying and modifying factors associated with site-specific intervention successes or failures for different populations. For example, these studies might examine the relative effectiveness of different interventions at late, rather than early to middle, stages in the disease or focus on interventions with specific strategies aimed at drawing underserved minority caregivers into formal care services that are culturally tailored to meet their needs. While some policymakers assume that increased service use is detrimental due to the increased costs involved, research and practice professionals may be able to demonstrate that such an increase is an appropriate response to overwhelming caregiving stressors and that the costs associated with caregiver interventions may actually be lower than those associated with adverse caregiver outcomes such as acute and chronic physical illness. As a result, this line of research may effectively influence support for existing and future caregiver services.

Another future activity would be to see if merging different successful strategies might be a viable next stage of research. One specific activity might be the translation of these findings into programs and services that can be easily adopted by practitioners, with an emphasis on interventions that broaden caregiver options and increase communication between informal networks and formal services in order to more effectively balance informal and formal care provision. Researchers, practitioners, and policymakers alike need to move away from simplistic views of family versus societal care and begin to frame research questions and service policies in terms of a partnership between family care and social services.

This next generation of intervention research might also focus on uncovering which interventions are most effective for caregivers with certain characteristics or individual difference variables identified during the intake process. By carefully studying aptitude by treatment interaction effects, researchers can develop an empirical base to decide who is most likely to benefit from a given intervention (Snow, 1991). Investigators from the California site, for example, found that two groups of caregivers with contrasting anger expression styles responded differently to two separate types of psychoeducational classes designed to improve their emotional well-being (Gallagher-Thompson, Coon, & Thompson, 1996). This kind of information could conserve program resources by streamlining the treatment process and increasing treatment success and maintenance of gains.

While the REACH Program's common data set will enable the assessment of intervention effects on caregiver well-being and burden and other variables through preplanned meta-analytic strategies, not all domains measured in the battery are assessed with the same rigor, given the availability of psychometrically sound and relatively brief measures. For example, although the Core Battery does gather some cost data that may help guide the future expansion or reduction of intervention resources necessary in order to achieve successful outcomes, the data are not intended to represent a definitive test of intervention cost-effectiveness. Therefore, additional research is needed before definitive conclusions can be drawn based on meta-analyses of REACH cost data and other less rigorously assessed domains. Still, both the Core Battery and the site-specific measurement batteries do afford the opportunity to expand caregiving norms, compare this sizable group of caregivers with national norms on well-established measures, investigate relationships between measures, explore less well-known but promising constructs and their measures in site-specific cases, and collect additional data to further explore the psychometric properties of measures for future research. In doing so, the REACH Program will shed light on several important areas of caregiver research for the decade ahead.

Finally, it is of critical importance to continue to gain understanding of the caregiving experiences of ethnic and racial minority caregivers and other minority groups neglected in the literature (male caregivers, gay and lesbian caregivers, friends and neighbors, the poor), for they too shoulder many of the burdens of informal care. Information regarding caregiving and caregiver interventions among Asian Pacific Islander groups and Native American tribes is noticeably absent. The door is still open to specify and examine theoretically sound and creative interventions for dementia caregivers in a variety of minority caregiving populations and to extend our knowledge about effective caregiver interventions among these populations with regard to other types of disorders (e.g., the functionally impaired and mentally ill). Given the heterogeneity of caregiving experiences reported within the majority community, there is no reason to expect homogeneity within or across minority caregiving communities. Even caregivers and their families do not always share common beliefs and expectations regarding the roles and responsibilities of caregiving. Therefore, future research might benefit from exploring how caregivers try to maintain optimal caregiving conditions within their own understanding of their sociocultural context (Gallagher-Thompson et al., in press). Researchers could then incorporate many of these beneficial strategies into the most successful interventions and disseminate the results across sociocultural contexts where appropriate.

Thus, the REACH Program will provide a systematic test of well-specified and theory-based interventions designed to strengthen the capacity of family members to care for their loved ones with ADRD. Although new scientific breakthroughs may help postpone or ameliorate the symptoms of dementia, researchers, service providers, and policymakers must remember that there still exists an urgent need to assist the growing number of ADRD caregivers of the foreseeable future.

REFERENCES

Archbold. P. G., Stewart, B. J., Harvath, T. A., & Lucas, S. A. (1986). *New measures of concepts central to an understanding of caregiving.* Unpublished manuscript. School of Nursing, Oregon Health Sciences University.

Bandura, A. (1977). Self-efficacy: Toward a unifying theory of behavioral change. *Psychological Review, 84,* 191–215.

Bandura, A. (1982). Self-efficacy mechanism in human agency. *American Psychologist, 37,* 122–147.

Bandura, A. (1989). Human agency in social cognitive theory. *American Psychologist, 44,* 1175–1184.

Barrera, M., Sandler, I., & Ramsey, T. (1981). Preliminary development of a scale of social support: Studies on college students. *American Journal of Community Psychology, 9,* 435–447.

Barris, R., Kielhofner, G., Levine, R., & Neville, A. (1985). Occupation as interaction with the environment. In G. Kielhofner & J. Burke (Eds.), *A model of human occupation: Theory and application* (pp. 42–62). Baltimore: Williams and Wilkins.

Beck, A. T., Rush, J., Shaw, B., & Emery, G. (1979). *Cognitive therapy of depression.* New York: Guilford Press.

Becker, M. N. (1992). Theoretical models of adherence and strategies for improving adherence. In S. A. Shumaker et al. (Eds.), *The handbook of health behavior change* (pp. 5–43). New York: Springer.

Berkman, L. F., & Syme, S. L. (1979). Social networks, host resistance and mortality: A nine-year follow-up study of Alameda County residents. *American Journal of Epidemiology, 109,* 186–204.

Bourgeois, M. S., Burgio, L. D., Schulz, R., Beach, S., & Palmer, B. (1997). Modifying repetitive verbalization of community dwelling patients with AD. *Gerontologist, 37,* 30–39.

Bourgeois, M. S., Schulz, R., & Burgio, L. (1996). Intervention for caregivers of patients with Alzheimer's disease: A review and analysis of content, process, and outcomes. *International Journal of Human Development, 43,* 35–92.

Burgio, L. D. (1997). Behavioral assessment and treatment of disruptive vocalization. *Seminars in Clinical Neuropsychiatry, 2,* 123–131.

Burgio, L. D., & Bourgeois, M. S. (1992). Treating severe behavioral disorders in geriatric residential settings. *Behavioral Residential Treatment*, *7*, 145–168.

Burgio, L. D., Jones, L. T., Butler, F., & Engel, B. T. (1988). The prevalence of geriatric behavior problems in an urban nursing home. *Journal of Gerontological Nursing*, *14*, 31–34.

Burgio, L. D., Scilley, K., Hoar, T., Washington, C., & Tunstall, A. (1993). Behavioral interventions for disruptive vocalizations in elderly nursing home residents with dementia (Sepcial issue #1). *Gerontologist*, *33*, 110.

Cobb, S. (1976). Social support as a moderator of life stress. *Psychosomatic Medicine*, *38*, 300–313.

Corcoran, M., & Gitlin, L. N. (1991). Environmental influences on behavior of the elderly with dementia: Principles for intervention in the home. *Occupational Therapy and Physical Therapy in Geriatrics*, *9*, 5–21.

Czaja, S. J., Guerrier, J., Nair, S., & Landauer, T. (1993). Computer communication as an aid to independence for older adults. *Behavior and Information Technology*, *12*, 197–207.

Dean, A., & Lin, N. (1977). The stress buffering role of social support: Problems and prospects for systematic investigation. *Journal of Nervous and Mental Disease*, *165*, 403–417.

Evans, R. L., Smith, K. M., Werkhoven, W. S., Fox, H. R., & Pritzl, D. O. (1986). Cognitive telephone group therapy with physically disabled elderly persons. *Gerontologist*, *26*, 8–11.

Finch J. F., Okun, M. A., Barrera, M., Zautra, A. J., & Reich, J. W. (1989). Positive and negative social ties among older adults: Measurement models and the prediction of psychological distress and well being. *American Journal of Community Psychology*, *17*, 585–605.

Folkman, S., Schaeffer, C., & Lazarus, R. (1979). Cognitive processes as mediators of stress and coping. In V. Hamilton & D. Warburton (Eds.), *Human stress and cognition* (pp. 265–298). Chichester: John Wiley & Sons.

Folstein, M. F., Folstein, S. E., & McHugh, P. R. (1975). Mini-Mental State: A practical method for grading the cognitive state of patients for the clinician. *Journal of Psychiatric Research, 12*, 189–198.

Gallagher-Thompson, D. (1994). Direct services and interventions for caregivers: A review of extant programs and a look to the future. In M. H. Cantor (Ed.), *Family caregiving: Agenda for the future* (pp. 102–122). San Francisco: American Society on Aging.

Gallagher-Thompson, D., Coon, D. W., Rivera, P., Powers, D., & Zeiss, A. M. (in press). In M. Hersen & V. B. Van Hasselt (Eds.), *Handbook of clinical geropsychology*. New York: Plenum.

Gallagher-Thompson, D., Coon, D. W., & Thompson, L. W. (1996, November). *Anger expression by type of treatment interaction predicts treatment outcome in family caregivers.* Presented at the annual meeting of the Gerontological Society of America, Washington, DC.

Gitlin, L. N., & Corcoran, M. (1996). Managing dementia at home: The role of home environmental modifications. *Topics in Geriatric Rehabilitation*, *12*, 28–39.

Gold, D. P., Cohen, C., Shulman, K., Zucchero, C., Andres, D., & Etezad, J. (1995). Caregiving and dementia: Predicting negative and positive outcomes for caregivers. *International Journal of Aging and Human Development*, *41*, 183–201.

Gonyea, J. G. (1989). Alzheimer's disease support groups: An analysis of their structure, format and perceived benefits. *Social Work in Health Care*, *14*, 61–72.

Granger, C. V., Hamilton, B. B., & Sherwin, F. A. (1986). *Guide for use of the uniform data set for medical rehabilitation.* Buffalo, NY: Department of Rehabilitation Medicine, Buffalo General Hospital.

Guy, D. H. (1995). Telephone care for elders: Physical, psychosocial and legal aspects. *Journal of Gerontological Nursing, 21,* 27–34.

Haley, W. E., Levine, E. G., Brown, S. L., & Bartolucci, A. A. (1987). Stress, appraisal, coping and social support as predictors of adaptational outcome among dementia caregivers. *Psychology and Aging, 2,* 323–330.

Haley, W. E., Roth, D. L., Coleton, M., Ford, G. R., West, C. A. C., Collins, R. P., & Isobe, T. (1996). Appraisal, coping, and social support as mediators of well-being in black and white family caregivers of patients with Alzheimer's disease. *Journal of Consulting and Clinical Psychology, 64,* 121–129.

Haley, W. E., West, C. A. C., Wadley, V. G., Ford, G. R., White, F. A., Barrett, J. J., Harrell, L. E., & Roth, D. L. (1995). Psychological, social and health impact of caregiving: A comparison of black and white dementia family caregivers and noncaregivers. *Psychology and Aging, 10,* 540–552.

Katz, S., Ford, A. B., Moskowitz, R. W., Jackson, B. A., & Jaffe, M. W. (1963). Studies of illness in the aged. The index of ADL: A standardized measure of biological and psychological function. *JAMA, 185,* 914–919.

Knight, B. G., Lutzky, S. M., & Macofsky-Urban, F. (1993). A meta-analytic review of interventions for caregiver distress: Recommendations for future research. *Gerontologist, 33,* 240–248.

Kramer, B. J., & Kipnis, S. (1995). Eldercare and work-role conflict: Toward an understanding of gender differences in caregiver burden. *Gerontologist, 35,* 340–348.

Krause, N. (1995). Negative interaction and satisfaction with support among older adults. *Journal of Gerontology: Psychological Sciences, 50B,* 59–73.

Lawton, M. P., & Brody, E. M. (1969). Assessment of older people: Self-maintaining and instrumental activities of daily living. *Gerontologist, 9,* 179–186

Lawton, M. P., Moss, M., Kleban, M. H., Glicksman, A., & Rovine, M. (1991). A two-factor model of caregiving appraisal and psychological well-being. *Journal of Gerontology: Psychological Sciences, 46,* P181–P189.

Lawton, M. P., & Nahemow, L. E. (1973). Ecology and the aging process. In C. Eisdorfer & M. P. Lawton (Eds.), *The psychology of adult development and aging* (pp. 619–674). Washington, DC: American Psychological Association.

Lazarus, R., & Launeir, R. (1978). Stress-related transactions between persons and environment. In L. Pervin & M. Lewis (Eds.), *Perspectives in international psychology* (pp. 287–325). New York: Plenum.

Leirer, V. O., Morrow, D. G., Tanke, E. D., & Pariante G. M. (1991). Elders' nonadherence: Its assessment and medication reminding by voice mail. *Gerontologist, 31,* 514–520.

Lewinsohn, P. M., Munoz, R. F., Youngren, M. A., & Zeiss, A. M. (1986). *Control your depression.* New York: Prentice-Hall.

Lewinsohn, P. M., Sullivan, J. M., & Grosscup, S. (1982). Behavioral therapy: Clinical applications. In A. J. Rush (Ed.), *Short-term psychotherapies for depression* (pp. 50–87). New York: Guilford Press.

Lichstein, K. L., Riedel, B. W., & Grieve, R. (1994). Fair tests of clinical trials: A treatment implementation model. *Advances in Behavior Research and Therapy, 16,* 1–29.

Lockery, S. A. (1991, Fall/Winter). Family and social supports: Caregiving among racial and ethnic minority elders. *Generations, 15,* 58–62.

Lubben, J. E. (1988). Assessing social networks among elderly populations. *Family & Community Health, 11,* 42–52.

Mittelman, M. S., & Gallagher-Thompson, D. (1996). Valuing intervention research. *Journal of Gerontology: Social Sciences, 51B*, S268.

Montgomery, R. J. V. (1996). Advancing caregiver research: Weighing efficacy and feasibility of interventions. *Journal of Gerontology: Social Sciences, 51B*, S109-S110.

Ory, M., & Schulz, R. (1996, November). *Resources for enhancing Alzheimer's caregiver health (REACH): Innovative approaches to AD caregiving interventions.* Symposium at the annual meeting of the Gerontological Society of America, Washington, DC.

Pearlin, L. I. (1992). The careers of caregivers. *Gerontologist, 32*, 647.

Pearlin, L. I., Mullan, J. T., Semple, S. J., & Skaff, M. M. (1990). Caregiving and the stress process: An overview of concepts and their measures. *Gerontologist, 30*, 583–595.

Radloff, L. S. (1977). The CES-D scale: A self-report depression scale for research in the general population. *Applied Psychological Measurement, 1*, 382–401.

Russo, J., Vitaliano, P. P., Brewer, D., Katon, W., & Becker, J. (1995). Psychiatric disorders in spouse caregivers of care-recipients with Alzheimer's disease and matched controls: A diathesis-stress model of psychopathology. *Journal of Abnormal Psychology, 194*, 197–204.

Scharlach, A. E. (1994). Caregiving and employment: Competing or complementary roles? *Gerontologist, 34*, 378–385.

Schulz, R., Newsom, J., Mittelmark, M., Burton, L., Hirsch, C., & Jackson, S. (1997). Health effects of caregiving: The Caregiver Health Effects Study. *Annals of Behavioral Medicine, 19*, 110–115.

Schulz, R., & O'Brien, A. T. (1994). Alzheimer's disease caregiving: An overview. *Seminars in Speech and Language, 15*, 185–193.

Schulz, R., O'Brien, A. T., Bookwala, J., & Fleissner, K. (1995). Psychiatric and physical morbidity effects of dementia caregiving: Prevalence, correlates, and causes. *Gerontologist, 35*, 771–791.

Schulz, R., Visintainer, P., & Williamson, G. M. (1990). Psychiatric and physical morbidity effects of caregiving. *Journal of Gerontology: Psychological Sciences, 45*, P181–P191.

Shank, C. J., Murphy, M., & Schulte-Mowry, L. (1991). Patient preferences regarding educational pamphlets in the family practice center. *Journal of Family Practice, 23*, 429–243.

Skaff, M. M., Pearlin, L. I., & Mullan, J. T. (1996). Transition in the caregiving career: Effects on sense of mastery. *Psychology and Aging, 11*, 247–257.

Snow, R. E. (1991). Aptitude-treatment interaction as a framework for research on individual differences in psychotherapy. *Journal of Consulting and Clinical Psychology, 59*, 205–216.

Spielberger, C. D., Gorsuch, R. L., Lushene, P. R., Vagg, P. R., & Jacobs, G. A. (1983). *State-Trait Anxiety Inventory for Adults (STAIS-AD) Manual.* Palo Alto, CA: Consulting Psychologist Press.

Szapocznik, J., Kurtines, W. M., Perez-Vidal, A., Hervis, O. E., & Foote, F. (1989). One person family therapy. In R. A. Wells, & V. J. Giannetti (Eds.), *Handbook of brief psychotherapies* (pp. 493–510). New York: Plenum.

Teri, L., Truax, P., Logsdon, R., Uomoto, J., Zarit, S., & Vitalino, P. P. (1992). Assessment of behavioral problems in dementia: The Revised Memory and Behavior Problems Checklist. *Psychology and Aging, 7*(4), 622–631.

Thompson, L. W. (1996). *Self-efficacy for caregiving: Shortform.* Unpublished manuscript, Stanford University.

Villa, M. L., Cuellar, J. B., Gamel, N., & Yeo, G. (1993). Aging and health: Hispanic American elders (2nd ed.). SGEC Working Paper Series: No. 5, Ethnogeriatric Reviews. Stanford, CA: Stanford Geriatric Education Center.

Vitaliano, P. P., Russo, J., Young, H. M., Teri, L., & Maiuro, R. D. (1991). Predictors of burden in spouse caregivers of individuals with Alzheimer's disease. *Psychology and Aging, 6,* 392–402.
Weeks, J. R., & Cuellar, J. B. (1981). The role of family members in helping networks of older people. *Gerontologist, 21,* 388–394.
Wright, L., Clipp, E., & George, L. (1993). Health consequences of caregiver stress. *Medicine, Exercise, Nutrition, and Health, 2,* 181–195.
Zarit, S. H., & Teri, L. (1992). Interventions and services for family caregivers. In K. W. Schaie & M. Powell Lawton (Eds.), *Annual review of gerontology and geriatrics* (Vol. 11, pp. 287–310). New York: Springer.
Zeiss, A. M., Gallagher-Thompson, D., & Bandura, A. (1992). *Self-efficacy for caregiving.* Unpublished manuscript, Stanford University.

Appendix

The principal investigators of the REACH Study Group include:

Louis Burgio, Ph.D., University of Alabama, Birmingham in Birmingham, Alabama
Robert Burns, M.D., Veterans Affairs Medical Center, Memphis, Tennessee
Carl Eisdorfer, M.D., Ph.D., University of Miami, Miami, Florida,
Dolores Gallagher-Thompson, Ph.D., Veterans Affairs Palo Alto Health Care System and Stanford University School of Medicine, Palo Alto, California
Laura Gitlin, Ph.D., Thomas Jefferson University, Philadelphia, Pennsylvania
Diane Mahoney, Ph.D., Boston Medical Center, Boston, Massachusetts
Richard Schulz, Ph.D., University of Pittsburgh, Pittsburgh, Pennsylvania

Conclusion

This volume has presented information, with contributions from authors representing a number of disciplines and professions concerned with human services, about a variety of practice and service delivery innovations for a wide array of problems with a range of population groups across the lifespan.[1] Innovations presented include a multiplicity of practice and service delivery approaches that require the use of multidisciplinary teams. These presentations reinforce our conviction in designing this volume that the development and implementation of innovations in service delivery and practice benefit from the contributions of a wide variety of disciplines and professions.

Having reviewed the range of innovative programs representing the work of authors from different disciplines and focusing on different vulnerable populations across the lifespan, what general themes can we identify? While there are many differences, a number of similarities are apparent.

First, vulnerable populations that are often viewed as homogeneous groups are, in fact, more heterogeneous than might be anticipated, and, for services to be effective, subgroup analyses leading to differential practice and service delivery approaches must be undertaken. We must move beyond the "one size fits all" approach that offers the same programs and services to broad groups of at-risk individuals, such as high-risk infants, and instead tailor services to at-risk subgroup populations. Although this is already being done in a number of fields, further research is needed to more fully understand what programs and services work best for what subpopulations under which conditions.

Second, vulnerable populations have multiple needs and, thus, require multiple services. The design of the services therefore needs to draw upon a wide range of theories and intervention approaches. Service programs should be comprehensive, and their design requires that the parts be interrelated. These requirements reflect much greater complexity than traditional programs and represent major issues in management. Particular attention needs to be paid to populations whose problems span the boundaries of more than one service delivery system, for example, adults with severe mental illness who also abuse alcohol or drugs.

---

[1]Except where noted by a full reference, text citations refer to authors of chapters in this volume.

Third, increasingly, the assessment of the needs of vulnerable population groups goes beyond individual assessment and stresses the context of the problem, including family, social network, community, and environmental factors as the focus of interventions. Even for problems that have a medical basis, interventions identify and address the social consequences, both as a buffer to prevent future difficulties and as an adjunct to treatment. Increasingly, the use of developmental and strengths-oriented theories, rather than a pathological orientation, gives direction to needs assessments.

Fourth, based on this broadening of the assessment process, a wide range of interventions are being utilized in a wide variety of combinations. For example, as will be seen later, skill learning, resource acquisition, social activities, use of the arts, and work preparation have been added to approaches that previously relied solely on relationship and verbalization as the basis for bringing about change.

Fifth, many of the innovations presented in this volume require additional and new staff skills and the ability to function as a member of a multidisciplinary team. As several of the authors identify, professional education has been slow in responding to these needs and often acts as a barrier to needed change, rather than as a leader or supporter of innovation. Too often, students do not get experience in working as members of multidisciplinary teams and lack opportunities to interact and learn from professionals in related disciplines. For example, despite the fact that institutional care for the aged requires social workers, nurses, and physicians to collaborate regarding patient care and communications with families, social work, nursing, and medical students often do not have any opportunities to interact with one another as part of their professional training.

Sixth, with the exception of the chapter by Lorion and colleagues, which calls for a public health, preventive approach to urban violence, the innovations presented in this volume do not address prevention as a major goal of the programs. This omission is probably an artifact of the editors' instructions to the authors to focus on an identified "problem" population, and, therefore, populations that already displayed the problem were chosen.

Seventh, not surprisingly, the innovations presented in this volume vary considerably in the degree to which they have been put to empirical tests. Though the need for further research to examine the effectiveness of interventions is an issue for the entire human services field, it is particularly important with regard to the examination of innovative practice and service delivery approaches. We have some concern, based on past experience in the human services field, that the search for panaceas for the difficult and often seemingly intractable problems faced by vulnerable populations may lead to the widespread adoption of ideas that are attractive and cost-effective and that seem to make sense but that in reality may not work well at all.

Although, as we have seen, there are a number of cross-cutting themes in this volume, we find ourselves left with the same concern we raised in the Introduction, namely, the need to develop a more systematic approach to the analysis of innovations that could be applied across problems and populations. This could offer a means whereby we could better synthesize the knowledge being developed by the various disciplines. Building on previous work (Blum,

1994) and utilizing the chapters in this volume, we have developed a framework for analyzing innovations in service delivery and practice. Our objective is to present an analytic framework that represents a disaggregation of service delivery and practice into common components across substantive areas and populations. This disaggregation will help to address the nagging question of what we really mean by "innovation." Utilization of the framework is intended to permit systematic comparison among programs and practices as to their theoretical rationale and structure, to identify common themes or program elements, and to highlight gaps and areas for which the need exists for innovation.

Goals of the Framework

Our framework has three goals as follows:

Goal I. *To disaggregate service delivery and practice into* common *components that would permit systematic analyses of innovations across fields and substantive areas.*

The word "innovation" has been used to depict any changes that have occurred in service delivery and practice without clearly identifying what elements have changed or the specifics of the changes that have taken place. This has made it difficult to systematically compare changes across innovations. As the field of human services has become more and more specialized and compartmentalized, mechanisms and classification schemes are needed to assist in knowledge transfer among disciplines and across substantive areas. Innovations that are developed in a particular field or substantive area are often unknown to practitioners in other fields and areas and, thus, are not available for consideration as to their usefulness. The framework provides a set of common components that cuts across fields and substantive areas and provides a means of classifying and bringing together knowledge in a way that permits easy access and analysis. The use of a common components approach can address barriers to knowledge exchange on alternative ways of designing and delivering services. Thus, the use of a framework that has common components helps neutralize one of the negative consequences of specialization.

Goal II. *To provide a systematic means for undertaking comparisons among programs.*

Once a way of disaggregating service delivery and practice has been established, we can begin to compare programs as to their similarities and differences in relation to each program component. Program titles are often deceptive when we begin to probe similarities and differences for each component. Also, agencies often tend to make adaptation in programs or adopt changes that apply to only selected components of an innovation. Thus, if we rely only on program titles for comparison, we will often be comparing apples and oranges, or undefined salads, in our evaluations across programs. In recognition of past shortcomings in comparisons of programs that were the same in title but inherently different in substance (e.g., case management programs in the mental health field and family preservation programs in child welfare), researchers have begun to develop empirical measures to examine program fidelity to the consistency between the theoretical design and the actual program delivery.

Also, if there is an intent to replicate programs, it is essential that not only the general thrusts of the programs be the same but that they be the same in relation to the various components identified in the framework. Comparison and replication require much greater specification than is often provided in program descriptions. Thus, attention to the fidelity of a program requires examination of its program components.

Goal III. *To provide a means for identifying common themes among innovations and gaps related to the various components.*

Are there common themes emerging in the development of innovations that address the needs of vulnerable populations across the life cycle? If such themes can be identified, they would provide direction for future developments. Likewise, if gaps can be identified and related to specific components, this could lead to greater specification and concentration of future efforts. With these goals in mind, we turn next to a presentation and discussion of the framework.

Framework for the Analysis of Service Delivery and Practice

Service delivery, as used in this chapter, includes all those activities that an organization must perform to fulfill its mission, beginning with a definition of the population to be served and proceeding through follow-up services and monitoring and evaluation. Agencies may include in their system multiple services and practices such as counseling, housing, financial assistance, and medical care. Thus, a much more detailed analysis of services is required. In addition to the broad components of a service delivery system outlined in our framework, practice is further disaggregated into its common elements in Section VI of the framework. Our framework is not intended to deal with administrative, management, policy, or fiscal considerations, as important as they are, but focuses solely on services.

The nine identified service delivery components in the framework and the seven practice elements listed in Section VI of the framework represent an attempt to strike a balance between creating a too-detailed list of categories, on one hand, or a too-broad set of categories, on the other. We believe that the nine service delivery and the seven practice elements represent the essential elements and major areas in which service delivery and practice innovations can and are taking place.

Discussion of each of the components follows, together with examples of innovations related to each of the components, drawn for illustrative purposes from the chapters in this volume. Space does not permit us, nor is it our objective, to present a comprehensive application of the framework to each of the chapters.

I. DEFINITION OF THE SERVICE POPULATION, NEEDS ANALYSIS, AND THE RANGE OF SERVICES TO BE OFFERED

Each of the chapters addresses the parameters of the vulnerable population to be served and demonstrates the variability and gaps in available data. The authors, however, stress the importance of careful definitions of the populations

I. Definition of the Service Population, Needs Analysis, and the Range of Services to be Offered
II. Case Finding
III. Screening Clients for Services Within the Organization
IV. Referral to Other Agencies for Services
V. Assessment for Specific Service Needs and Setting of Outcome Goals
VI. Analysis of Services
  1. Developmental and Intervention Theories
  2. Target and Foci of the Intervention (Individual, family, group, community, etc.)
  3. Duration and Intensity of the Intervention
  4. Setting of the Intervention (Agency, home, community, etc.)
  5. Medium through which Change or Learning Occurs
    a. Relationship
    b. Verbalization
    c. Skill Learning (skills of daily living, problem solving, coping, parenting, etc.)
    d. Resource Acquisition
    e. Social Activities
    f. Arts (visual, dance, music, etc.)
    g. Preparation and Adjustment to Work
    h. Religious Faith and Spirituality
  6. Background of the Staff
  7. Role of the Worker and Use of Multidisciplinary Teams
VII. Linkages Among Services and with Other Organizations
VIII. Follow-up as a Service
IX. Monitoring the Service System and Evaluation of Outcomes

Figure C.1 Framework for the Analysis of Innovations in Service Delivery and Practice

and, most important, the identification of subgroups for whom differential services may be required.

Needs analysis of the population and the identification of population subgroups stress the variations in the needs of subgroup members and the complexity involved in designing differential programs to meet differential needs. Consistently, however, the analyses in the chapters in this volume, as previously noted, encompass not only the individual but the context within which the individual functions and thus also include a focus on the family, the community, and the environment. Multiple explanatory theories drawn from a number of disciplines characterize the theoretical orientations used to understand the needs of vulnerable populations and to give direction to the development of needed services.

To address the multiple needs of specific subpopulations, a wide range of services is suggested, including sociopsychological, educational, resource acquisition, work preparation, medical, housing, and other services. Many services are community based and targeted to individuals, families, groups, communities, and institutions.

II. CASE FINDING

A characteristic of many vulnerable populations is their reluctance to utilize existing services or to respond positively to traditional methods of case finding that depend on voluntary, self-motivated initiatives. Lee, in this volume, stresses the need for aggressive, street-level outreach to the homeless and the use of community-based workers located in homeless shelters. Zweben and Rose propose that nondependent drinkers can be identified within the current caseloads of social service, mental health, and medical organizations if assessment for this problem is added to intake procedures. The ACT program, discussed by Solomon, contacts persons with mental illness while they are still in the hospital in order to enlist them for community-based services. Groza discusses the use of computers and the Internet to recruit adoptive parents.

New approaches are being developed that recognize the characteristics of vulnerable populations and decide which are better tailored to recruit the hard to reach groups. However, case-finding continues to be a major service delivery concern. Even with highly targeted case-finding approaches, service systems must monitor their programs to see if they are indeed recruiting clients whose characteristics are representative of the service population and its subgroups.

III. SCREENING CLIENTS FOR SERVICES WITHIN THE ORGANIZATION

Screening represents the "gatekeeping" function of service delivery. Case-finding approaches, however carefully designed, recruit some clients who do not meet the criteria for services. Littell and Schuerman call attention to the problem of inappropriate referrals of clients who do not meet the service criteria for family preservation programs. A number of the authors raise concern about the current trend in case management, which could result in screening out and denying services to some of the most vulnerable populations. Among these groups are clients who do not have resources, such as insurance, or who represent subpopulations that are difficult to serve and that will not enhance the organization's success rates. Historically, the most needy populations have been underrepresented in service programs. This is expected to become even a more critical problem with the growth of managed care health and social welfare programs. Monitoring who survives the screening process and how representative they are of the defined service population is therefore a critical endeavor.

IV. REFERRAL TO OTHER AGENCIES FOR SERVICES

Given the multiple needs of vulnerable populations, few service programs can meet these needs within a single organization and therefore must refer clients to other organizations for additional services. In addition to individuals who have been inappropriately recruited, services to specific populations, such as high-risk infants, neglected and abused children, the mentally ill, and the homeless, must access services provided by a number of organizations. The authors in this volume consistently recognize that many of these populations often lack knowledge of available services, are unable because of their problems to pursue these services, and need assistance with forms and screening procedures if they are to survive the intake processes. Thus, assistance beyond information giving is often required.

Programs have developed procedures to address these issues, ranging from telephone calls, assignment of staff who assist clients with forms, to actually accompanying clients and offering support throughout the intake process. In some instances, such as programs for the homeless, mentally ill, and the retarded, agencies have taken proactive roles in advocating, along with clients and caregivers. for the development of needed services not currently available in the community, More formal arrangements and linkages among organizations are discussed in component VII.

V. ASSESSMENT OF SPECIFIC SERVICE NEEDS AND SETTING OF OUTCOME GOALS

Although some assessment is undertaken during the screening process, more intensive procedures are required to specify the nature of specific services to meet specific outcome goals. Repeatedly, authors in this volume stress the importance of specifying outcome goals both as a guide for services and as a requirement in order to evaluate the effectiveness of programs. Goals may change during the treatment process, as demonstrated by Zweben and Rose in the treatment of nondependent drinkers, or goals may build through a sequence of services, as discussed by Solomon and Lee in relation to persons with mental illness and the homeless, respectively, but, for each stage of the treatment or service process, goal specification is required.

Assessment protocols have been broadened to include, along with assessment of individual needs, assessment of the family, support networks, community influences, and environmental conditions as a means of specifying needed interventions in some, or all, of these areas. Singer and colleagues, Zweben and Rose, and Coon and colleagues all suggest the use of scales, measurement instruments, and checklists during the assessment process in an effort to make assessment more systematic, to achieve added insight into client functioning, and to establish baseline data that can be used in evaluating outcomes.

VI. ANALYSIS OF SERVICES

To analyze innovations in services, this component of the service delivery system, which can be considered by itself as a subframework for analyzing innovations in practice, must also be disaggregated. We propose an examination of each of seven elements that together constitute a service. The programs discussed in the volume include wide variations in relation to each of the elements.

Developmental and Intervention Theories

Turner, in the first chapter, identifies the dramatic increase in the number and richness of developmental and intervention theories that has taken place over the past three decades in human services. We now have available a wide variety of theories from which to draw upon in our attempt to assess and assist vulnerable populations. As can be seen in a review of the theoretical rationales for the interventions described by the authors of each of the chapters in this volume, we find support for Turner's assumption that to serve vulnerable populations, we can draw from a wide assortment of theories. What is critical is that each of the many theories that were utilized provided clear direction to the nature of the interventions and impacted on each of the components in our analytic framework.

Although the innovations were based on different theories and were applied to design interventions to meet differential needs, there was agreement on the necessity for a clear theoretical rationale for the innovation. It is only as we develop theory-driven programs and undertake systematic evaluations that we can test the theories and the derived interventions to determine which theories are helpful and which should be modified or discarded.

Target and Foci of the Intervention

On the basis of different explanatory theories, we can target our interventions differentially at individuals, families, groups, communities, and the environment. The foci of the intervention goes a step beyond an identification of the actors and calls attention to what is to be changed. For instance, family interventions can focus on changing the behavior of individual family members or on changing the interactions within the family and, through these changes in interaction, impact the behavior of individual members (as discussed by Groza in relation to work with adoptive parents). Although the desired result are changes in individual functioning, these can brought about by interventions directly targeted to the individual (Zweben and Rose, Camp and Mattern), to the family (Singer and colleagues, Groza, Littell and Schuerman), to the group (Lee), to the community (Solomon, Lorion and colleagues, Braddock), to the institutional environment (Kahana and colleagues), or to a combination of these. The choice of both targets and foci, however, is dependent on the developmental and intervention theories utilized to give direction to the program. Overall, most of the described innovations differentially utilize multiple targets and foci to meet multiple needs.

Duration and Intensity of the Intervention

Depending on the theory utilized and the outcome goals of the intervention, both intensity (length of an interview) and duration (length of the treatment process) varied greatly in the described interventions. Zweben and Rose in their presentation of brief therapy suggest changes in both intensity and duration of interventions with nondependent drinkers. In their research with caregivers of Alzheimer patients, Coon and colleagues describe a systematic, theory-derived set of planned variations in duration and intensity of interventions that test the impact of variations on outcomes. The chapters by Solomon and by Lee call attention to the need for ongoing care and support of persons with serious and persistent mental illness and the homeless. Singer and colleagues also suggest long-term approaches for infants at risk, including periodic examination for delayed responses to early deficiencies. A number of the authors warn against the dangers involved in managed care, which may limit duration and intensity solely on the basis of fiscal concerns, rather than because of a theoretical understanding or the setting of appropriate outcome goals.

Setting of the Intervention

A wide variety of settings, such as an agency, client's home, workplace, and community, can be utilized in human services programs depending on explanatory theories, the client's needs, and established outcome goals. In addition, the recognition that some target populations have multiple needs has led not only to the creation of multiple service networks, but also to discussion of where each of the services should be located and provided. Considerations of appropriateness of setting have also included concerns about access, transportation, and decentralization.

Examples of the use of a range of possible service settings can be found in the chapters of this volume. Among these are the community (chapters by Lorion and colleagues, Solomon, Braddock, and Lee); family residence (Singer and colleagues, Groza, and Littell and Schuerman); agency (Zweben and Rose, Camp and Mattern, and Coon and colleagues); institution (Kahana and colleagues); and a combination of these. The setting in which interventions are delivered must be responsive to the needs and characteristics of vulnerable populations.

Medium Through Which Change or Learning Occurs

The listing in the framework of the range of potential approaches that can be employed to meet the client's needs (see Figure C.1) represents both the wide range of potential intervention theories that can be utilized and the setting of differential outcome goals. The innovations presented in this volume include the utilization of this entire range of approaches and various combinations. For example, skill learning (Camp and Mattern), problem solving (Zweben and Rose), resource acquisition (chapters by Solomon and Lee), social activities such as meals (Kahana and colleagues), and preparation for work (chapters by Solomon and by Lee) represent only a small sample of the variations discussed in this volume. These variations in approaches reinforce Turner's identification of the wide range of options that is currently available and the need to make systematic and theory-based choices as to which interventions in order to test which are most effective.

Background of the Staff

As new theories and intervention approaches have been developed, consideration of the theoretical background and skill repertoire of the staff has become as important as or more important than professional identity. Staff training is an essential component of many of the programs discussed in this volume, regardless of the professional background of the staff, since the theoretical orientations and related worker skills are not currently included in professional education. Other variables such as gender, race, socioeconomic status, indigenous status, and recovery from an illness such as alcoholism must also be considered. In comparing and replicating programs, staff background variables must be identified and be comparable.

Role of the Worker and the Use of Multidisciplinary Teams

New explanatory and change theories have led to new definitions of worker roles that expand traditional designations such as caseworker or therapist to include educator, enabler, mediator, consultant, and advocate. Each of these new designations involves specific worker tasks, goals, and, often, new required skills. Professional education has not, in many instances, included training for these new roles, and, thus, in-service training in these roles is required in many programs.

To meet the multiple needs of vulnerable populations, such as infants at risk, persons with mental illness, or persons with mental retardation, it has been necessary to develop multidisciplinary teams. Depending on the needs of the population, a variety of different combinations of disciplines is represented on these teams. Repeatedly, in those programs that utilize teams, the authors in this volume note a lack of preparation and experience among all the professionals in the team process and the role of team member. Current professional education does not adequately address this development, nor are team experiences provided as an integral part of the curriculum.

VII. LINKAGES AMONG SERVICES AND WITH OTHER ORGANIZATIONS

Rothman, in his research review of innovative organizations, finds that organizations that are innovative have more extensive linkages with other organizations. In order to create the range of necessary services, organizations must create linkages among service providers. These arrangements can take various forms—coalitions of agencies, formal arrangements, informal agreements, or referrals through the normal intake channels.

Likewise, coordination of multiple services within a multiservice agency is essential. A number of the authors of chapters in this volume discuss the development of case managers whose role it is to develop a system of services around the needs of the clients through both coordination of services internal to the organization and linkages with other organizations. Formal agreements among organizations greatly assist in this process and smooth the way for successful coordination and referral. A caution is raised, however, that for case managers to coordinate services, these services must be available in the agency or community. Increasingly, it has been necessary to be able to pay for these services in order to access them.

VIII. FOLLOW-UP AS A SERVICE

Follow-up services are defined as agency-initiated plans for periodic checkups with clients over an extended period of time. Like regular dental examinations or physical examinations or special diagnostic tests for successfully treated cancer patients, these ongoing evaluation and support services are needed by the vulnerable population. Too often, agencies terminate services as if the problem were "fixed" or with an indication that the client, if necessary, can reenter the system in the future as a new case. Singer and colleagues indicate the need for continual follow-up with high-risk infants regarding possible delayed responses; Solomon points out the need for long-term care for persons with severe mental illness, as does Braddock for persons with mental retardation. Coon and colleagues describe planned telephone and group meetings with caregivers after initial interventions. Other authors call attention to relapses after the planned services and the need for support during these periods. Overall, however, this component of service delivery is not dealt with in the same depth in the human services, and there is a lack of clearly designed programs and specificity as to the types of interventions or assessments needed. The characteristics of the clients at termination and the environment within they must function need careful consideration in designing follow-up services. As essential as these services are, resistance can be expected, since these services will be the most difficult for which to find funding.

IX. MONITORING THE SERVICE SYSTEM AND EVALUATION OF OUTCOMES

Each component of the framework should be monitored to evaluate whether the program is functioning as designed. In reviewing innovations, several of the authors in this volume call attention to the need to assess fidelity—is the program being administered consistent with its design? Ongoing assessment is needed to judge whether the program is servicing the defined population, whether procedures of case finding, screening, referral, assessment, linkage, and follow-up, as well as the elements included in the intervention, are being performed consistently.

For all the programs, systematic outcome evaluation is required if we are to test and refine the programs and to identify what really works. The authors consistently point out the need for additional research into all aspects of the programs and make specific suggestions concerning the needed research.

In conclusion, we hope that this volume, the first in our *Innovations in Practice and Service Delivery with Vulnerable Populations* series, stimulates interest in the examination of innovative approaches to better serve the needs of vulnerable populations. While much work remains to be done in this area, exciting developments are currently taking place in many fields, as the chapters in this volume demonstrate.

Arthur Blum and David Biegel
December 1997

REFERENCE

Blum, A. (1994). *Innovations in practice and service delivery: A framework for analysis*. Unpublished manuscript, Center on Practice Innovations, Mandel School of Applied Social Sciences, Case Western Reserve University, Cleveland.

About the Editors

David E. Biegel, Ph.D., is the Henry L. Zucker Professor of Social Work Practice and Co-Director, Cuyahoga County Community Mental Health Research Institute, Mandel School of Applied Social Sciences, Case Western Reserve University. Dr. Biegel has been involved in research, scholarship, and practice pertaining to the delivery of services to hard-to-reach population groups and the relationship between informal and formal care for the past 20 years. His recent research activities have focused on natural support systems for persons with chronic mental illness, family caregiving, and mental health and aging. Dr. Biegel is the author of more than eighty publications about mental health, caregiving, self-help, and social networks and social support.

Arthur Blum, D.S.W., is the Grace Longwell Coyle Professor of Social Work Emeritus, Mandel School of Applied Social Sciences. He retired from the Mandel School in June 1991, after 31 years of teaching. While at the Mandel School, Dr. Blum served as Director of the Doctoral Program, Director of the Practice Demonstration Program, Acting Director of the Mandel Center for Nonprofit Organizations, and Director of the Center on Juvenile Delinquency. He is a recognized expert in the areas of social group work and human service delivery and has published widely in these fields. His current area of concentration is the design of service delivery systems with an emphasis on support networks and self-help activities.

Professors Biegel and Blum serve as coeditors of the *Innovations in Practice and Service Delivery with Vulnerable Populations* series, published by Oxford University Press.

About the Contributors

Robert E. Arendt, Ph.D., Assistant Professor, Department of Pediatrics, School of Medicine, Case Western Reserve University, Cleveland, Ohio

David Braddock, Ph.D., Professor of Human Development and Director, Institute on Disability and Human Development, College of Associated Health Professions, University of Illinois at Chicago, Chicago, Illinois

Anne E. Brodsky, Ph.D., Assistant Professor, Department of Psychology, University of Maryland at Baltimore County, Baltimore, Maryland

Cameron J. Camp, Ph.D., Research Scientist, Myers Research Institute of the Menorah Park Center for the Aging, Cleveland, Ohio

Heidi T. Chirayath, B.A., Doctoral Student, Department of Sociology, Case Western Reserve University, Cleveland, Ohio

Michelle Cooley-Quille, Ph.D., Assistant Professor, Department of Mental Hygiene, School of Hygiene and Public Health, The Johns Hopkins University, Baltimore, Maryland

David W. Coon, Ph.D., Project Manager, Older Adult and Family Center, Veterans Affairs Palo Alto Health Care System, Stanford University School of Medicine, Menlo Park, California

JoAnn Damron-Rodriguez, Ph.D., Assistant Professor, School of Public Policy and Social Research, University of California, Los Angeles and Associate Director, VA Geriatric Research, Education and Clinical Center, West Los Angeles, California

Victor Groza, Ph.D., Associate Dean of Academic Affairs and Associate Professor, Mandel School of Applied Social Sciences, Case Western Reserve University, Cleveland, Ohio

Boaz Kahana, Ph.D., Professor of Psychology, Cleveland State University, Cleveland, Ohio

Eva Kahana, Pierce T. and Elizabeth D. Robson Professor of Sociology and Chair, Department of Sociology, Case Western Reserve University, Cleveland, Ohio

Judith A. B. Lee, Ph.D., Professor, School of Social Work, University of Connecticut, West Hartford, Connecticut

341

Julia H. Littell, Ph.D., Assistant Professor, Graduate School of Social Work and Social Research, Bryn Mawr College, Bryn Mawr, Pennsylvania

Raymond P. Lorion, Ph.D., Professor of Psychology and Chair, Department of Psychology, Ohio University, Athens, Ohio

Jeanne M. Mattern, Ph.D., Lecturer, Department of Sociology, Case Western Reserve University, Cleveland, Ohio

Sonia Minnes, M.A., Research Coordinator, Department of Pediatrics, School of Medicine, Case Western Reserve University, Cleveland, Ohio

Marcia G. Ory, Chief, Social Science Research on Aging, Behavioral Social Research Program, National Institute on Aging, Bethesda, Maryland

Susan Rose, Ph.D., Assistant Professor, School of Social Welfare, University of Wisconsin, Milwaukee, Wisconsin

Jack Rothman, Ph.D., Professor Emeritus, School of Social Work, University of California, Los Angeles, California

Richard Schulz, Ph.D., Professor of Psychiatry and Director of Gerontology, Department of Psychiatry, School of Medicine, University of Pittsburgh, Pittsburgh, Pennsylvania

John R. Schuerman, Ph.D., Professor, School of Social Service Administration, University of Chicago, Chicago, Illinois

Lynn T. Singer, Ph.D., Professor of Pediatrics and Psychiatry, Department of Pediatrics, School of Medicine, Case Western Reserve University, Cleveland, Ohio

Phyllis Solomon, Ph.D., Professor, School of Social Work, University of Pennsylvania, Philadelphia, Pennsylvania

Francis J. Turner, Ph.D, Professor Emeritus, Faculty of Social Work, Wilfrid Laurier University, Waterloo, Ontario, Canada

Allen Zweben, D.S.W., Director, Center for Addiction and Behavioral Health Research, and Associate Professor, School of Social Welfare, University of Wisconsin, Milwaukee, Wisconsin

Index

Page numbers followed by "n" refer to notes; those followed by "t" refer to tables.

Mobility, programs to enhance, 259–60
Model drift, 109, 117
Montessori, Maria, 287
Montessori-based program. *See*
    Intergenerational Montessori-based
    program
Morton, Margaret, 222
Motivational enhancement therapy (MET),
    206, 210
Motivational psychology, 202, 205, 206
Multidisciplinary teams, 336
Multifamily Group Therapy, 156
Multifinality, 22, 27
Multisystems approach, 117
My Sisters' Place (MSP), 231–40
    background and description of, 231–32
    intergenerational case study, 235–37
    substance abuse and, 232–35
My Sisters' Place II (MSP II), 227, 232,
    237–38
My Sisters' Place III (MSP III), 228, 232,
    238, 239–40

Narrative theory, 21
National Cancer Institute, 47
National Center for Medical Rehabilitation
    and Research, 190
National Conference on Self-
    Determination, 183
National Institute for Nursing Research
    (NINR), 297, 298
National Institute of Mental Health
    (NIMH), 187. *See also* Community
    Support Program
National Institute of Neurological Diseases
    and Blindness, 57
National Institute on Aging (NIA), 297,
    298
National Institute on Alcoholism and
    Alcohol Abuse (NIAAA), 211
National Institute on Child Health and
    Human Development, 187
National Institute on Disability and
    Rehabilitation Research (NIDRR), 190
National Institute on Drug Abuse, 64
National Institutes of Health (NIH), 297,
    298
National Survey of Supported
    Employment Implementation,
    184
Native Americans, 320
    fetal alcohol syndrome in, 59
    prematurity in, 67
Natural recovery, 202
Needs analysis, 330–31

Neonatal intensive care (NICU), 68–69
New Hampshire
    mental illness interventions in, 155, 157
    mental retardation services in, 174, 176,
        178, 189
*New Work Habits for a Radically Changing
    World* (Prichett), 43
New York
    foster care in, 105, 115
    mental retardation services in, 173
New Zealand, brief intervention in, 209
Nisonger Center, Ohio State University,
    185
Nondeclarative memory, 282, 286
Nondependent (nonhelp-seeking) alcohol
    clients, 8, 197–98, 200, 201, 215, 332,
    333, 334. *See also* Brief intervention
Normalization, 173, 182, 208
Nursing homes, 9, 249–70
    empowerment of residents, 254, 255,
        263–64
    family- and community-oriented
        programs in, 261–62
    goals and approaches of intervention in,
        250–52
    health and physical function
        enhancement in, 256–60
    management-oriented processes in,
        253t, 254–55, 258, 260
    patient-responsive care in. *See* Patient-
        responsive care
    program innovation in, 252–63
    prosthetic processes in, 253t, 254–55,
        256, 259
    psychosocial well-being enhancement
        in, 260–61
    staff-centered programming in, 262–63
    therapeutic processes in, 253t, 254–55,
        256, 258, 260
Nutrition, 257–258

Office of Special Education and
    Rehabilitative Services, 190
Ohlson, Joan E., 227
Ombudsmen programs, 249
Omnibus Budget Reconciliation Act, 114,
    116
Open Door, 225
Operation PAR (Perinatal Awareness), 62
Opiates, 60–61
Opinion leaders, 47
Optimizing, 204
Organizational innovation, 5, 32–49
    communication and contact in, 45–46
    discontent and advantage of, 44–45